WITHDRAWN
UTSA LIBRARIES

FOR A
PROPER HOME

PITT LATIN AMERICAN SERIES
John Charles Chasteen and Catherine M. Conaghan, Editors

FOR A
PROPER HOME

Housing Rights in the Margins
of Urban Chile, 1960–2010

EDWARD MURPHY

UNIVERSITY OF PITTSBURGH PRESS

Published by the University of Pittsburgh Press, Pittsburgh, Pa., 15260
Copyright © 2015, University of Pittsburgh Press
All rights reserved
Manufactured in the United States of America
Printed on acid-free paper
10 9 8 7 6 5 4 3 2 1

Cataloging-in-Publication data is available at the Library of Congress.

CONTENTS

ACKNOWLEDGMENTS   vii
INTRODUCTION   1

PART ONE. UNSETTLED FOUNDATIONS

Chapter 1. The Urban Politics of Propriety through Revolution and Reaction   23

Chapter 2. Property, Governance, and the City: A *Longue Durée* Perspective   40

PART TWO. INSURGENT OWNERSHIP

Chapter 3. A Place in the State: Housing Activism and the Seizure of Land, May Day, 1969   71

Chapter 4. Specters in the Revolution: Dilemmas of Home during the Chilean Path to Socialism   101

PART THREE. REACTIONARY TURNS

Chapter 5. Locating States of Emergency: The Politics of "Normalization" after the Military Coup   135

Chapter 6. Aesthetics of Order: Forging Spaces of Distinction amid Neoliberal Expansion   164

PART FOUR. DOMESTICATED PERIPHERIES

Chapter 7. Containing Protest in the Transition to Democracy   193

Chapter 8. Fractures of Home and Nation: Property Titling after the Dictatorship   219

Chapter 9. The Indignities of Home in the Margins of Modern Urban Life   242

CONCLUSION   264
NOTES   273
GLOSSARY AND ACRONYMS   305
REFERENCES   307
INDEX   335

ACKNOWLEDGMENTS

When it comes to acknowledgments, academic practice privileges the professional over the personal, the public over the private. Given my approach in this book, I have to throw such a problematic convention on its head. Christina Kelly has been with me through all of the twists and turns of this project as we have built a home together. She knows all too well how much I have depended on my personal relationships in writing this book. Thank you, *mi amor*, for being a steadfast support and an ongoing inspiration. I am also grateful to my parents, Anne and Dennis Murphy, who granted me the security and freedom to travel widely and think expansively.

I reserve a special thank you for the people whom I interviewed for this book, whose names, when I identify them, appear in the text. More than informants, they were intellectual interlocutors and friends who demonstrated a remarkable generosity. Many in Renca, the *comuna* in Santiago where I did my ethnographic research and conducted oral histories, helped me establish contacts and develop various parts of this book's research, including Pablo Vargas, Paula Cruz, Silvia Contreras, Maria Osorio, Maria José Maldonado, and Emilio Reyes Osorio. Each one also provided crucial camaraderie and support. A particular thanks to Patricio Cáceres for his dedication in helping me develop the oral histories, not to mention his humor, insights, and friendship. Elsewhere in Santiago, the Lillo Román family and the Moya Gómez family have hosted me and made me feel at home on more occasions than I can recall. Thanks to *Tía* and *Tío*, Marco and Miguel, in addition to Matti, Lucho, Claudio, Mauricio, Nacho, and Felipe. Thanks as well to Daniela Paz Jara, Kate Goldman, Carlos Figueroa, Alejandra Moreno, and Gonzalo Pérez.

Mario Garcés and Eduardo Morales were both crucial academic contacts in Chile. Their insights and suggestions have helped me enormously. Numerous archivists facilitated my explorations in the often labyrinthine pathways of library and archival holdings. Thanks to the staffs at the Fundación de la Vicaría de la Solidaridad, the Biblioteca Nacional (Hemeroteca and Periodicals sections), the Archivo de la Administración, the Biblioteca del Congreso (especially in the Recortes de Prensa Annex), and the Municipalidad de Renca.

In my academic life, this project has roots stretching back to a master's thesis I completed at Georgetown University. Thanks to John Tutino for his infectious passion for Latin American history; to Joanne Rappaport for introducing me to the rich possibilities of historical anthropology; to Arturo Valenzuela for sharing his deep knowledge of Chile; and to Gillian McGillivray for friendship and intellectual support.

I developed an initial, rough draft of this book as a dissertation in the doctoral program in Anthropology and History at the University of Michigan. For my dissertation chair, Fernando Coronil, I offer my deepest thanks. My gratitude, however, is touched with the worst kind of sorrow, as Fernando died in 2011. Both a friend and a mentor, Fernando helped push the intellectual boundaries of my work while reminding me of the critical importance of remaining ethically and politically engaged with the people and dynamics I am studying. Julie Skurski has not only offered warm friendship but has helped me to look unflinchingly at themes of power, violence, and hierarchy. David William Cohen has been a generous reader and provocative interlocutor. Perhaps beyond all else, he has given me the courage to make risky intellectual choices. In navigating me through Latin American gender historiography, Sueann Caulfield opened up new and provocative avenues. Rebecca Scott has always kept me focused on the poignant struggles that this book documents, reminding me of the importance of maintaining a critical distance from academic fads.

A number of other faculty members who were at the University of Michigan helped shape my thinking on this project, including Nancy Rose Hunt, Geoff Eley, Ann Laura Stoler, Ruth Behar, Janet Finn, Webb Keane, and Katherine Verdery. Numerous doctoral students and friends at Michigan have provided camaraderie and intellectual engagement since I started this project, including Paul Eiss, David Pedersen, Chandra Bhimull, Genese Sodikoff, Eric Stein, Jill Constantino, Michael Baran, Patty Mullally, Shannon Dawdy, Naisargi Dave, Frank Cody, Bhavani Raman, Natalie Rothman, Jessaca Leinaweaver, Kim Clum, Rebekah Pite, Jonathon Larson, Juan Hernández García, Marie Cruz, Isabel Córdova, Juliet Erazo, and Leslie Williams. For words of encouragement in difficult moments, in addition to ongoing friendship and close reads of much of the manuscript, thanks to John Thiels, Michael Hathaway, and Karen Hébert.

As a faculty member at Michigan State University, I have had the fortune of support, friendship, and intellectual engagement from a great many people. If the following lists are long, they are also heartfelt. Thanks to Pero Dagbovie, LaShawn Harris, Denise Demetriou, Michael Stamm, Karrin Hanshew,

Charles Keith, Helen Veit, Mindy Smith, Suman Seth, Walter Hawthorne, Laura Fair, Lewis Siegelbaum, Leslie Moch, John Waller, Brandt Peterson, Kirsten Fermaglich, Robert Blake, Anne Ferguson, and Laura Reese. Ben Smith, Peter Beattie, Sean Forner, Jim Porter, Steve Stowe, Lisa Fine, Chantal Tetreault, Najib Hourani, David Wheat, and Erica Windler all provided helpful feedback on parts of the manuscript. Cristián Doña Reveco and Alex Galarza aided with research and the bibliography.

In the many years of working on this book, I have presented parts of it in a number of forums and discussed it with a great many academics. I appreciate the comments I have received from Setha M. Low, Ida Susser, Catherine Fennel, Brodwyn Fischer, Javier Auyero, Bryan McCann, Dennis Rogers, Emilio Kourí, Margaret Power, Leandro Benmergui, Lessie Jo Frazier, and Chris Boyer. Jadwiga Pieper Mooney and Alison Bruey, perhaps without even knowing it, offered important insights in conversations along the way. For encouragement in Chile from historians working at North American universities, I am grateful to Karin Rosemblatt and Patrick Barr-Melej. Steve Stern and Thomas Klubock offered crucial support and advice toward the end. Jeff Maskovsky and James Holston provided thoughtful and critical reactions to the entire manuscript, vastly improving the final product. Kathy White gave significant editorial help.

At the University of Pittsburgh Press, Joshua Shanholtzer has been a patient and friendly acquisitions editor, while John Charles Chasteen has both believed in this project from early on and provided important words of encouragement. Finally, I thank the institutions that have offered me the grants and fellowships that have paid for my research trips and given me the time I needed to write. This includes the United States Fulbright Commission, in addition to a number of sources at the University of Michigan, including the Doris G. Quinn Dissertation Finishing Fellowship and a postdoctoral fellowship at the Eisenberg Institute for Historical Studies. The College of Social Science and the Department of History at Michigan State University provided important funding for a semester on sabbatical and three research trips to Chile.

Much of chapter three appeared previously as "In and Out of the Margins: Urban Land Seizures and Homeownership in Santiago, Chile," in *Cities from Scratch: The Informal City in Latin America*, edited by Brodwyn Fischer, Bryan McCann, and Javier Auyero (Duke University Press, 2014). Some material in many of the chapters comes from "Introduction: Housing Questions Past, Present, and Future," in *The Housing Question: Tensions, Continuities, and Contingencies in the Modern City*, edited by Edward Murphy and Najib Hourani (Ashgate, 2013).

FOR A
PROPER HOME

INTRODUCTION

Perhaps I was overstepping my bounds. It was obvious that Roberto and Carmen—two of my long-term acquaintances in Villa Topocalma, a low-income neighborhood on the outskirts of Santiago, Chile—could use the forty thousand pesos (about US $750) I was thinking of giving them. They faced expenses they could hardly afford and obligations to extended family members that would be nearly impossible for them to meet. Two of their nephews had recently been arrested and accused of forcing supermarket cashiers to empty their registers at knifepoint. When Carmen told me about this, she had asked, with tears in her eyes, "How could they do such a thing? They've left their families alone, with nothing."

Following the arrests, Carmen and Roberto had been busy, fulfilling the reciprocal ties of kinship and *compadrazgo* ("fictive kinship") that Larissa Lomnitz (1977), in a now classic study, describes as a key social practice of the unemployed and underemployed in Latin America's urban environment.[1] Roberto had met almost daily with three of his siblings, including the father of the two arrested young men. From what Roberto told me, their conversations were often heated, as the siblings were angry with their circumstances, frustrated by their obligations to each other, and uncertain about how to proceed. They did not trust the competence of the public defender who had been assigned to the case. But could they afford a lawyer who would make a difference?

Doing so would be a major financial strain, as the siblings would split the costs of the initial US $2,000 that they would need to hire someone of quality. In order to pay his share, one of Roberto's brothers, an itinerant salesman who sold fruits and vegetables, was considering selling his horse, an animal he depended on in order to cart around his merchandise. For his part, Roberto was also going to raise money by selling off parts of his livelihood. A small storeowner, Roberto sold cigarettes, soft drinks, candy, and such staples as bread, cheese, and milk out of his home. He also earned money from two video arcade games that he owned and neighborhood children used. Roberto was planning to sell at least one of the games and buy less merchandise in the coming months. This would force Roberto and Carmen into further debt and make more difficult the care of their three children, Roberto's father, and a grandchild, all of whom lived in their home. From what I could gather, they had discussed whether or not making these sacrifices was the appropriate thing to do. In the end, however, the importance of supporting kin won the day: the extended family mobilized to help the two brothers and their families.

Carmen began to invite her nephews' families over for meals more frequently. She had already been doing this at times, helping out because the two brothers had been unemployed before their arrests, a situation that had led to considerable strain inside their homes. One of the brothers had recently lost his job, in early 2009, at a small shoe factory, a casualty of the layoffs and downsizing that had taken place in Chile in the wake of the 2008, US-centered global financial crisis. At the time, an insecure, volatile, and poorly remunerated job market for low-income, urban workers in Chile had become even bleaker.[2]

As part of her support for the two nephews' wives, Carmen accompanied them on their first visit to prison. What Carmen had seen there horrified her. She later told me of the bruises and lacerations that the elder brother had on his face: one eye had been swollen shut and his upper lip was cut open and puffed out. While the younger brother looked better, he had bruised ribs and had received a blow in the back of the head. In the legal proceedings, it would be an important issue to determine whether or not the guards and the police had acted improperly and perhaps illegally in detaining the two brothers. There was no doubt, however, that they had been violent, as they had beaten the brothers with batons and forced them to the ground.

For Roberto and Carmen, the beatings confirmed their sense that the *pacos*, a somewhat disparaging term for police officers, tended to be corrupt and could act with impunity, a feeling shared by many of their neighbors. Police patrols rarely came around this part of the city, part of an uneven provision of urban services. When the police did come, they tended to take part in larger-scale raids in search of drugs, stolen goods, or weapons. Residents generally indicated that such raids were intimidating and marked by petty forms of corruption. Most felt a sense of impotence in facing the criminal justice system. Such skepticism had led Roberto and Carmen to have little hope in the fate of their nephews.

For my part, giving the money to Roberto and Carmen would not be too much of a sacrifice. I had, in fact, spent more than what I was thinking of offering them in order to come to Santiago for a six-week follow-up on my long-term research. My university was even going to reimburse me for the trip, and it paid me an annual salary equal to what Roberto (the primary breadwinner in the family) might perhaps earn in twelve years.

Still, I hesitated. As an ethnographer and historian, I took seriously the need to be engaged in the lives of those I studied. Yet I was also a professional from the outside whose offer of money would introduce potentially troubling dynamics to my relationship with Roberto and Carmen. The money could be a financial help for them in a time of family crisis, but it could also, I feared, be a slap in the face. Each had a strong sense of dignity and self-respect, both of which could be offended by an offer of money, especially if word of it got out to friends and neighbors. In attempting to act on the specific circumstances that had strained their finances and familial ties, I was intruding, to a greater or lesser degree, in the intimate, emotional, and vitally important spaces of Roberto and Carmen's private home lives. Was giving the money the appropriate thing to do?

Born from the immediacy of participant observation—one of the varied methodologies from anthropology and history that I adopted in undertaking this study—this question forced me to confront some of the central dynamics that give the themes I explore in this book their power and force. In modern urban societies such as Chile, developing the home and respecting its boundaries of privacy and propriety are ongoing tasks of enormous productivity. Such phenomena are a crucial part of everyday practices and expectations, while also unfolding in an at times uneasy relationship with labor regimes, inequitable social and spatial developments, and the citizenship dynamics of the state. Homes are often under great pressure, especially for low-income groups. Homes can be insecure and a threat to sensibilities of status, belonging, and dignity. A critical pressure point in the making of home is the extent to which its occupants can consider home and many of the relations that go into developing it secure, desirable, and socially appropriate.

While this pressure point is an ongoing, private concern, it invariably has consequences for the public sphere, if under very different circumstances and frameworks. In this book, I explore how certain practices and expectations of propriety have oriented the political field of housing since the mid-twentieth century among low-income urban citizens in Santiago (whom I'll call *pobladores*, following the Chilean nomenclature). During this period, pobladores have taken part in combative forms of housing activism. This includes hundreds of well-organized land seizures, the bulk of which took place during an era of reform and revolution from 1967 to 1973. Over the course of these six years, some 350,000 pobladores—about 14 percent of the city's population at the time—seized land in Santiago (see table 3.1). Through these seizures, residents and activists established hundreds of neighborhoods that still exist. The central government has often harshly repressed this kind of mobilization, especially during Augusto Pinochet's dictatorship (1973–1990). At the same time, it has also attempted to implement ambitious low-income housing programs, generally in conjunction with transnational development bureaucracies. (The notable exception to this trend, however, was in the first six years of the dictatorship.)

Both these state programs and the housing activism of citizens have helped to bring about a stunning transformation in the home lives of the urban poor in Santiago from the 1950s to the 2000s. During this period, the vast majority of the city's low-income residents have come to live in legally sanctioned homes with such infrastructure services as potable water, electricity, and plumbing. In the 1950s and 1960s, most low-income residents in Santiago lived in either ramshackle settlements without legal sanction or in run-down tenement rental units. Today they generally occupy homes with property titles in well-established neighborhoods. This transformation has helped give Chile a rate of homeownership that is relatively high internationally, especially compared to the rest of Latin America and the global South (see Angel 2000, 328 and 373; UN Habitat 2005, 66; Ronald and Elsinga 2012). Illegal housing lots and squatter settlements have declined significantly. Between 1960 and 2002, the last year for which, as of this writing, rough statistics are available, the percentage of households in Santiago that have property titles rose from 70 to more than 95 percent.[3]

A highly charged, public politics has made this change possible, in which citizen activism and state policies around urban housing have been front and center. This politics has taken place, however, in a dynamic, often tense interrelationship with the making of the private domain of the home, in which evolving expectations about its minimally acceptable constitution carry great weight.[4] Yet this interrelationship is often lost within the categories and debates that frame the public politics surrounding housing programs and urban settlement. State housing policies and public debates about them generally frame questions of housing development in restricted ways.[5] They might focus, for example, on measurements of the housing stock, the provision of housing subsidies, the role of the state in enforcing private property laws, the regulation of real estate markets, legal codes and enforcement, and the rights and responsibilities of homeowners and citizens. As important as these issues are, the manner in which they are framed misses or all too easily glosses over how, in Clara Han's (2012) term, a "weave" of social and spatial relations has inescapable force in the making of home.⁶ Such framings cannot adequately account for home's complexity, nor can they practically recognize home's centrality to the making of personhood and status.⁷

In an effort to foreground the multifaceted relationships, practices, and expectations that go into the making of the home, I begin this book in its often unsettled spaces. I do so even if my central empirical focus in this study is on the public, political field of housing, including its citizenship rights, forms of social activism, ideological visions, and the policies and regulations of the state. In tracking the historical evolution of the politics of low-income housing, I seek to constantly recognize how home is a central site of social reproduction and distinction. I specifically attempt to account for the troubled interrelationship between, on the one hand, the formation of the state and the public sphere and, on the other, the making of home for low-income city residents. For these residents, as with members of other socioeconomic groups, the private sphere of the home has subtle yet also potent and far-reaching boundaries. Ultimately, the issue of how to have proper respect for the integrity of the home is of paramount importance for both private lives and public policies.

In exploring the evolution of low-income housing in Santiago from the mid-twentieth century through the 2000s, I argue that expectations of a home considered appropriate have played a significant role in governance and in the evolution of low-income housing in Santiago. The question of what a proper home life is has been important in state institutions and international development organizations. It has animated the formation of social movements and claims involving the rights of citizenship. In making generally successful claims that they deserve to have a minimally acceptable home life, the urban poor in Santiago have mostly become homeowners. As I explore in this book, they have done so by working within a governing order that links property with forms of propriety. I call this crucial connection the urban politics of propriety.

This politics has been enormously productive, acting as a field of force that has given shape and meaning to struggles over housing. Within this field, the urban poor have taken part in a kind of insurgency in which they have received a right to housing, a historic achievement. In creative and courageous ways, pobladores have challenged dominant governing practices and transformed housing conditions. Over the long term, many of them have successfully demanded that the state legalize residential homes initially established through land seizures. As they have pursued homes they would consider appropriate, they have pushed the boundaries of acceptable forms of land tenancy, social activism, and governance. As a result, the vast majority of poor urban residents have come to live in legally sanctioned homes. In radical and defiant ways, activists in the realm of housing have changed the sociopolitical footing and left a significant imprint on land tenure in Santiago during the first decades of the new millennium.

At the same time, they have also nevertheless helped to instantiate and extend a liberal notion of citizenship, one bound to forms of property and expectations of propriety. This is an enduring, if evolving, cornerstone upon which Chilean state making has rested and within which pobladores have been enmeshed in their struggles for housing. Ultimately, mobilization on the part of pobladores in the realm of housing presents a seeming paradox. On the one hand, such activism has expanded the boundaries of citizenship and the ways in which low-income groups have accessed homeownership. On the other hand, however, it has also reinforced the power of liberal state making and its connection to private property. In taking part in struggles over housing, low-income urban groups have taken part in a process that I refer to as insurgent ownership.

In becoming insurgent homeowners, former squatters have helped to transform the state. Yet they have also been ensnared within its web. Within state relations, specific notions of poverty reduction, crisis conditions, and minimally acceptable urban homes have shaped housing activism. Squatters, moreover, have faced powerful interests, at the same time that they have had to comply with the bureaucratic requirements of the state and prove they are deserving of the benefits of citizenship. During the dictatorship and afterwards, the legacies of state violence have left an enduring impact. The dictatorship also first implemented the technocratic and pro–free market policies that came to be known as neoliberalism. In general terms, these policies, and their continued implementation in the post-dictatorship democracy, have played a problematic role in how pobladores have come to occupy their homes and act as citizens.[8]

Without question, in forging a right to housing and establishing their own homes, pobladores can rely on a crucial buffer against the harsh effects of neoliberal restructuring. Through their activism, pobladores have helped to limit neoliberalism's extensive reach.[9] Yet low-income urban Chileans still live in an often harsh, inequitable, and insecure environment, as Roberto and Carmen's case illustrates. Ultimately, then, this history of insurgent ownership is far from a simple narrative of a triumph of activism and rebellion in the area of housing rights for the urban poor.

The Limits of Homeownership and Housing Rights

In addition to underscoring the underlying importance of the borders of propriety in home life, Roberto and Carmen's story is also a cautionary tale about the value of homeownership and becoming propertied. In their own

Figure I.1. Villa Topocalma in 2009 (photo by author).

way, Roberto and Carmen have taken part in the great transformation in land tenure that has taken place among pobladores since the 1950s. When I first came to know the two of them in 2002, they lived in a squatter settlement, or, as Chileans refer to it, a *campamento*, literally an encampment. Along with the vast majority of their neighbors, however, they moved into Villa Topocalma not long after I met them. At the time, the complex was brand new, one of the many developments of so-called social housing subsidized by the Center-Left governments that had been in power from 1990 to 2010 following Augusto Pinochet's military dictatorship. In the campamento, Roberto and Carmen had lived, like most of their neighbors, in an illegal wooden shack with dirt floors. They did not have potable water in their home (they shared a spigot with others), and they had an unauthorized connection to the electrical grid. They also did not have a legal title to their home. But all of that had changed in the villa.

When Roberto, Carmen, and their neighbors moved to the new complex, media outlets covered the event and national and local municipal politicians celebrated it. For these observers, the move was an example of how state programs that razed squatter settlements and developed subsidized housing could contribute to the "eradication of extreme poverty," a term used to describe property titling and campamento removal programs since the early years of the dictatorship. The use of the term has had important consequences for how Chileans have debated and implemented policies in low-income housing and urban development.

Among certain powerful observers, including the influential Peruvian economist Hernando de Soto and transnational development bureaucracies such as the World Bank, the United States Agency for International Development, and the United Nations, Chile has been a model for how the provision of legally sanctioned homes is a key to better governance and poverty reduction within neoliberal policy frameworks.[10] For analysts such as de Soto (1989, 2000, 2004), property titling is a way for the urban poor to have more secure forms of land tenure and to profit from the homes they have built, phenomena that will supposedly foment broader economic growth. It also permits governments to institute social housing policies cheaply, following neoliberal policy prescriptions of fiscal discipline.

As critics have pointed out, however, there are fundamental flaws in de Soto's approach. Timothy Mitchell (2005, 310) notes that de Soto's view "assumes that a world without formal property rights is anarchic, and that once the proper rules are in place, a natural spirit of self-interested endeavor will be set free." Given such problematic assumptions, studies undertaken by de Soto and his followers have suffered from both faulty methodologies and mistaken conclusions. In the Chilean case, this includes a belief that the change in property titling in Santiago is both an ultimate good and that it has occurred as a result of neoliberal policies. This perspective fails to account, however, for how past forms of housing activism have shaped present conditions, especially the role that Leftist political organizations played in sponsoring them.[11] Beyond these interpretive problems, de Soto does not consider the forms of dispossession, inequality, and volatility that contemporary real estate market forces entail. In furthering the spread of potentially dangerous forms of finance capital, property titling programs extend debt to the most vulnerable of populations (Elyachar 2005; Harvey 2012).

Such critiques point to important shortcomings, but they do not address how the making of home and property is also a crucial element in the formation of the state, the dynamics of citizenship, and the building of subjectivity. They also leave unexamined the extent to which social actors might aspire to own their own homes. In the Chilean case, gaining a home of one's own has also been tangled up historically with the provision of "dignified" housing, as both outside observers and beneficiaries have put it in Chile since well before the dictatorship.

Given this, it is not surprising that Roberto and Carmen had shared in the enthusiasm about moving from a squatter settlement to a subsidized apartment complex. Shortly after the move took place, Roberto indicated to me how transformative the process had been. "When I first saw the villa . . . for me it was a truly beautiful dream," he said. "I'm the proudest, most pleased man about my home; [thinking about] how we lived before, and now we have this apartment. I'm as happy as I could be with my precious house." Roberto's

Figure I.2. "Smiles of Women," the caption that *El Mercurio*, Chile's newspaper of record, used to describe the above image, in which a mother and her daughters received a property title to their new apartment through a housing subsidy (*El Mercurio*, Sept. 7, 2002, c2).

pride was tied to the sense that he had earned a proper place for himself and his family, following a long struggle that included saving money and demonstrating personal discipline, both necessary steps for completing the state housing program that he and his family had been in. He had also helped to organize his neighbors, serving as the treasurer of the housing committee that represented the neighborhood to government and donor institutions. In summing up these experiences, Roberto adopted a familiar and yet very personal expression, "I have fought so hard to improve myself and my family."

Some seven years later, after his nephews had been arrested, Roberto was still proud of having left an illegal and precarious campamento and having moved into a well-constructed villa. He was now a homeowner, something he could not have been as a squatter. Occupying a legally sanctioned home of his own granted Roberto a certain status and greater security. He did not fear that his house might be demolished, as he had in the campamento. This gave him the confidence he needed to make longer-term plans.[12] When things had gone well, Roberto and Carmen had been able to invest in home improvements and expand their store. Yet they still lived in a context of insecurity, economic hardship, criminality, mass inequality, and social stigmatization. Developing their home was an ongoing and often precarious task. Their home could be upset by such unforeseen crises as the global recession and their nephews' arrests. Roberto and Carmen's experience thus underscores how the provision of property titles is not, by itself, a key to poverty reduction and social well-being.

Santiago's poor have come to make their homes in a generally fractured urban landscape. A dense nomenclature particular to the Chilean context has given meaning to this landscape, helping to shape identities in the city, including those of Roberto and Carmen. Not surprisingly, this nomenclature is intimately tied to the making of homes and neighborhoods. It also invariably cast a shadow over how I went about doing research and fieldwork. Before proceeding to the main narrative section of this book, in addition to a first chapter that will provide a deeper engagement with the specialized literatures that have informed my interpretations, it is crucial to have a better understanding of the terms for the places and people in the city. Foregrounding these terms further underscores the delimited ways in which governing policies and activism over urban housing have unfolded, in spite of the dramatic conflicts, rich symbolism, and sociopolitical importance that these policies and struggles have had.

Coming to Terms with Santiago's Fractured Urban Landscape

As should not be surprising for a city so integrated into the contemporary forces of global capitalism and shaped by intertwined, long-term histories of hierarchical social relations, Santiago has great divides between its wealthiest and poorest residential sectors. Chile has one of the highest rates of inequality in Latin America (itself the most inequitable region in the world). Such levels of inequality greatly increased following the implementation of neoliberal policies and have generally remained in place subsequently (see Winn 2004a and 2004c, 56). The dictatorship also implemented an aggressive slum removal program that heightened socioeconomic segregation in Santiago, a process I discuss in chapter six. Through this program, low-income populations ended up being further segregated, primarily consigned to the periphery of the city, at least to the south, north, and west.

Chileans reinforce the segregation in their cities by referring to all low-income area residents as *pobladores*. They also broadly term the neighborhoods that pobladores live in as the *poblaciones*. When used in this manner, the *poblaciones* are all of the peripheral, marginal, and low-income areas of the city. As with many labels for low-income groups generally, the term *pobladores* has at times been a source of pride, even as the weight of its negative associations is unavoidable. Throughout this book, I employ the terms *pobladores* and *poblaciones* as a general referent for the urban poor and the neighborhoods they live in, but I also attempt to show the specific, varied, and at times contested meanings that these words have had.

Yet as two terms I have already mentioned—*villa* and *campamento*—indicate, there is also a more complex lexicon at play in describing the peoples and places of low-income Santiago, in which a mosaic of socioeconomic distinctions fractures the urban landscape. Such distinctions become further refined when taking into account the historical development of these neighborhoods, in which social activism and political affiliations have provided important strands that have become interwoven in the urban tapestry. In general terms, all pobladores do share a kind of cultural identity, in which a sense of shared historical struggle, social distinction, and common experience carries weight. Yet as with any such group, this class- and place-based identity is neither entirely bounded nor devoid of internal variation and conflict. In spite of persistent myths about the singularity of a culture of poverty, urban marginality, and class identities more generally, people who live in the urban periphery are a heterogeneous group and form an integral part of broader sociospatial relations.[13]

During the thirty months' worth of research that I undertook for this book from 1999 to 2011, I sought to account for this heterogeneity. In my archival work, I cast a wide net across the entirety of Santiago in housing and urbanism, with forays into the designs, consumptive practices, and neighborhood settings of homes. These sources include media accounts, in addition to the plans, reports, debates, and legislative initiatives of government officials, from presidents, congressional representatives, ministerial bureaucrats, and mayoral representatives to social workers. I also examined hundreds of letters, requests, and applications completed by individual citizens and civic organizations seeking legal recognition, infrastructure services, and housing development for their homes and neighborhoods.

My ethnographic and oral history research was more delimited in spatial focus, even as it inevitably forced me to confront the dense network of practices and relations that constitute home in everyday life, not to mention its desires and expectations. In this research, I focused on four neighborhoods with unique historical trajectories in Renca, a low-income municipality in the northern section of greater Santiago. (Greater Santiago is today divided into thirty-three municipalities.) This work led me into local municipal archives at the same time that I established crucial contacts with nongovernmental organizations, charities, and community organizations active in the area. My primary focus, however, was on generating a set of oral histories and on ethnographic observation. The oral histories were participatory in nature, forming the basis for a book I released in Chile in 2004, in which many, but not all, of the testimonials we produced appeared. Through multiple interviews, a process of revision, and a series of workshops, the research participants and I collaborated in developing their testimonials (see Murphy 2004a; in this book, citations of this source refer to these oral histories).

The first neighborhood in which I undertook this kind of research is Población Primero de Mayo, a neighborhood originally established through an urban land seizure on May 1, 1969, the date from which the settlement originally took its name. Residents adopted the name May Day as a deliberate statement of solidarity with international labor and the Left. The neighborhood's Leftist ties preceded even its founding, as the Chilean Communist Party provided crucial organizational support for the seizure and the subsequent establishment of the neighborhood. Following the September 11, 1973, coup that established the dictatorship, the neighborhood assumed the name Huamachuco, a reference to a pivotal 1883 battle won by Chilean military forces over their Peruvian counterparts in the War of the Pacific (1879–1883).

This abrupt name change illustrates not only the military regime's efforts to whitewash the past and celebrate the past victories of Chile's armed forces, but also how important the politics of representation has been to the urban poor and for social movements more generally. For many Leftists in the late 1960s and early 1970s, land seizures such as the one that established Primero de Mayo were a demonstration of a burgeoning "popular power." Reactionaries tended to view the seizures with a mix of disdain, fear, and opprobrium. They viewed such outbursts of activism as subversive and criminal, a danger to the existing order. No matter the interpretation, however, pobladores like the residents of Primero de Mayo who seized land formed a part of the dramatic forms of social activism that shook Chile during the Christian Democratic reformism of the late 1960s and Salvador Allende's Socialist regime from 1970 to 1973. Pobladores established hundreds of neighborhoods that are generally poblaciones today.

Beyond generally referring to a poor neighborhood, the term *población* signals a settlement that is legally established. In poblaciones, houses have property titles and such infrastructure services as potable water, electricity,

Figure I.3. Housing in a población, 2009 (photo by author).

and plumbing. Poblaciones also have diverse forms of housing, reflective of the varied purchasing power and social resources of their residents. Such neighborhoods often have small, single-story houses that are poorly constructed and have been fashioned over the years from wood, pieces of aluminum, sheets of plastic, and perhaps cardboard or bricks. But they also have two-story houses made of cinder blocks and plaster, with patios and gardens. Most poblaciones, like Primero de Mayo, were once squatter settlements. But this is not true in every case. Many began as state-subsidized neighborhoods, usually with very small, basic forms of housing designed to be added onto.[14]

The second neighborhood I worked in, Población Lo Velásquez, began in this way. The neighborhood was built in the early 1980s with state-subsidized loans and funding from the Inter-American Development Bank. For some residents in Lo Velásquez, the fact that the dictatorship provided the subsidies to build their neighborhood helped cement their loyalty to Pinochet's regime. Yet other residents remained highly critical of the dictatorship, having earlier developed their solidarity with Leftist political groups. Some of this affinity for the Left, surprisingly enough, had roots in the formation of the same neighborhood. Before moving to Población Lo Velásquez, the residents of the neighborhood had lived together in a campamento that they had established through a land seizure in 1973 with the sponsorship of the Movement of the

Figure I.4. Housing in a población, 2009 (photo by author).

Revolutionary Left (the MIR), a radical socialist party formed in the 1960s. In terms of its broader political connections, Población Lo Velásquez has both radical and conservative origins, an indication of how multiple actors have supported the drive for urban property and housing, if often in conflicting and varied ways.

The third neighborhood I focus on is Campamento Lo Boza, a neighborhood that squatters established in the 1980s, but slowly over time and not through a land seizure. According to state categories since the 1950s, *campamentos* are "irregular" neighborhoods without services and property titles, a sure sign of lack of development. They are abnormal spaces that need to be cleaned up and legalized. Less technically, Chileans who don't live in these areas often see them as places in need of assistance and charity. Many also view them warily: they are supposedly neighborhoods where violence, crime, and drug running hold sway. Historically, such visions of danger overlapped with fears of subversion and radicalism, especially in campamentos established through land seizures. In all of these conceptions, campamentos are unruly spaces in need of interdiction. They are neighborhoods without legal sanction, often with precarious housing. Chileans generally view them as inappropriate spaces for hardworking citizens, an affront to decency, fairness, and propriety.

Villas—such as Villa Topocalma, the fourth neighborhood I did fieldwork in and the only one I have given a pseudonym—are composed of apartments and row houses. Private, professional developers have built these villas and sold individual units to pobladores who have received public subsidies (a policy in place since the dictatorship). Villas have legal sanction and property titles. Most tend to have athletic fields and common spaces for children to play. In many instances, however, such spaces are of a poor quality: jungle gyms are broken down and sprayed with graffiti, concrete surfaces can be full of cracks and broken bottles, and dirt fields are often littered with rocks, uneven playing surfaces, and holes. The domestic spaces of villas can at times be quite cramped, especially when extended family members and fictive kin live there.

Yet villas are solidly built and have infrastructure services often lacking in campamentos. They thus protect residents from the elements, an important difference from campamentos and many poblaciones, where flooding and poor insulation are common. In her assessment of her home in Villa Topocalma, Carmen pointedly juxtaposed her current living conditions to the rats, mud, and leaks that she dealt with in the campamento. For many, villas also signal a higher status for their residents. When I was leaving the home of a family who lived in a villa of two-story row houses, the middle-aged mother of the family said to me as she was pointing to a población across the street, "This is a villa here. Not like over there; not like the people over there."

On balance, then, there are hierarchical divides between campamentos, poblaciones, and villas. Yet the fact that all of these areas can be subsumed into

Figure I.5. Campamento Lo Boza, 2007 (photo by author).

the general category of *poblaciones* underscores how middle- and upper-class Chileans often stigmatize all pobladores in the same way. Because of this, residents in the municipalities of Santiago where pobladores are concentrated will often lie about their addresses on job applications. It is also for this reason that it has been a challenge to market new, suburban-style middle-class housing developments in these municipalities, despite their increasing numbers. Though these developments are often at a remove from the neighborhoods of pobladores, and protected by the private security guards and the walls and gates of what Teresa Caldeira (2000) describes as "fortified enclaves," they still suffer from stigma by association.[15] Historically and into the present, outsiders have tended to condemn pobladores for living in certain areas. If this condemnation has contributed to segregation, stigmatization, and suspicion, it fuses a superficial understanding of the city's geography with the moral worth of its residents. It has also tended to obscure political economic and class relations, assigning inherent character to surface appearance.[16]

Given such dynamics, villas can ultimately have a public image far removed from the promise of social integration and personal dignity that homeownership appears to offer. This has occurred despite the fact that villas have become ubiquitous in Santiago's urban periphery, as aggressive programs to provide subsidized housing to the urban poor have, with varying degrees of intensity and success, dominated state policy since the 1960s.[17] But the continued stigmatization of pobladores in villas highlights the troubling fate that can potentially await the beneficiaries of these programs.

Stigmatization and Propriety

As this review of the different categories of low-income neighborhoods and housing suggests, "territorial stigmatization"—to borrow a term from Loïc Wacquänt (2007, 2008)—is an important characteristic of Santiago's urban milieu. Such stigmatization was an ongoing source of frustration for Roberto and Carmen in their home. They ruefully expressed their disappointment at the nickname that their section of Villa Topocalma had acquired following their arrival: *la manzana podrida*, "the rotten apple." A play on words, the term refers not only to an apple but also to a block of housing. In the assessment of many of their neighbors, Roberto and Carmen lived among a rotten group of poorly behaved and dangerous pobladores.

For Carmen and Roberto, other memories of denigration and stigmatization weighed heavily on their life histories, as they had for many pobladores whom I spoke to. Such reminiscences often related how indignities could be woven into the fabric of everyday life. In one example, a pobladora from Campamento Lo Boza described to me how the residents in her neighborhood stained their shoes and clothes on the narrow dirt pathways of their neighborhood. In a city where concrete had long been a sign of modern urban development, having dusty and muddy attire was an embarrassment. At school, students from neighboring poblaciones and villas teased the children in the campamento about it; this had even caused fights to break out (Cecilia Castro in Murphy 2004a, 56). In another memory, Carmen and Roberto recalled that they were often ignored or met with skepticism as they and many of their neighbors organized to move out of the campamento they had lived in. Officials from the municipality of Renca were particularly harsh, often dismissing the pobladores as unorganized and suspect, treating them as "pests" (*chinches*) who were unworthy of attention.

There were also recollections of very specific instances of prejudice, ones that could add humiliation and stress to already trying circumstances. Throughout Roberto's childhood, his father often went through long bouts of drinking during which he could be abusive. According to Roberto, if it had not been for his mother, Roberto and his siblings would have ended up on the streets as "drug addicts or criminals." During one of her husband's drunken spells, however, Roberto's mother fell ill and could no longer care for the family, leaving Roberto and his six siblings to fend for themselves. In response, Roberto went out in the streets to panhandle. In Roberto's recollections, strangers did give him money and food, sometimes with words of encouragement. But many insulted him for begging, while some threw food away that they could have given to him. Roberto also claimed that one "well-dressed man with a jacket and tie" spit in his hand as Roberto was holding it out. In assessing the experience, Roberto said simply, "he humiliated me."

The nature of these specific memories—in addition to the broader social forces that contributed to their making—convinced me that I needed to tread carefully in offering money to Carmen and Roberto. Beyond feeling like an intrusion into an area where I did not properly belong, giving the money potentially concretized a hierarchical relationship between us and failed to recognize the sense of self-reliance and dignity that I believed Carmen and Roberto had long sought to cultivate. It would, in any case, undoubtedly change my relationship with them.

I had often listened to Roberto and Carmen as they related painful memories and circumstances. At the same time, I had socialized with them by watching television, attending family meals and gatherings, and making jokes (often about my gringo sensibilities and accent). In addressing me, Roberto tended to call me his friend. Yet I was not his *compadre*, someone who would have been counted on for discretion and help during this kind of situation. While the term *compadre* literally means "godfather," it more generally refers to the close bonds of trust, loyalty, and mutual dependence that tie kin together, fictive or otherwise.[18] To a degree, such ties establish a basis for equality. They provide crucial buffers against the pressures and potential crises that the urban poor experience. But such relationships can also be volatile as they demand constant attention and can be strained by trying circumstances and perceived slights. In intimate, private relationships, greater obligations often accrue. I was ultimately not in a position to be Roberto's compadre, given that I lived a busy life in the United States, far from the circumstances in the rotten apple. Building up the reciprocal, long-term ties that are a part of compadrazgo was not, at that point anyway, how I could interact with Roberto.

As I continued thinking about what to do, I took my concerns to another friend of mine, a poblador who had originally introduced me to Carmen and Roberto and had long been a social worker and community organizer in the area. He helped me to obtain some initial, free legal advice for Roberto and Carmen. He also indicated that merely handing over money would be "very cold" and could lead to troubling ties of dependency. I had experienced this problem previously, the only other time I had explicitly helped a family financially. In that case, the family's home had been largely destroyed in a fire, a not altogether uncommon experience in campamentos and poblaciones. I had dealt mostly with the mother, who subsequently asked me on a number of occasions if she could work for my wife and me as a maid. This is a dynamic that often plays out with the numerous nannies, servants, and handymen who labor for middle- and upper-class Chileans, in which servitude, dependence, and beneficence coexist in a complicated knot.

As a way out of either creating this kind of relationship or insulting Carmen and Roberto, my friend advised me to soften the emotional impact of giving them cash by explaining that they had already helped me in my research and career. When I finally went to Roberto and Carmen's house with the money strapped around my waist in a money belt, I was ready to follow my friend's advice. Yet as I raised the possibility of giving the money to Roberto, his initial reaction surprised me. He said, "I don't want to take advantage of you." Roberto evidently had his own sense of propriety and respect, with his own concerns about how he was treating me. I told him the generosity that he and Carmen had shown me over the years had helped me to do my research, which eventually played a role in my finding an academic job. On hearing this, Roberto asked me what my salary was, a question that again caught me off guard. For Roberto's part, the answer I gave him was a surprise: American salaries are generally on an even higher scale than he had imagined.

But at least from my perspective, having this information out there made it sound less like Roberto was inappropriately taking advantage of our relationship. I untucked my shirt and gave Roberto the cash I had stowed away in a money belt. It was something that I could give in order to support Roberto's familial ties and financial situation, both of which were now in crisis and had placed the development of his home in jeopardy. It was not the kind of thing I would or could do all of the time. It did not resolve the kind of debt I owe Roberto and Carmen for granting me an ethnographic window into their lives. The gift I offered them did not neatly close a tight circle of reciprocity between us in which we all benefited and came out basically even.[19] Much more importantly, it was far from resolving the insecurities that Roberto, Carmen, and pobladores like them face. Upon receiving the money, Roberto quickly put it away before anyone else could see. We have not spoken of it since.

In the histories that this book explores, many residents have taken part in their own decisions—as controversial, imperfect, and as often unsatisfying as they sometimes were—to develop, protect, and maintain their families and homes. Occasionally, as in the land seizures that pobladores have taken part in, such struggles would garner a great deal of public scrutiny. At other times, these attempts formed part of mundane, daily decisions and practices that hardly seem worthy of attention at all. But whatever the case, efforts to create and maintain a minimally acceptable home would reverberate in multiple domains. Such efforts have invariably been wrapped up within the great transformations, emblematic events, and intense conflicts that characterize Chilean history and the evolution of Santiago since the 1950s.

PART ONE

UNSETTLED FOUNDATIONS

CHAPTER 1
THE URBAN POLITICS OF PROPRIETY THROUGH REVOLUTION AND REACTION

CHILE HAS LONG HELD A POTENT international symbolism, despite its relatively small size and distance from the centers of global power. The country's political trajectory, especially in the post–World War II era, has made it stand out as a beacon for visions of development that have driven the political Left, Right, and Center throughout much of the world. In moving from a unique experiment in socialism to a dictatorship that was at the forefront of neoliberal restructuring, the country has been an emblem of the promises, tragedies, and conflicts that marked the global Cold War.[1]

The dramatic turns of the Chilean presidency point to a history of extreme ruptures and ideological polarization. To a remarkable degree, competing groups of Chileans have had the opportunity to plan for radically different political projects by controlling the presidency. From 1964 to 1970, Eduardo Frei Montalva led a Christian Democratic government that sought a "Revolution in Liberty." A recipient of substantial support from the United States, Frei Montalva's government attempted to achieve social justice and inclusion through reform. Salvador Allende's election in 1970 inspired radicals across the globe, who saw in Chile an opportunity to follow a peaceful and democratic "Chilean Path to Socialism." For their part, supporters of Augusto Pinochet's military regime rallied around the dictator's goal of ridding the country of communism and creating a free-market society. With democracy's return in 1990, many again looked to Chile for the enchanting prospect of realizing an alternative future. During the presidencies of the Center-Left Concertación (1990–2010), this prospect included the promise of crafting a form of neoliberal governance that would build channels of citizen participation and achieve "growth with equity."

Few in Chile have been left untouched by the country's diverse presidential projects. The dictatorship's volatile mix of right-wing nationalism, intense anticommunism, national security state impunity, and free-market fundamentalism left a particularly enduring and scarring mark. The brutal demise of Chilean democracy became a lightning rod for controversy and played a significant role in galvanizing an international human rights movement.[2] It was also important to a general turn to right-wing dictatorships in Latin America, the tragic result of a period of ideological hardening and increased polarization and militarization. As Grandin (2004) points out, the US-sponsored 1954 overthrow of Jacobo Arbenz in Guatemala heightened conflict in the Americas, often pushing the Left to take up arms (as in the Cuban Revolution) and making the Right more reactionary and authoritarian. Frei Montalva's reformism and Allende's commitment to a peaceful revolution seemed to offer ways out of the violent spiral. But the US-supported coup in Chile only further spread the terror fomented by the counterrevolution that engulfed much of Latin America. This violent reaction was a crucial factor in laying the foundation in Chile and far beyond for the establishment of neoliberal policy frameworks.[3] These frameworks, in turn, contributed to heightened individualism and social fragmentation, foreclosing many of the broader, social democratic options available in much of Latin America immediately following World War II.

Given this general trajectory, most observers, both academic and otherwise, have narrated Chile's political history since the 1950s by using a clearly demarcated timeline. There are good reasons for doing so, and the chapters of this book thus generally unfold following a chronology based on the turns of the Chilean presidency. Through a focus on the establishment and consolidation of campamentos and poblaciones, this book highlights how pobladores have been embroiled in vastly different governing projects, each with important implications for citizen relations, social activism, and urban settlement. If numerous pobladores played a central role in the forms of popular mobilization that marked the period leading up to the military coup, they also disproportionately suffered from the human rights abuses and neoliberal restructuring of the dictatorship.

Yet in spite of such intense changes, it is also necessary to track continuities in order to unweave how the deep-rooted relationships between property and propriety have operated in the settlement of low-income areas of the city. In general terms, time is trickier and more elusive than a singularly linear account provides, especially when necessarily understood in interrelationship to spatial relations.[4] Scholars of the city point out that the urban tapestry is woven from multiple, overlapping strands, stitched together at different moments in time.

As such, David Harvey (2003) warns that one of the "myths of modernity" is the idea that wholesale change across state-led political projects is possible. In Chilean historiography, scholars who analyze the workings of gender and violence in the formation of the nation-state have underscored persistent dynamics in the country's political culture.[5] Such perspectives form part of a broader trend among Latin American historians and beyond, in which analysts emphasize the entangled intersections that produce sociopolitical power and spatial relations.[6]

In seeking to integrate these perspectives with those on squatters and citizenship, I explore in this book how the relationship between property and propriety is intertwined with varied domains of social and political life, including the production of space in the city. In the case of pobladores, the links between property and propriety have provided a grounding upon which they have become significant actors on the national scene. Such links underscore the ongoing ways in which liberal forms of state making based on a private property regime have endured through the conflicts of the Cold War in Chile. These links have given impassioned meanings and embodied substance to how pobladores seeking housing have interacted with Chile's diverse presidencies through processes of reform, revolution, and reaction. They have provided unsettled foundations to a volatile and conflict-ridden history, in which a clear resolution has still not been reached.

In exploring these foundations, I have primarily relied in my research and writing on interweaving approaches from anthropology and history. Approaches from each discipline have helped me to explore how, as C. M. Hann (1998) insightfully argues, property's dynamics are embedded in sociospatial and political economic contexts. Far from being a mere legal contract, property is a relationship that comes together at the intersection of domains generally treated as wholly separate: the social, the economic, the political, the cultural, and the spatial. Perspectives from both anthropology and history have provided me with crucial guidance as I have sought to reveal how the multidimensional connections between property and propriety operate in the making of both home and citizenship.

In bringing these disciplines together, I have not sought to privilege one over the other. Instead, I have attempted to interweave and transform my understanding of each, with an eye toward critically evaluating and pushing their limitations.[7] As I have done so, my focus has been on developing an integrated perspective that simultaneously accounts for limits, margins, and conflict. This approach has three advantages: First, it has been crucial in revealing obscured connections, the kind that have bound the urban politics of propriety together and made this politics such a potent and unsettled historical force.

Second, in focusing on limits, I have sought to reveal how the boundaries of what is understood as normal have had particular importance for squatters who become homeowners, whose homes have straddled divides between the illegal and the legal, the formal and the informal. In this regard, exploring the liminal margins helps to reveal not only the overall, evolving spaces of social acceptability and public legitimacy, but also forms of hierarchy and difference.[8]

Finally, my anthropological and historical perspective has helped me to view the unfolding of Chilean history in a new light, one that takes account of the country's dramatic ruptures and turns, yet sets them simultaneously within a context of entangled legacies and continuities. This, I argue, has important implications for how to account for conflict and political transformation on the one hand and persistence and intersectional relations on the other. Such a perspective can help, in turn, to provide a broader interpretation of urban land tenure processes, ideological conflict, and the dynamics of citizenship across the twentieth century and into the present in the many cases that share a range of dynamics with the Chilean one. Such interpretations need both a theoretical and a historical grounding. I'll continue to develop mine by beginning here with the very core of this book: assessing the significance of private property itself.

Connecting Property to Propriety and Governance

Scholarship on property, particularly in anthropology, addresses how it is not merely a legal arrangement among people and things and/or land. It is, rather, an unfolding set of shifting social and spatial relationships among these elements, in which the values and meanings assigned to each is paramount. Each element, furthermore, is not isolated from the others. Instead, as people come into a property relation with things and/or land, they influence the status and value of the other elements. Each element, in other words, exists in a dynamic interrelationship.[9] Things and land enmeshed in a property relation have particular "social lives," with values and attachments that are both crucial for economic exchange and carry weight in the sociopolitical and moral standing of people.[10]

These entailments underscore how dominant property relations are embedded in and constitutive of context, from state and legal frameworks to spatial relations and sociocultural practices and expectations. Liberal states codify and enforce private property relations, with a reliance on coercion and its threat. Yet such relations also become real through what Nicholas Blomley (2003, 131) calls "an environment of the everyday," one that he describes as being "divided into thine and mine and more generally into public and private domains, all of which depend upon and presuppose the internalization of subtle and diverse property rules that enjoin comportment, movement, and action."

Given property's interrelationships between such domains as legal codes, policing, spatial boundaries, and everyday practices and expectations, Katherine Verdery (2003, 32) notes that the study of property relations can be "about everything: power, practices, institutions, land, the transformation of value, social relations, privatization, class formation, and so on." Such a perspective can quickly become unwieldy. But it has the advantage of recognizing the constructed nature of property regimes, in which cultural norms, spatial practices, and historical processes are all of paramount importance. At the same time, it underscores how issues of power and inequality in the distribution of resources, land, and things must be taken into account.

In this book, I attempt to both recognize and tame the all-encompassing nature of an analysis of property relations by returning to my object of study: the manner in which low-income residents in Santiago have come to live in legally sanctioned homes and the consequences this change has had.[11] This grants the narrative a kind of historical skeleton at the same time that it permits the complex assemblage of dynamics and processes that give flesh and life to this skeleton to come to light. Elements of citizenship and state formation are central to this assemblage. But these elements themselves do not exist in a vacuum.

The focus on propriety provides a further delimitation to my analysis. Carol Rose (1994) has shown how the links between property and propriety have an old genealogy in liberal property regimes.[12] When property holding was the domain of a small elite, a justification for the holding of property was that property holders would ensure an appropriate order. Property holders thus had a special status in the polity. Property, of course, was an initial requirement for citizenship in many newly formed republics across the Atlantic in the late eighteenth and early nineteenth centuries. In mass-market, democratic societies, private property regimes have retained certain exclusive and hierarchical characteristics, forming much of the material ground upon which class distinctions develop. Yet such regimes have also maintained the link between property and propriety, in that they emphasize how property relations are supposed to be, in Rose's term, a "foundation of decency and good order" (1994, 64).

Such a foundation links individual comportment with spatial relations, the distribution of resources, and governance. It has implications for ideas of both social standing and justice. In the former instance, gaining access to property is about gaining a place in the social order. Provided that property is recognized as having been legitimately acquired or earned, it tends to serve as a sign of status and acceptability. For this reason, having property can often be a source of pride and an instantiation of personal worth: as Roberto indicated about becoming a homeowner, "I'm the proudest, most pleased man about my home." The link between property and propriety underscores how property relations are inextricably bound to notions of personhood, in addition to basic understandings of the proper order of things.

In this latter sense, questions of citizenship and state formation come into play, especially in polities that emphasize the point that citizens have a right to a minimally acceptable set of conditions and a life of dignity. To state the formulation succinctly, proper citizens have a right to living conditions considered appropriate to their status. In the Chilean case since the mid-twentieth century, this has included a right to minimally acceptable forms of housing for pobladores, forms that have generally been tangled up with homeownership. Such a right, however, depends on citizens fulfilling a number of requirements. As Holston (2008, 115) argues in reviewing the Lockean and Hegelian traditions of property, this right entails "a close connection between property and the fundamental qualifications of citizenship: freedom (economic and intellectual independence), capacity (agency, mastery, responsibility), dignity, respect and self-possession." Rights to property should thus lead to dignity and respect, but they depend on citizens who can properly fulfill their roles as responsible individuals capable of possessing themselves and their properties.[13]

In developing the links between property and propriety, I must stress two differences between my approach to property and propriety and that of John Locke ([1689] 1988), the figure who has perhaps most influentially connected property to propriety. First, I do not presume that a legally sanctioned, well-regulated private property regime necessarily creates a stable, vibrant, and wealthy system. Both Locke and many of his intellectual descendants today, such as Hernando de Soto, make this assumption. But a private property regime does not tend to create an order that all actors in a polity will consider proper. Instead, tensions, insecurities, crises, and inequities are invariably woven into property regimes within capitalist relations.

This often gives birth to conflicts and contradictions, since the *idea* that property relations should be an instantiation of a proper order still carries weight. As such, links between property and propriety can serve as a kind of pressure point, providing openings in which citizens can denounce what they perceive as the improprieties of property relations, including how such relations might violate their rights. This has at times included critiques of the broader sociopolitical order, and, in cases of certain segments of the Left in Chile and globally, an outright rejection of private property. In general global terms, however, by the early twenty-first century, private property has expanded, even as it is also set within the context of nation states that oversee mixed kinds of property, including public forms and exceptions to the sanctity of private property. The making of these mixed property regimes generally entails compromise, negotiation, conflict, and coercion, including the workings of propriety.

The second way in which I differ from Locke is that I emphasize how the practices and expectations of propriety within property regimes must be understood in their specific contexts. Locke presumed that forms of propriety in property relations remain constant across time and space. In doing so, he made universal claims about specific types of propriety that grew out of his own English enlightenment milieu. But it is crucial, as Dipesh Chakrabarty (2000) asserts, to provincialize such perspectives.

Such provincialization, however, should not obscure how private property regimes do entail some fundamental, shared elements that resonate widely in the modern world. These include a notion of individual ownership, a separation between the public and the private (including expectations of the sanctity of home life), suppositions about the autonomy of the individual, and the sovereign power of the state to protect both the rights of citizenship and private ownership. All of these elements have an increasingly global relevance for politics, spatial practices, and social relations.[14] At the same time, they are each ideological and forged in the dynamics of history.

To reemphasize the point, such guiding elements do not preclude contingencies and highly differentiated, place-specific ideas about propriety. The notion, for example, that citizens who act in ways considered proper have a *right* to housing has had a particularly strong pull in Chile, a phenomenon tied to the country's tradition of popular social movements. While the urban politics of propriety in Chile supports a particular regime of liberalism and private property, it has never been solely about unfettered free-market relations.

In some cases, the link between propriety and property has tended *not* to serve as the basis for claiming a right to housing as a part of citizenship among low-income groups. This is generally true in the United States, despite the fact that several cities, particularly in the Midwest and Northeast, have long suffered from mass foreclosures and the large-scale abandonment of homes, a process that the 2008 financial crisis both accelerated and made more general. Some collective movements for housing rights have responded to the crisis, but without great effect.[15] In the United States, the dominant notion of homeownership is that it is properly one's personal responsibility, neither the duty of the state nor a part of social rights.[16] The US case, however, tends to be different from much of the global South and especially Latin America, as

Holston (2013) suggestively discusses. In Latin America, powerful movements for housing rights have often taken root in squatter settlements, especially in the second half of the twentieth century.

Yet no matter the situation, the issue of appropriate housing raises fundamental questions about justice, living conditions, and governance. As an issue with particularly strong political and moral implications, it links property dynamics to the rights and duties of citizenship, spatial relations, understandings of personhood, ideologies of nation, and elements of state formation. These links matter in multiple settings, particularly in the urban slums and squatter settlements that as many as one billion people live in today.[17] In such settlements—the number of which has exploded throughout the world in the past century of unprecedented urbanization—residents often live on the borders of legality in informal housing. For an already suspect and stigmatized population, occupying such a liminal space tends to raise further questions about their social acceptability and the propriety of their actions. The answers to these questions, in turn, matter deeply for their respectability and whether or not they will be able to take part effectively in broader social structures, including the rights of citizenship. Given this, informal squatter settlements have become an important arena for struggles over the meaning and possibilities of citizenship.

Citizenship, Informal Housing, and States of (Un)Exception

There is a certain paradox at play in squatter settlements made up of informal housing, a paradox that has important implications for the citizenship status of their residents. For many observers, including many squatters themselves, squatting and informal housing have been a sign of unjust living conditions and the failures of the governing order. Squatter settlements, moreover, have also represented breakdown, danger, anomie, and subversion. Residents of these neighborhoods often face legal prohibition, harsh forms of policing, and other kinds of social sanction. Seen in this light, squatter settlements are exceptional spaces within which both states and citizens have mobilized resources and energy.

At the same time, however, neighborhoods made up of squatters have also been a pronounced feature of innumerable cities throughout the course of the twentieth century and into the twenty-first, especially in Latin America and other areas of the global South. Such ubiquity is a characteristic of the informal sector generally. Far from being set apart from the rest of society, this sector has been central to modern urban processes, as it has been integral to social and economic relations, in which all sectors of society have been involved.[18] In the field of housing, informal squatter settlements have been a crucial means through which the urban poor have been able to reside in the city and carve out a life for themselves. At the same time, informal housing settlements have allowed an untold number of urban societies to maintain a cheap and accessible labor force in their principal cities. Swindlers and speculators, moreover, have been able to profit from squatter settlements. State officials and politicians, for their part, have often benefited from such areas as they have doled out favors and developed networks of patronage that are cheaper than providing formal housing and the range of urban services that other residents have.[19] From the perspective of their practicality and ubiquity, squatter settlements are unexceptional, even ordinary.

In curious ways, then, informal squatter settlements are both exceptional and unexceptional, a boundary that the residents of such neighborhoods uncomfortably straddle. This boundary is important to how such residents have claimed the rights of citizenship and interacted with state frameworks and institutions. In the Chilean case, urban squatters have always operated in a field of state relations, but on their tense and at times contested margins. Boundaries have been integral to how squatters have made claims to the state. This includes not only demonstrating that they can fulfill the duties and responsibilities of citizenship and landownership, but also establishing limits around the minimally acceptable conditions that citizens can assert as their rights.

From the 1960s to the present in Chile, squatters have often been able to demand that the state establish or restore the conditions they consider minimally necessary for daily life in the home and in the city. If this has been a particularly important issue for squatters, they have not been alone in making this claim. While referring to family and home, citizens have, for example, publicly protested against the lack of minimally acceptable housing, shortages of consumer items such as food, and human rights abuses. Throughout this book, I analyze each of these forms of activism. In doing so, my aim is to underscore how squatters' struggles have been enmeshed in broader processes in which the formation of the home, including ideas about its minimally acceptable constitution, has contributed to the making of the Chilean state and citizenship.

Crises in the home have elicited intense responses precisely because they were out of the ordinary. In reacting to these crises, Chileans have sought to define the boundaries of what they find to be appropriate and inappropriate. They have attempted to denounce what a problematic state of exception is and to determine if out-of-the-ordinary steps should be taken in order to resolve the aberration, perhaps even by instituting a new order. Yet the limits of what is understood as normal have had particular importance for pobladores, and especially squatters, whose very homes and neighborhoods have had a status as marginal, problematic, and illegal.

Inside state frameworks, Chilean legislation and law since the 1930s have cast squatter settlements as being "irregular" and in a state of "emergency," similar to legislative efforts elsewhere in Latin America and beyond.[20] Going back to the early twentieth century, the state adopted emergency legislation in the areas of housing and urban reform in response to housing shortages and exceptional moments of crises such as earthquakes. Such legislation has increased the bureaucratic power and jurisdiction of the state, augmenting its role as an enforcer and arbiter of what certain everyday conditions should be like.[21] The assertion of state control over these spaces has overlapped with assumptions about how to establish proper regulation, sanitation, and minimally acceptable conditions.

Such assumptions point to the existence of a powerful discourse of modern urban governance. This kind of discourse, as Foucault (1975, 1991) emphasizes, has repressive and productive effects, simultaneously disciplining populations and making possible new sociopolitical forms. In Santiago, this has meant that pobladores have often faced particular pressures to demonstrate their worth as well-behaved citizens. Yet it has also made them deserving of certain kinds of state resources. As a sign of Chilean poverty and backwardness, the campamentos are areas in need of interdiction, a target for social programs and development. For their part, pobladores have often been able to argue that their lack of appropriate housing has given them the right to protest. Ultimately, the notion that the city should conform to both specific norms of social order and particular forms of living conditions has had multiple and even contradictory effects.[22]

As legislation toward the "irregular" housing of pobladores underscores, the declaration of states of emergency and exception has been an important part of governing frameworks in the city. As Agamben (2005) explores, the declaration of a "state of exception" permits states to suspend normal governing practices and protections, even granting governments complete control over certain subjects. The power that governments wield in states of exception often pushes questions of legitimacy and popular consent to the side, especially given the use of violence and secrecy, as in the Pinochet dictatorship.[23] Yet Agamben also points out that states of exception can also be creative and productive, as when they involve the passing of social legislation. They are, moreover, uneasily bound up with popular forms of democratic sovereignty and sociopolitical legitimacy. This dynamic has been important for squatters and housing rights activists. In seizing land, squatters have acted within the same kind of logic that a government uses in declaring a state of exception:

they transgressed normal legal limits, but on the supposition that they were realizing a proper state of affairs.[24] They asserted a right to popular sovereignty, in which they could take the exceptional and normally illegal step of seizing lands. But they ultimately sought to gain access to property titles, a pillar of order within liberal forms of rule. They thus had to fulfill expectations that linked appropriate citizen behavior with the rights to property. It is through this dynamic that Chileans who have seized land and established homes have taken part in a process of "insurgent ownership."

Insurgent Ownership, Urbanization, and Sociopolitical Conflict

The insurgent ownership that pobladores took part in had radical elements, and it was often conjoined with the Chilean Left, especially in the land seizures. To a degree, it was part of a "generalized insurgent threat" that, as Grandin (2004, 178) argues, challenged Latin America's ruling classes for much of the twentieth century and helped to fuel the conflicts of the Cold War in Latin America. Laborers in the countryside, unionized workers, and the urban poor, among others, sought more expansive forms and meanings of citizenship, especially in reformist, revolutionary, and populist regimes. As they did so, they sought to overturn existing exclusions, privileges, and inequities. However, conservatives and reactionaries, often with the support of the U.S. government, took part in a general counterrevolution, putting in place dictatorships and policies that brutally repressed such insurgencies and turned much of Latin America into a field of killing and torture. This violence helped pave the way for the neoliberal era.

Chilean squatters became wrapped up in these processes, actively contributing to the processes of insurgency. Their struggles, however, must also be understood within the particularities of their experiences in the city, especially in their efforts to occupy homes that would be both socially and politically acceptable. If, as Grandin (2004, 2010) asserts, there has been a dialectical relationship between revolutionary and counterrevolutionary forces across the twentieth century and into the present in Latin America, such a relationship is not the singular motor of the region's historical development and conflicts.

The movement that squatters in Chile took part in also grew out of the struggle to reside in the city, forming part of what Holston (2008) labels an "insurgent citizenship." While Holston develops his argument in examining the case of São Paulo, he asserts that his interpretation has much wider relevance, taking place in cities throughout much of the global South (see especially Holston 2013). In these cities, massive population growth has not been met by a concomitant increase in legally sanctioned housing and the equitable provision of urban services. Those left without legal and secure forms of housing, however, have contributed to changing their destinies. Through the experience of organizing social movements, building their own homes, and finding ways to access infrastructure services, the urban poor have demanded, and often received, greater rights in the city. While this has not necessarily led to unambiguous legal title to their homes, it has at least included a general acceptance of their right to their homes and neighborhoods.

In his analysis, Holston does not integrate certain crucial elements about the insurgency that inform Grandin's interpretation: the generalized nature of the rebellious threat, the dialectical movement between insurgency and counterinsurgency, and the forceful turn to neoliberal restructuring. Each of these elements, however, is important historically and should be more fully integrated into analyses of citizenship, social movements, and low-income urban settlement in Latin America since the mid-twentieth century. On balance, Leftists and reformers played an important role in organizing movements for housing rights in the city (Fischer 2008 and 2014c; Way 2012; McCann 2014). Leftists did so even as they generally continued to look toward the mobilization of organized labor as the key to revolution and transformation. But in taking part in the nitty-gritty of working with the lower classes, the Left has invariably needed to address the issue of more secure forms of urban housing. As Fischer (2014c, 30) points out in excavating the largely forgotten role that communist organizing played in Rio de Janeiro's favelas, the "Left has been shaped by a troubled and dialectical tension between ideology and grassroots experience."

This tension often leads to paradox and contradiction, two characteristics that both Grandin and Holston argue are keys to understanding the insurgent challenge. While the insurgency I examine in Chile has expanded the boundaries of citizenship, it has also been entangled with citizenship's inner workings, as Holston asserts. Within this dynamic, encumbered social expectations and identities have been at play (Grandin 2004, 193–94; Joseph 2008, 23). This includes the weight of powerful special interests. It also involves the interrelated links between socially accepted landholding and political forms of propriety, in which state regulations and legal frameworks matter intensely. In these latter areas, expectations of home and family invariably play a role. All of these elements have been important for how squatters have sought greater citizenship rights and a change in their land tenure status.

Since the first half of the twentieth century in Latin America, squatters and low-income groups have generally achieved more secure forms of housing. Through the 1940s and 1950s, it was primarily organized laborers integrated into the coalitions of state-led development projects who became homeowners, an important indicator of the exclusions and inequalities built into Latin American regimes of citizenship at the time.[25] Yet in the aggregate, this situation overall changed. Continued struggle on the part of low-income urban citizens has made this happen, in addition to mass housing development projects and the support of neoliberals for property titling programs. Both the weight of the insurgent challenge to occupy the city and the dominance of private property as a governing regime have produced cities that have much higher rates of legally accepted housing. This has happened, however, in variable and not always straightforward or linear ways. As in Chile, many former squatters have received full rights and de jure recognition.[26] In a number of other cases, however, they have received partial rights and de facto acceptance.[27]

The range between these cases is an indication of the varied trajectories that squatters have gone through within their distinct national and local contexts. Squatters and former squatters, moreover, can be relatively secure or insecure in their land tenure. Such distinct paths, however, should be understood as being on a continuum, part of a family of experiences that have shaped how low-income urban groups have come to occupy their cities. In important ways, the difference between areas that have unambiguous legal title to housing tenure and other areas that have forms of state-accepted housing tenure is not necessarily as great as one would suppose. Historically, all of these areas have come into being through an entanglement with land titling regimes and urban regulations, a struggle over the meanings and possibilities of citizenship, and the housing projects and failures of the state. Mass inequalities and exclusions have weighed on each of these interrelated phenomena, in which residential segregation and labor markets have played critical roles. Throughout, possessing more secure, socially appropriate homes has been an ongoing desire and challenge.

In whatever circumstance, acceptance of squatting creates a new possibility in the acquisition of property, one that moves beyond such standard practices as market exchange, inheritance, and gift-giving. Given this, the process of insurgent ownership creates a new form of state-sanctioned property relations. Still, the break is far from complete. In order to be successful, and notwithstanding cases of corruption or forgery (which can often be widespread), squatters must present themselves as particular kinds of citizens.[28] In the process of gaining legally sanctioned housing, squatters enter a specific space of claims making, in which state frameworks reassert themselves. To a degree, the rupture caused by squatting is repaired. In the Chilean case, the practices and expectations of family and home—including gender dynamics and ideologies—have been a crucial part of this process.

Gender and the Space of Claims Making

Throughout the period analyzed in this study, women, primarily acting as *dueñas de casa*, "housewives"—literally female "masters of the house"—have often stepped into the public sphere to demand the restoration or creation of homes considered appropriate. These women have generally protested as suffering mothers, appealing to a seemingly natural order of family and motherhood.[29] Activists have repeatedly claimed that their primary goal is to ensure that Chilean mothers can properly care for their homes. The public and partisan world of politics was not supposed to sully their cause, a supposition generally at work in forms of female civic engagement. Even Michelle Bachelet, Chile's first female president (2006–2010, 2014–), has often presented herself as an empathetic woman above the fray of political wrangling.[30] She has done this at the same time that her personal biography as an agnostic, a former political prisoner, a single mother, and a trailblazing politician has pointed to significant change in what is possible in Chile and in notions about the proper makeup of a family.

In a growing body of literature that explores female activism in Chile and Latin America, debate tends to founder on whether it needs to be understood as transformative or constrictive.[31] This dispute underscores a broader, problematic fault line between certain poststructural thinkers who stress the diffuse and persistent nature of formations of knowledge and power and those who emphasize ideological conflict and change.[32] But rather than choosing one or the other of these positions, careful integration of the two provides a better accounting of the more embedded, intersectional workings of gender. Bachelet's case demonstrates that the seemingly apolitical register of motherhood and family protection is both powerful and persistent but neither static nor all-encompassing. Feminists have criticized this register, while female activists have often creatively worked within it to become participants in the world of sociopolitical organizing and to partially change the nature of public debate.

Still, the deep sympathy that suffering motherhood evokes has invariably lent moral legitimacy and emotive power to the protest movements in which women have publicly projected this identity. Several scholars have pointed this out, but they have not stressed how women have been in an apt position to appeal to the transcendent promise of justice that the state is supposed to offer. As a liberal government, the Chilean state should ensure that justice encompasses all citizens equally and impartially, irrespective of politics or personal point of view. Yet this is a fetishized understanding of the state, masking the fact that it is neither an impartial nor a unified entity.[33] In practice, states are made up of diverse institutions that are weighed down by power dynamics, from influential special interests to cultural practices and expectations. Corruption is always a possibility. But even if the idea of the state as an impartial arbiter of justice does not match state practice, it matters. It can motivate actors, from citizens to government officials, to realize the promise of fairness that the state offers (Coronil 1997; Trouillot 2001).

This is a critical dynamic in the urban politics of propriety. Urban squatters seeking a legally sanctioned home have often claimed that they deserve the justice that the state should offer. Successfully making this argument has been crucial in granting them legitimacy. But in order to do so, squatters must present themselves in ways that comply with the ideals of fairness that the state is supposed to safeguard. As a part of this compliance, squatters have received access to legally sanctioned homes if they present themselves as being able to fulfill a series of duties that appear outside of politics. The seemingly apolitical nature of claims making helps to explain why women have often played such a prominent role in squatter mobilization, neighborhood organization, and the acquisition of homes. Just as the state has magically projected the appearance of being outside of politics, so has female mobilization. Such activism has thus fit naturally with the cause of granting pobladores housing, a right that is also supposed to supersede politics.

Seen from this perspective, housing activism on the part of pobladores has always depended on whether or not they could perform appropriately in the institutional settings of government and in moments of public spectacle, as in the land seizures.[34] The boundaries of what constitutes acceptable performances have changed over time. The urban politics of propriety is neither inert nor uncontested: there have been intense disagreements about what proper actions pobladores can take and what demands they can legitimately make in seeking homes. Not surprisingly, the revolutionary challenge from Salvador Allende's government provided the boldest test of these boundaries. Overall, however, the socialist regime not only left residential ownership generally intact, it even encouraged it. This was one element of sociospatial and governing relations that was too basic to change wholesale.

Housing Rights and the Question of Dignity

When pobladores receive property titles, they not only obtain state benefits but also improve their status in the social and moral order. It is a demonstration of personal worth and propriety. They become legitimate citizens deserving of homes of their own. The trouble, however, is that claims to a right to homeownership unfold under constraints. Within the institutional frameworks of the state, such claims conform largely to a vision of establishing a particular kind of urban environment, one in which neighborhoods will no longer be "irregular." This vision hinges on a particular understanding of housing and need. Even if pobladores can claim a right to property titles and certain public services, they can claim little else. Pobladores come to have homes of their own, but the benefits they receive hardly broach forms of consumption, taste, and social distinction. They also do not significantly deal with the question of employment, and only partially with debt. But these phenomena are of obvious importance to social actors who wish to establish homes in a commodified mass market.

For their part, pobladores must largely deal with these phenomena by privately mobilizing their own resources. State programs, especially in the neoliberal era, have primarily concentrated on providing legal housing that conforms to zoning practices and codes. They assume little responsibility in other areas. Such programs provide limited forms of housing. Chilean governing elites, the international press, and development experts who support neoliberal policy frameworks look to the provision of property titles and housing to pobladores as a success. But precisely because of this understanding, pobladores find it more difficult to articulate a further critique of the conditions they occupy. They have thus come to live generally in what I call a domesticated periphery, especially between the late 1980s and 2006. As they are domesticated in the home, so they are politically.[35]

Still, the urban politics of propriety is not entirely settled, even as pobladores have homes of their own. If the everyday expectations, practices, and desires that are central to the making of home are often publicly pushed to the side when pobladores become homeowners, they have also weighed on and even haunted debates about housing. They have publicly surfaced at certain points, perhaps in no way more powerfully than in the recurring assertion that deserving citizens have a right to a home life of dignity. Latin American historians and certain social analysts have recently called attention to the importance of ideas of dignity in claims for the rights of citizenship (Elena 2011; Scott 2013; Grovogui 2009).[36] Dignity, these scholars note, is an expansive category: its fulfillment includes notions of justice, respect, and fairness, in which living conditions and patterns of consumption matter intently. It is thus not surprising that the term surfaces in public discussions of housing.

Throughout the histories I explore in this book, Chileans have claimed that being a homeowner holds out the promise of a life of dignity. As we have seen, however, homeownership is not a panacea. Even for pobladores with legally sanctioned properties, home life can be insecure and tense, threatened by a volatile and inequitable political economic context, troubled by unrealized expectations and desires, and disturbed in many instances by gendered forms of domestic violence. Such a tension between actually existing housing and home lives of dignity has ultimately left the housing question in Chile without a satisfactory answer. In the end, the urban politics of propriety has been both enormously productive and restricted, a tension that I seek to illuminate throughout *For a Proper Home*. Within a context of inequitable, insecure, and fractured forms of urbanization, homes provide unsettled foundations for politics and land tenure in the city.

In the second decade of the twenty-first century, Santiago no longer has a large number of campamentos that stand as an affront to the dignity of the squatters who inhabit them, the rights of citizenship, and the development status of the nation. If tensions and discontent still exist, they tend not to coalesce around the cause of housing for pobladores as they once did. In the 1960s and 1970s, pobladores took part in a movement for housing rights that had considerable power and helped to shape the revolutionary activism of the time period. As part of an insurgency, most pobladores would come to have homes of their own. In becoming homeowners, pobladores achieved a status that had once been representative of some of the most profound exclusions in Chile. They achieved this status, however, during the dictatorship and afterwards, when the provision of housing entailed neither forms of social democracy nor socio-spatial inclusion. In the end, pobladores gained homes of their own while entangled in an unfolding web of state and property relations, in which everyday forms of propriety had an inexorable pull.

CHAPTER 2

PROPERTY, GOVERNANCE, AND THE CITY
A *Longue Durée* Perspective

WHILE THE CONNECTION BETWEEN PROPERTY and propriety extends into basic practices and expectations—such as the everyday making of a private, domestic sphere—it also operates in particular ways within the public domains of state formation and citizenship. This chapter untangles some of the strongest and deepest historical roots that made the urban politics of propriety so consequential for state formation, citizenship, activism, and residence among pobladores by the mid-twentieth century. Some of these roots precede even the founding of Santiago, such as the value and prestige that Spanish colonists granted to urban property holding. Still others began to grow when urban civic associations, often in conjunction with reformist and radical political groups, first sought improved home lives for the urban poor in the late nineteenth century. Other roots took hold in the mid-twentieth century, as transnational development bodies, political parties, and popular organizations gave unprecedented resources and attention to the question of housing for the urban poor. Throughout, evolving practices and expectations of family life and gender were of critical importance. Developing a *longue durée* view on the urban politics of propriety, this chapter places the struggles over residence in Santiago during the second half of the twentieth century within histories that tie together the city's property regimes with legacies of Spanish colonialism, the making of the lower urban classes and their living spaces, and key elements of citizenship and state formation.[1]

During the colonial period, homeownership was highly exclusive. As in later periods, however, it generally stood as an instantiation of social belonging and political and legal inclusion. This served as an important foundation for urban citizenship in the national period. By the early twentieth century, homeownership and legally sanctioned residence in the city would generally rise along with the expansion of mass politics. But this would be an uneven, conflictive process. Housing markets were often insecure and corrupt, with dispossession a constant danger. Homes for the urban poor—just like those of anyone else in Santiago—developed in conjunction with the unfolding of class distinctions, residential segregation, family practices and expectations, and insecure and inequitable labor and real estate markets. Yet the homes of the urban poor tended to exist on the margins of legal frameworks, simultaneously stigmatized and segregated. When state bureaucracies focused on these homes and spent resources on them, they generally did so by attacking the effects of poverty, not its causes. These policies targeted decrepit homes for demolition, removal, and (less frequently) improvement, while singling out poor residents for reform, discipline, and criminalization.

Still, the urban poor periodically made their homes a center for activism and protest, at times even helping to change the state's direction. As the twentieth century progressed, pobladores could increasingly point to their precarious housing conditions as a sign that the promises of citizenship had failed to reach them. As citizens, they deserved to live in proper homes. Such a claim entailed two elements: First, it included ideas of what were minimally acceptable housing conditions. Second, the claim itself could only succeed if there was a sense that the claimant was a deserving, legitimate citizen. These two elements developed over time in conjunction with the making of Chilean housing law, social conflicts and popular mobilization, and transnational expertise in urban planning. These elements served as key, *public* foundations that shaped how the links between property and propriety have mattered.

The notion of a minimally acceptable home was, to adopt Paul Rabinow's (1989) formulation from another context, a "norm and form of the social environment." Yet given the volatility and inequity of Chile's urban property regimes, many could not realize this norm and form, a dynamic that could spur both citizen activism and state intervention. Because of this, Santiago's property regimes were politically contentious. They did not lay the basis for a well-functioning city and polity, free of conflict and contradiction. Homes were often the site of unmet desires and struggle. The relationship between the development of homes and evolving norms about proper living conditions and appropriate forms of citizenship provided unsettled foundations for the making of the state and the homes of the urban poor.

Mass Urbanization and State Relations in Fin-de-Siècle Santiago

In the second half of the nineteenth century, in the period right before the term *pobladores* became a catchall referent for the urban poor, one of modernity's principal tensions came more centrally to the fore in Santiago's development. On the one hand, the city experienced a series of tumultuous and destabilizing changes, in which capitalist and state relations relentlessly transformed everyday life. New habits and tastes developed, while political options expanded and social identities based on, among other things, style, residence, work, and inequitable access to commodities spread. On the other hand, however, the normalizing frameworks also at the heart of modern states achieved a more diffuse efficacy. Forms of discipline, conformity, and regulation would be crucial features in the unfolding terrain. Each of these impulses would play an important role in the development of the urban politics of propriety, often standing in tension with each other and providing a basis for state reforms and citizen mobilization.[2]

These dual impulses were at work during the famous projects that Benjamín Vicuña Mackenna, as the provincial governor of Santiago, implemented in the early 1870s. Vicuña Mackenna admired Baron von Haussman's ambitious reworking of Paris under the dictatorship of Napoleon III, and he himself had visited the imperial City of Light and effusively praised Parisian transformations. While Vicuña Mackenna's projects were not on the scale of what Haussman unleashed, they were nevertheless both wide-ranging and an indication that Chilean society was undergoing a profound restructuring.

Vicuña Mackenna was able to implement his reforms only because of the growing size and power of the central state. Unlike much of Latin America, Chile had a relatively stable national government shortly following independence. Such centralization developed in conjunction with the growth of the economy, a general and occasionally volatile expansion that had begun in the second half of the eighteenth century. Based primarily on agricultural exports, this expansion buttressed the authority of an increasingly wealthy oligarchy that had important ties to foreign investors. The elite also depended on the development of markets abroad and a cheap labor force. The central state grew, in no small measure, from the tax receipts of the export trade, a mutually reinforcing relationship that has had long-lasting implications (Salazar, Mancilla, and Durán 1999; Loveman 1988 [1979]).

Chile's successful nineteenth-century military campaigns helped to further consolidate the central state's power. These campaigns—including the War with the Peruvian-Bolivian Confederation (1836–1839), the drawn-out conflicts against groups of the Mapuche in what is now southern Chile, and the War of the Pacific (1879–1883)—established a heroic place in the Chilean imaginary for the military as an apolitical protector of the nation (Frazier 2007; Skuban 2007).[3] The military's prestige only increased with the economic windfall that these wars entailed, especially the War of the Pacific, which gave Chile the northern third of its present territory and included nitrate and copper fields. Exports in nitrates and later in copper made possible an unprecedented expansion in the size and reach of the state bureaucracy by the early twentieth century, something that planners after Vicuña Mackenna took advantage of.[4]

For Vicuña Mackenna, reforming Santiago represented a chance to propel the city and its residents into the very latest in urban design and governance. New tendencies, however, overlapped with enduring legacies. Vicuña Mackenna hoped for a "*policía* of health" and a "*policía* of security." In emphasizing health and security, he drew on emerging, transnational paradigms in public health and criminology.[5] The term *policía*, however, harkened back to conceptions of a proper urban order during the colonial period. Recent scholarship has emphasized that translating the term *policía* as "polity" or "police"—as historians often used to do—hardly does justice to the broad range of meanings and attachments that colonial officials gave to it.[6] While policía was a political community, it was one in which, following Aristotle, good governance reigned supreme. Such governance itself entailed a number of domains in which the just and benevolent reign of rulers was only a starting point.

Quite crucially, proper governance included the form of the built environment. A well-ordered city was to have a rational, attractive, and hierarchical layout, based on the classic grid pattern of Spain's colonial cities.[7] The central *plaza mayor*—boasting the monumental architecture of the city's cathedral and central government buildings—should lead visitors and inhabitants alike to feel a sense of wonder and respect. If the city was to be well organized, it was also to be beautiful, possessing an underlying urban aesthetic of order that served as a basis upon which to judge the merits and grandeur of the city and the polity. Chilean cities, and Santiago itself, had long fallen short of this ideal. They had been relatively modest cities on the Spanish frontier, lacking in resources and designed more with military defense in mind than for aesthetic reasons (Guarda 1966). While Santiago eventually did establish a grid pattern and monumental architecture, it remained a second-tier city in the colonial order. In the national period, Vicuña Mackenna and other urban reformers showed great concern for improving Santiago's international standing.

From Santiago's founding through the mid-nineteenth century, elite men, along with their families and servants, lived next to the city center, a geographic instantiation of their place in society. In the colonial period, they were the only ones who had a right to take part in the *cabildo*, the town council. Outside of the church, these men tended to be among the few property holders, although there were a small number of women. Beyond the city center, Spaniards and mestizos of lower rank lived a ring farther away. When not living in the homes of the elite as servants and laborers, the lowest classes occupied dwellings on the outskirts of town. The geography of the city dynamically reinforced its social hierarchy. Full political and social belonging, moreover, was inseparable from sanctioned residence in the city, in which owning residential property was paramount.

As a governing paradigm, policía not only connected ideas about just rule and the orderly layout of the city, it also entailed forms of behavior and discipline. The attractive harmony of the city landscape and the benevolence of its rulers should be matched by proper forms of comportment among the populace. Questions of residence, honor, faith, sexual propriety, civism, charity, industriousness, and appearance all carried weight in assessing social worth. As a part of policía, subjects should keep the city clean and orderly. Numerous ordinances demanded the maintenance and upkeep of cities (de Solano 1996, xxxvii; Lechner 1981). Those not properly settled in the city were the most suspect: the crown and local officials passed a string of regulations against vagrancy, prostitution, and public drunkenness, in addition to the making of temporary shanties.[8]

Policía thus developed links between an orderly sense of aesthetics, social hierarchies, sociopolitical belonging, appropriate governance, and the urban landscape. These links tended to elide the ways in which Chile's inequitable and often volatile economy constantly upset the ideal of urban development. Dependent on healthy agricultural production and exports, the economy lacked size and dynamism. In Santiago, many could not live up to the ideals of residence and behavior, even if they had wanted to (which, of course, should not be taken for granted). The sense that order depended on proper forms of urban residence and clearly demarcated social and spatial boundaries sat uncomfortably with the everyday workings of the city. In colonial Santiago, officials continually filed reports registering their disgust and frustration at being unable to clean up the outlying areas of the city, prevent the building of temporary housing, and otherwise properly constrain the activities of poor residents (see de Ramón 2007, 32–59). But even if the elements of policía were ideals far from being carried out in practice, they still carried weight. They would continue to do so in the national period, though from a more diverse array of ideological perspectives and within a context of emerging forms of popular sovereignty.[9]

A half century after independence, Vicuña Mackenna continued to follow elements of the perspective entailed in policía. Consider, for example, his hierarchical vision of the city and its residents. Vicuña Mackenna divided the city in two. He defined "proper Santiago" (la ciudad propia) as "polished," "elegant," "civilized," "enlightened," and "Christian." Areas outside of proper

Santiago were, in Vicuña Mackenna's racialized terms, "barbaric," the home of "African hordes" (de Ramón 2007, 145–46). These areas included overcrowded *conventillo* tenements and poorly constructed *arrabales*, another term that had colonial roots and referred to neighborhoods made up of Arabs.

Residents of conventillos and arrabales were not property owners; arrabales, in fact, lacked titles entirely. Residents in arrabales could not access a baseline basket of services that others should enjoy, something also true for many in the conventillos. It was only in the civilized, proper city that the government implicitly promised to provide what Vicuña Mackenna termed "necessities": paved roads, sidewalks, public lighting, potable water, law enforcement, and schools. The notion that the state should ensure these services to deserving urban citizens was becoming a significant norm of governance.

The exclusive nature of this norm played a crucial role in Vicuña Mackenna's plans. He oversaw, for example, the construction of a barrier around Santiago, a so-called sanitary cordon that consisted of the Mapocho River, agricultural estates, certain parks, and roads designed to be more easily patrolled. According to planners, the barrier would protect proper Santiago from the "pestilential influences of the arrabales" that bordered the city.[10] It would thus keep the civilized safe and healthy while segregating and controlling the popular classes (Vicuña 2001; de Ramón 2007; Hidalgo 2005, 32–33).[11] Those inside should have access to infrastructure services considered basic. If citizenship entails boundaries of inclusion and exclusion, the "sanitary cordon" was a remarkable physical manifestation of how officials such as Vicuña Mackenna sought to manage the limits of urban citizenship.

Vicuña Mackenna also administered the demolition and, to a lesser degree, the improvement of arrabales and conventillos in Santiago itself, especially following an outbreak of smallpox in 1871. In response, urban planners sought neighborhood demolitions and improvement projects, which included efforts to identify residents and verify their property status. In doing so, planners sought to *sanear* these neighborhoods, a verb that simultaneously means to "regulate," "sanitize," and "make well." Importantly, the term *sanear* continues to be used into the present day.[12] The assertion of state control over the arrabales and conventillos thus overlapped with assumptions about how to establish proper regulation, sanitation, well-being, and minimally acceptable conditions. These neighborhoods had a status that marked them as pathological and impure, criminal and dangerous, unhealthy and unattractive, immoral and in need of remediation. Arrabales and conventillos thus stood in contradistinction to presumably normal and healthy neighborhoods. Notions entailed in policía ultimately fused with more contemporary discourses in public health, hygiene, and criminology, discourses that resonated far beyond

Santiago's borders and would continue to circulate well into the future. Such discourses had an important regulating element, but they often superseded the control of government officials. They were an important element of state reform initiatives, while also, as I discuss below, helping to lay the groundwork for forms of protest.

In their projects to *sanear* neighborhoods, officials evicted residents but did not generally improve the affordable housing stock. This dynamic would become a pattern. Vicuña Mackenna's planners did attempt to provide incentives for construction companies to build low-income homes, but these incentives were largely ineffective. The displaced subsequently had few legal housing options. They often went to live in the informal arrabales and *rancherías* that lay just beyond the city's borders (Espinoza 1988, 16). When government bodies helped to upgrade existing housing, this tended to increase its value, a process that often made these properties more expensive. When this happened in the conventillos, the urban poor could often no longer afford their rent (de Ramón 2007; Hidalgo 2005, 27, 33). Instead of providing homes for low-income residents, the slum improvement and removal programs contributed to real estate booms in certain parts of the city, heightened residential segregation, and reinforced the bias toward urban property holding.

As a part of his vision to bring civilization and progress to the city, Vicuña Mackenna extended the central street grid and widened the main thoroughfares. As in Paris, these projects facilitated mass circulation and the rapid deployment of police forces. Planners also demarcated the city into residential, commercial, industrial, and recreational zones. They bolstered efforts to contain trash, helping to prevent the outbreak of certain diseases while fortifying a general sense of disgust at noxious smells and dirtiness. Intertwined notions of beauty and order were a constant concern, demonstrated most spectacularly by the construction of public parks and "green spaces" (the so-called lungs of the city), monumental architecture, and a pedestrian-friendly central core. Downtown Santiago still bears the mark of these efforts, from tourist attractions such as the oft renovated Cerro Santa Lucía to the numerous storefronts, restaurants, and cafes that surround the Plaza de Armas.

Vicuña Mackenna's projects also facilitated the expansion of capitalist relations. Yet far from the regimented order that he sought, this expansion was often destabilizing and chaotic, helping to release what Marshall Berman (1982) calls a "maelstrom of modernity." It contributed to destroying older economic relationships and eroding preexisting hierarchies, while creating an unemployed and underemployed segment of the lower classes. Crucially, Chile's agrarian capitalism undermined previous forms of rural settlement. Wheat production for the international market expanded dramatically from the 1840s to the end of the century, doubling between 1880 and 1895. Large, specialized estates became dominant, spreading throughout the central valley that surrounds Santiago. These estates tended to force out small landholders and certain agricultural workers (Hurtado 1966, 96, 161).

Vagrancy laws sought to keep laborers tethered to estates, but a significant number left the countryside. By the early twentieth century, agricultural development had stagnated. Yet rural landownership remained concentrated, a dynamic that would last until the early 1970s. These processes, in conjunction with other factors such as the allure of city life, expanding urban industries, a growing state sector (with central bureaucracies concentrated in Santiago), an overall increase in the national population, and the demise of nitrate production in the 1920s, contributed to explosive growth in the size of the capital city. The city grew from 177,271 people to 542,432 between 1885 and 1930 (DeShazo 1983, 4).[13]

As all of this was unfolding, Santiago's downtown streets increasingly became the site of collisions and interactions between different groups and classes. For the elite, such a dynamic had long been a concern, but it now occurred on an unprecedented scale. The visible existence in the city center of itinerant street vendors, vagabond children, and prostitutes undermined the urban aesthetic of order that Vicuña Mackenna and subsequent officials sought to cultivate. Danger, disorder, and insecurity were seemingly all too present, concentrating concern on the much discussed "social question."

Santiago's residents formulated responses to the social question amid a deepening commodification of social relations in the city. If the downtown area became a gathering place for people from all walks of life, it was also a place where one could easily find the attractions of a mass consumer market, including storefronts filled with foreign items. Styles proliferated, contributing to new expectations in everyday life and emerging forms of class distinction. The lower classes were themselves a part of the act, if in somewhat limited and insecure ways. By the late nineteenth century, they tended to have at least one store-bought outfit, their "Sunday clothes." Most assumed that imported teas and sugars would be a relatively affordable part of their diets, not to mention domestically produced breads and alcohol. A more privileged sector of the lower classes expected meat, although its regular consumption was beyond the means of many. It carried a certain prestige in the arrabales and conventillos. Mass-produced household furniture and accessories became relatively common, if of a poor quality (DeShazo 1983; Orlove 1997).

Members of the upper class, for their part, established new forms of privilege as elements of Chilean capitalism and republican governance undermined older forms of hierarchy. By the end of the nineteenth century, wealthy residents had begun to move away from the central Plaza de Armas. They built a number of neighborhoods in an expanded downtown area and to the east and south. These neighborhoods featured opulent and walled-in two- and three-story homes in gothic, neoclassic and baroque designs, with extensive inner courtyards. Such homes, in addition to the proliferation of elite clubs, pastimes, and networks, signaled a further privatization of privilege and a remaking of Santiago's fractured urban landscape. The elite lived in a tight-knit, exclusive environment, in which even political opponents tended to be tied together through extended business, leisure, and kinship connections (Vicuña 2001, 43–50; Brito 1995). This general characterization of wealthy Santiago would continue to be important throughout the twentieth century (Zeitlin and Ratcliff 1988).

The importance of family and kinship relations was far from limited to the upper classes. Such relations were central to the social reproduction of all socioeconomic groups. But amid the creative forms of destruction that capitalist relations unleashed, many could not live in the single, patriarchal family homes that elites and social reformers embraced. Many did not have the resources needed to live up to this ideal, even if they had the desire to do so. Since the independence period, Chilean presidents and legislators had promised to protect the family and the home (Thomas 2011, 34–41). By the second half of the nineteenth century, the ideal of developing a nuclear family became ever more important to legal frameworks and institutions committed to the "social question." Charity organizations and state agencies focused increasing attention on those who moved around, did not live in legally sanctioned properties, and breached expectations about proper family roles. As with Vicuña Mackenna's reforms, norms about behavior were of great significance.

Yet state frameworks in the area of family relations, as with housing demolitions, often contributed to the conditions they ostensibly sought to ameliorate. They also reinforced standards about the proper makeup of families. Consider, for example, the 1857 civil code, which stiffened the means by which sons and daughters born out of wedlock could establish paternity and the concomitant rights that filiation offered. As Nara Milanich (2009) demonstrates, this law, which was a model throughout Latin America, excluded a large underclass from the expanding entitlements offered by the state. When children were not recognized by the courts as legitimate, they could neither officially marry nor take part in a number of state-sanctioned economic activities. This helped to create a legally kinless underclass that faced crippling obstacles in the labor market. Worse, this underclass tended to pass their status on to their offspring. As with housing and the creation of arrabales and rancherías outside of Santiago, such a situation contributed to the making of informal, extralegal relationships and activities. Yet it simultaneously reinforced normative frameworks; having family relations considered proper and legitimate ultimately had significant advantages. Family law thus helped to shape class inequities and social stigmatizations.

In this context, state agencies and charity organizations looked with alarm at how low-income groups often had to maintain their livelihoods. A number of these bodies concentrated on the increasing number of women who began to enter a growing industrial labor force. Nearly 30 percent of factory workers from the 1880s through the 1920s were women. Reformers and philanthropists sought to educate these women on the finer points of domesticity and keep them in labors appropriate to their sex, as Elizabeth Hutchison (2001) puts it.[14]

They also concentrated on the many economic activities that fell outside of legal boundaries (Salazar 2000 and 1992; Milanich 2009; Brito 1995; Zárate 1995). As they did so, they focused on the lower classes, despite the fact that all classes took part in such informal practices and that state policy had directly contributed to their making. Both the upper and middle classes hired domestic servants, did business with street vendors, slept with prostitutes, contributed to the circulation of children without legally recognized family ties, and bought and sold contraband, including illegal housing. Given the ubiquity of these phenomena, state institutions could at times have relative tolerance for them. On a very basic level, such informal practices helped to constitute social and economic relations in the city. Far from being outliers in the making of urban modernity in Chile, they were integral to it.

For their part, the popular sectors often had a higher tolerance for extralegal activities, including informal housing. Such practices, after all, formed a part of how many in the lower classes negotiated the obstacles of everyday life, especially as formal jobs were not widely available to them. Tolerance for these practices, however, should not be taken to mean that the popular sectors occupied a world either autonomous from state frameworks and capitalist relations or in singular opposition to them.[15] The informal was not simply a parallel realm that highlighted the state's failings and allowed the lower classes to resist dominant labor dynamics, disciplinary paradigms, or property regimes.[16] Though informal practices were often necessary, they also tended to be insecure and fraught, entangled with the formal sector and set within a broader context of sociospatial relations, cultural expectations, and legal and policing paradigms.

Still, the fact that informal practices tended to be concentrated among the lower classes and were more visible in their neighborhoods had significant consequences. It reinforced territorial forms of stigma, making it easier to blame the lower classes for their living conditions and subjecting them to state and social sanction. Many in the lower classes, moreover, could quite naturally be desirous of the privileges that full legal and social belonging entailed. Yet if they wished to access these privileges, they would have to change their behavior or at least present themselves in ways considered appropriate. Such pressures only became greater as the lower classes began to take part in more visible, public forms of activism, in which their status as legitimate and proper citizens became paramount.

Popular Mobilization and Ideological Conflict

During the Parliamentary Republic (1891–1924), numerous civic associations, including renters' leagues, consumer societies, sports clubs, and cooperatives came to the fore in low-income urban neighborhoods. These associations often worked in conjunction with militant labor unions and mutual aid societies.[17] Some of these organizations drew on strands of socialism and anarchism. They often formed part of an increasingly combative opposition, one that valorized working-class struggles and celebrated a militant popular subject. This opposition provided a language of class exploitation to interpret social life, singling out a predatory and unjust oligarchy that stood against the values of national identity and kept the lower classes from assuming their proper place in society.[18]

Importantly, however, the new urban civic associations, no matter their political character, acted as citizens' organizations. They claimed to represent dignified Chileans, whose propriety made them deserving of better treatment. As Brenda Elsey (2011, 28) asserts, the "pursuit of respectability and the embrace of radicalism often came together." These civic associations tended to work within the prevailing frameworks of governance, even if they could push the boundaries of what was possible in the state. In organizing around specific causes, these groups generally sought to achieve baseline standards of living for the citizens they represented. There was a great deal of conflict over these standards and the conditions of the popular classes. As mass politics and competing ideological visions increased in importance, more sectors in Chilean society would publicly weigh in on the question of what kind of living conditions citizens could appropriately demand.

This issue was central to the activism and violence that characterized Red Week, a series of riots and violent reactions that shook Santiago in 1905.[19] In a city of some 350,000 at the time, anywhere between twenty thousand and fifty thousand took part in the demonstrations. Denouncing a rise in food prices that exacerbated an eight-year shortage of meat and the pain caused by high levels of unemployment, protestors responded to a crisis in everyday forms of consumption. Made up primarily of artisanal, manufacturing, and transportation workers, demonstrators tended to be from a more privileged sector of the lower classes. Many were recent migrants from the countryside who had been *inquilinos*—tenant sharecroppers with long-term residence in rural estates. Notably, inquilinos had greater social prestige than *peones*, seasonal workers who occupied the most difficult jobs. Inquilinos lived in solid houses of a good quality and generally had meat as a relatively frequent part of their meals. Peones, meanwhile, lived in poorly constructed, temporary *ranchos* with a more limited diet. As such, home life conditions were a clear indication of status.

In the mobilizations, protestors drew on a particular moral economic framework. As Benjamin Orlove (1997, 235) argues, they interpreted contemporary conditions as violating "deeply held views about proper economic relations." This included expectations about the everyday constitution of the home, from the consumption of meat to housing conditions. Certain neighborhood organizations involved in the riots demanded that landlords improve the quality of their housing or cancel their rents. Initially, centrist newspapers expressed sympathy for the protestors, asserting that the working classes were suffering undue hardships. Such arguments implied that citizens could properly demand that the state ensure affordable living conditions, a claim that would have enduring resonance.

Building on this support, protestors attempted to deliver a petition to President Germán Riesco. Yet police officers prevented them from doing so. A group of activists then threatened to overtake La Moneda, the presidential palace. A mass confrontation followed, in which the police wounded fifty-three and arrested 148 more. The riots then began in full. Protestors constructed street barricades, cut electricity and telegraph wires, burned street cars, and attacked a senator's house. They also took part in targeted looting, especially of warehouses that stored meat and pawnshops where many owed debts. The boldness of these actions, however, came at a price: protestors soon began to lose the support of centrist politicians and media observers.[20]

In response to the extraordinary circumstances, the prefect of Santiago and the minister of war adopted exceptional measures. They not only called in military units that had been away from Santiago on exercises but also authorized firefighters and a number of civilian "white guards" to help put down the protests. Soldiers from the war department handed out weapons to men who gathered at the prestigious Club de la Unión. The armed civilians subsequently went on rampages. After a week of mass arrests and street conflicts, government forces and their civilian allies had killed two hundred to three hundred people. Class and ideological hatreds fueled their actions, spurred on by the fear that the popular classes were occupying areas of the city that did not belong to them, upsetting the proper order of things. To devastating effect, reactionaries acted on their own sense of propriety in sociospatial and political relations.

The carnage of Red Week was part of a broader cycle of reactionary violence. A major strike in the port city of Valparaíso resulted in thirty deaths in 1903, while a mass protest in Santa María de Iquique, in the nitrate region, led to a massacre of some three thousand protestors in 1907. As Mario Garcés (2003, 81) points out, such reactions underscore how violent and coercive the state could be. Officials did not enter into meaningful dialogue with the opposition. They did not seem to be much concerned with developing consent and forging popular legitimacy.

Yet coercion alone does not explain how Chilean state relations continued to unfold. Despite repression and moments of authoritarianism, democracy would remain a cherished national myth, granting greater weight to the idea that the state could be a true expression of popular sovereignty and will (Elsey 2011). Many activists, civic associations, and labor unions may have firmly believed in the violent and exploitative nature of the opposition they faced, but they generally adopted legal means in working for change. These same groups developed memories of events such as the 1905 riots and the 1907 Santa María de Iquique massacre that shaped how they viewed themselves as oppressed historical actors who could mobilize and protest (Frazier 2007). Such memories would be crucial to the formation of the Left and its ties to popular activism.

For their part, legislators and state planners eventually implemented reforms that responded to some of the demands that had been made during the cycle of protests. The government lifted tariffs against Argentine beef in 1909 and began to implement new policies in housing and urban development. In taking these actions, officials sought to quell popular discontent and provide an effective answer to the social question. Such reforms were far from radical. Officials implemented housing and urban reforms in dialogue with transnational public health and urban planning paradigms, as similar legislative efforts were happening elsewhere. They also drew on private initiatives that were already in place.[21] The reforms, moreover, expanded capitalist relations and propagated a series of privileges. Still, they implicitly included promises of fairness and improved circumstances for the lower classes, based on evolving standards about minimally acceptable living conditions. As the twentieth century progressed, such promises would become even more important, as Santiago continued its massive growth and housing for the poor became even more volatile, insecure, and controversial.

Housing Reform and the Status of Pobladores

As state relations unfolded, they had contradictory impulses, something particularly evident when looking at how they contributed to the making of popular groups such as the pobladores. On the one hand, the state propagated inequitable class relations and contributed to the stigmatization of pobladores and the places they called home. On the other hand, however, the state also provided a forum for protest, a space within which alternative political visions could flourish, and a site within which rights could be claimed and secured. In related fashion, pobladores occupied a pronounced, if particular place in the contested national imaginary: viewed, alternatively, as a dangerous and barbaric people in need of discipline, an impoverished group deserving of charity and support, and as an oppressed and potentially revolutionary subject whose struggles offered liberation and redemption. Given the multiple, conflicting, and even contradictory places that pobladores have occupied, it is little wonder that relations with pobladores have often been inflamed and explosive.

In the field of housing, the government passed the Ley de Habitaciones Obreras, the Law of Worker Housing, at the height of the cycle of protests in 1906. Legislators publicly supported the law in order to both strengthen Chilean families and overcome social conflicts. One deputy claimed that proper housing supported the "healthy moral and legal constitution of the family, a fundamental base for every society . . . and for social peace."[22] With homes of their own, workers would be more productive and orderly, focused on their families and on paying off their debts. Such an attitude linked elite opinion to emerging transnational attitudes toward governance and homeownership.[23]

Practically speaking, the law permitted the state to take a more proactive role in regulating housing and developing policies that would allow the lower classes, and especially workers, to access it.[24] It created local housing councils that consisted of officials from the central government, the municipalities, and the church, in addition to state-appointed representatives from worker societies. Of great significance, the legislation helped to bring beneficiaries into banking and credit institutions, many of which were new.[25] Recipients of housing subsidies, generally organized in cooperatives, had to assume down payments and pay off mortgages. This meant that middle-income sectors and a more privileged sector of the working classes entered the programs established by the law. The poorest tended to be excluded from state housing benefits. Beneficiaries, meanwhile, could face foreclosures when they could not pay off their mortgages, something that invariably happened, especially in periods of crisis.

Ultimately, legally sanctioned, affordable housing was not possible for many. During the nineteen years the law was in effect, the state demolished more housing than it subsidized, built, or improved, by a margin of nearly two to one (Hidalgo 2005, 67–82). State housing policies thus continued to exacerbate poor housing conditions by focusing on its effects rather than its causes. Still, the new laws built on preexisting legislation that had sought to ensure a minimal set of conditions for homes in legally established urban neighborhoods. Citizens in these areas had a right to such municipal services and utilities as sidewalks, paved roads, lighting, potable water, sewer systems, law enforcement, schools, and garbage removal. They should also have access to forms of recreation and green spaces, helping to create a healthy and vigorous population. Soccer fields and clubs were particularly important (Elsey 2011).[26] Homes for low-income residents should also meet certain building standards and provide access to fresh air and sunlight. By the 1920s all of the political parties promised to ensure the delivery of these benefits and services (Walter 2005, 100). Yet the housing councils and other regulatory bodies generally did not provide effective enforcement for the relevant legislation, which made it relatively easy for landowners and developers to ignore it (Espinoza 1988, 45; Hidalgo 2005, 93).[27]

Neighborhood civic associations and housing cooperatives often decried the impropriety of this situation, "making use," as one group put it, "of their rights in defense of their homes and families."[28] They wrote letters to newspapers, sought the support of elected officials, and denounced their situation to government representatives. In 1925, workers' associations, neighborhood organizations, and consumer groups, many of which had the support of anarchists and the recently formed Communist Party, took part in massive renters' strikes in both Santiago and Valparaíso. Demands for housing took center stage. These protests did not achieve the more radical goals of some of the groups involved, but they did further ensure that the quality of urban home life for the poor would remain an issue of critical political importance (Espinoza 1988, 47–120; Elsey 2011, 90–126; Salazar, Mancilla, and Durán 1999).

They also kept the pressure on to make homeownership a right of citizenship. All the way up to the present, this demand has sat in tension with the notion that housing is merely a good in the marketplace (Gómez Leyton 2004; Bruey 2012). A representative from the Renters' League, the umbrella organization that had spearheaded the protests, argued that unhealthy conventillos were a "national shame." He made the following demand: "We want each worker or employee to have their own comfortable and hygienic home, without a down payment.... That is patriotism."[29] Subsequent laws, including a Renters' Law (Ley de Arrendatarios) and a Law of Affordable Housing (Ley de Habitaciones Baratas), both passed in 1925, improved regulatory oversight and helped to establish the state's responsibility in ensuring affordable housing of a minimal quality. The government's housing programs would subsequently become more ambitious. But a great number of Santiago residents would continue to live either as renters or in homes without legal sanction. They would not have homes of their own. Private property would remain dominant, enshrined anew in the 1925 constitution. Yet there were exceptions "in favor of the general interests of the state [and] of the health of the citizens."[30] Both officials and citizens would take advantage of these exceptions in the ensuing decades.

Beyond new housing laws, other reform efforts held out the promise of legally sanctioned residence in Santiago. Yet these efforts also generally fell short, if in often unintended ways. Legislation in 1906 established a number of new municipalities in greater Santiago. This included Renca and a number of others to the south, north, and west of downtown. Many of these municipalities had large rural estates, in addition to arrabales and rancherías, the informal neighborhoods that had fallen outside of Santiago's jurisdiction. The new legislation was meant to change this, making the new municipalities an administrative part of greater Santiago. As such, these municipalities were now responsible for providing services considered basic to urban areas. They were also expected to offer legally sanctioned houses, perhaps even homeownership.[31]

The process of settling these newly established urban areas, however, did not go according to plan. Municipal officials, in addition to the owners of a number of agricultural estates, sold off large swaths of land to developers. A great number of middle- and lower-income neighborhoods came into being. Developers advertised many of the neighborhoods sprouting up as *poblaciones obreras*, workers' neighborhoods, meant explicitly for wage earners of the working classes who could now have homes of their own.[32]

The development of these neighborhoods, however, tended to be muddled and chaotic. There was a great deal of speculation and corruption in the land grab (*El Mercurio*, Feb. 23, 1929, 5; Walter 2005, 138; Hidalgo 2005, 125–28, 146–47). Municipal officials and estate owners profited handsomely from the selling of land, while regulatory bodies often provided insufficient oversight of the new neighborhoods. The developments often did not include services when residents moved into their homes, something subsequent laws sought to forbid. Certain landlords established modest forms of legally sanctioned rental housing. In other cases, however, residents of new neighborhoods found themselves the holders of fake land titles. They lived in so-called phantom subdivisions, neighborhoods that swindlers had created, often fraudulently acting as the heads of housing cooperatives (Hidalgo 2005, 128).[33] Such neighborhoods would be a part of the urban landscape until the last decades of the twentieth century.[34]

The people who lived in these areas often found themselves in a troubling legal bind. Since they did not have legitimate property titles, their land tenure was insecure. Moreover, they could not legitimately ask for the provision of services unless they could prove that they were proper citizens and could show that they had been cheated. Yet legal responses, if they happened at all, were extremely slow, often stretching out for decades. Residents of the already existing arrabales and rancherías experienced similar difficulties, although their problems could be worse since they did not hold even contested land titles.

Legislators had not designed housing laws in such a way that state institutions would completely take over the administration of neighborhoods. Through subsidies and the provision of urban services, state housing programs worked in conjunction with private developers and financial institutions. Yet neither government bureaucracies nor private businesses wished to take on the task of transforming "phantom" and "irregular" subdivisions, as it was a costly and laborious process. In the end, the number of these subdivisions increased dramatically in greater Santiago, especially following the economic depressions of the early 1920s and 1930s.

Santiago's volatile real estate market only exacerbated the problems. There was a brief, spectacular boom in the late 1920s, including an expansion in credit to the lower classes.[35] The Law of Affordable Housing, enacted in 1925, had facilitated this expansion by granting credit preference to housing cooperatives (Gross 1991, 31). With the onset of the Great Depression, however, this boom came to a crashing halt. As unemployment rose to unprecedented heights, many indebted Chileans left their mortgages or ceased paying their rents, leading to an increase in evictions and abandonment (Espinoza 1988, 121–29; Gross 1991, 31).

This development, coupled with a rise in immigration to Santiago, meant that many looked to informal forms of housing, including squatting. Squatters could take advantage of the fact that there was a large number of legally dubious homes without services and established titles. They often set up makeshift housing on the edges of the phantom subdivisions, further complicating efforts to legalize these areas. Squatters also built precarious homes in undeveloped areas that were undesirable or unsafe. They took over areas prone to flooding, especially along the banks of the Mapocho River and its tributaries; at the same time they could live next to or even in garbage dumps (de Ramón 2007, 237). Squatters not only faced extreme environmental hazards, they also confronted the hostility of neighboring communities and officials, including the police.

Given that both state agencies and private institutions often failed to take a leading role in providing services and property titles, residents of phantom subdivisions and squatter settlements increasingly built up their neighborhoods and houses on their own. They literally became builders of the city. As they did so, residents developed collective ties and organizations that reinforced class and neighborhood solidarities.[36] Crucially, both state programs and charities, especially those in the Catholic church and in mutual aid societies, began to support these efforts. These organizations provided technical help in building infrastructure and small, "emergency" housing structures. Hogar de Cristo, one of Chile's largest and best-known Catholic charities today, cut its teeth in this arena (Magnet 1978, 58–63). Through these processes, residents made their informal neighborhoods more permanent, bolstering their claims to the land as they demonstrated discipline and commitment.

Beginning in the 1930s, certain state housing programs institutionalized the notion that residents could acquire homes by building them along with neighborhood infrastructure. In designing these programs, lawmakers drew on the clauses of adverse possession in the 1925 constitution, which stipulated that citizens could claim a right to property if they occupied it and put it to good use. Housing and neighborhood development programs subsequently began to rely on the labor that residents provided in order to develop their homes and *sanear* their neighborhoods.[37] In these cases, state-subsidized developers would provide access to land, but with only minimal forms of housing and services. Residents could become homeowners, at least in part, by providing construction labor. This dynamic bolstered the move toward increasing access to homeownership that was not solely dependent on market exchange. It reinforced the notion that work and sacrifice should be rewarded with property, something which housing rights activists had long been arguing.[38] This would set an important precedent. In the land seizures, pobladores could strengthen their claims to land tenure by building their own homes and neighborhoods. Making a legitimate, proper use of land was a key to acquiring housing rights.[39]

It would also be important in the land seizures for pobladores to demonstrate personal discipline and appropriate forms of behavior. The link between comportment and residence, of course, had a long historical trajectory in Santiago. But the housing cooperatives codified this link based on standards of the time period. For members of cooperatives, familial status and personal behavior were paramount. To access loans, applicants needed to have already saved a sufficient amount and to have dependent children. They had to agree to dedicate their homes to proper, residential use. They were not allowed, for example, to sell liquor, rent rooms, or establish places of gambling or prostitution. Moreover, as the Law of Affordable Housing put it, they could not take part in "immoral conduct . . . against the good customs and morality of neighboring pobladores" (Hidalgo 2005, 114). Individual housing cooperative covenants had clauses that sought to ensure the "intellectual, moral, physical, and economic well-being" of associates, keeping them from falling into the kinds of "pernicious vices that corrupt humanity."[40] They were not supposed to drink excessively, take part in illegal activities, fight with family members or neighbors, or miss taking part in collective forms of labor. In the cooperatives, norms about appropriate behavior were integral to the extension of homeownership. Moral expectations were woven into the social and spatial landscapes of the city.

In such an environment, Chileans began to develop a new vocabulary through which to describe urban residential settlement. By the 1920s, Chileans talked about the *callampas*, the "mushroom" neighborhoods that seemed to grow uncontrollably and haphazardly in the middle of the night. The term *pobladores* also became a blanket term for the urban poor. Yet the expression still referred, as it had since colonial times, to inhabitants who had legal residence and deserved to be a part of the polity.[41] It was thus very different from other terms for the lower classes, such as *rotos*, "the broken ones," or *huachos*, abandoned orphans without "appropriate" kin relations.[42] As a term, *pobladores* conveyed a sense of belonging. By living in homes of their own, pobladores presumably worked in the legal economy and had the right kind of families. They should, therefore, enjoy the full rights and privileges of citizenship.

Yet many of the pobladores in the emerging urban landscapes did not live in legally sanctioned neighborhoods. Instead, they lived in poorly constructed, insecure areas, on the borders of legality. Outsiders generally conceived of these neighborhoods as dangerous, indicative of a moral and social breakdown. Marked as belonging to the lower classes, legally sanctioned but also not, pobladores occupied a shifty and contested position. The tension between the two connotations in the term *pobladores* would have long-term significance. The status of pobladores and their housing conditions would remain an unresolved, contentious issue.

The Housing Question under State-Led Development

The central state adopted a more proactive role in Chile's development in the wake of the tremendous dislocations of the 1920s and 1930s. A quintessential example of a country that relied on exporting primary products with little added value, Chile depended on healthy foreign markets and capital flows from abroad. By certain indicators, the Great Depression devastated Chile more than any other nation in the world, a sign of the country's deep integration into global trading networks. For a brief period in the late 1920s—following a severe recession in the early 1920s—foreign investment had poured in, contributing to Santiago's real estate boom. But by 1930, mass unemployment took hold, construction foundered, industries folded, and foreclosures increased.

During the crises, migrants increasingly streamed into Santiago from the northern mining areas and the agricultural zones. Even with a relative recovery in the economy in the late 1930s, mass immigration to Santiago continued to take place. Between 1940 and 1970, the city nearly tripled in size, growing from 1,075,000 to 2,779,499.[43] (This growth has continued, although at a slower rate: in 2002 the city's population stood at 5,822,316 [INE 2005].) This expansion far outpaced the population growth in the country as a whole, as Santiago's share of the national population rose from 21 to 31 percent between 1930 and 1970. Several low-income municipalities saw their populations increase exponentially. The municipality of Renca, for example, grew from 16,262 to 72,829 during this period.[44]

This demographic explosion compounded the poor housing options that pobladores faced. Population growth contributed to rising housing demand, even as many of the conventillos in the city center became further run-down and overcrowded. Housing prices generally increased, despite efforts at rent control. In response, many slept in temporary shanties in squatter settlements, while others, especially in the 1930s, camped out in public parks, under bridges, and in the Cerro San Cristóbal (Walter 2005, 168–69). In municipalities such as Renca, a number of new neighborhoods appeared. But some of these neighborhoods fell short of following the norms and forms of urban development. Even neighborhoods with legitimate land titles at times lacked the infrastructure that they should have had. According to the 1952 census, 36.2 percent of Santiago's residents lived in "poor" housing conditions, including homes in callampas, run-down conventillos, and phantom subdivisions (INE 1952a).

The grim housing options for most pobladores underscore limitations in the project of state-led development. The state's policies to promote industrialization had initially led to an impressive expansion in manufacturing. But high tariff walls and subsidies for Chilean businesses could not make up for the limited size of the national market. Moreover, the country continued to rely on exports, principally of copper, in order to generate the foreign exchange that would pay for factory inputs, infrastructure, and imported manufactured goods and luxury items. Copper accounted for more than 80 percent of Chile's exports and from 10 to 15 percent of the GNP from the 1940s to the 1960s (Moran 1974). Copper's revenues were volatile, however, and did not permit a broad industrialization and diversification of the economy, especially given the size of the domestic market. Manufacturing remained largely limited to producing such goods as furniture, food, and textiles. Because of this, few new industrial jobs were created during the 1950s and the 1960s.[45]

Yet the size of the state bureaucracy continued to grow, becoming an increasingly important source of employment and investment. By the late 1960s Chile had the second largest state sector as a percentage of GNP of any country in Latin America (Valenzuela 1978, 13). Given the foundering process of industrialization and continued reliance on state spending and foreign goods, inflation was a perennial problem. Following the advice of the Klein-Saks Mission, a North American delegation that came to Chile in the mid-1950s, President Carlos Ibáñez del Campo adopted austerity measures. This led, however, to unemployment and eventual discontent, including another round of bloody riots in Santiago in 1957 (Salazar 1990, Milos 2007).

In Chile, as elsewhere, the project of state-led development confronted basic issues about mass consumption, everyday living conditions, and fairness and inclusion.[46] This ultimately made the project a tense one. Deep social schisms remained at the same time that promises of greater inclusion and improved living conditions were only partially met. State-led development generally left many of the privileges of the Chilean elite intact. They continued to dominate agriculture and industry. Despite the increasingly contested nature of the polity, elite interests still weighed heavily on the workings of the state. The tariffs and subsidies offered under the policies of import-substitution industrialization served certain members of the elite more than anyone else.[47] A middle class had largely succeeded in finding employment and gaining access to housing, health care, education, and pensions.[48] Some other sectors had carved out an important space for themselves in Chilean society and in its political life. But agricultural laborers and unemployed or underemployed urban groups did not generally enjoy many of the benefits offered by state-led development.

Still, the possibility of greater inclusion, and perhaps radical transformation, remained. Despite often intense repression, Leftist unions, civic associations, and political parties grew stronger, offering alternative visions of Chile's future, in which the struggles of the past and present would lead to a more just and inclusive society.[49] Leftists had revolutionary transformation as their ultimate goal, but they still tended to work within electoral, bureaucratic, and legal structures. Neither the Socialist Party (formed in 1933) nor the Communist Party generally supported violence. They sought to make the rights of citizenship more expansive and inclusive. The Left thus offered a kind of radical transformation, but did so while being firmly rooted in the dominant practices and expectations of citizenship and residence.

The Socialists and the Communists helped to shape the emerging social welfare state, most notably as a part of the Popular Front governments of the Center-Left from 1938 to 1948.[50] The organized working classes played a key role in this process. By the 1920s labor unions in the cities and in copper and coal mines supported reform and legislation that would sustain homes with stable nuclear families.[51] Following Fordist principles, both Chilean industrialists and foreign companies, particularly US-based copper corporations, had generally supported efforts to domesticate laborers in this way. They had done so, however, for reasons that were largely different from those of the unions: they sought to control their workers through closer surveillance. Paternalist in outlook, these capitalists believed that their social programs could forge loyalty and compliance. Quite often, however, laborers had neither the wages nor the conditions necessary to live in minimally acceptable homes.

Such failures contributed to labor militancy in the copper mines, the ports, and the cities, often supported by Leftist political parties. In supporting this activism, the Left quite naturally sponsored initiatives to transform working-class homes. They had a certain level of success. In 1943, Law 7,600 mandated industries to put 5 percent of their profits into constructing housing for workers. The law also granted a number of tax breaks for low-income housing (Gross 1991, 37). By the 1950s and 1960s unionized, fully employed workers, especially in the copper mines, generally lived in legally established residences, if not always in homes of their own. In the cities, factories with large labor forces often supplied housing for their workers.[52]

While these changes were significant, they also involved what gender historians have called a "restructuring" or a "modernization of patriarchy," in which notions of proper homes carried great weight.[53] In the Chilean case, such a modernization drew on prevailing ideas of property and propriety. There was a link between receiving greater political rights and conforming to seemingly proper forms of residence and family. State institutions sponsored benefits for legally constituted and deserving homes, including family allowances, disability insurance, social security, and housing benefits. In such an environment, more and more Chileans became a part of legal regimes that regulated domestic relations. In the 1940s and 1950s formal marriage rates underwent an unprecedented increase, while illegitimacy dropped by half (Milanich 2009, 233). Everyday domestic relations and expectations were part and parcel of the kinds of political inclusion that were available. But as generally happened throughout Latin America at midcentury, a more privileged sector of the working classes ultimately enjoyed the benefits of sociopolitical inclusion, including housing.[54]

Given the emphasis on family and home, urban and housing reforms became increasingly important issues for politicians, including presidential candidates, to address. The number of government bureaucratic organizations dedicated to urban development, housing, and public health consequently multiplied from the 1930s to the 1960s. This process culminated in the 1965 establishment of the Ministry of Housing and Urbanism (MINVU). As before, the new government bureaucracies had significant ties to international development institutions, both financially and intellectually. At midcentury, however, the links became stronger and the level of monetary support greater. By 1955, housing and urban development received 20.4 percent of the national budget, rising to nearly 25 percent in the 1960s (Collier and Sater 2004, 289; Hidalgo 2005, 229).

Such impressive spending responded to the long-standing importance granted to residence, infrastructure, and architecture in the city. There were, however, also more immediate reasons behind the spending—not least the fact that special interests and political concerns shaped policies toward housing and urban development. Spending in these areas provided jobs in construction, an important goal for a government committed to Keynesian economic policies. This kind of spending also served as an important means for state institutions to reinvest capital and support the financial sector.

As a result, government bodies developed intimate connections to the construction industry, real estate developers, and banking interests. State bureaucrats in housing and urban development worked closely with the Chilean Chamber of Construction, a powerful private research and advocacy organization formed in the early 1950s (Cleaves 1969 and 1974; Cheetham 1971; Hidalgo 2005, 181–90). In terms of housing policy, the Chamber of Construction sought subsidies for middle- and low-income sectors in an effort to extend private real estate markets. They successfully lobbied for the creation of state-backed mortgages that would expand levels of debt and investment, enshrined in the 1949 Pereira Law under a president of the Center-Left and then again in a 1959 law under the conservative presidency of Arturo Alessandri.[55] The role of the state in this legislation was crucial: the new programs contracted private real estate developers and worked as intermediaries between beneficiaries and lenders. In 1953 the government established the National Corporation in Investments in Social Welfare and the State Bank of Chile, two institutions with mandates to expand credit for housing. Inspired in part by US efforts to increase homeownership, the State Bank acted like the American institution

Fannie Mae. It could buy mortgages from lenders and then extend new credit to low- and middle-income borrowers, most often organized into cooperatives. Both the US Agency for International Development and the Inter-American Development Bank provided important funding for these new initiatives, as did private capital (Hidalgo Dattwyler 2005, 238).

State bureaucracies and the Chamber of Construction publicly emphasized their desire to support building for the lower classes. They undertook a handful of very large and ambitious popular housing projects, at the same time that more low-income Chileans did become homeowners. Yet middle-class housing was more lucrative, as was the building of urban infrastructure, public parks, and monumental architecture. Low-income housing ultimately occupied a small part of the state's housing and urbanism budget. Far more houses were built for middle-income sectors. In the end, the middle class, construction companies, and financial institutions benefited the most from the new legislation and terms of financing (Cheetham 1971). Economic recessions, moreover, led not only to foreclosures but to major decreases in construction. These processes undermined state plans for the extension of homeownership and the housing stock.

Figure 2.1. Juan Antonio Ríos, a subsidized housing project inaugurated in 1959 on the edge of the municipality of Renca (photo by author).

Pobladores had generally not come to have minimally acceptable housing. State programs consistently fell short of their promises, while economic conditions for pobladores remained generally woeful. According to one survey of a number of low-income neighborhoods in the mid-1960s, the percentage of pobladores without full-time employment was close to fifty percent. Those with stable, full-time employment worked in such areas as industrial labor, construction, transportation, clerical work, and low-level services, including domestic employment. The informal sector, meanwhile, thrived on, and many plied their trade in this often insecure and stigmatized area.[56] Only a small number of pobladores could formalize their housing status without the support of state institutions. The harsh insecurities that most pobladores faced underscored some of the unfulfilled promises of citizenship under state-led development.

Housing as an Urban Crisis and Priority of the Cold War

In the context of shortcomings within state-led development, housing for pobladores remained a highly charged public issue. At a rate never before seen, popular forms of activism and political party organizing began to take place in low-income Santiago. Government officials, transnational development experts, and media commentators found in the burgeoning urban shantytowns clear signs of Chile's status as a "third world" and "underdeveloped" nation. For these observers, the issues of squatting and squalid living conditions were of great humanitarian concern, representing a profound urban crisis across the third world.[57] This crisis, moreover, placed Chilean national prestige on the line.

For non-Leftists, the situation was all the more concerning since there appeared to be increasing signs of danger and subversion. Pobladores might be worthy of charity and state support, but they would also need to be closely watched, especially given the increasing involvement of Leftists in organizing them. During the 1950s and 1960s broader geopolitical concerns helped grant the perennial issues of social marginality, urban housing, and political inclusion a more potent charge. These issues became wrapped up in the conflicts, activities, and constructs of the early stages of the Cold War. As an indication of the urgency of these issues, the callampas and campamentos, and certain conventillos, received special legislative treatment. The presidency and the legislature passed emergency decrees and laws to deal with what they considered to be the exceptional circumstances inherent in this kind of urban poverty.

These laws both extended earlier trends and had significant consequences for governing relations. The fact that campamentos and callampas existed in a state of emergency reinforced their "pathological" and "abnormal" status.

This status potentially placed these neighborhoods and their residents in extreme danger. Police and military forces could undertake special operations in the campamentos and callampas, something that the Pinochet dictatorship would take full advantage of when it launched military raids in these areas. Pobladores in these neighborhoods could thus face the overwhelming coercive power of the state's sovereign authority. Yet being in a state of exception could also be productive. The emergency legislation permitted state agencies to make use of special funding sources to *sanear* the campamentos and callampas, thus providing these areas with infrastructure services, housing construction, and property titles. Moreover, residents of these areas could denounce the emergency conditions they lived in and even justify their own exceptional actions in the land seizures by claiming that they were seeking nothing more than to live in a normal urban neighborhood.

Consider, for example, the land seizure in 1957 that established the iconic neighborhood of La Victoria in the municipality of San Miguel, southwest of downtown Santiago.[58] Pobladores took part in the land seizure after losing their homes in a well-publicized fire in a callampa on the banks of the Zanjón de la Aguada, a canal in southern Santiago. After suffering through such a well-publicized catastrophe, these pobladores had greater success in organizing and mobilizing sympathy for their cause. They subsequently took part in the exceptional act of seizing land and abrogating property laws in response to their own out-of-the-ordinary conditions. Yet they did so with the expectation that they would develop their own neighborhoods and homes, ultimately restoring a proper state of affairs in the city.

In the La Victoria land seizure, Communist Party activists provided logistical and moral support to the pobladores who took part in the action. Government officials and non-Leftist observers looked to this development with alarm. Since the Communist Party's inception in 1922 it had been involved in urban housing and neighborhood development issues. It had done so despite the fact that some prominent Chilean Communists, following Marxist theory, viewed the housing question and property rights as issues that detracted attention from labor exploitation, class conflict, and the possibility of revolution.[59] Yet in working as grassroots organizers, the Communists quite naturally gravitated toward activism that bolstered lower-class homes, including property rights. Through the mid-1940s, the Communist Party had concentrated most of its organizing efforts on the labor unions. But following the implementation of the Law for the Permanent Defense of Democracy, the ironically titled legislation that outlawed the Communist Party from 1948 to 1958, party members found it increasingly difficult to continue working in their union strongholds. In response, they fortified their links to urban neighborhood organizations, especially taking on the cause of granting pobladores legally established neighborhoods and homes (Schneider 1995).[60]

The Communists did this right as pobladores were beginning to take part in organized land seizures in Santiago during the second half of the 1940s (Garcés 1998, 32; Red de Organizaciones Sociales de La Legua 1999, 86). Increased Communist involvement with pobladores thus occurred precisely at the moment when a controversial and combative form of urban activism appeared on the national scene. Pobladores would subsequently take part in dozens of organized land seizures through the mid-1960s in Santiago, often—but not always—with the sponsorship of the Communists. No matter the situation, however, many observers interpreted Communist involvement in the land seizures as a radicalization of pobladores. Most in the Center and Right viewed this with apprehension and disdain, while Leftists generally greeted it as a sign that popular demands for social justice were gaining momentum.[61]

These interpretations took root even as the distinction between neighborhoods established through land seizures and previous forms of squatting was not, at least in certain respects, that great. Both involved the illegal taking of land. They both established communities and homes on the borders of legality, raising suspicion about the character and legitimacy of their residents. In the callampas, however, squatters sought to maintain a low profile as they took over lands in the middle of the night, often in areas that already had questionable forms of land tenure. The land seizures, by contrast, were combative and public acts. They included more sophisticated forms of organizing and explicit efforts to denounce and confront the shortcomings of the governing order. Pobladores often seized state-owned lands set aside for parks, housing, or other forms of development. Not surprisingly, the government often reacted quite harshly to the seizures. The Ministry of the Interior had a well-armed riot police at its disposal that it was not afraid to deploy. The situation was becoming increasingly tense and dangerous, full of risk and conflict.

Yet the moment was also one of modernist promise. Pledging a more just and equitable order, the political parties of the Left and the Christian Democratic Party, formed in 1957, advocated fundamental changes to society. Each of these parties promised to redistribute wealth, implement aggressive agrarian reforms, foment industrial development, and seize greater control of national resources. They also promised to provide more secure and minimally acceptable homes for pobladores. Still, these parties had fundamental disagreements. They competed intensely with one another, as they did with the Rightist National Party. Each held firm convictions about what society should become. The Right, Left, and Center were capable of organizing substantial bases in civil society and forming formidable political blocs that could potentially assume the presidency.[62] Yet in spite of the intense polarization, Chile's competing ideological projects led largely through the transformative power of the state as political parties and civic associations generally sought redress within existing state structures. This was the case even as these projects had radically different visions of reform, revolution, and order.

But what kind of place would the mobilized social actors of the 1960s find in the state and in sociospatial relations? How far would reformist and revolutionary projects be able to go? In the spaces of Santiago, in which unprecedented resources and attention were being paid to pobladores, what kind of transformation would heightened activism and state development projects offer? Would pobladores be able to find an appropriate place in the Santiago landscape that matched their status as citizens and their visions for the future? Would they live in minimally acceptable conditions, outside of a state of emergency, in which they could take part in the promises of inclusion entailed in citizenship? The answers to these questions would play out in bureaucratic offices, street protests, land seizures, legislative debates, media coverage, and neighborhood and political organizing. To an unprecedented degree, Chileans would start to grapple with the long-standing disparity between the promises of citizenship and the home life of pobladores. The relationship between propriety, residence, and citizenship, an issue central to urban property relations since the colonial period, would now help to fuel the unprecedented mobilization and ideological conflicts of the late 1960s and early 1970s.

PART TWO

INSURGENT OWNERSHIP

CHAPTER 3

A PLACE IN THE STATE
Housing Activism and the Seizure of Land, May Day, 1969

AN UNREALIZED, IF EXPECTED, STATE of being can provide motivation for action. For many low-income residents in Santiago during the late 1960s, expectations of what home life should be fueled collective struggle, as many did not consider their individual living conditions to be in accord with their rights. Over the course of the twentieth century, important forms of labor mobilization, state development efforts, and housing rights activism had been dedicated to the cause of creating an appropriate domestic life. Yet this activity rapidly increased with the heightened mobilization of the late 1960s and early 1970s.

Many came to see their circumstances as fundamentally out of line with their expectations, lending the situation particular urgency. This tension is evident in the way that Ana Valdés related her life history to me, as she emphasized how her home failed to meet her standards, ultimately leading to her involvement in a land seizure.[1] She began her story by indicating that she was born into "a well-constituted family," a state of being that Karin Rosemblatt has identified as central to the goals of the state's social welfare institutions and Leftist political movements during the period of state-led development.[2] Ana's "well-constituted family" was precarious, however. When she was four, her abusive and alcoholic parents split up, leaving Ana and her siblings in the care of others. The Valdés children eventually moved in with another family, the Recabarrens, who raised them almost as if they were their own.

The Recabarrens belonged to the Communist Party, and Ana attended party meetings from a very young age, joining the Communist Youth when she was barely a teenager in the early 1960s. As a young militant, Ana was proud of her close relationship with the Recabarren family. Not only were the Recabarrens respected Party members in Renca, the municipality in Santiago where they lived, they also shared the last name of Emilio Recabarren, the labor agitator and writer whose activism and fame had contributed to the formation of the Chilean Communist Party (PC) during the first three decades of the twentieth century. Recabarren's memory remained a rallying point for Leftist activists: his image adorned the walls in Communist meeting halls, journalists and politicians often cited his speeches and publications, and interpretations of his life were a standard part of Leftist histories of Chile. Leaders in Ana's neighborhood had even named their community Población Recabarren. In doing so, they both symbolically connected themselves to the figure of Recabarren and attempted to associate the term *población* with pride and working-class solidarity. For her part, Ana enjoyed a certain status among Leftist militants through her close association with the name Recabarren.

Her relationship with the Recabarrens also granted her relative financial security, at least in comparison to many of her neighbors in Renca. During the mid-1960s, when they were in their teens, Ana, her siblings, and the Recabarren children sought to channel their privilege into the kind of solidarity work that became increasingly common in Chile's poblaciones and campamentos at this time. Among other activities, they helped with the construction of houses, dug outhouses, leveled footpaths and roads, took part in literacy campaigns, and organized neighborhood celebrations. At Christmastime, Ana helped to plan parties at the neighborhood council headquarters, raising money and putting together gifts for families who could not otherwise afford them. The festivities, Ana recalled, often lasted late into the evening and included folk music, dancing, fried empanadas, poetry readings, and theater sessions.[3] Over the years, the ties between the Recabarrens and the Valdés children grew to be very strong: two of Ana's siblings married into the Recabarren family, and Ana almost did the same. The affection that Ana feels for the Recabarren family pervades her often pleasant and nostalgic memories of the period. Yet despite Ana's relatively happy recollections, she was still not part of a "well-constituted family" for some, as her home was made up of siblings and fictive kin, not the nuclear norm that so powerfully mattered, even as it was far from being universally practiced.

When Ana was sixteen, she married a man she met in the Communist Youth. By the time Ana turned nineteen, she had two children. But Ana and her husband were unable to buy their own house, lacking the income they needed to join a government-subsidized housing program. They moved in with her in-laws and became, like many of her friends and neighbors who lived with people outside of their nuclear families, *allegados*. As an allegada, Ana lived in what she considered to be unacceptable housing: her family slept on two beds in a room that was barely large enough to fit the four of them. Her family shared a house with six others, a fairly common experience in the burgeoning poblaciones, campamentos, and run-down tenements that housed the urban poor in the 1960s. Despite being married, and having her own children, Ana did not have the space that she felt was appropriate for a well-constituted family. Like other allegados and families who rented or lived in illegal settlements, Ana was *sin casa*, "homeless," without a home of her own. In the Chilean context, this did not mean living on the street or in a shelter, but it did mean being without the appropriate kind of home.

Unsatisfied with this status, Ana and her husband joined PC members to mobilize the homeless of Renca in early 1967. In building their movement, the PC organizers, as was typical, built a large network and focused on specific neighborhoods, forming committees of the homeless in ten different poblaciones, including Recabarren. By 1969, approximately 1,200 families had joined the committees, giving the umbrella organization, the Communal Command of the Homeless of Renca, a certain amount of clout and considerable responsibility. Nevertheless, by the end of April of that year, Renca's homeless had been unable to receive housing, despite the arduous planning and labor they had put into organizing more than six thousand people. For more than two years, the homeless committees had negotiated with officials and had sought to comply with the bureaucratic requirements expected of housing applicants.

On the morning of May 1, 1969, as a steady rain fell, Renca's homeless decided on a bold, if increasingly common, option. At dawn, several hundred homeless committee members marched from the PC headquarters in Recabarren and seized uncultivated land on a local vineyard. Through this action, they sought to establish, once and for all, proper homes. Ana was taking an important step toward living in a well-constituted family whose housing conditions would live up to that status.

A Place in the City, A Place in the State

The May Day seizure formed part of the unprecedented activism in Chile during this time period. From 1967 to 1973, the last three years of Eduardo Frei Montalva's presidency and the three years of Salvador Allende's, workers, peasants, and pobladores seized factories, rural estates, and urban land at a rate that far eclipses anything witnessed before or since. While land seizures had taken place in Santiago since 1947, they remained relatively rare events until the late 1960s.[4] However, between 1967 and 1972, according to one source, 279,000 people took part in successful seizures.[5] The rate of the land seizures

Table 3.1. Urban land seizures in Santiago and in Chile, 1967–1971

	1967	1968	1969	1970	1971
Santiago	13	4	23	103	350
Chile-total	NA	8	35	220	560

Note: A research team working in 1971 and 1972 under the direction of Manuel Castells compiled the statistics on the seizures in Santiago, except for 1971. The total number of seizures follows figures provided by the Dirección General de Carabineros, as cited by Castells (1983, 200). Leeds and Leeds (1976, 228) report the number of seizures in Santiago for 1971. These figures represent general trends, and diverge from numbers provided by other sources. For an alternative estimate on the number of seizures that nevertheless follows a similar pattern, see Schneider (1995, 53–54). In a personal communication, Garcés confirmed the decline in land seizures following the great surge in their number in the months leading up to and following Allende's election, but nevertheless claimed that they had continued importance, especially outside of Santiago.

increased rapidly through 1971, as table 3.1 demonstrates. For months in 1970 and 1971, the land seizures became quotidian events, as Santiago averaged nearly one seizure per day (Leeds and Leeds 1976, 228). The seizures had a major impact on the landscape of Santiago, accounting for approximately 40 percent of the geographic expansion of the city between 1969 and 1973 (Schneider 1995, 45).[6] In all, perhaps 14 percent of the city's population seized land between 1967 and 1973.

Through this heightened mobilization, homeless committees successfully articulated a critique of the state, often leading government institutions to respond to their demands. This, in turn, permitted many to improve their living conditions, particularly the "homeless." Because of this success, many Leftist observers celebrated the activism of the pobladores, and particularly the event of the land seizures, as a triumph of *el pueblo* and its collective struggle for a more just society. Others, on the opposite side of Chile's increasingly polarized ideological divide, claimed that this activism would inexorably lead to society's breakdown. This could, in the words of one conservative editorial writer, return Chile to the "chaotic forces of the jungle."[7]

While such views were typical of the time period, they failed to recognize how the mobilization of the homeless occurred within established practices and expectations of state formation, citizenship, and home life. As a movement about the construction of the home, it forcefully raised the issues of what were the appropriate, minimal kinds of living conditions that citizens felt they deserved. The members of the homeless movement argued that the state should assure the rights of low-income Chileans and grant them a respected place in the city. As they sought to inhabit legally sanctioned, well-constituted homes, the homeless focused attention on the inability of the state to fulfill its promises of development and modernity to a vast segment of the citizenry. By exposing this contradiction, and demanding that it be eliminated, they helped to transform and, to an extent, revolutionize the state.

Yet many of the foundations of state power proved resistant to change. Special interests weighed heavily in how state bureaucracies operated, hampering efforts at reform and redistribution. Squatters, moreover, had to prove themselves to be proper, disciplined subjects worthy of the state's assistance. Their activism could be successful only if it built on sensibilities of justice embedded in state frameworks and national imaginaries. And even in cases where pobladores eventually became legally recognized homeowners, they received only state benefits and protections of a particular kind. This included the right to have small plots of land, property titles, and access to urban services considered basic. Though these gains were of critical importance, they were also circumscribed.

Ultimately, as groups of the homeless challenged and transformed the state, they also entered its sinuous web, where their activism became ensnared within the material, symbolic, institutional, and performative frameworks of state power. This happened as the homeless set themselves on a path toward being legally sanctioned homeowners. In seeking a proper state of affairs, the homeless carved out a place for themselves not only in the city but also in the state and in the nation. They did so, however, not necessarily under conditions of their own choosing.

In taking part in the radical politics of the period, squatters and housing rights activists formed a powerful social movement that tested existing legal structures and government frameworks. Yet they also sought to become property owners, a foundation of order within the liberal state. They thus took part in the seemingly contradictory process of insurgent ownership. In exploring this process, this chapter interweaves the radical and conventional elements that came together in the housing movement. As part of an insurgency, the land seizures were an important part of revolutionary activism and symbolism. They represented struggle, collective sacrifice, and radical transformation: the fruition of "popular power." Yet in order to establish homes and neighborhoods, the homeless movement also had to work through the procedures of government bureaucracies. As insurgents, squatters would test and expand the state's boundaries; as legally sanctioned homeowners, they would confirm important elements of its power. In each case, squatters gained access to property and carved out a place in the state depending on the perceived propriety of their actions.

Justifying the Land Seizures, Celebrating a New Subject

As Ana and her homeless neighbors organized their movement, their efforts to realize the dream of living in well-constituted homes led them to the bureaucracies of the central government. They also approached municipal officials and private bodies, particularly Catholic and student solidarity organizations. These latter groups often offered significant logistical support and helped to form networks of solidarity. They were, however, a means to an end, as the homeless movement was ultimately about the acquisition of state-sanctioned housing. To achieve this aspiration, the homeless had little choice but to bring their claims directly to the newly formed Ministry of Housing and Urbanism (MINVU). Given the dominance of the central government in dispensing the benefits and services of the state, the pobladores had to work through such a large bureaucracy.[8]

MINVU was often exasperating and slow-moving. Moreover, homeless pobladores faced a number of dangers and threats as they worked their way through both MINVU and the other institutions of state. The homeless, after all, could face sanctions and prosecution, especially after they took part in such acts as seizing land. Yet if the homeless hoped to access certain benefits and be included in the exclusive company of citizens, they had to work through these state bodies.[9]

In approaching MINVU, the Communal Command of the Homeless of Renca often relied on the support and mediation of PC politicians, especially Gladys Marín, a young parliamentarian who was making a name for herself as a leader of the Communist Youth and as an advocate of housing rights.[10] Marín's work with the homeless of Renca was typical of the actions of many politicians who provided a crucial link between citizen organizations and state bureaucrats.[11] In sponsoring these claims, deputies and senators focused attention on the plight of specific homeless committees, recording their complaints in the official congressional records and often publicizing the inability of state bureaucracies to respond appropriately.[12] Given the importance of the political parties in this process, individuals or neighborhood groups without support from elected officials could often feel isolated and impotent, unable to voice their causes effectively.[13]

In working with Marín and the PC, Renca's homeless committees joined forces with a party organization that had been prominently involved with pobladores and in many of Santiago's largest and best-known land seizures. As they privileged the movement of the pobladores, the PC assigned it an activist, heroic role that fit within the Left's general interpretation of Chilean society. The lack of appropriate housing symbolized the failures of the bourgeois state, while the homeless response expressed a class organization and militant consciousness that would help to develop a more just and humane society. By seizing land, the pobladores took part in a struggle that would end in revolutionary transformation, encapsulated in the motto of many PC-sponsored homeless committees: "From the seizure of land to the seizure of power."[14]

Through her work with housing rights activists, Marín was at the center of this narrative. In 1967, she made national headlines through her sponsorship of homeless committees in Barrancas, a municipality just to the north of Renca. At 2:30 in the morning on March 16, 1967, these committees had led more than five thousand people in one of the largest land seizures in Santiago's history.[15] Shortly after the seizure, nearly four hundred police officers attempted to remove the pobladores, resulting in a confrontation that lasted for seven hours. The scene was violent and chaotic. The police shot off tear gas canisters into the settlement, blasted squatters with water cannons, and hit several of them with batons. In the commotion, a fire broke out that destroyed a number of the pobladores' temporary shelters. Several squatters were wounded and many others were taken into custody.[16] A number of Communist and Socialist politicians arrived at the scene, drawing public attention to the seizure and the police response. Marín was one of the first to show up, receiving a slight injury when she joined the pobladores. More prominent figures such as Salvador Allende, the president of the Senate, arrived later and sought to defuse the conflict from behind the scenes, meeting with the minister of the interior and police officials.[17]

During the standoff, one injured woman left the area with her nine-day-old daughter, who was suffering from a fever. That night the child was brought to the hospital, but it was too late. The infant died of bronchopneumonia. A few days later, the leaders of the homeless committees in Barrancas held a well-publicized funeral for the baby. During the ceremony, a priest named the child Herminda and baptized her. Marín and another PC representative, Luis Neira, became the godparents, cementing their relationship with the pobladores in the neighborhood through ties of compadrazgo. In doing so, Marín and Neira went well beyond merely being political patrons; they were now, from a performative perspective at least, fictive kin, a part of the family. Addressing the crowd, Juan Araya, the leader of the Barrancas homeless committees, declared that the new campamento would be named Herminda de la Victoria in honor of the child. What happened to Herminda symbolized the brutal injustice that pobladores faced. But her death, Araya argued, would not be in vain. The painful sacrifices borne by the pobladores would lead to their ultimate victory, as their organization and suffering would eventually allow them to have homes of their own.

Araya's prediction turned out to be correct. Two and a half months after the land seizure, Christian Democratic officials negotiated a settlement with the homeless committees of Barrancas, attempting to avoid any further embarrassment that the government would receive from the incident. In doing so, they generally conceded that the claims made by the pobladores were legitimate, and granted them a means to become homeowners in a legally sanctioned neighborhood.

They did this, however, only after completing a survey by the Ministry of the Interior. Placing the squatters into the categories of the state, the survey determined that there were 1,098 families among the squatters, 601 of whom had been allegados and 431 renters, many at risk of being evicted. The vast majority, in other words, fit the definition of being homeless. Importantly, those who didn't were not permitted to stay. In addition, over half earned less than the minimum wage, granting them access to certain housing subsidies. Finally, 642 of the families were enrolled in state housing programs and had paid a series of monthly quotas.[18] MINVU officials demanded that the pobladores produce a down payment and assume monthly mortgages for three years in order to partially reimburse the government for the land and the provision of such services as potable water. The pobladores also agreed to provide labor for the construction of houses, roads, and sewers. Through these processes, the pobladores demonstrated that they had the discipline and resolve to fulfill the state's requirements. They could thus have homes of their own. The victory of the residents from Herminda de la Victoria ultimately depended, in no small measure, on properly following the prosaic tasks and requirements of state bureaucracy.[19]

Yet the Left also seized on the fact that activism had made this victory possible. In legislative debates, in the press, and even in a best-selling 1972 album by the famous folk singer Victor Jara, memories of Herminda and the heroic establishment of the campamento named in her honor were kept alive.[20] For the Left, these memories focused attention on how the governing order had failed to supply basic shelter to families and children. Instead of providing hope for the future, the state defended a bleak and morally bankrupt status quo that produced violence and trauma. But through collective struggle, pobladores had overcome these constraints and produced a more appropriate order. Finally, their grievances would be heard, as reporters, politicians, and pop musicians lavished attention on their activism.

In an excerpted interview on Jara's album, two pobladoras involved in the land seizure shared their memories of Herminda's death. The first woman to speak claimed that Herminda's mother was pregnant and that the police raid caused her to suffer an accident. The other pobladora interrupted her, correctly stating that Herminda was a newborn. This second woman, nevertheless, did not mention that the infant was sick, letting stand the implication that the violent intervention of the police was ultimately responsible for Herminda's death. For these pobladoras, the police were illegitimate state agents who contributed to the misery and oppression that pobladores had to suffer. Despite such hardship, these pobladores had demonstrated their determination and resolve, establishing homes and neighborhoods for their families. As a third woman on the album asserts, "Thanks to our triumph, now we are living like people, we have our place, our house, Población Herminda de la Victoria" (Jara 1972). The story of Herminda thus stood as an example of how popular struggle could lead to a better life, where the oppressed could be treated like human beings. Rather than living like "marginals in subhuman conditions"—as many Chileans, and particularly Christian Democratic officials, referred to the homeless during the 1960s—the pobladores in Herminda de la Victoria now had a place to call home, where they could live like normal, respected citizens.

As the godmother of Herminda, Marín could claim a special solidarity with the cause of homeless pobladores, and she lost few opportunities to publicize the uplifting message of activism. In an event held shortly before the May Day land seizure in 1969, Marín addressed Renca's Communal Command of the Homeless. In her remarks, Marín celebrated the "maturity of the consciousness of the pobladores." They had demonstrated resolve in their "long fight." Marín also praised the pobladores for complying with state programs, noting how they had deposited monthly quotas into the savings accounts that MINVU had established on their behalf. By faithfully making their monthly deposits, the homeless had demonstrated that they could pay dividends and be homeowners.[21]

But while Marín praised Renca's homeless for having complied with legal requirements, she ended her speech by hinting that more transgressive means might be necessary. Calling for "unity, organization, and decisiveness in the fight," Marín recalled how other homeless committees had recently established exemplary neighborhoods by seizing land, including Campamento Herminda de la Victoria and Campamento Violeta Parra, a neighborhood formed in 1968 and named after another famous folk singer. For Marín, seizing land, while a revolutionary and illegal act, was also justified, since the pobladores had complied with state requirements. Such a balancing act between transgression and legitimate propriety, revolution and respectability, marked the process through which pobladores would establish neighborhoods throughout the period.

Generally speaking, the Communist Party constantly worked at the line between revolution and institutional processes, as it was committed to radically transforming Chilean society through existing legal frameworks. Given this, it is not surprising that the party was crucial to making the land seizures a generally acceptable practice by the middle of 1970. As the principal sponsor of the land seizures from 1947 until the late 1960s, the Communists, through their affiliated homeless committees, provided the pobladores who seized land with an impressive party apparatus that granted them critical logistical support, legal counsel, access to prominent legislators, and publicity. Through these activities, the PC helped to articulate a justification for the land seizures and to establish new modes of activism. Most importantly, the party helped to ensure that the provision of minimally accepted housing conditions for pobladores was understood as a right of citizenship and a central obligation of the state.

During the 1960s this was often an insurgent challenge, permitting certain pobladores to act as rebels outside of the law in their struggles to receive housing. By the end of the decade, groups of homeless pobladores increasingly went beyond the officially sanctioned channels of signing up for government programs, writing petitions to ministry officials, and seeking support from political party leaders. More and more, they demonstrated in front of government buildings, took part in sit-ins, blocked traffic, and, in more extreme cases, seized land. Through these tactics homeless groups demanded, and often received, direct meetings with government officials.

In their recollections of these meetings, pobladores tend to stress how they could both voice their displeasure at government intransigence and demand respect from officials. The homeless committees of Renca, for example, were able to speak with the regional governor following a two-hour protest in front of his office. Eliana Parra remembered that during the meeting, the governor interrupted one of the homeless committee members, shouting "¡Cállate pajarón!" ("Shut up, idiot!"; literally, "Shut up, big bird!"). Angered by this insult, Eliana claims that she said to the governor, "We're not being arrogant, why do you have to come and insult a homeless *compañero*?" She went on, saying that he had to listen to them and that "he couldn't, just because we were poor, have us taken away." She claims that she then reproached him, saying, "More than anyone, you, as the governor, shouldn't treat us like that." For Eliana, the exchange ended favorably, as the governor apologized and asked for forgiveness. The homeless pobladores thus gained some measure of respect, even if, as in this case, they still did not receive housing. Eliana's narrative privileges the action of pobladores and their ability to directly confront officials in the government. In its favorable ending, it satisfies a desire on Eliana's part to be treated properly, with respect and dignity. For the pobladores, long accustomed to being stigmatized and dismissed, their insurgent activism had helped to change the social footing upon which everyday interactions had generally taken place.[22]

In flyers, posters, song, and the mass media, Leftist narratives of this kind of activism connected efforts to be treated properly with the promise of revolution. These narratives, in fact, depicted the pobladores as rebellious subjects who acted with singular resolve in assuming their class interests and transforming society. Communist newspaper reports cast the land seizures as watershed events that represented the emerging consciousness of Chile's pobladores. Through their exemplary activism, the pobladores would help to create a new Chile. This redemptive narrative also provided a blistering critique of the Christian Democratic government, whose efforts at reform had fallen short of responding to the needs of the homeless.

Ideological Conflict and the Suppositions of Reform

The criticism that Marxists launched at the Christian Democrats underscores the increasingly intense and volatile ideological competition that the Left and Center were taking part in during the 1960s. This competition linked particular dynamics in Chile with transnational development paradigms and the policies and ideological constructs of the Cold War. For policymakers in Washington and Santiago, Eduardo Frei Montalva's government represented an important opportunity: a chance to demonstrate that capitalist modernization was possible and that it could uplift the lower classes. The Christian Democrats adopted an ambitious program, including land reform, a deepening of the policies of import-substitution industrialization, increased expenditures in social welfare, a diversification of Chile's export base, and greater control of national resources, especially copper. As a moderate alternative to the Cuban Revolution, the Christian Democratic "Revolution in Liberty" held out the promise of creating fundamental change while building on Chile's liberal democratic tradition. Famously, the country was a model for the US-sponsored Alliance for Progress, a hemisphere-wide effort to implement reform, blunt the appeal of revolution, and support militaries and counterinsurgency forces in the region.[23]

Officials sought to mobilize the lower classes through their program of "Popular Promotion." As they did so, they had bitter conflicts with Leftists over how to involve such sectors as the pobladores in political and social processes. Marxists and Christian Democrats each claimed they represented the popular classes and held the keys to changing their position in Chilean society. In order to make this transformation possible, the Left and the Center both stressed that they needed to mobilize popular groups on an unprecedented scale. The Left and the Center longed for both the support of the popular classes and their active transformation, a change that was central to their broader visions of national progress.[24]

Providing housing for the homeless became a wedge issue upon which Marxists, Christian Democrats, and their international supporters competed. To an important degree, the ideological conflict between the Chilean political Center and Left played out within the contours of the urban politics of propriety. Clearly, the conflict was an indication of the heightened polarization, expectations, and mobilization of the time. It was a part of broad international struggles about the nature of capitalism, the forms that democracy could take, and the social, political, and economic rights of citizenship. If these were the kinds of struggles that ultimately animated the Cold War in Latin America, they not surprisingly involved conflicts over housing and rights in the city.[25] In the poblaciones and campamentos of Santiago, these conflicts coalesced around the idea that homelessness was an inappropriate condition. If there had long been a gap between expectations of a proper home life and living conditions for low-income Chileans, this was now an imminent and unavoidable public issue.

As had many presidents before him, President Frei promised to resolve the problems of housing and urban order during his administration. Yet he committed an unprecedented amount of publicity and resources to realizing this vision. His government, moreover, cast Santiago's development as a pressing national problem. The minister of housing and urbanism, Andrés Donoso, claimed that one had only to "take a look at the areas that encircle the center of Santiago in order to realize that there isn't any situation that could more clearly illustrate the social injustice, the economic anarchy, and the underdevelopment of our deteriorated, unhealthy, congested, archaic, and unattractive [anti-estética] capital city."[26] For Donoso, the transformation of the city was an urgent task, the realization of which would propel Chile into an attractive modern order characterized by social justice, development, and a healthy cityscape. Transnational development experts in Chile, working with crucial links to experts and resources in the United States, emphasized urban housing reform as a means to provide stability, create modern citizens, and prevent subversion among the urban poor.[27]

Given the importance of urban housing, when Frei assumed the presidency in 1964 the Christian Democrats made the creation of MINVU a centerpiece of their reform efforts. As a part of the Alliance for Progress, the bureaucracy and its programs received support and loans from the US Agency for International Development, the Inter-American Development Bank (IDB), and even the American Federation of Labor.[28] Many of Chile's programs, moreover, became international models for programs in housing and poverty reduction

(Cleaves 1974, 217). The programs were ambitious: Frei promised to resolve the housing crisis through an unparalleled effort to build 360,000 new housing units from 1964 to 1970.[29] Critics, especially Leftists, pointed out that this would fall short of the problem, since the 1960 census had identified a deficit of 488,000.[30] But the Christian Democrats countered that producing sixty thousand units per year was far beyond anything the country had yet produced.[31] Besides, officials asserted, government subsidized housing would now be of a better quality. As President Frei put it, the developments would not simply be a "row of houses on an unpaved street, but rather fully constructed neighborhoods where a family can develop with dignity."[32]

This kind of promise touched a nerve. In their dealings with government officials, pobladores often expressed how important the stakes were for them to receive dignified housing. In a plea to the minister of Housing and Urbanism in 1967, the directorate of one neighborhood committee pointed out how stigmatized and denigrated the homeless could be: "*Señor Ministro*, excuse our frankness, but when some families don't have a meter of their own land, people often say that they are naked, beggars, without any moral or patriotic honor. . . . [They say] that they walk like gypsies from one place to the next, like birds without nests."[33] Given such assumptions, seeking a proper place to live had potent status implications. Those without homes considered appropriate suffered from a powerful stigmatization: they were morally reprehensible and unfit to be a part of the nation.

If state programs held out the promise of helping the homeless to overcome this, they nevertheless did not subvert the understandings that made the stigmatization of the homeless possible in the first place. To the contrary, the very categories that state technocrats used to administer their programs reinforced this stigmatization. Beginning in the national census of 1952, housing and urban planners began to use the terms *campamentos* and *poblaciones callampas* to describe "irregular" neighborhoods that lacked property titles and basic services. These terms helped officials classify urban neighborhoods, as they referred to areas that consisted of poorly constructed houses fashioned over the years from wood, cardboard, and tin. In the first Chilean housing census in 1952, surveyors used these terms to describe areas that were built "clandestinely" and made from "scrap" materials (INE 1952a, V–VI).[34] But the terms *campamento* and *callampa* were not merely technical: they marked neighborhoods as the poorest and the most backward.

In order to transform the "irregular" and "unhygienic" campamentos and callampas, planners at MINVU continued to seek to *sanear* these areas. To accomplish this task, state bureaucracies would need to provide the residents of these areas with both property titles and neighborhoods that would have the

Figure 3.1. An "irregular" campamento, shortly after its establishment (*El Siglo*, May 8, 1967, 5).

spatial and design qualities of modern planning. As such, the neighborhoods would include relatively uniform lot sizes designed for single family homes, a street grid pattern, and houses built of solid materials (apartments could also work). The neighborhoods should also have "basic urban services," including electricity, potable water, sanitation facilities, and paved roads, in addition to relatively close access to health clinics, police services, and schools. In many cases, officials only considered it possible to properly transform the "irregular" campamentos by "eradicating" them, razing the neighborhoods and removing the pobladores to other areas of the city.

As medical metaphors, "sanitizing," "healing," and "making well" presume a normal and healthy bodily condition, outside of which lies pathology and illness.[35] The sensibility behind this metaphor affected not only how officials approached the spaces of the city but also how they viewed the city's inhabitants. One of the underlying assumptions of MINVU's housing policies was that nuclear families who lived in "hygienic" neighborhoods would be better citizens. A basic MINVU principle stated that housing was a right of all Chilean families, and the conditions in the houses and the neighborhoods must be adequate to "permit the normal development of the family and . . . of the community."[36] In defending the creation of MINVU, a Christian Democratic deputy argued that the ministry's projects developed "the necessary conditions of hygiene to prevent the promiscuity and degeneracy [that exists] in the campamentos, and resolve the misery of the workers."[37] This deputy assumed that the conditions in the campamentos produced abnormal, destructive, and pathological behavior. But this would change in a "hygienic" environment, where nuclear family structures and appropriate personal conduct would be insured.[38]

There were many ways in which officials and experts assumed that low-income populations were abnormal and deviant. The Marginality School, a transnational school of thought based in Santiago that helped to justify Christian Democratic policy, asserted that low-income sectors were marginal to the economic and social structures of the nation.[39] Urban poverty, in this view, represented a moral failing, as the urban poor were excluded from society's benefits. The marginal, moreover, were susceptible to crime, subversion, anomie, and even subversion.

In order to overcome these problems and make the marginal "modern," Christian Democratic planners argued that it was necessary for state projects to "integrate" them into socioeconomic structures. In order to do this, officials sought to foment the participation of the pobladores by funding, training, and granting legal status to neighborhood councils, mothers' centers, sports clubs, and youth groups. This led to an extraordinary mobilization of the citizenry. Popular Promotion programs helped to establish as many as 21,917 organizations, with over 660,000 participants, in Santiago from 1964 to 1970 (*Mensaje Presidencial* 1970, 148).[40] These efforts reflected a firm belief in the vitality and virtue of existing social structures: the marginal needed to be brought into them so as to experience their benefits.

Christian Democratic planners granted MINVU an important role in Popular Promotion, seeing the creation of property owners and neighborhoods considered appropriate as crucial elements in the transformation of "economic" and "ecological" marginality. In order to facilitate these goals, MINVU, working in conjunction with USAID and the IDB, designed a "popular savings plan" in which the homeless "marginals" would assume ten- to fifteen-year mortgages through government-subsidized housing programs. Marginal peoples would thus work within the banking system, becoming consumers in the marketplace. Once established in homes of their own, marginals would also become involved in neighborhood institutions, a process that would make them active citizens. From this perspective, homeowners who paid mortgages and participated in social and political structures were the norm, outside of which lay the marginal, a homogeneous social group defined primarily by its deviance.

In casting the urban poor as an undifferentiated population, the Marginality School failed to recognize the extent to which pobladores remained heterogeneous and fluid. (The Left tended to make the same error, even as it emphasized the role that broader structures played in shaping the lives of the urban poor.) Pobladores were often mobile, as many held temporary jobs in agriculture, construction, domestic service, or street vending that could take them away from their homes for extended periods of time (Maltes, Bessone, and Cabala 1970, vol. 2, 36). Approximately a third of pobladores were first-generation migrants from the countryside, where they maintained contacts and often returned.[41] There could be fairly large income disparities among neighbors; while the vast majority of the people were low-income, wealthier residents could earn five times as much as their neighbors (Barahona 1966, 37). Pobladores, moreover, supported a variety of political platforms. Certainly, electoral support for the Left, and particularly the Communist Party, tended to be stronger in the lower-income municipalities. Numerous poblaciones, campamentos, neighborhood organizations, and households, moreover, nurtured a militant working-class identity. Yet *pobladores* also voted for the Christian Democrats and, to a lesser extent, the Rightist National Party.[42]

Critics have pointed to other problematic assumptions embedded in the thinking of experts from the Marginality School. To begin with, the school failed to recognize the extent to which low-income urban residents could share the dominant ideologies of society.[43] Moreover, the school tended to ignore the extent to which the Chilean economy had left a large percentage of Santiago's residents, and particularly *pobladores*, chronically unemployed or underemployed. Far from being outside of socioeconomic structures, many of the *pobladores* held crucial positions in the Chilean labor market. They worked as factory laborers, janitors, construction workers, low-level clerical staff, and in services. They also took part in "informal" labor as gardeners, maids, wait staff, itinerant salespersons, prostitutes, or drug and illegal alcohol dealers. An inequitable labor structure played a central role in producing the conditions of marginality, something that the proponents of the Marginality School tended to overlook. Even as the broader Christian Democratic platform sought to transform the Chilean economy through structural reforms, the Marginality School still fundamentally misrecognized poverty, seeing it as a deviant condition unconnected to socioeconomic processes.[44]

This misrecognition fit with the then dominant theory of modernization, one that teleologically supposed that modern social actors (and societies) would follow a singular development path, eventually leaving behind "poverty," "backwardness," and "underdevelopment" if the right conditions were in place. In terms of policies toward pobladores, this meant granting them such tools as access to credit, education, homeownership, and community organizations. With these in place, marginal pobladores would leave behind their impoverished and pathological condition. Some of these prescriptions could offer substantial benefits. Yet they had a dark side. They ignored the historical context that gave rise to marginality and they reinforced hierarchical social relations.[45] Reports on marginality asserted, in line with long-standing stigmatizations of the urban poor, that the marginal were violent, had poor family structures, lacked education, and were prone to crime, delinquency, and radicalism. These were characteristics inherent to poverty. Taken to their extreme, these suppositions viewed poverty as a condition endogenous to the urban poor. If the poor were marginal to social, economic, and political structures, there was little room to set their lives in broader context.[46]

For all its faults, the Marginality School was nevertheless influential as it tapped into widely accepted notions about the proper order of things and the place of pobladores within that order. In accord with the urban politics of propriety, the school presumed that there are norms and standards that outline how proper citizens should behave. Properly behaved citizens, in turn, would naturally live in certain conditions. There was much to debate about this politics. Leftists asserted that the social pathologies of the urban poor resulted from socioeconomic conditions and a morally bankrupt political process. Many on the Right presumed that these pathologies were the result of the poor's own deficiencies. Perhaps it was some combination of the two, as the broader Christian Democratic reform program seemed to recognize.[47]

As important as these impassioned debates were, they took shape on the shared assumption that properly behaved citizens deserved living conditions commensurate with their status. In their struggles, homeless activists and squatters did not necessarily reject this assumption. To the contrary, the moral authority that the homeless could gain as they sought housing depended on their ability to demonstrate that they were responsible and of good character. Through their compliance with official programs, they proved this. The state, therefore, had failed them, unable to fulfill its obligation to provide proper housing.

The homeless, moreover, often warned of the potential harm that their living conditions could do to them, and especially to their children, as they waited to receive housing and services. In a letter to the minister of housing and urbanism in 1969, the president of a homeless committee, Eduardo Toledo, angrily denounced the seemingly endless and futile bureaucratic processes that the 910 families he led had been subjected to. More than a year and a half earlier, a MINVU social worker had completed a survey of Toledo's committee. After reporting that the pobladores in the committee had met the required savings quotas and were responsible workers and family members, the social worker had concluded that the pobladores deserved to receive housing. But nothing had happened. Toledo claimed that the pobladores continued to live in the "deplorable conditions" of a callampa, a situation that was both unjust and dangerous to Chile's development. He thus pleaded to government officials: "The greatest aspiration of these families is to have their own plot of land where they can build their own houses and allow their children to have a better standard of living. The children need to be taken out of the miserable environment in which they now live and away from the bad examples, vices, and promiscuity that surrounds their young existence. We know that the future of our beloved nation [*patria*] depends on the formation of these young children in a healthy and orderly environment." The undersecretary of housing and urbanism replied that all of the slots for subsidized housing in that sector of the city had already been filled. It would therefore be impossible to grant the committee's request, even though its claims were legitimate.[48]

The Failures of State Reform

These kinds of rejections were common, an indication of Christian Democratic housing programs falling short of their initial goals. In response to budget shortfalls and rising inflation that began in 1967, the Christian Democratic government generally scaled back its more ambitious spending policies (Castells 1975, 266). In the end, Chile produced a total of 228,398 housing units during Frei Montalva's six-year term. While this goal was a record for any six-year period, the total still did not meet the original target of 360,000 (Bravo Heitmann 1993, 45). In low-income housing, Chile produced only 121,000 units, a figure also below the original promise of 213,000 (MINVU 1972, 23; Arellano 1976, 12).

The weight of special interests exacerbated the state's budgetary problems. As had happened previously, the privately controlled Chilean Chamber of Construction and the savings and loan institutions took advantage of their close relationships with MINVU. They effectively lobbied officials to build more middle-class housing in publicly financed programs than had been the initial intent. This process undermined efforts to provide low-income housing, as private developers sought more lucrative real estate deals (Cheetham 1971).[49] The effects of this were perverse, especially as immigration from the countryside and population increases continued to swell the size of Santiago. By the end of the decade, the Chilean housing deficit had actually increased, climbing to 585,000 units in 1970 (Equipo de Estudios Poblacionales CIDU 1972, 55). As housing became scarcer and as more of it was developed for middle- and upper-income sectors, it became considerably more expensive. Between 1960 and 1968, the average price of a square meter of housing tripled in Santiago, while the average rent rose even more.[50]

As the Christian Democrats scaled back their plans for housing construction, they began to rely more on programs that were in line with the practices of squatting and self-construction common in the campamentos and callampas. These programs reduced costs by taking advantage of labor that the pobladores would themselves provide. In a signature program, "Operation Housing" (Operación Sitio), the government provided neighborhoods divided into lots with twenty-square-meter "sanitary huts" and urban services considered basic.[51] But pobladores were required to build the rest of their houses and complete the urbanization of their neighborhoods, a requirement that reinforced the importance of adverse possession.[52] It was therefore common for pobladores to create work teams in order to build latrines or pave neighborhood streets.[53] For officials, the labor that pobladores would provide gave them an opportunity to "participate democratically" in community development and government programs. But even in these pared-down programs, MINVU rejected or postponed the applications of thousands of the homeless who had fulfilled the government's requirements and had sufficiently met the savings quotas.

At the same time, MINVU tended to develop low-income housing that maintained the socioeconomic segregation of Santiago, a policy at odds with the goal of integrating the marginal. Middle- and upper-income neighborhood organizations would have it no other way. Leaders of these organizations often claimed that the construction of low-income housing projects near their more established neighborhoods would inappropriately undermine their property values and social status. In a July 1969 letter, representatives from four neighborhood councils wrote to Minister Donoso asking that MINVU cease construction on an Operación Sitio. As residents of villas, the leaders noted that they lived in a "residential area" and that, according to the law, any new developments should be similar to the style of their neighborhood. Since villas consisted of single-story homes with urban services, it would be illegal to construct a neighborhood in the area without complete housing. As "popular representatives," the leaders argued that they had a right to "have a responsible voice before public organizations." They claimed that the proposed housing development would put their neighborhoods in "danger," since such an area would be both a "center of infection and of delinquency." They thus asked that the government retain what they considered to be the proper separation of their villas from the new neighborhood.

In an indication of the power that middle-class neighborhood councils wielded, Minister Donoso personally replied, something he hardly ever did in responding to groups of pobladores. Donoso wrote that "it is necessary to remember" that, although the residents of an Operación Sitio were unable to afford completed housing, they would, through successive stages of self-construction, eventually produce a "fully constructed and urbanized neighborhood." Furthermore, he promised that the two sectors that bordered the villas would consist of single-story brick homes. Besides, parks in the new neighborhood would be built between the fully constructed neighborhoods and the villas. Finally, the Minister promised that the paths in the new neighborhood would lead pedestrians away from the villas. While the neighborhood council leaders failed in their attempts to prevent the construction of the new neighborhood, they did succeed in maintaining certain physical barriers that preserved distinct neighborhoods.[54]

In general, it was not necessary for officials to go to such lengths to reassure wealthier residents that government programs would protect class distinctions. The housing projects that MINVU subsidized were most often built on the outskirts of the city, in predominately low-income areas.[55] Still, the land seizures and the placement of subsidized housing caused increasing concern among many that the socioeconomic and spatial boundaries that wealthier residents had long been used to were breaking down. The "Revolution in Liberty" did put in place significant reform, but established and powerful organizations reacted, limiting the effects of change, particularly efforts like those to integrate the marginal. Such processes bedeviled other Christian Democratic programs and the Alliance for Progress more generally.

Leftists and housing activists often pointed to these contradictions when they defended the right of the homeless to seize land. Such arguments placed the Christian Democrats in an awkward position. While officials could plausibly condemn the land seizures as an illegal tactic that upset the state's housing plans, they nevertheless conceded that the demands that homeless groups had were often legitimate. It was thus generally difficult for them to adopt a hard line against the land seizures. If officials ordered the police to break up the land seizures, this inevitably led to violent confrontations, including deaths and injuries. Such an outcome clearly contradicted Christian Democratic plans for Popular Promotion and a Revolution in Liberty. Police violence against pobladores could thus be easily exploited by opponents of the Christian Democrats. This became particularly apparent in February 1969, when the police killed eleven homeless pobladores who had taken part in a land seizure in the southern city of Puerto Montt. The massacre became a national scandal and contributed to divisions among the Christian Democrats. Following this event, the police used force much less often during urban land seizures, which was the most important, immediate factor in their increase in number.[56]

Ultimately, the rise in activism around housing demonstrated a central contradiction and dilemma of governance. Facing budgetary constraints and powerful private interests, overwhelmed state bureaucracies often fell well short of realizing the promise of transformation embedded in state programs. Yet many pobladores continued to be inspired by visions of development and the possibility for fairness and propriety. These visions undoubtedly developed out of a fetishized understanding of the state as both an impartial arbiter of justice and an expression of popular sovereignty. To be sure, many pobladores had few illusions about the exclusions and power interests they faced. But visions of change and justice were nevertheless important. They fueled action that ultimately contested the contours of state politics as dreams of future transformation animated action in the present.

Neighborhood Organization, Gender, and the (A)Political Nature of Activism

As the homeless mobilized, their activism took shape along very particular lines. One of the most important was organizing as a potential neighborhood (or as an existing one, if they already lived in a campamento or a callampa). The claims of neighborhood organizations superseded those of individual families in the attempts of low-income citizens to gain access to government benefits.[57] In most cases, pobladores had to collectively assume payment plans and labor responsibilities when they became involved in housing programs. Such obligations continued when squatters sought to "regularize" neighborhoods following land seizures.[58] After seizing land, homeless pobladores formed neighborhood councils that worked with government agencies in order to create more ordered conditions.

Planners claimed that the neighborhood councils would grant pobladores more autonomy in deciding how they would develop their living spaces.[59] Yet this autonomy had its limits. Expectations of what "neighborhood development" was supposed to be framed the claims that pobladores could make. This framing fit within the goals of "sanitizing," "regulating," and "healing" the "irregular" campamentos and callampas. These goals delimited the claims of the homeless to property titles, basic housing, and neighborhood services. Both Leftists and, to a lesser extent, Christian Democrats often sought to push the boundaries of what citizens could receive, but pobladores ultimately faced the constraints of a powerful framework that defined urban development in particular ways.

Somewhat paradoxically, while homeless pobladores were a central part of the intense political debates and plans of the day, they could successfully mobilize to receive housing only if they publicly presented themselves as being apolitical. Proselytizing the cause of the political parties was not an effective means of mobilizing citizens to claim their housing rights. These rights, after all, were supposed to transcend political interests and positions, as they were a part of the liberal contract of justice and fairness between citizens and the state.

Given this, homeless committee organizers in Renca quite naturally claimed that they were only interested in the needs of the homeless as they formed committees and signed pobladores up for housing programs. As Eliana Parra recalled about the long hours spent searching for Renca's homeless, "we were looking for people who didn't have their own house[s]. We spoke with everyone; we didn't care if they were Catholics or evangelicals, nor were we interested in what kind of politics they had. We didn't care about that; what we did care about was if they had a place to live, if they had a roof and if they had a place to shelter their children at night" (Murphy 2004a, 28).[60] For an issue such as housing, all Chileans were expected to rise above parochial interests, not sullying the sanctity of the home with the rough-and-tumble of political life.[61] Proper Chileans, no matter their politics, deserved an appropriate standard of living that the state should ensure.

Within this context, dueñas de casa played an important role in organizing the homeless committees, since they occupied the private, domestic sphere, an arena largely cast as feminine and apolitical. These women emphasized their position as mothers who cared, above all else, about the well-being of their families.[62] Women involved in the land seizures generally framed their activism as a step that they had to take in order to overcome hardship and fulfill their responsibilities as dueñas de casa. Given the transgressions of the state and the desperation and abnormality of their domestic situation, they simply had to enter the public arena.[63]

Renca's homeless committees initially planned their actions in accordance with MINVU's requirements, as they sought to enroll eligible pobladores from Renca in the government's popular savings program.[64] In order to do so, they had to identify Renca's homeless, and volunteers from the committees spent long hours searching for them, posting flyers, going door to door, holding organizational meetings, and making announcements on local radio stations (Parra and Valdés in Murphy 2004a). The volunteers sought to find families who did not have legal property titles, whether they lived as allegados, renters, or squatters in informal settlements. These homeless did not live on the street, but nevertheless had been unable to establish "well-constituted homes." MINVU heavily favored applicants for low-income subsidized housing who fit the gendered definition of being homeless, permitting only families to sign up for the programs. Such a guiding framework had been a cornerstone of state housing programs since the first half of the twentieth century.[65] These policies often left individuals, especially men who did not live in legally sanctioned families, at a disadvantage in receiving help from state institutions.[66]

The May Day Land Seizure

The homeless committee leaders in Renca found the symbolism of seizing land on May Day to be an important statement of solidarity. Knowing that tens of thousands from Chile's labor union confederations would march in Santiago's main thoroughfare later in the day, the leaders hoped that the land seizure would be received as a statement on working-class power and the possibilities of revolutionary activism. As they began their march in the cold, rainy dawn, the homeless pobladores carried Chilean flags. Their cause was a national one, representative of what they deserved as Chileans. Two days before the seizure, in an attempt to rally support for continued mobilization, one pobladora invoked an oft repeated saying credited to Manuel Rodríguez, a hero of the Chilean wars of independence and an icon of the Left: "'We still have fatherland [*patria*] citizens.' We too are Chileans, and we have a right to live here. And there are lands here, and we should fight for them."[67]

Almost immediately, the seizure gained significant public attention. Shortly after the march began, two elected Communist officials, including a senator and Gladys Marín, joined the homeless pobladores. Morning radio and television programs provided live coverage of the seizure. More ominously, several dozen police officers, dressed in riot gear, encircled the pobladores. Yet they did not impede the pobladores' progress, having evidently received orders to act with restraint. Once the pobladores arrived at the field that they had chosen to occupy, the police immediately cordoned off the area, and they permitted only food, water, and temporary materials for shelter to enter. This uneasy standoff, where the police controlled any movement in and out of the new campamento, would last for five days. During this period, the PC organized a number of relief and solidarity efforts. Committees from Herminda de la Victoria and Violeta Parra held vigils and donated food, while university students, labor organizations, and volunteers from *El Siglo*, the Communist daily, provided clothing and temporary shelters.[68] The pobladores camped out in tents, placing numerous flags throughout the land they now occupied.

In hopes of resolving the new campamento's legal status, homeless committee leaders, with the support of PC parliament members, entered negotiations with government officials. The leaders defended their actions by pointing out that the homeless pobladores had savings quotas, that they had seized the lands without causing disorder, and that they were well organized. As one pobladora commented to the press, "We aren't afraid. We're organized, we have rights, and we'll defend them, and we've done this seizure in an orderly manner, without provoking anybody.... If there's a fight, well, this wouldn't be the first time that some fall for the good of everyone else. Today we fight

Figures 3.2a and b. With flags waving, pobladores and others begin to set up Campamento Primero de Mayo (*El Siglo*, May 2, 1969, 1).

for tomorrow, for our children. . . . The struggle continues, and our children will have conquered a piece of land where they can live."[69]

On the day of the seizure, MINVU officials began a survey of the campamento.[70] Minister Donoso claimed that the survey would allow planners to understand the "true dimension of the housing problem" in Renca. According to Donoso, there were many squatters who legitimately had enough savings in housing programs, but there were several others who did not. Some had taken part in the seizure because they had been "pushed by political forces." Others, the minister alleged, already owned houses and were only trying to profit from the seizure.[71] But the survey would clear these issues up. To accomplish this, the survey assessed where and under what conditions the pobladores had previously lived, the nature of their families, their ability to make dividend payments, and whether or not they owned other properties.[72]

The squatter leaders did not object to the survey.[73] They viewed it as an opportunity to validate the propriety of their goals and actions.[74] They had, after all, already spent two years establishing the "homeless" status of committee members and enrolling them in government housing programs. The pobladores jealously guarded the records of their housing savings, referring to them as their "golden ledgers" (*libretas de oro*, as opposed to their *libretas de ahorro*, savings ledgers). Eliana Parra recalled not being worried about what the government might find, since all of the homeless were "married and lived in families" (Murphy 2004a).[75]

Still, negotiations between squatter representatives and officials were often tense. On May 5, more than one hundred homeless from Renca went to the regional governor's building to show their support for the land seizure.[76] Homeless committee leaders, Marín, the minister of the interior, Housing and Urbanism Minister Donoso, and the regional governor entered negotiations. Despite their obvious anger over the land seizure, Christian Democratic officials were under intense pressure to resolve the standoff, particularly since a baby had died from pneumonia the day before in the campamento, raising the specter of another young martyr.[77] On May 6, following a lengthy series of meetings, officials permitted the pobladores to stay, implicitly validating their claims.[78]

Such recognition, however, did not necessarily resolve many of the practical concerns that the pobladores had. Much planning remained to be done. Attempts to transform the campamento into a población would drag on for years, not being completed until well into the military dictatorship. The Homeless committee leaders, now recognized as a neighborhood council, worked with architects and planners from MINVU to organize the neighborhood. Establishing security patrols and work teams, the neighborhood council sought to provide for the safety of the población and for the construction of a meeting hall, latrines, and footpaths. Council members also often met with organizations willing to donate medical supplies and building materials, including university student groups.

But these efforts to transform the campamento into a población were short-lived. As often happens in the winter wet season in Santiago, sustained rains descended on the city in late May. Lacking sewers, the Primero de Mayo campamento, like many other new settlements, flooded, destroying many of the insecure housing structures that pobladores had cobbled together. By early June, the campamento was uninhabitable. Residents took shelter in a local parish and in the homes of extended family members or friends. The pobladores organized security patrols to return to the site of the seizure, guarding against theft and maintaining their claims to the land.

As families slowly returned to the campamento during the second half of 1969, negotiations continued over what the government would eventually provide and how many pobladores could remain on the land. This was often a fractious process, including challenges from groups of pobladores sponsored by the Christian Democrats.[79] Ultimately, the neighborhood council, Communist Party representatives, and government officials agreed that the ten homeless committees could stay. However, there was not enough room in the area to house all of the pobladores. In response, the negotiating parties agreed to two stipulations. First, MINVU would buy sections of a few adjacent properties to create more space.[80] Second, each committee had to identify twenty "families" who would have to leave.[81]

Homeless committee leaders had considerable leeway to decide who these pobladores would be. They thus had the authority to act as state-like administrators. Inclusion in the newly formed community depended on expectations that the homeless committees themselves established. This was true not only in the May Day land seizure, but also in committees that legally became a part of government-sponsored housing programs.[82] As these committees had the autonomy to make up their own minds about who to include and exclude, they had some flexibility in coming to their decisions. They could, for example, place more emphasis on the extent to which an applicant acted in honorable, neighborly, and communal ways, in which they fought for not only the betterment of themselves, but also their neighbors. Such criteria could become more important than financial requirements and a normative understanding of idealized nuclear families, although these still mattered.[83] The land seizures had opened up a broader space through which to establish a proper home life. Still, however, norms and expectations of propriety carried great weight, a supposition shared by both the homeless and state officials.

Inside the new campamento, leaders stressed the importance of individual conduct in meetings with the pobladores. Eliana Parra remembered it this way:

> We explained to them . . . that each resident was going to live in the neighborhood as if they were in their own home, without making any scandals, without anyone who would get drunk, without people who were looking for fights. . . . We also explained to them that the children should go to school, that the men had to go

to work, and that the women should stay in and take care of their houses, keep everything clean. . . . When it was seen that people made scandals, that husbands arrived home to the campamento drunk or something like that, people would come look for the directorate and call our attention to the bad behavior. On a number of occasions, I had to go speak to the people and some of them had to leave the campamento. (Murphy 2004a, 33)

Council leaders such as Eliana thus attempted to regulate behavior, establishing codes of personal conduct that stressed appropriate comportment, including hygiene, family relationships, work, and relative abstinence from alcohol and fighting. Individuals had to demonstrate that they were capable of conforming in this way if they wished to stay.

Such efforts to police the behavior of residents were common in neighborhoods established by land seizures.[84] Expectations of propriety in citizenship, class relations, and neighborly comportment drove these efforts to order the neighborhood through the internal policing of residents. These expectations were a diffuse and yet critical part of the social landscape, influencing the plans of anyone who sought to construct a proper and distinct home sanctioned by state institutions. By demonstrating that they were responsible and disciplined, pobladores showed that they deserved, as citizens, to be homeowners who would have access to basic city services. They could then be defined as living in a población or a villa, not a campamento or a callampa. Having these basic services and land titles was thus an important form of distinction, reflective of personal status. By gaining these benefits, pobladores achieved a different state of being in which they could demonstrate that they were full, not marginal, members of the imagined national community. The benefits that they received proved this. In this context, local groups carried on state practices of inclusion and exclusion, as they decided who could be a part of the new neighborhoods and gain access to better housing conditions. In other words, they helped to establish who deserved to shed the stigmas associated with being "homeless" and who could become full citizens with homes considered proper.

But the pobladores in Primero de Mayo were far from having appropriate homes, since they continued to live in a campamento. They thus continued to plan for the construction of their new neighborhood. The emerging spatial organization of the new campamento conformed to expectations of proper family relationships, neighborhood development, and home life. Once the pobladores returned to the May Day campamento after the floods, MINVU organized the campamento into ten distinct sections, which eventually became city blocks.[85] Each committee of the homeless occupied a different block, following a common practice that preserved the neighborhood identity that the pobladores had before the land seizure. MINVU granted each housing lot approximately sixty square meters. Beyond this, however, MINVU provided little else when residents moved in, angering many of the pobladores. As Ana Valdés recalled, "With everything that we had saved, [President] Frei should have given us an urbanized neighborhood, with electricity, water, sewer services, the lots divided, and street lights, but he only gave us lots that were chalked off; I'll never forget how they were simply chalked off" (Murphy 2004a; 42–43).[86]

The burdens placed on pobladores in this situation were onerous. At first, residents had to walk several blocks to wells for water or pay inflated prices for water drums.[87] They were also forced to dig their own latrines. The responsibility for the building of houses fell on individual households, although pobladores received help from architectural students at the University of Chile and from PC solidarity campaigns. In theory, a single family occupied each lot. However, allegados often moved in, at times reproducing the kinds of cramped quarters many had sought to escape.

Household and neighborhood designs were similar to those in place with government housing programs for low-income Chileans. The kitchen was a small room, where women did the cooking, separate from the living room where meals were eaten. The kitchen therefore tended to be an isolated space, demarcating where women worked.[88] Residents sought to keep the passageways small in the campamento, in order to facilitate foot traffic and aid in its fortification. They did this against the recommendations of professional architects, who generally planned for neighborhoods that would be accessible to cars, a feature that was well beyond the purchasing power of the vast majority of pobladores.

As had happened in the Herminda de la Victoria land seizure, the PC neighborhood leaders debated organizing living spaces in more revolutionary forms. One proposal included the creation of a communal kitchen and eating area. This was ultimately rejected, however. In a press report of the Herminda de la Victoria campamento, Juan Araya explained why the homeless committee leaders decided not to implement the communitarian option: "For the executive command of the campamento, the integrity of the home and private life is fundamental. [We have] agreed not to have a common kitchen [*olla común*]. Each mother will prepare, as is the custom, the food for her children. . . . With good will, the familial intimacy can prevail."[89] There was, ultimately, a certain amount of agreement about how neighborhoods should develop.

Even so, residents were unable to establish a proper población. The government did not provide a number of infrastructure services, prompting renewed activism.[90] On May 15, 1970, more than a year after the initial land seizure, several hundred pobladores from Campamento Primero de Mayo demonstrated in MINVU's central office building. They seized the first floor, demanding a meeting with Minister Donoso. Eventually, the Minister received the President of the Communal Command of the Homeless and promised that the campamento would receive running water, street pavement, and, further in the future, electricity. While the meeting had a favorable ending for the pobladores, it was also tense. The police forcibly removed several of the activists, wounding three of them and arresting eight others.[91]

After Allende became president, officials proposed apartment buildings as the way to transform the campamento. Popular Unity planners offered this solution to pobladores throughout Santiago, adopting the motto "let's move on up" (*vamos pa' arriba*). Nevertheless, in Primero de Mayo, as in many other areas, pobladores rejected this solution, preferring single-family homes. By the time of the military coup, the neighborhood was still a campamento. As Ana indicated, it "remained incomplete."[92]

Such an anticlimactic conclusion for pobladores who had seized land was not an isolated experience. While homeless pobladores throughout Chile's urban areas became particularly visible actors on the national scene during this period, seizing their place, as one author has described it, they could not entirely change the stages upon which they acted, nor the roles that they played.[93] If they were able to ensure that state functionaries would listen to their demands for acceptable standards of housing, they were nevertheless often stuck within a setting and with props that did not let them realize their desire to act as full citizens. Government bureaucracies were not able to provide the services and infrastructure that the pobladores demanded, even if there was a general consensus that they should have.

In many cases, as in the Primero de Mayo land seizure, the pobladores, rather than ceasing to be "homeless," found themselves in unfinished settlements without full legal sanction on the day of the coup. During the years that followed, planners in the dictatorship would target these areas as both hotbeds of Marxist "subversion" and as areas that needed to be "developed" and "modernized." By the beginning of the 1980s the pobladores of the May Day land seizure would have undisputed property titles and live in a neighborhood with urban services considered basic. But this "victory" followed violent dislocations during the military regime that the pobladores could hardly have imagined on that cold and rainy May Day in 1969.

Between Revolution and Continuity

The outpouring of activism in the land seizures represented a sense of the possibilities and promises of transformation in the poblaciones in the late 1960s and early 1970s. State actors, from officials determined to end "marginality" to the homeless committees that sought to establish legally constituted neighborhoods, undertook bold plans to create new conditions. They committed resources and took part in mobilizations that were unprecedented in scope. In this ferment of heightened activism and planning, pobladores and the spaces that they occupied were central objects of the desired changes. Improving their status would, after all, help to develop a new kind of nation, whether this meant the government's ongoing attempts to reform Santiago's shantytowns or the more revolutionary project that sought to construct vanguard neighborhoods in the poblaciones. As they sought change, various actors, but particularly the political parties, fought over what kind of citizens these homeless pobladores should become. In doing so, they followed different conceptions about what the appropriate role of the state should ultimately be and what role the pobladores should play in the new Chile.

But whether or not these futures would be revolutionary or simply reformist, or even provide for the more tangible goals of providing shelter and access to services, pobladores occupied a landscape in which naturalized practices, expectations, and categories persisted. The extent to which the land seizures became a means for producing proper homes underscores this point. Amid the revolutionary promise that the seizures engendered, structures and expectations of domesticity persisted, including gender relations, the discipline and personal habits of residents, and the layout and upkeep of living spaces. While they acted in insurgent and revolutionary ways by seizing land, pobladores also operated within established forms of citizenship and state formation as they became homeowners.

Through their activism, squatters pushed the boundaries of acceptable action and received state benefits that had previously been denied them. Leftist activists, moreover, celebrated the land seizures as an indication of the possibilities of emerging forms of "popular power." Yet this insurgent challenge also led directly through the symbols, bureaucracies, practices, expectations, and interests that gave shape to the state. In this environment, pobladores had to demonstrate their worth as proper citizens in order to become homeowners. Housing rights activism thus unfolded at the treacherous edge between revolutionary transgression and state conformity, legality and illegality, formality and informality. Ultimately, the struggles of housing rights activists help to reveal the unsettled and contested boundaries of hegemonic state frameworks during a tense period of conflict and unprecedented activism. In this landscape of promise and peril, transformation and continuity, the status and living conditions of pobladores hung in the precarious balance.

CHAPTER 4

SPECTERS IN THE REVOLUTION
Dilemmas of Home during the Chilean Path to Socialism

IN HIS MEMOIR, ARIEL DORFMAN, a cultural critic and prolific writer who held posts in the Popular Unity (UP) government, describes the exhilaration and release he felt while participating in the massive demonstrations that became common in the central streets of Santiago during Allende's presidency. In the midst of the boisterous crowds, Dorfman rubbed elbows and joined voices with socialists from across Chilean society, as labor unions, peasant organizations, student confederations, political party militants, and homeless groups seized the streets. They all shouted support for *poder popular* (popular power). Dorfman felt a sense of euphoria as the bodies and voices of the UP's followers came together to build solidarity, to affirm the revolution, and to construct a participatory form of democracy based on equality.

The marches were demonstrations of strength, illustrative of what the revolution might be capable of as the diverse bases of support for the UP found a place to articulate a shared vision of the future. For supporters, this mobilization was a sign of Leftist momentum. But while the performance had the power to unify and display revolutionary might, it nevertheless remained essentially a show of possibilities, a vision only of what could one day be. After the marches, Dorfman and his militant intellectual friends from the universities returned to the wealthier sections of Santiago's east side, while the other demonstrators would head home to their respective neighborhoods, often the campamentos and the poblaciones (Dorfman 1999 [1998], 244–45).[1]

With Allende's election, it was clear that certain stages of the Chilean social drama had shifted. As never before, Leftists were mobilized, ready to act toward the realization of an alternative future. For supporters of the UP, expectations were high; dreams of radical change were all around. These supporters had succeeded, after all, in transforming the social footing in a number of settings. Throughout the country, they filled stadiums and meeting halls; their demonstrations overwhelmed the streets; and many had taken part in seizing urban land, rural estates, and factories. But such activism only led to particular forms of change; other social stages, such as Santiago's stratified neighborhoods, would prove to be more resilient in the face of the revolutionary challenge.

Forces from the past would persist in the midst of the tumultuous changes of Salvador Allende's presidency, providing implacable and devastating obstacles to the socialist project. Two flashpoints of conflict during the UP years illuminate this theme: urban land seizures and the shortages that first developed in late 1971. These flashpoints underscore how the gap between the practices and expectations of home life were an unresolved tension that haunted the revolution. Despite the extraordinary transformations that occurred during the "Chilean Path to Socialism," citizenship claims cohered, as they often had in the past, around conceptions of a well-constituted and proper home. Based on the idea that they led a moral home life, citizens voiced their expectation that they should live in a minimally acceptable home. This included both a home's physical structure and its everyday patterns of consumption.

Planners in the UP government, however, ultimately did not have the means to provide a proper home life for many. Despite some initial success, by 1972 these planners faced a troubling panorama. They had not succeeded in solving the problems of the homeless, who continued to seek a right to housing in the city through urban land seizures, even as officials became increasingly concerned about them. At the same time, the shortages of such everyday items as food and milk contributed to a tense social environment that rallied the opposition and contributed to strains within the Left.

In much of the social mobilization, women played a crucial role. As they stepped into the public sphere, women tended to do so in a gendered register in which they played particular roles as mothers, consumers, and dueñas de casa. They often claimed to be defending the sanctity of family life. As in the past, this task was supposed to transcend narrow political interests. Defending the home remained an important grounding upon which elements of sociopolitical legitimacy stood. Sectors of the Left and the Right both argued that they were the ones who were truly protecting Chilean families. The question of home thus remained of crucial significance to the body politic.

Ultimately, obstacles to creating a home life considered appropriate posed significant challenges to the viability of the UP government. Understanding the nature of these challenges underscores how the production and consumption of home was a central aspect of Chile's capitalist state formation, before, during, and after Allende's government. As such, the power relations that formed at the crossroads between domesticity, capital, and the state were central to the exceptional years of the Chilean Path to Socialism. The crises and the revolutionary project led Chileans to debate elements of these relations publicly and vociferously. The revolutionary project, however, did not transcend these relations. Formed largely in the Chilean past, they were an anxious point of contention that the revolution unsettled but could not overcome. They were specters that haunted the revolution.

"The Most Generous Utopias of the Past" Confront the Limits to Governability

In his first address to Congress in May 1971, Salvador Allende asserted that Chileans were living in an unlikely era, one "that provided the material means to realize the most generous utopias of the past" (quoted in Martner 1992, 327). A committed Marxist, Allende argued that his government would transform the means of production. At the time of his address, several banks had already been transferred to the "Area of Social Property." The legislature would soon nationalize the copper mines, an industry that accounted for close to 80 percent of Chilean exports and more than 10 percent of the gross national product.[2] The UP government would then move forward to place several industries, mines, and agricultural estates under state control, focusing on enterprises that were "inefficient," monopolies, or foreign-owned, in addition to "strategic" industries that were important for achieving Chilean economic autonomy.

In realizing these goals, the Allende administration would redistribute wealth and, ultimately, create a new kind of Chilean social life in which the individual would work for collective ends. By changing the social conditions and building on the sacrifice and solidarity of all Chileans, the revolution would make possible the development of the "new man" who was aware of his duty to the revolution.[3] Allende called for sacrifice in the realization of this project, warning against presuming that the rewards of the revolution could be received without hard work.

But while Allende exhorted Chileans to work, he also promised that they would achieve new standards of living through the possession of material objects. One of his slogans in the 1970 elections had been "empanadas and red wine for all." Understood as quintessentially Chilean, these two products had often been beyond the reach of many. The slogan made clear that this would change. The revolution would achieve economic independence, completing the process of political sovereignty begun by the break from Spanish colonial rule. As the country finally broke the bonds of its persistent neocolonial relationships, all things Chilean would be for all Chileans. The working classes would have access to the fruits of the nation's labor and land as the country's wealth would neither leave the country nor serve the exclusive interests of the bourgeoisie.[4]

Allende's utopian vision included both the Socialist revolution and increasing levels of consumption. For UP planners, these two processes would unfold together in the creation of a new society. Yet Allende recognized that there was a potential conflict between these objectives and he urged his followers to remember that material benefits were only assured through social obligations and labor. As Allende put it, one should not confuse "personal interest" with the "generous conduct of collective work." "It is with reason," Allende argued, "that they write on Parisian walls: 'The revolution happens first in people and later in things'" (quoted in Martner 1992, 295).

But things were embedded in Chilean social life, forming a central part of self-definition and personhood.[5] Allende's promises and goals—and the ensuing experiences of the UP years—put the question of material distribution at the forefront of public discourse. Allende's project threatened to radically alter the intertwined patterns of Chilean production and consumption. Of course, this was precisely what made the Chilean Path to Socialism so controversial and threatening to powerful interests. For their part, UP planners walked a kind of tightrope. On the one hand, they sought to transform the means of production by undermining the power of the business class and breaking Chile's ties of economic dependence. On the other hand, however, officials sought to provide Chileans—and especially the working class—with increased access to consumption. For most, this meant fulfilling the kinds of desires that having consumer goods in the capitalist market had long held out. Plans for radical transformation thus confronted preexisting desires and expectations, presenting a fundamental dilemma for the revolution.

The ambitious scale of the UP project confronted a number of other obstacles, not all of which were readily apparent to government planners. Providing the means to produce and consume well-constituted homes was a complex and vexing problem. As officials moved forward, they found themselves in often uncomfortable binds, unable to control and transform the array of forces that their project unsettled and the interests that it potentially threatened.

Analysts have previously focused on three crucial areas in describing the difficulties that the Allende government faced.[6] First, the Allende administration sought to implement its programs from a weak governing position. The coalition had far less than total control of government bodies, let alone the multiple bases of state power. UP officials dominated only the executive branch, while the opposition political parties had majority control of the legislature and the judiciary. Despite increasing its support during municipal elections in 1971 and congressional ones in 1973, the UP coalition never enjoyed more than minority support at the ballot box.[7] (Allende himself won the 1970 election with only 36.2 percent of the vote.) Many of the UP's plans were held up in the governing process. Numerous UP officials faced inquiries and impeachment trials, as the opposition used the power of the legislature and judiciary to frustrate and slow down the Allende presidency.

The second obstacle that Allende confronted came from within the ranks of the Left itself. More radical sectors, including elements of Allende's own Socialist Party and the Movement of the Revolutionary Left (MIR), adopted a "maximalist" approach that sought immediate socialization and, in certain cases, armed conflict. Many labor unions, agricultural cooperatives, and neighborhood organizations often demanded a more rapid transition to revolution than the "gradualist" approach favored by UP leaders. This often forced officials to move at a faster pace or in ways different from what they would have liked.[8] In order to realize their plans, officials thus had to overcome both the discord within the UP's bases of support and the outright hostility of sectors of the opposition.

Third, the government faced a difficult financial situation. The sources of revenue and foreign exchange that the Chilean state had long depended on were scarce during Allende's tenure in office. International copper prices had recently fallen, restricting the government's largest single source of revenue (Loveman 1988, 308).[9] Furthermore, the nationalization of the copper mines did not initially generate the kind of economic boost that planners expected, as the costs of transferring them to state control proved to be a financial burden (Boorstein 1977, 133–36; Moran 1974). Compounding this, capital flight became a serious problem. Many Chilean investors, fearing that the UP would confiscate their assets, moved their capital and money abroad. Perhaps most importantly, the US government, in the words of President Nixon, sought to "make the economy scream," implementing a campaign that largely suspended US development aid (with the important exception of that going to the military) and sought to block Chile's access to international credit.[10] Groups such as the World Bank and the Inter-American Development Bank severely reduced loans to Chile, while international business investment sharply declined.[11]

The problems with copper production and the major reduction in aid, credit, and investment made it increasingly difficult for the Chilean government to acquire foreign currency. To support its ambitious programs, the government eventually had to spend its reserves and go into debt. As a result, the Chilean currency devalued. While this helped exports, it contributed to increasing

Figure 4.1. "Cigarettes? Tea? Rice? Sugar? Milk? Coffee? Oil?" "Out of stock," says the store owner (*Chile Hoy* 1 [32], 1972; image courtesy of the Biblioteca Nacional de Chile).

the prices that several industries had to pay to gain access to essential inputs from abroad. Production began to fall, contributing to the shortages. As UP planners sought to overcome this situation, it became clear that they were not able to control many of the distribution circuits in the country, despite the nationalization of three hundred "strategic" industries. Opposition groups retained an important means of sabotage, often hoarding goods and refusing to produce more. They thus were able to upset the circulation of commodities, as sectors of the Left were often quick to point out (see figure 4.1). The devastating truckers' strikes of October 1972 and August 1973 best illustrate the ability of the opposition to disrupt the flow of goods. The truckers received covert financial support from the executive branch of the US government, part of a secret ten-million-dollar campaign to destabilize the country and undermine the Chilean Path to Socialism. (Given the black market price of dollars, this campaign was probably worth closer to forty million dollars, a significant sum in Chile at the time [Angell 1993, 167].)

In addition to the truckers, US government funds supported political opposition parties, media outlets, trade associations, small business groups, and far-Right organizations such as Patria y Libertad (Fatherland and Liberty). Some of this money probably also went to groups that supported the Marches of the Empty Pots, protests initiated by right-wing women in December 1971. Assessing the precise impact of these covert operations has provoked a long-running debate.[12] Certainly US covert operations often failed to achieve their immediate goals, most famously in a bumbling, if deadly, effort to prevent Allende from assuming office following the presidential elections.[13] But regardless of whether or not they were immediately successful, these operations had toxic effects. They heightened conflict, sowed confusion and uncertainty, and emboldened the opposition. They were particularly effective at making everyday living conditions worse. Ultimately, they undermined the Allende government in ways similar to the effects of earlier US covert operations in such places as Guatemala. They polarized social relations and irrevocably damaged democratic processes.[14]

Planning to Produce Revolutionary Consumption

Despite the formidable array of forces aligned against him, Allende enjoyed a successful first year in office. Money flowed as the government went on an extraordinary spending spree. The country broke out of its economic slump from 1968 to 1970 as UP planners adopted a series of ambitious plans. They focused, in particular, on reaching out to low-income wage earners and providing these Chileans with greater access to goods and services. Yet officials experienced a number of difficulties as they confronted persistent inequities, practices, and expectations, many of which were at odds with their vision of revolutionary change. Dynamics from the past endured, often confounding government programs, tempering revolutionary fervor, and contributing to a tense social environment.

Initially, government agencies adopted a Keynesian approach that sought to stimulate the overall production and consumption of goods and services in Chile. This included plans for the construction of more than eighty thousand new housing units in 1971, a target that, if met, would approximately double the best annual total in Chilean history (Gobierno de Chile, *Mensaje Presidencia,* 1971, 582).[15] The UP government focused most of these programs on low-income sectors, seeking to overcome the tendency of past government housing subsidies to benefit the middle classes.[16] The generous spending initially contributed to an 8 percent rise in the GNP during 1971, even as substantial inflationary pressures began to appear.

Through these policies, officials sought to grant the popular classes access to a different lifestyle, one to which wealthier Chileans were already accustomed. As the minister of the economy Pedro Vuskovic made clear, the policies of increasing the money supply and stimulating employment were meant to grant low-income groups enhanced purchasing power, a central part of a strategy to increase support for the government.[17] During Allende's first year in power, the government was able to grant the lower classes greater access to such consumer items as radios, gas stoves, furniture, and, just as Allende had promised, *empanadas y vino tinto*.[18]

Both government bureaucracies and private organizations launched a series of artistic initiatives and leisure activities aimed at the popular classes. Cultural events happened all over Santiago and many pobladores were swept up in the festive atmosphere. Several popular artists played free concerts, including stops in the poblaciones (Jara 1984, 164). Classical orchestras and operas traveled to neighborhood councils and union meeting halls (*Ramona* 1 [2], Nov. 5, 1971, 46). Certain works of art were meant to refine tastes and be accessible to all. The government sponsored mural brigades and the display of public art throughout the city.[19] More books were published in Chile in the three years that Allende was president than in all of the preceding years of the nation's history. In subsidizing these publications, the government assured their cheap, mass distribution (Dorfman 1999; Fernández Labbé 2003). There were even efforts to support "popular tourism," as the UP government sponsored programs to help pobladores travel to beaches and mountain resorts for vacations.[20]

Yet if UP planners sought a fundamental shift in the state's approach toward the popular classes, they also implemented certain policies that reflected familiar patterns in state programs toward low-income sectors. Plans for modernization formed an integral part of many projects, based on paradigms that borrowed from international development models. The notion that the poor were outside of the dominant governing and market structures of society continued to resonate with planners. In this view, the poor needed to be included in the protections and benefits that citizenship offered. While many government programs had long been designed with these goals in mind, they had not been undertaken with the same kind of ambitious scope that UP planners sought. These planners, after all, hoped to guarantee all Chileans a high standard of living, well above thresholds defined merely by levels of poverty. This was a radical project, even as it sought to push the promise of modernization to one of its logical ends.

In certain areas, UP planners strengthened programs already in place, as in the highly publicized program designed to transform the campamentos and to "regularize" some two hundred thousand properties (Gobierno de Chile, *Mensaje Presidencial*, 1971, 294). Three MINVU officials wrote that the UP government was to undertake the "gigantic task of getting 40,000 families out of the mud who live in the so-called 'campamentos,' a heavy inheritance that the new government has received from the past" (Wong, Lawner, and Cortés 1971, 1). This included efforts to "sanitize, regulate, and make well" the campamentos, as officials adopted the familiar verb *sanear* to describe their efforts to transform the campamentos into healthy, developed, and modern city spaces.

The UP also initiated several programs designed to provide low-income sectors with better services. Some of these efforts were similar to the policies of the Christian Democratic government, even as they superseded them in scope. For example, officials hoped to provide low-income neighborhoods with access to athletic fields, pools, libraries, and youth centers.[21] They also targeted the lowest-income sectors through programs that provided free milk, granted school uniforms to children, and established mobile health units that would tour recently established squatter settlements (Gobierno de Chile, *Mensaje Presidencial,* 1971). In one emergency program, "Operation Winter," officials sought to improve infrastructure in the campamentos to protect them against seasonal floods.

UP planners cast these initiatives as an attempt to transform the conditions of the working class and overcome existing distinctions and privileges. This would include making fundamental changes to the spaces of the city. According to housing and urbanism officials, the ultimate goal of their policies was to create a city that "would no longer be an expression of class."[22] In order to achieve this goal, however, officials often followed a sensibility about living arrangements that conformed to middle- and upper-class standards. In their housing programs, planners sought to build new apartment buildings for the lower classes, promoting their efforts, as previously noted, with the motto "Vamos pa' arriba." For officials, this would permit the "popular classes" to live in conditions that only the wealthy had occupied. It would also help to build a "modern" and more "rational" city.

The attempt to move on up remained largely an unrealized goal. By the end of 1971, UP planners massively scaled back their construction plans for apartment buildings (see Gobierno de Chile, *Mensaje Presidencial,* 1971, 592). These initiatives were expensive and they proved to be unpopular, often at odds with what many pobladores wanted. Neighborhood councils and housing organizations generally rejected MINVU's offers to move to subsidized apartments.[23] For their part, officials in the government sought to convince pobladores of the value of "movin' on up." Speaking to a homeless group in August 1971, Carlos Cortés, the minister of housing and urbanism, rhetorically asked, "So, only the rich can live in apartments?"[24] Three housing officials wrote that the policy had forced them "to have a patient dialogue with poblador organizations, who have been reticent to accept apartment buildings because of their family background in the countryside but who have nevertheless understood the need to control the irrational growth of the cities that each year cuts into important agricultural areas that are indispensable for the food supply of the country" (Wong, Lawner, and Cortés 1971).

These arguments, however, tended to fall on deaf ears, and only partially because many had recently arrived from the countryside. Pobladores preferred to live on their own property lots, in houses that reflected the existing architectural patterns of single-family homes for middle- and lower-class residents. This was undoubtedly an aesthetic choice for many, but pobladores also had more flexibility in controlling their own space and in adapting to changing conditions. In lots of their own, they could do such things as build additions, raise chickens, or have a garden. It would thus be easier for them, as Chileans tend to put it, to overcome (*superarse*) the often harsh situations that they faced.[25] The diverse styles, designs, and sizes of houses that one generally sees in the poblaciones reflect these historically necessary adaptive practices, in addition to the varied purchasing power of pobladores and the extended social networks that residents have been able to mobilize.

The allure offered by "movin' on up" also encountered another difficulty. For many pobladores, moving to an apartment would not necessarily be a desirable form of upward mobility. Pobladores tend to refer to themselves proudly as neighbors, *vecinos*, who can depend on the people who live around them for companionship and help. As we have seen, during the land seizures and the resettling of neighborhoods, pobladores most often moved together, reflecting the importance that they put on the relationships they built with neighbors, often cast as a form of solidarity. By contrast, Chileans often refer to the upper classes as residents, *residentes*, who largely ignore their neighbors in the comings and goings of daily life as they live in exclusive apartment complexes or in fortified houses. Today, pobladores often dismiss the wealthy as cold and impersonal, pointing to their seemingly hermetic lifestyles, as evidenced by their closed-in houses and their quiet and anonymous streets.

Government planners, in their attempts to move the city on up, thus faced embedded practices, expectations, and social divisions that proved to be at odds with their visions of transformation.[26] As Allende had warned, there were potential dangers for the path of the revolution in the acquisition of material objects. But this went beyond Allende's observation that "personal interest" potentially conflicted with "collective work." The "most generous utopias of the past" were born from the often contradictory social pressures and formations that had developed within Chilean capitalism and in urban living conditions. In the case of efforts to move the city on up, elite visions of modernity and transformed social relations clashed with the survival strategies, expectations of home and neighborhood, and the class perspective of many pobladores. For many pobladores, high-rise apartment living was an inappropriate response to the conditions they had long endured.

Revolutionary Governance and the Problem of Seized Land

Urban land seizures presented a series of dilemmas for UP officials. Before Allende's election, the seizures had become a well-publicized mode of Leftist activism, symbolizing the radical potential of militant organization to overcome the injustices of Chilean capitalism and the inadequacies of the state. The land seizures thus represented a threat to the status quo and to the legal system. Pobladores who had been killed by the police during the land seizures became martyrs in the memory of the Left. Allende, in fact, emphasized this point in his inaugural address. Beginning his speech solemnly, Allende asserted, "There are others [who] share in our victory . . . and they are here with us." Allende recalled figures who he felt had made possible the ascension of the Left: Lautaro and Caupolicán, two indigenous leaders who had resisted Spanish imperialism; Manuel Rodríguez, a guerrilla leader from the Chilean wars of independence; the late nineteenth-century president José Manual Balmaceda; and Luis Emilio Recabarren, the labor leader and founder of the Communist Party. At the end of this history of sacrifice and struggle, Allende honored as heroes the pobladores who had died while taking part in land seizures, including those killed in the 1969 massacre in Puerto Montt (Salvador Allende, in Martner 1992, 287).

Given the importance that the land seizures played in the revolutionary imagination, how would Leftists in the government respond to them as they sought to establish a legal path to Socialism? How would the social solidarities of the Left, forged through years of oppositional activism and negotiation with the Chilean state, adjust to having Leftists in the presidential palace? As officials assumed their new posts in MINVU in November 1970, they immediately had to respond to these questions. Throughout 1970, the number of urban land seizures drastically increased, particularly in Santiago. During the frenetic two months between Allende's electoral triumph and his ascent to the presidency, a number of groups seized neighborhoods under construction, including some that were part of subsidized housing programs.

In January 1971—two months after Allende assumed power—one MINVU functionary wrote that the proper response to the land seizures was to follow "the social spirit that animates us" and the "attributes that the law grants."[27] But even if MINVU officials could make the attributes of the law adhere to their wishes, they still had to contend with an animating social spirit that, while revolutionary, had been forged within the contours, dynamics, and desires of Chilean capitalism and state formation. Such a historical weight often contributed to making the Path to Socialism a difficult and confusing route to follow. The weight of governing frameworks, including their norms and stigmatizations, still pressed down upon citizen relations and processes of urbanization. As the following example illustrates, such dynamics remained an important force in the negotiations between homeless citizens and state functionaries.

On October 21, 1970, Leticia Román de Morales penned a lengthy letter to Salvador Allende.[28] Román was from Green Valley, an area settled in 1960 by squatters in San Bernardo, a rapidly growing municipality just outside of Santiago. As the president of the Green Valley Women's Committee, Román expressed her elation at Popular Unity's electoral victory, proudly noting that on the day of Allende's triumph, her committee had hosted a celebration. Under a banner that read *Venceremos* (We'll win, or, We shall overcome), pobladores danced and sang until late into the night, joining Allende supporters throughout Chile who had taken to the streets to proclaim their solidarity.

In her letter, Román expressed confidence that the new government would transform her neighborhood. After having seized Green Valley, Román and her neighbors had been unable to legalize their housing lots following indecisive negotiations with the landowner and potential developer of the site, María Luisa Contreras Jofré. In 1960, the pobladores had signed a contract with Contreras in which they promised to buy their properties after they had received basic infrastructure services. Green Valley, however, had remained undeveloped, as both residents and Contreras had waited in vain for subsidies from one of MINVU's subdepartments to contract the provision of water, sewage systems, and electricity.

This situation left pobladores in Green Valley in an unresolved administrative bind. Legally, Román and her neighbors were "occupants" of privately owned land. Because of this, MINVU and other government bodies could not proclaim Green Valley an "irregular area," an important bureaucratic procedure that would permit residents to receive "emergency" services from MINVU. This situation was further complicated by the fact that other squatters and allegados had continued to come to Green Valley throughout the 1960s. Despite the work that Román and her neighbors had put into building their houses and organizing their neighborhood, they continued to suffer the indignities and hardships of being without basic services.[29]

Román, however, expressed hope that this would soon change. Quoting a campaign speech of Allende's that she had attended in San Bernardo, Román claimed that the "compañero presidente" had promised a complete "clean up" if the UP won. Román assured Allende that Green Valley desperately needed such a crackdown: despite the efforts of her committee, the campamento had far too many "thieves and muggers." It also had a reactionary and rival committee in the neighborhood that supported Arturo Alessandri, the former president from the Rightist National Party and the runner-up in the 1970 presidential elections. If the "filth" (*mugre*) would leave the campamento and if the remaining pobladores received land titles, Green Valley would develop into the kind of neighborhood that Román had dreamed it could be. Allende's election, Román rhetorically assumed, assured this happy outcome.

Román's expectations, however, were misplaced. The MINVU officials who responded to Román's letter, the chief of the Section of Irregular Neighborhoods and an undersecretary of the ministry, quickly brushed aside Román's request for land titles. Dismissing the pobladores as illegal occupants, the officials argued that they did not have the right to stay in Green Valley.[30] This was especially clear, they claimed, since the residents had shown little ability to organize their neighborhood properly. Using the precise language that a Christian Democratic official had used the year before to describe Green Valley, the undersecretary wrote in his reply to Román that Green Valley was in a "most anarchic" state. The housing lots spilled chaotically one on top of the other. There were, the undersecretary noted, 170 houses in an area that should have had only one hundred, thus making it impossible for the neighborhood to have a proper street plan. As bad as that was, the disorder and overcrowding was even more serious: a number of the pobladores permitted allegados to build ramshackle rooms behind their houses. Given all of this, the undersecretary concluded, it would be impossible for MINVU and the Ministry of Public Works to build sewage systems in Green Valley and "regularize" the neighborhood.

The MINVU officials thus condemned Román and her neighbors, seeing them as dirty, disorganized, and undeserving of the benefits of citizenship. Ignoring Román's fervent support for President Allende, officials at MINVU made the same assessments and recommendations for Green Valley's improvement as had the previous Christian Democratic administration. In the eyes of these planners, Green Valley was a failure, an assessment that Román probably found insulting and unfair. She was, after all, the president of an organization of dueñas de casa who had taken it upon themselves to fight for the proper development of their neighborhood. Through mobilization and planning, dueñas de casa like Román sought to construct dignified living arrangements that protected the sanctity of their families. Beyond receiving basic services and land titles, they sought to inhabit a landscape where they received respect and where they comfortably fit in, free from stigmatization. Given the necessary resources, they would achieve this goal once they inhabited a proper home.

This was, of course, a very common desire, crosscutting political and class interests. Inclusion in the exclusive company of citizens had long hinged on the ability of the homeless to demonstrate discipline, in conformity with dominant expectations of appropriate domestic practices, personal comportment, and neighborhood spatial arrangements. As the Green Valley Women's Committee discovered, failure to display proper discipline could carry sanctions. Developing a well-constituted home was thus a tremendous social force, exerting an inexorable pressure that was particularly potent for homeless pobladores. It had led them to seek redress and dignity within the state, allowing them to rally around a common cause and to act in solidarity. Homeless pobladores during Allende's government continued to utilize a similar conceptual framework in order to seek legitimacy in state bureaucracies.

Planners in the UP government, in turn, often responded to the homeless in ways that mimicked their predecessors. For example, the housing surveys that they used were largely the same. They sought to discover whether or not the applicant came from a nuclear family. They also asked other familiar questions: Would the applicant be able to save and responsibly assume mortgage payments? Was the applicant part of a neighborhood council, a committee of the homeless, or some other neighborhood organization? What were the personal antecedents of the applicant? All of these factors remained important in determining the extent to which government agencies would assist the pobladores in gaining access to a house in the spree of seizures and building that took place during the Chilean Path to Socialism.[31]

There were then elements of continuity, even as the government sought radical transformation and much of the context had changed. To be sure, the mechanisms in place to police the requirements for homeownership had shifted. The official policy of the UP government was to discourage the land seizures, but state bureaucrats would not use the most coercive forms of state violence to stop them. The risks taken by squatters were thus greatly reduced, as had been the case during the last year of Frei Montalva's government. Land seizures remained relatively common, despite the priority that officials placed on attempting to dissuade groups from taking part in them.

Shortly after becoming president, Allende told a group of pobladores in Campamento Che Guevara that although he had supported land seizures in the past he would no longer do so. The "popular government," Allende asserted, would work harder to resolve the housing crisis than had any previous government. UP officials, however, would only "appeal to reason" to convince the pobladores not to seize land.[32] From his perspective as the new minister of housing and urbanism, Carlos Cortés argued that the seizures harmed planning efforts, fomented intraclass conflict, and made it more difficult for state bureaucracies to provide infrastructure for the newly settled areas.[33] To a certain extent, government bureaucrats sought to support their "appeals to reason" with the force of law. But many of the proposed laws regarding the land seizures were never implemented and officials generally sought to avoid conflict, hoping to manage the seizures and limit the damage that they could cause.[34]

Overall, officials were strictest with three types of land seizures: First, they often refused to help pobladores when the land seized had provoked a conflict with another group of pobladores.[35] Second, officials were reticent to help establish neighborhoods that would put further strains on the government's budget.[36] Last, they sought to prevent the establishment of neighborhoods that would harm the country's agricultural or industrial output.[37]

Such concerns, however, were often overridden by, as one MINVU official put it, the "political effervescence" of the day. In one case, Juan Araya—the famous housing activist who had led the Herminda de la Victoria land seizure in 1967 and who now held a post in MINVU—sponsored a group of squatters who seized land in an area that had been zoned as industrial. Araya, by this time an icon of the Left, had always worked tirelessly to ensure that the neighborhoods his committees established were well organized and strictly disciplined. Given Araya's involvement, it is not surprising that officials acquiesced to the demands made by his committee, despite the fact that its members had seized land set aside for factories.[38]

In general, MINVU bureaucrats grudgingly tolerated the seizures. At times, they legally sanctioned the right of the squatters to remain where they had established a neighborhood.[39] In one illustrative case, a neighborhood council president wrote a letter to the minister of housing and urbanism in which he admitted that the members of his committee seized land adjacent to the campamento that he and his neighbors occupied. In justifying this act, he pointed out that many residents of the campamento had lived as allegados and that the owner of the adjacent property had not put his land to productive use. He asked that the minister legalize the status of the squatters and expropriate the land, so that, in his words, "we, the needy workers, will have a place to live . . . and so that we can leave a roof to our children and wives." Following an investigation, officials acquiesced to the seizure, even supporting the homeless committee as it sought to procure basic infrastructure.[40]

In managing the fallout from the seizures, officials faced a difficult set of options. Legal solutions were expensive and demanded technical expertise.[41] Unlike in the past, private contractors often refused to work with MINVU.[42] Allende's opponents vociferously denounced the seizures as an indication of social breakdown and government ineptitude. Over the long term, the situation was not tenable. As officials readily admitted, "regularizing neighborhoods" established through seizures would put their other ambitious plans at risk. MINVU officials generally responded by denying the squatters legal status and the services that the bureaucracy offered. But they did not force the pobladores to leave.[43] This contributed to the fact that, by the time of the military coup, there were hundreds of "irregular" campamentos in Santiago that had not received legal recognition and were without basic services. These neighborhoods ultimately looked much like Green Valley: a sure sign of stigmatized underdevelopment.

Mobilizing the Homeless: New Faces, Old Claims

Many of the elected officials who had been most involved in sponsoring homeless groups when they seized land before Allende's inauguration—such as Gladys Marín, Laura Allende, Mario Palestro, Volodia Teitelboim, and Mireya Baltra—did not do so once Salvador Allende assumed power. These officials, particularly those from the Communist Party, followed the stated policies of the UP leadership, tending not to grant overt support to the seizures.[44] Other political groups, however, perhaps sensing an opportunity to embarrass the UP and build up support among the pobladores, began to sponsor land seizures. This included Christian Democratic activists, who started to seize land in the year leading up to the 1970 presidential election after it became obvious that the Frei Montalva government would no longer stop the seizures. In a few exceptional cases, even the Rightist National Party and the fascist organization Patria y Libertad sponsored land seizures, sometimes as part of efforts to "recover" already seized land.

More radical sectors of the Left—particularly the MIR and "maximalist" factions of the Socialist Party—also became increasingly involved in the land seizures, garnering much public attention.[45] MIR and Socialist housing activists attacked bureaucrats at MINVU for their recalcitrant attitudes. They argued that it would not be possible to achieve a transition to socialism using government institutions that continued to respect legal frameworks and remained mired in bureaucratic procedures.[46] Denouncing the UP government in the press, they often led acts of civil disobedience in which they blocked traffic and led sit-ins at government ministries. Through their protests, these groups sought to negotiate access to services and benefits, just as their Communist Party predecessors had done before Allende's presidency. In doing so, they could point to the discipline and sacrifice they enforced in their campamentos, as they demanded adherence to the conduct embodied in the Socialist "New Man." Through their actions, the members of these homeless committees articulated a critique of the conditions they lived in and laid claim to a place in the state. But rather than being a source of Leftist unity as it had been in the past, mobilization of this kind often exacerbated fissures within the UP and led to contradictory government policies.

The MIR sponsored a few highly publicized land seizures in Las Condes, the wealthiest municipality in the country. For more exuberant MIR militants, these seizures would both promote revolutionary consciousness and provide important beachheads for the impending armed conflict. Not surprisingly, these kinds of seizures provoked strong reactions. Right-wing vigilantes often went to the MIR's campamentos to demonstrate and beat up residents. The opposition press printed alarmist stories about these seizures, claiming they were an indication of the violent and radical turn that the revolution was taking. According to these reports, MIR leaders were subversive and dangerous. Not only that, they were depraved, a threat to proper manhood and character with their long hair, beards, and *guerrillero* style. The reports labeled them *miricones*, playing on the term *maricones*, a derogatory term for homosexuals that included a sense that they were untrustworthy.[47] As these reports would have it, duplicitous and sexually questionable men were thus illegally seizing land and illegitimately transgressing spatial boundaries of property, class, and propriety.

For their part, UP officials publicly complained about the "sectarianism" that the MIR and the "ultra maximalists" fomented. Yet MINVU officials conceded that most pobladores involved in land seizures sponsored by the MIR deserved to have homes of their own. Crucially, they tended to recognize that the MIR's organization and discipline assured proper behavior on the part of squatters.[48] The result was a stalemate: officials neither forced the MIR to stop nor did they tend to go out of their way to provide neighborhoods settled by the MIR with services and land titles, although there were important exceptions.

The spike in the number of seizures and the ambitious construction projects initiated by the UP government meant that urban land was, on balance, easier to obtain. Yet for many, legally owned urban land was still scarce, insecure, and inequitably distributed. It became the site of intense conflicts and of rigorous defense strategies on the part of landowners and squatters. Before, seizures had generally occurred on the urban periphery. For the most part this was still the case, yet, as with the MIR in Las Condes, activists now seized land more frequently throughout Santiago, in neighborhoods of all classes. A few seizures occurred in apartment buildings and housing cooperatives under construction. While many homeless committees may not have wanted to move into high-rise apartment buildings, some groups were willing to do so, seizing new buildings in the *barrio alto*—the wealthy neighborhoods—including the one pictured in figure 4.2.

Figure 4.2. Squatters seized the middle building in 1972, just after its completion (photo by author).

For wealthier residents, the seizures generally heightened anxieties and fears that their homes and class privileges were under threat. Developers and neighborhood organizations hired security guards for protection, resulting in occasional confrontations.[49] Efforts to defend new housing cooperatives and recently seized land were also stepped up, with armed groups going out on patrol (see figure 4.3). In certain instances, Christian Democratic neighborhood organizations clashed with UP supporters in well-publicized confrontations that resulted in injuries and occasionally in deaths. Both Leftist and Rightist media outlets treated such violence as a breakdown in civility and as a portent of the "impending confrontation" or "civil war."[50]

As conflicts over land were increasing, government planners began to face serious budgetary constraints. The number of new housing starts dropped precipitously. Building materials had largely been depleted due to the general economic problems and the massive construction efforts of 1971. In addition, the building companies, well-organized in the Chilean Chamber of Construction, became increasingly unwilling to cooperate with the building plans of the government. For their part, UP officials began to promise less, pointing out in the legislature, the press, and their letters to citizens that Chile had a housing deficit of six hundred thousand, an existing stock of only 1.2 million, and a maximum capacity of building seventy thousand housing units per year. Change, they now argued, was not going to come quickly.[51]

Despite all of these tumultuous changes and confrontations taking place in Santiago, claims for housing continued to be made based on assumptions about proper gender and familial roles. In their letters seeking homes from UP officials, women often sought support as mothers and housewives. As one mothers' center wrote to Allende, "we hope that your Excellency of the Republic Compañero Allende will respond to our petition in order to help us proletarian mothers and children, who have for years hoped and had confi-

Figure 4.3. Armed pobladores protect a new neighborhood (González and Pino [1997], 1565; image courtesy of the Centro de Estudios Públicos).

dence that our compañero Allende would end our suffering and worries before we die so that our desire for the upbringing of our children can be fulfilled."[52] Many also wrote in efforts to keep their properties from being confiscated or lost. One neighborhood council, for example, wrote to Allende, explaining that through "an entire life of work and suffering" they had managed to build their houses, "95 percent of which are made from solid materials." It would be "unjust and highly unusual" if the municipality expropriated their lands, since "while you are making it possible for every Chilean to have access to a house, they are going to take ours away from us . . . your government would look badly if the municipal authorities expropriated our well-constituted and well-constructed homes."[53]

In seeking homes considered appropriate, Chileans assumed that their living spaces should have certain physical characteristics. In a letter from January 1973, a lieutenant from the National Armed Forces wrote to Allende in the hopes that the president could improve the "dramatic situation" that he lived in, in which he shared one room with his entire family. Such a situation, he pleaded, "causes many hardships and is very tight of space, insufficient for a well-constituted home."[54] A Christian Democratic deputy, writing a letter on behalf of a neighborhood council in a campamento, asked for help from MINVU, noting that residents had houses that were only eighteen square meters, a size that is insufficient "for a regular family."[55] Both of these claims reflected a familiar refrain: disciplined and hardworking families deserved minimal standards of living. One of the primary goals of the land seizures, after all, was to achieve living conditions considered basic, including land, neighborhood infrastructure, and the materials for a house. MINVU still responded to this, continuing to focus on minimally acceptable housing.

Between Housing and Home

Of course, much more actually went into producing an appropriate and dignified home than minimal forms of housing, from family and neighborhood relationships, material items to fill the house, and food for the table. UP officials implicitly recognized this as they tried to transform the lifestyles of the lower classes. But in newly established campamentos, it nevertheless remained largely the responsibility of household members to provide for the accoutrements of the house and most of the consumption needs of its occupants. The "collective work" of both neighborhood organization and government programs only laid the groundwork for establishing the right kind of home. If pobladores could organize in solidarity to receive basic housing, they needed much more in order to develop a home in a social world still marked by commodities and mass consumption. There continued to be a gap between the provision of housing and the development of a home.

The story of Rosa Cancino underscores how difficult it could be to establish a home considered appropriate. During the late 1960s and early 1970s, Rosa had four children whom she was raising on her own.[56] Between 1970 and 1973 she moved three times, taking part in the tumultuous settling and resettling of Santiago. In September 1970, during the wave of land seizures that gripped Santiago following Allende's electoral victory, Rosa's homeless committee established Campamento Blanca Vergara in Renca. In her recollections, Rosa emphasized how hard it was to "advance much" in Blanca Vergara. During her fifteen months there, the campamento's homeless committee was unable to legalize the neighborhood and provide the residents with property titles. Fearful of the uncertainty, Rosa did not commit to building a permanent house, using instead only a makeshift nylon tent with a corrugated roof for shelter. Without property rights, Rosa and her neighbors were in a weak negotiating stance, suffering from an insecurity of tenure. As an illegal squatter, Rosa had little autonomy and control over her home. But becoming a legally recognized homeowner would change this.

In late 1971, Rosa and her neighbors left the campamento, having grown impatient with time-consuming bureaucratic procedures and the intransigence of Blanca Vergara's landowner. They moved to an area named Las Cuncunas, possession of which they ostensibly took through a land seizure. They had, however, reached an agreement with the owner of Las Cuncunas, and they seized the land peacefully, without any resistance.[57] As a part of the process, Rosa and her neighbors formed a housing cooperative.[58] To be in the cooperative, residents had to follow standards typical of neighborhood councils and homeless committees. The housing contract stipulated that the pobladores "get along well" with their neighbors, maintain clean and orderly households, and avoid causing scandals such as public drunkenness or fighting. Members also had to participate in cooperative committees and in vigilance groups that would protect Las Cuncunas from squatters and thieves.[59] Rosa needed to demonstrate particularly exemplary behavior. She was one of only three single mothers in the cooperative and she desperately needed to build on her friendships and ties of compadrazgo: she could take her eldest daughter along to her work as a maid, but during the long days that she was gone she needed someone to care for her other children.

Beyond neighborly and familial forms of behavior, members of the cooperative also had to adhere to a monthly payment schedule. This obligation proved to be too onerous for many, and a number of pobladores from Blanca Vergara did not stay in Las Cuncunas. Newcomers arrived in their stead. Rosa indicated that these were people "from a little higher society than ours," people who had the means to more easily meet the financial requirements of the cooperative. In an important sense, the Las Cuncunas cooperative acted as a means to gaining a home of one's own along the lines of an emerging mass-consumer housing market. Since 1959, the year that the government passed an important housing decree, the state had helped to subsidize a boom in middle- and lower-middle-class housing starts. This funded the construction of apartment buildings and smaller houses, for both pobladores and middle-income sectors.[60]

These new dwellings could be difficult spaces to manage, particularly for those with very low incomes, despite the available subsidies and the support that homeless committees and neighborhood groups could offer. If homeownership pointed to one's status as a proper and respected citizen, developing the home and filling it with commodities depended on resources and time, both of which could be limited. Given that Chile's mass-consumer market included constrained choices and particular tastes, it was not necessarily easy to create desirable homes. During the late 1960s, women's magazines such as *Paula* appeared, advising dueñas de casa on how to develop their homes. *Paula* suggested interior decorating schemes for houses, including the thousands of new ones that could be as small as fifty-four square meters, or 486 square feet (see figure 4.4). But despite *Paula*'s advice and the "carnival of images" that bombarded Chileans with visions of domestic life, as Mattelart and Mattelart (1990) put it, many dueñas de casa were unable to produce these distinct kinds of houses.

Such a fate befell many pobladoras like Rosa. In Rosa's case, she failed to make her monthly payments a little more than two years after she moved to Las Cuncunas, and she was forced to leave. In recalling this, she claimed that she really had little choice: she would either pay to feed her children or make her monthly payments. And so she faced the complicated problem of having to move again. But she was not entirely alone. Because the president of the cooperative knew that she had three children in her care and, at least according to Rosa, saw her as a *luchadora* (fighter), he helped Rosa to find another place to live, vouching for her character to neighborhood committee leaders. Rosa even had choices, of a sort, and she considered three campamentos. In the first year of the military dictatorship, she moved to Las Palmeras, formerly Campamento Lenin.

A committee consisting mostly of militants from the MIR led the settlement of Campamento Lenin in March 1973.[61] Emilio Pastenes, a surviving leader from Campamento Lenin's organizing committee, remembered that the leadership demanded strict "moral requirements" of the homeless who wanted to live in the campamento (Pastenes in Murphy 2004a, 88–89). A resident, Erika Cereño, agreed, recalling how the neighborhood council enforced norms of personal conduct. As she said, "When the neighborhood leaders spoke to

Figure 4.4. *Paula* says that even though houses are small, "space is gold" (*Paula* 107, Feb. 1972; image courtesy of the Biblioteca Nacional de Chile).

us and called meetings, they did it in order to single out the people who were dirty [*gente cochina*], the people who fought and the people who drank. They would not tolerate these people; they threw them out. We therefore had a campamento that was completely clean. The people were modest, but they were clean." Erika's perspective is full of nostalgia: she went on to tell me that the discipline in the campamento is something that her neighborhood lacks today, as people now live as if they are "thrown-out trash" and "need someone to show them how to live" (Cereño in Murphy 2004a, 101).[62]

Ultimately, the disciplinary practices in Campamento Lenin point to the continued importance of the urban politics of propriety, even in neighborhoods organized and sponsored by the MIR. MIR activists were young and rebellious. They embodied all that was new about the late 1960s and early 1970s. Having developed out of the radicalized student movement of the 1960s, MIR militants drew inspiration from Che Guevara and the movements of the New Left. As such, they were generally unwilling to compromise with the UP coalition. They thus contributed to the era's polarization and to schisms within the Left. MIR militants hoped to construct a new society in which people would labor for reasons other than personal interest and capitalist relations. Yet for their activism to be effective, especially in the land seizures, they also had to respond to persistent, if also permeable, expectations of home life.

The MIR also drew strength from the many other nonconformist and rebellious currents of the time period. They could work with hippies and others who supported forms of popular power.[63] Emilio Pastenes is an example of this: he held his leadership position in Campamento Lenin while being a hippie and general supporter of the Left, rather than being a MIR militant. In his memories, Emilio recalled being swept up by the new lifestyles that the period offered. He threw himself into late-night gatherings, psychedelic and folkloric music, and traveling around the country. In the campamento, however, his life became more regimented and ascetic, as he had to be an example for how other residents should behave (Murphy 2004a, 86–90). The very success of the neighborhood depended on it.

During the UP years, as more and more pobladores seized land, the "homeless" did not have to always assume payments in order to obtain properties. They did, however, have to demonstrate disciplinary practices. Many homeless pobladores who took part in land seizures either paid much less on mortgage debt burdens or did not have to assume them at all. This was a major change in the obligations of citizenship. Yet pobladores still had to conform to the behaviors expected of good neighbors and family members. As before, the homeless committees and neighborhood councils had a degree of autonomy to determine these criteria, particularly as the official requirements for occupying property became more lax. In such a context, it was essential that the homeless demonstrate that they could be good neighbors and contribute to the neighborhood's development.

As Rosa indicated, extra pressure could be placed on single mothers. Single men could be left out entirely (Pastenes and Cancino in Murphy 2004a). Yet there was a more general tolerance for domestic arrangements that did not conform to the nuclear family ideal. This underscores two important points. First, feminism had begun, slowly and uncertainly, to affect the Left.[64] Second, home life for many in the conventillos, campamentos, and poblaciones had never followed the strictures of the nuclear family. The establishment of homes and neighborhoods through the land seizures reflected these realities. To a certain extent, the UP government adjusted their policies in response. Unlike in the past, the UP provided services for couples who were separated, allowing them to apply to housing programs and to receive the benefits that a married couple would.[65] They also sought to grant couples who were together but not married—as often happened in the campamentos—the same rights as legal conjugal unions.[66] Still, officials were unable to translate these evolving standards into law, although they did generally operate in practice.

In Campamento Lenin, due to the overall acceptance of pobladores who did not live in nuclear families, the number of single mothers and couples who were not legally married was relatively high. Moreover, neighbors in the campamento did not assume mortgage payments on their houses, a burden they would not have to take on until the 1980s (see Pastenes and Cereño in Murphy 2004a). When Rosa finally moved to the former Campamento Lenin in early 1974—now renamed Las Palmeras in order to avoid its affiliation with Leftist militancy during the dictatorship—she fit right in. In the new campamento, Rosa at long last established a more stable house.

Yet she faced harsh insecurities, beginning with the dictatorship's intense political repression, especially in places like Las Palmeras. Moreover, the economic restructuring put in place by the Pinochet military regime produced a major recession in the wake of the coup, making Rosa's home life that much more difficult. Back in 1972 and 1973, the fixed-mortgage payment schedule that Rosa had assumed in Las Cuncunas was relatively easy for her to pay off since money was plentiful even for someone like Rosa, who worked as a maid. But given the scarcities, Rosa at times had difficulty providing food for her children. She struggled to provide for her family and develop what she considered to be a proper home. This would become a common problem and complaint, causing a series of difficulties for the Chilean Path to Socialism and providing grounds for public opposition to the regime.

Responding to the Shortages

In their polarizing "Marches of the Empty Pots," right-wing women helped to galvanize opponents of the UP.[67] The first of these marches took place in December 1971, coming at the end of a well-publicized and controversial monthlong visit by Fidel Castro. The marches placed the supposedly feminine question of home at the center of contemporary political debates. For the leaders of the marches, the disappearance of everyday commodities represented an inversion of the normal. They denounced the revolutionary government for destroying the material constitution of a proper home and thus undermining gender roles. Because of the crisis, these women claimed they had been forced into an anomalous public role as protestors. They thus took to the streets, banging empty pots in the major thoroughfares of Santiago.

As dueñas de casa, the demonstrators argued that they knew firsthand the threat posed by the UP government. Nina Donoso, a leader of the Marches of the Empty Pots, claimed that the "insecurity of the situation caused by the scarcities was threatening the very bases of Chilean democracy," including the "stability of the home and the moral and physical health of our children."[68] As long lines to obtain everyday items became common, Chileans experienced a breach of normality that tested existing practices and expectations. The opposition press posted sarcastic headlines such as "The 'Socialist Paradise' Begins in the Stomach," accompanied by articles that reported on how supermarkets and street vendors did not have chicken, beef, butter, or milk in stock.[69]

In their marches, right-wing women claimed that they rose above politics.

As these women assumed increasingly public roles, they argued that they simply sought to defend their rights as dueñas de casa. Given the difficulties that they faced, they had been forced to step outside of their everyday domestic responsibilities. In entering the public sphere, they sought a return to normalcy. Once their goals were achieved, they would return to their private lives and recede, once again, into the political background. Their actions were taken, they claimed, only to restore a proper home life.

The majority of the activists in the Marches of the Empty Pots were wealthy women. For them, "normal" social conditions included class privileges and distinctions. The elite had previously maintained such differences through, among other things, conspicuous forms of consumption and the creation of exclusive social settings and residential segregation. Such options were now more limited, contributing to a moral and social panic for many.[70] In response, many fought intensely to maintain Chilean society as it had been. They did so in the courts, in the legislature, in acts of sabotage, in conspiracies, and in conflicts on the streets. For their part, protestors in the Marches of the Empty Pots responded to the threat posed by the revolution by denouncing it as illegitimate and claiming that it had upset minimally acceptable living conditions. In this, these protestors made the same kind of universal, nonpartisan claim to citizenship that homeless pobladores did in the land seizures. The marches thus gave the appearance of being not about class privilege, but rather about defending the basic rights of citizenship. In making these arguments, the most prominent of the organizations—the National Women's Union and Women's Power—attracted a modest degree of support from middle- and lower-class women (Power 2002 and 2004). They became instrumental in calling on the military to intervene in democratic institutions in order to save the nation. Apologists for the dictatorship have long cited the uncertainties in consumption during these years as a justification for military intervention (Power 2002; Stern 2004 and 2006; Valdivia Ortiz de Zarate 2003).

For the protestors, this intervention was one that men should undertake. Female activists often marched behind neofascist armed "guards" from the group Patria y Libertad (Winn 2010, 255). They also publicly threw chicken feed at military officers and chanted slogans that made fun of their lack of manly nerves for not overthrowing Allende (Spooner 1994, 26, 28; Power 2002, 217–47). In calling on the intervention of strong, patriarchal leaders, these women helped to grant the counterrevolution a transcendent moral justification. Overthrowing Allende was about protecting the right that deserving and vulnerable citizens had to minimally acceptable living conditions. This right superseded politics. In the hands of the women who opposed Allende and military leaders, it also became a justification for superseding the constitution.

While showing much greater respect for peaceful means and democratic processes, Leftists in the government also tended to approach women as apolitical actors who defended the integrity of both domestic life and the nation. When UP officials developed policies in response to the shortages, they called on women to become more active in organizations that would defend the rights of dueñas de casa. Through the National Directorate of Distribution and Commerce (DINAC), government planners established Supply and Price Control Committees (the JAPs) in order to coordinate the provision of a basic food basket to every family. DINAC urged neighborhood women to fulfill their duties to their families and to the Chilean nation. As a cartoon in the pro-government magazine *Chile Hoy* indicates, these women would work together to confront the bourgeoisie and the forces of reaction (see figure 4.5). For planners from DINAC, the provision of basic foodstuffs for families superseded political interests, as one of their advertisements suggests (see figure 4.6). All Chileans deserved a basic food basket, irrespective of their purchasing power. As the advertisement states, "money should not make a difference in either calories or protein. The simple fact of living should assure the right to nutrition."

In the poblaciones and the campamentos, residents who had led the land seizures often became the heads of local Supply and Price Control Commit-

Figure 4.5. Dueñas de casa confront the bloated bourgeoisie (*Chile Hoy* 1 [25], 1972, 13; image courtesy of the Biblioteca Nacional de Chile).

Figure 4.6. DINAC, "your friend in distribution," seeks support for "her" policies. "All children are equal. They all have the same needs. . . . It doesn't matter what your political ideas are. Don't you agree?" (*Chile Hoy* 1 [49], 1973, 27; image courtesy of the Biblioteca Nacional de Chile).

tees. It could be a thankless job. Ana Valdés, the leader from the Primero de Mayo land seizure described in chapter three, remembered being physically attacked by neighbors who believed that she was hoarding goods provided by the government. In her recollections, Ana took the step of opening her house up to inspection by neighbors to show them that she had nothing to hide (Murphy 2004a, 44–46). Many of the goods that people expected—onions, flour, eggs, bread, sugar, and oil—simply weren't available. In response, Leftist activists often acted as they had in the past to situations of need: they would march in demonstrations, occupy distribution centers, or block traffic. But these actions were controversial. Fellow Leftists often denounced them as counterproductive to the revolution.[71] More often, pobladores simply had to wake up early and wait in three- to four-hour lines to buy what was available. Or perhaps, if they could afford it, they might turn to the burgeoning black market where prices were significantly higher, but where more goods were available.

In the end, the situation led to a crisis of sociopolitical legitimacy. Debates raged about who was to blame. Allende and his supporters pointed to conspiracies and collusion, an international blockade, and ongoing forms of economic dependence. Many Christian Democrats and the Right argued that the Allende government was inept, misguided, and subversive, having provoked social conflict and collapse without regard for democratic traditions. For everyone, rumors swirled about what had happened and who had caused the situation. During fieldwork, I heard many explanations about the reasons for the missing commodities. Ana Valdés told me that "the people themselves" helped to provoke the coup, since they expected too much and focused too narrowly on their own personal interests, failing to properly sacrifice for the revolution. Erika Cereño argued that sabotage was the primary culprit, and she recalled seeing a delivery truck dump its merchandise into the Mapocho River. A middle-class woman related to me how her sister, a Christian Democratic organizer and small-shop owner, withheld foodstuffs from her neighborhood Supply and Price Control Committee on the orders of officials in her party. Emilio Pastenes blamed the "forces of reaction" for collusion and hoarding. He correctly pointed out that immediately following the coup, stores and outdoor markets were suddenly full of goods.[72]

These partial perspectives undoubtedly relate some important truths about what happened and who is to blame for the shortages and the breakdown of democracy. Yet the perspectives are also important for another reason. They seek to assign moral culpability and political responsibility. If the social relations that make commodities circulate are generally opaque and mystified, they were particularly confusing and uncertain at this time. Yet the issues of consumption and the development of minimally acceptable homes gained a powerful place in public debates during Allende's presidency. In a moment of confusion, uncertainty, and crisis, these issues were more directly and explicitly tied to narratives of the political than normal. Conflicting memories about what happened reflect how insecure and divisive the social context had become and how impotent some felt in their ability to confront the situation.

Plans for socialist transformation had foundered. Homes were coming apart and so too were the visions of the "most generous utopias of the past." Into this crisis of legitimacy stepped female activists, on both the Left and the Right. Each mobilized as a woman who had a higher moral legitimacy because of her role as a dueña de casa and a mother. If a great deal separated the two camps, the moment of crisis nevertheless called for the clarity that womanhood seemed to offer in assigning blame, establishing victims, and building unity. But the crisis was far beyond the means that most dueñas de casa could actually resolve.

Legacies and Contradictions in the Revolutionary Path

The Chilean Path to Socialism consisted of a thousand days of tumultuous conflict, bold inspiration, and aggressive mobilization. Yet for all its intensity, it never constituted a thorough revolution. Though all political revolutions are less than complete, the peaceful path in Chile was particularly limited. It did not have the means to control all sectors of government, let alone transform the multiple bases of state power. These bases had their roots in interconnected social domains, including the constitution of home life, the paths of commodity circulation, and the subjectivities of citizenship. An integrated perspective that points to how these areas overlapped during the Allende years demonstrates that the era should be understood less as a breakdown in socialism than as a crisis in Chile's capitalist state formation.

The Chilean Path to Socialism brought into the open many of the tensions that intertwined the legitimacy of the state with both the everyday practices of domesticity and capitalist forms of production and consumption. If these tensions had always been present, they were not necessarily publicly recognized. Yet they burst onto the political stage during Allende's presidency. UP officials and ordinary Chileans faced major obstacles in producing homes considered appropriate. This directly contributed to the intense activism of the time period, ultimately threatening governability itself.

Forces that had developed in the past placed constant pressure on the revolutionary project. UP officials sought greater forms of sovereignty and economic independence, but they nevertheless remained vulnerable to the very forms of power that they sought liberation from. The revolutionary government was still dependent on the foreign exchange that Chile's export-oriented terms of trade provided and it suffered from deliberate acts of sabotage and decreased access to foreign and domestic capital. As officials attempted to build a revolutionary society of solidarity and sacrifice, they also sought support by increasing the money supply. This policy responded to long-standing desires, in addition to recently developed expectations, that lower-class citizens would be able to consume more. Yet increasing the money supply contributed to inflation, a process that not only exacerbated the constraints that the economy faced but also provided an area that the enemies of the revolution could exploit. Each of these factors contributed to the shortages. Sectors on the Right were able to protest over this issue by arguing that their supporters suffered from deprivation and an improper home life.

If these dynamics put the revolution on the defensive, the Chilean Path to Socialism also faced dilemmas inside the Left. Hierarchical visions of development, modernity, and proper living remained embedded in governing paradigms, undermining efforts to create revolutionary social relations. Officials faced the unprecedented mobilization of the popular sectors, including urban squatters. In the case of land seizures, they responded by being sympathetic to the cause of popular mobilization but not the forms that it took. This tended to paralyze the government, pushing officials to move faster than they wanted to and undermining their efforts to plan for a carefully controlled revolution.

Each of these dynamics represented fundamental tensions that intertwined the state with the unfolding of home life and political economic processes. Clearly, these tensions came to the fore during the Popular Unity years because of the specific conditions that developed at the time. Yet they were also representative of long-standing dilemmas in Chilean society, in which mass inequality had meant that many did not have homes considered proper in an urban landscape defined by stratification and unrealized expectations and dreams. The circumstances of the time period exposed and exacerbated these dilemmas but could not overcome them.

The very specific conjunctures analyzed in this chapter elucidate larger processes that, while in constant flux, persisted through the Allende years. Clearly, individual actors contributed to the breakdown of democracy—including the political parties, radicalized groups, and particularly cold warriors in the US government and conspirators in the Chilean armed forces. Many colluded to help create the crisis conditions. Counterrevolutionary forces adopted violent and subversive tactics that undermined the socialist government. Such violence stands in stark contrast to the revolutionaries, who, as Peter Winn (2010) shows, were generally peaceful. Leftists did at times make mistakes that only made the situation worse. But the tragedy of the Popular Unity project must also be understood as a particular expression of the inequitable, contradictory, and fractured sociopolitical relations that had long been developing in Chile. These persistent legacies often overwhelmed the revolutionary path. Such inequities and contradictions would only deepen during the dictatorship, but the new regime would respond with harsh repression.

PART THREE

REACTIONARY TURNS

CHAPTER 5

LOCATING STATES OF EMERGENCY

The Politics of "Normalization" after the Military Coup

For many Chileans, the military coup of September 11, 1973, initiated a searing break with the past, tearing asunder the sanctity of private life, respect for individual rights, and social solidarities. Many pobladores who lived in neighborhoods established with the sponsorship of the Left felt this historical fracture right away. For them, the violations came early and often. A disproportionate number of those killed and tortured by state agents came from these poblaciones and campamentos. The military junta justified these exceptional measures by declaring that the country was in a "state of siege," which it defined as "a state or time of war" as the nation confronted civil strife and the prospect of a violent communist takeover.[1] Coup plotters justified their violent actions by claiming that Chile faced an international Marxist conspiracy. Yet this specter was part of a much larger understanding that cast Chilean social life in a profound state of crisis. The mission of the government was to overcome the crisis and return Chile to a state of order and normalcy. According to officials, the country needed wholesale change, even as the regime promised to reinstate tradition and stability.[2]

The regime combined a conservative celebration of the Chilean past with an ambitious, totalitarian effort to reshape social life. The dictatorship's defenders held impassioned but not always compatible views: intense right-wing nationalism, virulent anticommunism, respect for efficiency and hierarchy, and, after a short period, support for neoliberal economic restructuring. The regime furthermore sought discipline and conformity in everyday social practices, as dictatorial authority spread into the intimacy of private life. Bodily comportment, gender dynamics, and the regulation of living spaces all fell under the dictatorship's forceful sway. In these spaces, themes of propriety would continue to be paramount, as the building of a new social order invariably involved questions of proper behavior and appropriate living conditions.

Following the burst of repression that occurred immediately following the coup, officials began to seek the consolidation of the regime, a process that disillusioned many initial supporters who had believed that the military intervention would be short-lived.[3] In institutionalizing the dictatorship, junta officials often applied a "state of emergency" framework to their policies, taking advantage of their ability to adopt exceptional measures. The states of emergency were supposed to be a means to an end: through painful and disruptive measures, the regime's planners claimed they would heal a sick social body. This body would eventually recover and develop on its own, at which point the state would cease its exceptional forms of intervention.

In practice, however, states of emergency persisted. This was particularly true of the campamentos. Officials declared that squatter settlements were in a state of emergency in a decree law approved in October 1973, a law that would remain in effect throughout the military regime, even after the state of siege was lifted.[4] Soldiers, police forces, and agents from the regime's intelligence services targeted the campamentos and certain poblaciones. At the same time, planners in the dictatorship undertook ambitious efforts to *sanear* the campamentos, perhaps through "eradication." As both development planners and security officials focused on squatter settlements, they each sought to resolve "emergencies" and "normalize" a state of exception.

Elements of these policies were not without precedent. In certain respects, moreover, they granted the regime a degree of legitimacy. Policing services had long been more sporadic and spotty in the campamentos than in society at large, but police intervention, when it did come, had also been harsher and more violent. The regime's efforts to eradicate the campamentos, furthermore, grew out of preexisting expectations of what normal and developed urban neighborhoods should look like. As in the past, state technocrats focused attention on providing access to property titles and infrastructure services for squatter neighborhoods. If successful, the transformation of the campamentos would thus paradoxically respond to one of the primary objectives of the land seizures, even as it severed these efforts from attempts to make society more egalitarian and democratic. In theory, the dictatorship would overcome the crises of the moment, restore order, and set the country on a path toward development.

The dictatorship, however, created its own crises, beginning with the mutilated and tortured bodies languishing in secret detention centers or decomposing in unmarked graves. The crises included circumstances in everyday life, from housing conditions to forms of consumption. Many would eventually work to expose these contradictions, leading to an effective movement against the regime. The recognition of crises, emergencies, and states of exception thus had an intense and persistent politics to it. Right-wing reactions to the perceived social crisis under the UP government provided a justification for the type of order the dictatorship sought to implement. This justification granted legal cover to the regime's most severe human rights abuses and lent ideological fervor to its strict, moralizing campaigns. Yet the human rights abuses and the conditions produced by neoliberal restructuring placed an overwhelming burden on the ability of many, and particularly pobladores, to occupy homes considered appropriate. Military regime planners who sought to manage and control the situation were often confounded by their inability to produce the results they had hoped for. Fissures and crises were endemic to military rule, ultimately creating contradictions that would challenge its viability.

The Objects of Repression

A Cancer in the Social Body

Not surprisingly, reactions to the coup of September 11, 1973, were intense. Some Chileans greeted news of the takeover with street celebrations and glasses of champagne. In Santiago, this occurred generally, but by no means exclusively, in the wealthier sections of the city.[5] For many others, however, the events of the day had a far different meaning. In Campamento Primero de Mayo, Eliana Parra remembers crying as she set fire to the paraphernalia she and her husband had gathered over the years as Communist Party members: a red flag emblazoned with a gold hammer and sickle, party identity cards, posters and banners, certificates from workshops and meetings, and pamphlets and books. Among the books that Eliana cast into the flames were two historical accounts of Chilean Marxism that had been a gift from the head of Chile's largest labor federation to Eliana's husband (Murphy 2004a, 35).

While everyone seemed to recognize that the events of the day had initiated a momentous change, it was not clear what would happen next. Most imagined neither the scope of the ensuing violence nor the persistence with which the dictatorship would hold on to power. A number of Chileans initially showed remarkable deference to the regime. Even after the bombing of the presidential palace and the death of Salvador Allende, many placed on the regime's suspect lists voluntarily turned themselves in (see Constable and Valenzuela 1991, 30; Verdugo 2001). Such individuals were certainly under pressure and duress, but many expected the new government to respect their rights, presuming that democratic practices would ultimately continue. But such faith was often a cruel miscalculation, followed by detention, interrogation, and even torture and death.[6]

In hindsight, belief in the professionalism and rectitude of the military and police apparatus may seem surprising. But the respect that many showed for the armed forces underscores how powerful and widespread the notion was that proper liberal governance was a part of national identity and that it would endure. Such respect was, ironically enough, a crucial element in initial support for the coup. In an interview in October 1973, the former President Eduardo Frei Montalva expressed an oft repeated sentiment: military officials were like highly trained doctors who had the skills required to perform a necessary, if bloody, surgery on the social body. "You don't want to have a cancer operation, but there comes a moment when you are forced to have one," Frei declared. "Our surgeons are the armed forces, and the *pueblo* asked for their insistent, resounding, and heroic intervention."[7] In undertaking an emergency operation, the military would remove the sources of suffering, conflict, and breakdown in the country, restoring Chilean health and setting the country on a path of development and growth. For Frei and many other initial supporters of the coup, this meant that, after an initial rupture, the junta would take the steps necessary to restore democracy.

According to Frei, the task facing the regime was a massive and arduous one. His metaphorical use of cancer referred to much more than simply Marxism. Frei believed there were many causes of the crisis, including social conflict, disrespect for the constitution and legal precedent, and an environment conducive to the development of armed extremism. The "cancer" thus spread perniciously throughout the social body. Many military officials viewed the cancer in even more general terms, a position that contributed to Frei's move into the opposition by late 1974. They argued that the sickness stemmed from "demagogic" and "internationalist" political parties and, particularly after the rise of neoliberal policymakers in early 1975, the statist policies of the past. Through the use of military discipline and technocratic expertise, government professionals would seek to restore health and normalcy to the nation.[8]

From the beginning, the military and police apparatus led a repression that reached far beyond simply incapacitating Marxism. This apparatus sought to exterminate the Chilean Left, a phenomenon that Steve Stern (2004, 31) has referred to as *policide*, which he defines as "a systematic project to destroy root and branch . . . an entire way of doing and thinking politics." Stern's concept is crucial for understanding the specific plans and institutions that the dictatorship put in place in order to repress and coerce elements of the Left. Regime agents meticulously prosecuted an "internal war" that targeted individuals and devastated the networks that had supported the Socialists, Communists, and the MIR.

Yet while the dictatorship's project was systematic, it also included elements that grew out of less self-conscious frameworks, including gender ideologies, hierarchical deference, and assumptions about class and the location of subversion and danger. The order that the regime sought to implement included naturalized assumptions about proper behavior and spatial organization. In resolving "crises," regime agents would seek to restore their sense of a normal and proper social life. This helped to grant the regime's ideology a virulent and dangerous charge. It was an important part of what Greg Grandin (2004, 188) argues were the two factors that generally drove the Latin American counterrevolution: "precise counterinsurgent tactics and more furious sentiments and aesthetics."

The official line held that Marxism was foreign to Chile, an infection from abroad. The "security forces" acted decisively to eradicate Marxists. Officials quickly removed known Leftists in any position of authority and promptly outlawed Marxist organizations.[9] The regime proscribed political parties and purged state bureaucracies and companies, universities, labor unions, agricultural cooperatives, and neighborhood organizations. In the first six months following the coup, according to one estimate, some thirty thousand students were expelled, while one hundred sixty thousand workers suffered politically motivated job dismissals (Roberts 1998, 94). Many of the fired workers would be blacklisted as subversives, making it nearly impossible for them to find legal work. From September 11 to the end of the year, state agents killed at least 1,634 Chileans, a majority of whom were former UP officials and Leftist party activists. More than half of these victims came from Santiago.[10] Soldiers and police officers detained from forty to fifty thousand by the end of 1973 (Schneider 1995, 3). Under the dictatorship overall, some two hundred thousand people went into foreign exile, slightly less than two percent of the population on the date of the coup (Wright and Oñate 1998, ix).[11] Many others would go into "internal" exile.

The security apparatus also targeted the varied symbols and artifacts that had come to represent the Left. The regime banned Leftist literature, art, and music. Leftist publishing houses, newspapers, magazines, radio stations, record companies, and cultural groups ceased to exist in the open. Thousands of volunteers erased left-wing murals and slogans throughout Santiago. It was at this time, moreover, when the names of campamentos and other settlements that expressed solidarity with the Left were changed: Campamento Primero de Mayo became Huamachuco, Campamento Lenin became Las Palmeras, and Nueva La Habana became Nuevo Amanecer, or New Dawn.[12]

The dictatorship's forceful touch thus spread into several domains. It even affected bodily discipline and expression. Men who had emulated Che Guevara's scruffy beard or had adopted a countercultural style shaved and cut their hair (Spooner 1994, 10–11, among others). Familiar forms of expression, including the ubiquitous use of the terms *compañera* and *compañero*, vanished from public discourse. The curfews and bans on public gatherings made impossible the mobilization of the UP years (Garcés and Leiva 2005, 26; Valdés, Parra, Cancino, and Pastenes in Murphy 2004a). Informants and spies lurked, sowing fear and distrust. The regime, with CIA support, established secretive intelligence agencies that developed a bureaucratized form of surveillance in order to infiltrate Leftist organizations and keep a general eye on the citizenry.[13]

Regime agents also sought to reestablish what they considered to be traditional gender comportment, acting with wide latitude to enforce their sense of appropriate male and female behavior. Ana Valdés recalled how, shortly after the coup, one police officer attempted to force her to follow his conception of proper female conduct while she waited in line to buy bread. As she said nearly thirty years later:

> I had a big confrontation with an official . . . who came up to me and said, "And you [*vos*], why are you wearing pants?" I told him, "because I'm cold and if my husband doesn't make me take them off, nobody is going to." And he said, "Well what if I grab you [*te pesco*] right here and cut your pants."
>
> "*Bueno*, you'll have to pay for them if you cut them up."
>
> "You know," he said, "I could detain you."
>
> "If that's what you want to do, that's your problem, but I'm not going to let you rip up my pants." The people in line began to complain, to say no, that they had already cut up so many pants, and why were they going to continue to do so? In the end, he stopped. (Murphy 2004a, 46)

In this recollection, the soldier first acted in a cavalier and condescending manner by addressing Ana in the intimate *vos* form. Far from a friendly form of address, the soldier's use of *vos* is disrespectful, lacking in proper demeanor. As he demanded to know why she was wearing pants, he threatened her. Ana spoke back, saying that only her husband could make such a demand; whether or not she wore pants was an issue for the private sphere, and the soldier had no right to publicly order Ana to change her dress. After the soldier threatened to detain her and destroy her pants, Ana received support from the rest of the people waiting in line, a public who knew that soldiers had acted in the same way with many other women. This was a development that ultimately, at least in this recollection, made the soldier stop.

In telling this story, Ana had the opportunity to condemn the authorities, calling attention to their abuses of power, much as Eliana Parra was able to do when she denounced how an official had treated the homeless in Renca before the May Day land seizure. Like the anonymous people waiting in line, Ana expresses her indignation at the soldier's behavior. The extent to which the events occurred precisely as described is open to question, but the manner in which the narrative unfolds is nevertheless a tale of propriety and expectation. In her recollection, Ana is able to condemn the soldier and, more generally, the regime itself. By expressing her outrage, Ana criticizes the repression she faced and the individuals who enforced it. This was an important outlet: shortly following the incident, Ana began to wear skirts and dresses in public.[14]

Home Searches in the Campamentos

Much of the most controversial and destructive forms of domination that the dictatorship exercised rested on the ability of regime agents to control and violate the private sphere in the name of the sovereign state. The national state of siege authorized regime agents to act out extreme forms of violence and domination. As has been well documented, the violence of the regime descended into the most intimate areas of the body—for those detained or kidnapped, rapes, tortures, and even deaths were common. In detention centers, interrogation teams, often working in conjunction with doctors who verified that the "suspects" could withstand more, largely had a free hand to dominate and humiliate their victims, making them suffer unconscionable physical and psychological wounds. Electric shock treatments were used on genitalia. Victims were dunked in tanks of water and excrement. Torturers raped victims in front of family members, friends, or other prisoners. Burns, fractured bones, and severe beatings were common.[15] In an extremely low estimate, the official commission on torture in 2004 identified 27,254 who suffered these kinds of violations during the dictatorship.[16]

Torturers exercised a power based on the physical and often sexual domination of the tortured, a power that humiliated the sense of self-worth and dignity of the victim. They could penetrate and wound the most intimate, private areas of the body. The devastating horror of this form of repression took place within the cultural logic of a split between the public and the private; public agents had an exceptional ability to violate the sanctity of private bodies and space. In doing so, the regime's henchmen and torturers produced extreme forms of humiliation, stigma, and suffering.

Despite the magnitude of the violence, most Chileans were not cast as enemies of state, even if everyone was a potential suspect. As they prosecuted the "internal war," agents had to decide who would be targeted. This task was not always clear. The primary justification for the coup, after all, had been that Chile was facing an imminent civil war that involved a well-armed Left. Yet following September 11, the regime did not face any serious, organized armed resistance.[17] Still, the regime continued to speak of the Marxist threat, and the press constantly displayed arms found in raids and gave significant coverage to official reports—often false—of armed confrontations with "terrorists." The logic of a civil war was crucial to the state of emergency (Agamben 2005, 3). Despite a lack of armed confrontations, the "state of war" mentality persisted in the military and police forces. Torturers sought information about weapons and military plans in interrogation sessions.[18]

For their part, soldiers brought the tactics and attitudes of war to their raids of the poblaciones and campamentos, especially in the initial months after the coup. In their efforts to purify, cleanse, and purge the national body, the military junta placed particular attention on neighborhoods that had developed with the sponsorship of Leftists, presuming that Marxists actually had transformed these areas into centers of armed resistance.[19] Regime officials referred to these neighborhoods as "dangerous" and "subversive zones." Such a construction drew naturally from more common expressions that stigmatized these areas as "centers of delinquency" and, to a lesser extent, "centers of disease." The overlap between delinquency, danger, and subversion came together in raids, as military and police planners searched for both subversives and criminals.[20] Because of this, pobladores—particularly those in neighborhoods known for their Leftist militancy—disproportionately suffered the human rights abuses of the regime. While military forces targeted many, they only raided entire urban neighborhoods in the poblaciones and campamentos.[21]

The targeting of groups of pobladores began in the months leading up to the coup. Acting independently of the central government, the military swept through a number of poblaciones, campamentos, factories, political party headquarters, and agricultural cooperatives in order to discover potential sites of resistance and to confiscate weapons.[22] The intensity and frequency of these raids became much greater during the dictatorship, particularly in the four months following the coup. Using the emergency powers granted to them under the state of siege, the armed forces violated the sanctity of the private sphere through an overwhelming show of force. Fully dressed for war, with their faces painted black and green, the soldiers and policemen tended to be belligerent in the raids. Their commanding officers often gave them specific instructions to tear things up in their searches for subversive materials and weapons.²³ Such a policy was part of a larger strategy to intimidate target populations. In the immediate aftermath of the coup, disfigured and mutilated bodies were left in the streets of neighborhoods characterized as dangerous and subversive. Bodies dumped in the Mapocho River washed ashore in the western part of Santiago, where many of the land seizures had been concentrated (Rettig Commission 1991, 127). In many campamentos and poblaciones, soldiers and police officers killed dogs and other animals. They left the carcasses behind, a testament to the power that the regime possessed.²⁴

These arresting and provocative tactics left their mark indelibly on the sensibilities of residents, and the pobladores I interviewed each emphasized the climate of fear and violence they lived through. The raids of neighborhoods stand out as particularly exceptional, as armed strangers transgressed the boundaries that normally defined the privacy of the home. The raids led to intimate encounters between state agents and pobladores. In the memories of pobladores, this proximity often allowed them to question the actions of low-level representatives of state.

The memories that pobladores have of these confrontations help to reveal the boundaries of behavior that they consider appropriate from state security forces. This often centered on the particular conduct of police officers or soldiers and on the innocence of the pobladores involved. Importantly, pobladores who experienced police raids did not necessarily condemn the raids themselves as overstepping the bounds of acceptability. Some raids, in fact, were not seen as particularly exceptional: one pobladora in a community with a long tradition of Leftist activism described one of the raids as "normal" since nothing very serious happened.²⁵ Pobladores did, however, object to the specific ways in which the raids crossed into illegitimacy, either through acts of criminality or human rights abuses.

This attitude is understandable given that the raids were an existing part of the national security state; a "security" that, for many groups of pobladores, had not necessarily lived up to its name. Pobladores, after all, had a relationship with the military and the police that had long been ambiguous. Certainly, many pobladores distrusted the police. Pobladores who had seized Campamento Primero de Mayo, for example, well remembered how police forces had cordoned off their neighborhood when it was originally established. In their protests and demonstrations, pobladores had often experienced violent confrontations with the state's "security" forces. But the relationship between pobladores and the police apparatus was not defined solely by opposition or coercion. Before the coup, numerous neighborhood organizations in recently formed settlements had sought a greater police presence.²⁶ If many pobladores believed that police and military groups enforced an unjust order, there was also the countervailing idea that they could help to create a more secure environment. From this perspective, the lack of a proper police presence in poor neighborhoods was another example of the inequitable provision of services in the city.

The tensions in the relationship between pobladores and the security forces were particularly strong during the raids, since they were circumstances within which the legitimacy and security of entire neighborhoods were at stake. The specific circumstances and recollections of the raids in Campamento Huamachuco and Campamento Las Palmeras reveal the ways in which the pobladores I spoke to condemned or tolerated the tactics of the military. As these raids often led to tremendous dislocations in family and community life, they also put into stark relief the coercive power of the dictatorship.

Campamento Primero de Mayo/Huamachuco I

On most days in the early 1970s, Eliana Parra left her house before dawn to go to a local street market where she sold clothes. She didn't earn much; the blouses and skirts that she had sewn were similar to some of the other merchandise available at the street market. Still, it was important for her to make the effort. Her husband's salary as a construction worker was often sporadic, and her contribution to the family income was crucial. On the day that a military unit raided her campamento, however, Eliana had not been following her normal routine. Instead, she stayed home in order to care for her mother, who was sick with pneumonia. As Eliana was making a typical breakfast of tea, bread, and butter, she suddenly heard her front door open.

Looking up, she saw a *milico*, a soldier, in her living room. Startled, she cried out: "And you?" According to Eliana, the soldier responded, "Be careful." In her story, Eliana quickly retorted: "'But who gave you permission to come in? . . . You all arrive and come right in the house, that shouldn't be.' . . . And the *milico* said to me, '*Señora*, we are in a raid.' 'Well then say so, but call before you enter,' I told him. 'But what is it that you want? What is it that you want to see? Let's take a look; open up, there's my sick mother in bed, she has pneumonia, there is the bedroom of the children and here I am. There's the kitchen.'" The implication, of course, was obvious: Eliana had nothing to hide. The house was in a normal state.

In the end, the soldier did not do much to Eliana and her family. She said that the "idiot soldier" (*milico jetón*) only found some music albums of her daughter's by Quilapayun, a folk group with Leftist sympathies that had been banned by the dictatorship's censors. In concluding, Eliana said, "they never discovered that we were in the [Communist] Party" (Murphy 2004a, 36–37).

In her account, Eliana does not openly question the right of the soldier to enter private homes per se; rather, she questions the way he came into her house. Once inside, she sought to show him that he had no reason to be there, that his justification for searching the house had no merit.

Campamento Lenin/Las Palmeras

Three days after the coup, a contingent of soldiers came looking for the leaders of Campamento Lenin. In the words of Emilio Pastenes, these soldiers knew that the neighborhood was "politically marked by the MIR." Emilio asserted that before the coup, if there were one hundred flags flying in the campamento, seventy of them had been MIR flags, and thirty of them Chilean. There had also been other demonstrations of militancy: a number of pobladores from the campamento had joined marches organized by the Revolutionary Workers' Front, a labor organization with ties to the MIR. Emilio recalled that these pobladores "marched with hard hats, with batons, military-like, supposedly like guerrilla fighters." Dressed for combat and linked to the bearded young revolutionaries of the MIR, certain pobladores in Campamento Lenin thus played up a militant image. For Emilio, this granted the neighborhood's residents a certain amount of respect, since the campamento gained fame as a place of armed revolution, a place to be feared. Nevertheless, as Emilio also points out, the image of dangerous rebels was largely a façade: "there weren't any arms, there wasn't any training, there wasn't anything [except] . . . political effervescence."[27] But the reputation that the campamento had gained would still feed into assumptions on the part of military planners about the danger of the place. The "guerrilla" mystique associated with Campamento Lenin, once helpful, now marked it as a center of subversion.

In recognition of this danger, the leaders of the campamento who had been in the MIR left the neighborhood in the days after the coup. For his part, Emilio shaved his beard, knowing that it potentially distinguished him as a young radical. He also buried a number of the books he had been given as the "Secretary General of Culture" for the campamentos in Renca. In that position, Emilio had been in charge of gathering a library that would be installed in an old bus. With this mobile "popular library," Emilio and others had planned to visit Renca's various campamentos, making the literature widely accessible. The collection that Emilio had been able to gather included a number of pamphlets written for a mass audience by supporters of the UP, in addition to books written by Marxists such as Che Guevara, Lenin, and Herbert Marcuse.

In his testimonial, the precautions taken by Emilio and other pobladores did not come a moment too soon. The next day, a military unit from the Buín

Regiment arrived at dawn, looking for the neighborhood "command," including Emilio and the two other leaders who had remained in the campamento. After searching their shacks and the surrounding areas, the soldiers detained Emilio and the two others. According to Emilio, the treatment was rough. While being led at gunpoint to a military truck, one of the other leaders asked the soldiers if he could leave a gold chain with his son. The soldier responded by hitting him with a pistol, breaking open his lip and knocking out a tooth. In Emilio's recollection, the soldier said, "You must have something to hide if you want to leave that with him." After being taken to a detention center, Emilio said he received beatings and electric shocks. He was subsequently placed in a holding cell, next to where a former UP official from the municipality adjacent to Renca was locked up. Emilio recalled that throughout the night soldiers came to the former official's cell, and in a mocking tone said things such as, "Mr. Governor, Mr. Subdelegate, grant me a meeting."

Despite his experiences, Emilio was relatively lucky: he was let go after being held for less than a week; others were killed in the same detention center.[28] In Emilio's words, he convinced his captors that "he was only a hippie." He told them that while he was a neighborhood leader, he was not a member of the MIR. According to Emilio, during interrogation sessions he emphasized the entirely appropriate and seemingly apolitical work that he had done in the campamento. Rather than working to build up the MIR, he had sought his neighborhood's well-being: he had formed committees to build houses, patrol the streets, and provide day care. He had also led pobladores in petitioning ministries for housing materials, potable water, and the legalization of the campamento. This emphasis on practical, seemingly apolitical work was common among detainees.[29]

Several months after Emilio's return to Campamento Lenin, another military unit arrived, cordoning off the neighborhood and two adjacent campamentos in a predawn raid. Emilio remembers presenting himself to the commander, saying that he was "there to help them coordinate" their activities. The commander informed Emilio that he was still under suspicion and that the military had to do a "full cleanup of the campamentos." As the leader of Las Palmeras, the commander said, Emilio had to ensure that the neighborhood was safe from Leftist subversion and criminals. The commander instructed Emilio to call all of the men out of their houses and present their national identity cards. The soldiers corralled the men into a soccer field, forcing them at gunpoint to lie down on their stomachs as they checked their papers.[30]

While the men were being detained, soldiers began a house-to-house search through the entire campamento. Erika Cereño, a resident of the campamento, denounced the "wickedness" with which four soldiers entered her home. The soldiers became suspicious after they saw a poster of Aníbel Pinto, a former senator from the Radical Party who had been a minister in the UP government. The soldiers rifled through drawers, overturned furniture, and cut through Erika's pillows and mattresses. In reflecting on the destruction, Erika wondered, "Why so much damage, if they could see that we were only modest people? We didn't have hidden rifles or anything, we were peaceful people." Erika's indignation increased after the raid, when she discovered that soldiers had "confiscated" a knife set from one of her neighbors, another dueña de casa who had faced a police search after her husband was detained. "Why would they do such evil?" Erika asked. "They stole that [knife set] that had been given to her as a wedding gift" (Murphy 2004a, 104–5). Erika found these actions to be reprehensible, beyond the acceptable level within which state agents could act. The raid thus confirmed Erika's sense that the dictatorship was illegitimate.

For Emilio's part, the raid forced him to reconsider his position in the campamento, as he believed that his presence placed the neighborhood at risk. Regime agents might ask him to further help them in their search for "subversives" and "delinquents." In his recollections, Emilio left the campamento because of this, spending several months in hiding. He returned to a different población in Renca where his father-in-law had received a house as a textile worker in the 1960s. After Emilio left Las Palmeras, the dictatorship had entirely broken up the original leadership of Campamento Lenin, a change that Erika continued to lament in our conversations nearly thirty years later. "After the coup," she said, "there weren't any meetings. Nothing happened, no one helped anyone else. I wasn't involved with anyone else; there wasn't any type of organization" (Murphy 2004a, 103). In no small measure, the dictatorship had broken down much of the tenuous cohesiveness and solidarity that the neighborhood had built before the coup.

"Normalization" in the Home and in the Nation

The kind of fear and silence that Erika alludes to was, of course, not a part of the dictatorship's official discourse. In the midst of widespread social dislocation and state-sponsored violence, regime defenders insisted that the country was becoming more peaceful and calm. While these claims could border on the absurd, they did carry their own logic, responding to the process of normalization that officials hoped to implement. An essential part of the restoration of order included the reestablishment of appropriate homes. Officials often stressed that it was the duty of all Chileans to dedicate themselves to their families, not politics.

An army commander, in addressing prisoners about to be released from Tres Alamos, a detention and torture center, emphasized this point as he wished the political detainees well:

> "Arrive with complete happiness to your homes and have a happy reunion with your family members, with your loved ones. In the future, dedicate all of your mind, your efforts and your predisposition to worry about your loved ones, your mothers, etc. Here in the shadow of the national tricolors, I invite all of you in these moments to have this holy symbol be the only place for all of your thoughts and activities. That all of you go to your homes, I repeat, with calm, because in working for the home, you all will be working for the progress of the entire nation. At this time, you all are free, see you later and have a good trip."[31]

Given the torture that many of the prisoners in Tres Alamos had suffered, such good wishes acted as a cruel joke. They express some of the obvious contradictions between the actions and stated goals of the dictatorship. Yet for officials such as this army commander, a central part of the "apolitical reconstruction" of Chile would occur when citizens dedicated themselves to their homes. As the former prisoners worked for the "progress of the entire nation," they would learn to contribute to national reconciliation.[32] In making these assumptions, the commander did not mention the conflicts over home and housing rights that Chileans had taken part in. Instead, the commander reiterated the belief that dedication to family and home life was apolitical and inherently unifying for the nation.[33]

Such an assumption followed the claims that right-wing women had made in their protests against the UP. For the dictatorship, these women held a privileged place in Chilean history (see, among others, Power 2002; Baldez 2002; Stern 2006, 57–66). In a speech addressing Women's Power (el Poder Femenino), one of the groups that had been central in organizing the largest anti-Allende rallies, Pinochet said, "women wanted the fall of the Marxist government, which symbolized slavery for their children, but they also wanted a new order: women sought the protection of a strong and severe authority that would restore order and the moral public sphere in our society" (Molina 1989, 64, as cited in Franceschet 2005, 60).

Such an image effaces struggle, conflict, and repression, a convenient sense of history and of social relations for such a violent regime. Clearly, there was a wide disjuncture between the rhetoric of order, harmony, and justice that officials celebrated and the regime's coercion. Still, defenders of the regime often insisted that Chile was more peaceful during military rule, liberated from the "chaos" caused by "international Marxist subversion."[34] After the initial purges—with their widespread violence—the most egregious human rights abuses tended to be hidden from most. Many would claim ignorance of the regime's excesses, a position that is perhaps understandable given the climate of fear and misinformation.[35]

Ultimately, the focus on home life and harmonious gender relations fit in with the insistence of the dictatorship's defenders that the country was undergoing a process of normalization. Following the intense modes of activism that had marked the UP years, planners in the dictatorship sought a general withdrawal into the private sphere. Officials celebrated how they were able to put an end to much of the extraordinary, public phenomena that had marked the tumult of the UP period: gone were the land and factory seizures, demonstrators no longer took part in mass marches, and street clashes had ended. The caustic public, rhetorical debates were also over, as the Left no longer had the means through which to denounce the "reactionary mummies" of the Right.

There were other signs of normalization. In the days immediately following the coup, merchandise began to reappear in stores. Many would interpret this development as evidence of the collusion between suppliers and distributors in the shortages experienced during 1972 and 1973. The regime's supporters would nevertheless tout this as a return to normalcy.[36] For the women who had taken part in the Marches of the Empty Pots, the reappearance of these everyday commodities seemed to vindicate the actions they had taken. Public transportation, after being disrupted during the Allende years by the transportation strikes and street protests and conflicts, was largely restored.

Changes such as these, and the general promise of the military government to "reconstruct the fatherland," contributed to the support that a substantial number initially granted the military takeover.[37] In the weeks following the coup, many would offer their expertise and resources in support of the military junta. Thousands of couples donated their wedding rings to the new regime. In return, the military government sent the donors copper bands, thus recognizing this matrimonial patriotism with jewelry forged from the metal associated with Chilean national identity (Spooner 1994, 88). A number of other individuals and groups mounted similar efforts, responding to the regime's call for sacrifice in response to the "crisis." A group of sanitation contractors contributed a quarter of their monthly salaries to the government.[38] An organization of pobladores presented a donation to the minister of the interior during a press conference in which the minister promised that the regime would dedicate substantial resources in order to improve conditions in the campamentos.[39]

Some of these offers, no doubt, were part of a calculated effort to curry favor with the new officials. Still, most of the donors and volunteers tended to stress the specific reasons why the circumstances before the coup had been disturbingly abnormal for them and why they believed that the military regime could restore life to its proper order. In one case, the president of a construction federation wrote to the minister of housing and urbanism to offer his organization's labor "as a voluntary contribution to the titanic task of rebuilding Chile, in which all men of a clear conscience must participate." The federation provided materials and expertise to pobladores in order to help them build their own houses, a process that the president stressed would ensure the "care, effort, and sacrifice" needed to resolve the housing "crisis." During the UP government, the president wrote, a number of campamentos had sprung up in his municipality in northeastern Santiago, with more than two thousand families "in the most undignified conditions of the human being." This representative wrote out of self-interest: the kind of building his organization provided had officially been opposed by the UP government.[40] But at least on a rhetorical level, the resolution of this specific case was part and parcel of resolving the larger problems that confronted the country.

In these situations, petitioners claimed that the regime would restore fairness to social structures that had failed both themselves and the nation. In another example, Carmen Rodriguez wrote a letter to Pinochet dated October 10, 1973, thanking the junta for its "glorious and benevolent work." She recounted to Pinochet how she and her husband had signed papers to buy a small property on the outskirts of Santiago in early 1973. They did not, however, receive a property title, and thus could not build their house. For several months before the coup, they had lived in constant fear that squatters would seize their sixty-square-meter plot. To protect the site of their future home, Rodriguez's husband had slept there in a tent. However, "once the situation in the country . . . began to normalize," Rodriguez wrote, she and her husband were able to relax, secure in the thought that nobody would arrive to seize their property.[41]

If claimants expected a kind of normalization in social relations and property titling, they were often disappointed, as there tended to be a great distance between what they hoped for and what the new regime would actually provide. In another letter to Pinochet, Inés de Quintana apologized for bothering the president, but she was "desperate." She and her husband had been applicants in a housing program since 1971 and they had managed to save enough to qualify for benefits, but they had not been selected. Their circumstances were difficult: they lived in a borrowed house that was eighteen square meters, with a roof that often leaked and without plumbing, potable water, or electricity. "You understand, Señor Presidente," Molina wrote, "how difficult it is to live in conditions like this with my three children and my husband; you know what I suffer." Molina noted that during the UP years her family could have taken part in land seizures, but they did not do so, because, as she put it, "we are Christian Democrats. I suffered seeing every day all of those things that happened before the eleventh of September, now I'm happy because we are free thanks to the armed forces and the police." She closed the letter with her request: "I ask you, like I ask God, to give us a (government-subsidized) house . . ."[42]

But if Pinochet had godlike, sovereign powers, they were not of the kinds that Molina expected. The undersecretary of MINVU responded a little more than two months later, informing Molina that her husband was number 6,553 in a list of qualified applicants to receive housing. It was an orderly, enumerated response, the kind of clear and simple answer that state bureaucrats had long given hopeful applicants. But such a framework was granted renewed value under a dictatorship that emphasized the normalization of social life by, among other things, reestablishing and celebrating the regulatory power of bureaucracy.

Neoliberal Technocrats Map Out the Subjects of Dictatorship

As military commanders and right-wing technocrats began to occupy central posts in the government, they rallied behind the calls of national reconstruction and the development of a bureaucratic order that would operate outside of politics. Within this framework, the "Chicago Boys," a group of neoliberal economists trained at the University of Chicago under Milton Friedman and Arnold Harberger, began to assume the central leadership positions in the ministries devoted to finance and development by late 1974. The Chicago Boys provided simple and forceful arguments about how aggressive action would redress the errors of a politicized and inefficient state sector. Their reforms would set the country in a pathbreaking new direction. In a familiar metaphorical register, the Chicago Boys described their economic policies as the "emergency measures" of "shock therapy" that would cure a "sick patient." The prescriptions included constricting the money supply, selling off many state-owned industries, reducing tariffs, cutting fiscal spending, and opening the country to foreign investment.[43]

True to the metaphor of shock therapy, such policies induced severe pain. Already in the immediate aftermath of the coup, government planners had freed price controls and frozen wages and salaries. From September 11 to the end of December 1973, the price of bread rose more than 1,000 percent (Winn 2004c, 22). In early 1974 planners sought to control the runaway inflation by constricting the money supply, raising interest rates, and reducing fiscal spending. This policy was particularly hard on the many workers and pobladores who had gained unprecedented access to money during the UP years. Under Allende, the enhanced purchasing power of these groups had evaporated in the face of shortages. After the coup, the reappearance of commodities was accompanied by having little access to cash. In one of our conversations, Erika Cereño noted the irony: "Everything was available but money was suddenly hard to come by" (Murphy 2004a, 103).

By 1975, Chile was in its deepest recession since the Great Depression. During that year, the GNP contracted by 12.9 percent and unemployment rose to 17 percent, a level that it would average for the rest of the dictatorship.[44] As policymakers lowered tariff walls and cut back on subsidies, many pobladores lost their more secure sources of employment in state-protected industries. Santiago generally went through a process of deindustrialization as many of its textile factories and cotton mills shut down (Gatica Barros 1989). These processes took place at the same time that organized labor lost much of its power. The combined effects of repression and economic restructuring irrevocably changed the role that organized workers had played in Chilean society. These workers now had little ability to strike or enter labor negotiations, while regime agents decimated the leadership of several union and trade organizations.[45]

As these tumultuous transformations took root, planners throughout the government focused on what they considered to be the state of emergency *before* the coup. In the Ministry of the Interior and in MINVU, bureaucrats began to formulate policies to rid Chile of campamentos. In the months following the coup, a series of press reports claimed that Chile would "never again" produce the "national shame" of these neighborhoods, as the "supreme government" committed itself to "eradicating" them. For planners in the regime, the "unregulated" and "disorganized" spaces that squatters inhabited symbolized the breakdown of the Allende years and continued underdevelopment. The new director of MINVU put it plainly: "Chaos: that is what this government inherited in the area of housing. The magnitude of the problem reflects the demagogic promises of the Popular Unity. [We are left] today [with] the titanic task of reconstruction."[46]

In order to accomplish such a "titanic task," the military junta created a special commission to study the crisis conditions in the campamentos and the callampas. In the decree that created the commission one month after the coup, the undersecretary of the interior argued that the situation in the campamentos was grave. "Twenty percent of Chileans live in emergency poblaciones with subhuman conditions," he wrote. The residents of these neighborhoods, he continued, "lack an adequate organization that would permit them to

Figure 5.1. "This National Shame: NEVER AGAIN" (*Vea*, Oct. 25, 1973, 6; image courtesy of the Biblioteca Nacional de Chile).

resolve their minimum housing needs and access electricity, potable water, sewer services, health, schools, recreation, and provisions." The undersecretary proposed granting the chief of the Office of Emergencies in the Ministry of the Interior, a position initially established in 1968, enhanced administrative powers in order to overcome the problem.[47]

In dealing with the chaotic state in the "emergency poblaciones," regime planners sought to simplify the administration of these areas, streamlining state programs and dispensing services based on need. They would focus on "extreme poverty," a new discursive category circulating in international development circles through which to identify those with the most need.[48] As part of the emergency plan, the junta ordered the creation of the "Map of Extreme Poverty," a project taken up by technocrats in the National Planning Office (ODE-PLAN) and academics from Catholic University (Gobierno de Chile, *Mensaje Presidencial* 1974–1975, 272). Miguel Kast, an economist who had studied at the University of Chicago, and Sergio Molina, a former Christian Democratic minister, led a team of researchers in designing and drawing the map.

Locating poverty cartographically, the map ranked neighborhoods throughout the country by tabulating the number of dwellings within them that lacked solid building materials and infrastructure services such as potable water, electricity, and sewage systems. Kast and Molina then cross-referenced these criteria with how many occupants lived in a particular household and whether or not they held property titles. Last, they factored in the size of the lot. Areas defined as urban, with households that did not have infrastructure services, solid building materials, or property titles, but with the greatest number of occupants and the smallest-sized lots, became the most extreme cases of poverty. Granting these different criteria numerical values, the map's designers set a threshold by which to measure extreme poverty. The map's approach explicitly connected the state of housing and neighborhood development with social well-being, ultimately defining poverty in spatial terms. Within this framework, the map focused, unsurprisingly, on the campamentos in cities as those areas most in need of emergency funding (Kast and Molina 1975, 5–8).

To a degree, the criteria that Kast and Molina employed to identify extreme poverty were what squatters had sought in order to transform their campamentos into poblaciones. The standards that the map focused on thus built on preexisting assumptions about the nature of neighborhood development, poverty reduction, and the provision of services at the neighborhood level. But while achieving these standards had played a central role in the mobilization and planning of poblador organizations before the coup, it had been part of a larger, more flexible process that included neighborhood development, citizen empowerment, and social democracy. In employing the criteria of the map, regime planners hardened the standards by which to interpret minimal welfare standards, setting aside the questions of citizen participation and social rights. Such broader questions were not a part of how technical experts would find answers to the "national shame" of "extreme poverty." Instead, they would focus almost exclusively on the acquisition of property rights and infrastructure services.

In drawing the map, Kast and Molina used census data from 1970. Astonishingly, they insisted that this data was the best available for measuring the true nature of poverty, ignoring the significant number of land invasions that had occurred between 1970 and 1973, and, as I discuss below, the fewer public occupations of land that continued to occur following the coup. In spite of such an obvious flaw, the map's publication was a media event and Kast became the military government's primary spokesperson on issues of social welfare.⁴⁹ Technocrats drew a follow-up map in 1982 and a similar one in 1997. Through the use of refined criteria, these maps promised to conclusively define and locate poverty.⁵⁰

Like the notion that Chilean families were returning to normal, the simplicity and elegance of the map could border on the absurd. It ignored the complex and fractured social landscapes that had produced the campamentos. To a certain extent, the map didn't travel well. Regime opponents mounted strong criticisms, pointing out some of its obvious fallacies. They emphasized, for example, how neoliberal reforms had contributed to impoverished living conditions (Foxley 1986; Vergara 1990). One critic turned the map on its head, producing "A Map of Extreme Wealth," which described how wealth and capital became increasingly concentrated during the first five years of military rule (Dahse 1980). The military regime itself developed other tools with which to measure poverty, ultimately settling on surveys administered by the municipalities.⁵¹

Still, however, bureaucrats in the central government followed the map in dispensing many of the housing and infrastructure resources to the municipalities.⁵² The map gained such traction by tapping into assumptions that appealed to supporters of the regime's technocratic experts both within Chile and in international development and financial circles. For the map's defenders, it appeared to transcend the polarization and conflict of the recent past, seemingly untainted by the messy, contentious, and competing claims of politics. Building on established statistical methods, the map was an elegant artifact of governance, reinforcing a sense of control and assuredness. Kast (1976) claimed that poverty was a technical problem that could be solved by experts who would employ rational criteria, measuring precisely the communities that lacked basic infrastructure services and property titles. According to Kast, this kind of measurement was sorely needed, since evaluations of poverty in the past had been inappropriately made according to political interests and/or emotional assessments. Through the adaptation of supposedly standard and universal measures, Kast assumed that poverty could be defined in absolute terms.

Such standard measures stood outside of history, eliding the conflicts and controversies that had engulfed neighborhood development and urban transformation. In the map, these "universal" forms of measurement made the government's subjects intelligible and manageable. The map quantified the needs of these subjects, making it appear obvious what actions the government should take in response. In this process of measurement and prescription, the "extreme poor" played no role: they were to be the passive recipients of an efficient state sector that would target spending. In its design and application, the map is an extreme example of positivist, technical expertise, neutral and objective in appearance and antidemocratic in effect.[53]

Cracks in the Artifice of Order

Following the coup, officials from MINVU and the Ministry of the Interior moved quickly to establish clear and legally sanctioned criteria through which citizens could access housing. Invariably, however, they often found the order they hoped to impose upset by unforeseen problems and circumstances. Amid the tumult and dislocations caused by neoliberal restructuring and state-sponsored terror, not to mention the unsettled land status of the campamentos, the administration of the city was a complex and disorderly task.

As was only natural for them, housing planners gave particular emphasis to the military dictatorship's project to "depoliticize" the country. In doing so, they acted on a central justification for military rule and on the assumption that the development of the home lay beyond politics. As one general put it in a speech to a poblador organization, "The pobladores will have direct collaboration in the urgent [housing] plans through their neighborhood councils, fulfilling their basic function without politicking [*politiquería*]. Politics is over, we have to work now in order to recover the Chile that some sought to destroy . . . we are prepared to give priority to housing, but first the people must be organized under common motivations, not political ones."[54]

Given the climate of repression, the kinds of organizations that had been dedicated to housing and neighborhood development before the coup became significantly weaker. Moreover, officials now tended to favor dispensing services to individual applicants, a practice generally indicative of the move toward neoliberalism. As the minister of housing wrote in one decision, groups could not receive preference since that would mean that "individual applicants [would] see their possibilities to obtain housing made more difficult, in spite of the fact that they comply with all of the requirements in terms of savings, length of time in the program, and family size."[55]

In favoring individual applicants, officials often dismissed the tactics and practices previously employed by organizations of pobladores. In another letter to Minister Viveros, a legal representative of a housing cooperative sought to defend the right of the cooperative's members to remain on the lands they occupied. He argued that his clients had "sacrificed and fought" in order to establish their homes. Members, furthermore, had paid their debts and organized their neighborhood according to legal codes. By lauding the hard work, sacrifice, and legal rectitude of his clients, the lawyer sought to defend them by pointing out that they had fulfilled some of the central obligations of citizenship. Minister Viveros, however, rejected the request. Following the assessment reached by a social worker, Viveros argued that the cooperative's members had caused "disorder" in the past. They had seized the land they were now on and had taken part in a sit-in at MINVU's offices in order to receive infrastructure services. The cooperative's members would thus have to move.[56]

In cases such as this one, officials at MINVU justified their decisions by adopting a tone of judicious fairness. In doing so, they often cited established precedent. The applications for housing loans, for example, largely followed standards in place before the coup. Pobladores received more points for being a member of a stable nuclear family. They also had to be able to assume debt, an indication that they had proper work habits. The military regime generally enforced the number of savings quotas that applicants were required to meet in order to access government programs.[57] (In a number of cases, as in Campamento Lenin, this had become increasingly lax during the UP years.) In demonstrating that they had the discipline to fulfill these criteria, pobladores showed that they were responsible citizens.

As the dictatorship developed its housing policies, it gave particular emphasis to a liberal, individual subject. This fit within the broader project of the regime to disarticulate the social organizations that had been powerful before the coup and push for a focus on private life. In stressing these points, the dictatorship picked up on and reinforced only the part of the politics of propriety that emphasized individual responsibility and ownership. Yet if the dictatorship was contributing to a change in the urban politics of propriety, the persistence of the links between property, propriety, and home life also contained the dictatorship. As pobladores could not access homes considered appropriate, fundamental contradictions at the heart of dictatorial rule became evident.

The nature of the low-income housing market presented a particularly difficult set of challenges. Amid the economic crisis of the mid-1970s, a number of pobladores who lived in legally sanctioned homes defaulted on their loans. This problem was heightened by the fact that state-backed housing loans for lower-income sectors were readjustable, a long-term stipulation that had been suspended in 1971 under Allende but reinstated during the dictatorship.[58] After the Central Bank raised interest rates in order to counteract inflation, the banks that had supplied loans for the low-end housing market subsequently raised mortgage rates. This placed increasing pressure on housing committees and cooperatives. Despite some efforts to keep mortgage payments down for low-income housing applicants, officials generally permitted interest rates to rise.[59] Many pobladores lost their homes. This phenomenon, coupled with the harsh climate of neoliberal restructuring and the fact that little construction was taking place, made it increasingly difficult for many pobladores to access appropriate housing.

Until the late 1970s, the dictatorship did little in response. Despite the lofty rhetoric that officials employed in promising to end the "national shame" of "underdeveloped" neighborhoods, they committed few resources during this period, limiting themselves to finishing housing that the UP government had begun. In doing so, they made it appear statistically as if they had built more housing than had Allende's government, trumpeting the number of housing projects they had completed.[60] But new housing starts were few. Officials often replied to requests for housing or neighborhood services, even the most basic of *mediaguas*, by saying that none were available.[61]

In response to the increasingly bleak housing situation, many pobladores looked to unorganized, quiet seizures of land as an outlet. Since the large-scale seizures of the recent past were no longer possible, these pobladores packed themselves into existing neighborhoods. Household members often built beyond their property limits, constructing, in many cases, separate shacks for allegados.[62] In a number of cases, squatters slowly and almost imperceptibly moved into areas set aside as roads, passageways, or green spaces. The building was so widespread that in some areas entire street blocks disappeared (Morales 1983, 14).

In Renca, Las Palmeras and Huamachuco each saw a significant rise in population and houses, especially during the economic crisis of the mid-1970s: lots became crowded with second houses; allegados moved in; squatters encroached on thoroughfares and areas set aside as parks. As these neighborhoods were not yet "regularized," squatters took advantage of the opportunities to move in, at times provoking conflicts among neighbors. Divisions and conflicts between original settlers and newcomers arose, only partially mitigated by ties of compadrazgo and family. The building and settlement not only contributed to crowded conditions but also made it more difficult for these neighborhoods to go through a process of legalization, as they would not conform to the norms and forms proper to a población.[63]

The unplanned building and settlement made officials increasingly anxious. Compounding the problem, squatters and vandals often occupied or looted the apartment and housing complexes that were being completed. When residents moved into these new housing units, they often found a considerable amount of damage. Quite often, anything that could be removed had been taken away: doors, windows, sinks, piping, and toilets. For urban planners, such actions were infuriating, upsetting the strict order they had sought to implement.[64]

The artifice of control that officials sought to put in place was constantly breaking down. Ultimately, they were unable to restore many of the "normal" relationships and practices that the regime's supporters had expected. Following the coup, a number of landowners sought to recapture the properties they had lost in the urban land seizures by requesting evictions. Yet this created a number of problems for planners, since the legislation that guided official policies stated that anyone evicted in this way could apply to emergency housing programs.[65] Officials had little idea of where they would put hundreds of thousands of evicted squatters and they thus called on the former owners to have patience. While still promising they would eventually reinstate their properties, they sought to explain to landowner organizations the magnitude of the problems they would face if they evicted pobladores who had seized land.[66] As the years dragged on and the government failed to find a resolution, many gave up their efforts to recover their properties.

In this situation, officials at MINVU often found themselves compromising their positions, unable to do all that they had promised. As the policies of neoliberal restructuring and the national security state contributed to profound social dislocations, efforts to efficiently administer an orderly, clean, and healthy population proved unsuccessful. The desire to implement precise and simple paradigms in the pursuit of national reconstruction and normalization met a much more complex, fractious, and messy reality. Officials and citizens were left in the troubling position of having to deal with ongoing states of emergency. This produced both everyday hardship and openings for dissent and critique.

Managing the Crises as a Dueña de Casa

For pobladores like Ana Valdés, circumstances following the coup were particularly anxious. Ana recalls that during this period, "There was a tremendous misery . . . I had problems with my children, because before, my children were well dressed and well fed, but afterwards, it wasn't the same. As a dueña de casa, I had to get rid of my things; I began to sell the silverware that I had stored away, because we didn't have enough to eat. A sister of mine, who was unemployed, even got rid of her stove and her propane tanks" (Murphy 2004a, 48). In responding to the crises they were experiencing, Ana and her sister took exceptional steps to support their families, even if this meant the indignity, regret, and everyday difficulties presented by selling valued objects.

Ana's problems were compounded by the troubles that confronted members of her extended family. Long dependent on the relationships she had with these relatives, including her close ties to the Recabarrens, Ana had significantly less support in looking after the needs and safety of her family following the coup. Two of Ana's brothers lost their jobs and could not find legal work since they were on regime blacklists, one for having worked for a Leftist periodical and the other for having been in the central committee of the Communist Party. On the day of the coup, soldiers detained Ana's brother-in-law—one of the Recabarren children with whom Ana had grown up—and took him to the National Stadium. After being held there for nearly two months, he was transferred to a detention center in the north for more than a year.

Ana spent much time attempting to help her sister find him, largely stopping her work as a community organizer. The two sisters made queries and petitions to the Ministry of the Interior and the courts, attempting to work through the bureaucratic circuitousness and secrecy of the regime. They consulted human rights lawyers and joined efforts to document and call attention to the state-sponsored violence. After several months, they discovered where Ana's brother-in-law was being held and they made three trips to northern Chile in attempts to see him. Finally, on their last visit, they were granted a ten-minute conversation, a few months before he was released.

After her brother-in-law returned to the family, Ana turned to community organizing in Campamento Haumachuco. Along with other community leaders, Ana began a committee of the unemployed, in which neighborhood residents could labor toward collective ends. Working with the local Catholic parish, Ana helped to organize an *olla común*, a "community pot." Members of the olla común began their work by seeking donations from the grocers who ran stalls in local markets. Eventually, they received funds from the Catholic church and from a long-operating Catholic charity, Caritas de Chile. With this backing, they sought to provide such basics as bread, butter, oil, tea, and sugar to local residents, in addition to occasional meals. As in her work before the coup in Campamento Primero de Mayo, Ana acted in some ways as a state functionary. She contacted and surveyed heads of households. At first, the olla común provided food for free, but following arguments about the fairness and openness of the system, they began to charge a small fee. Ana justified this by claiming that "everything in this life has to cost something" (Murphy 2004a, 47–48).

The community leaders did much of this organizing under tense and difficult conditions. Through their links to the Catholic church and international NGOs, neighborhood groups like Ana's Committee of the Unemployed and the olla común could maintain autonomy from government-sponsored programs and survive in the face of official hostility. Ana's role as a woman was also important, as women increasingly held leadership positions in organizations throughout the campamentos and poblaciones.[67] Once again, Ana and her female neighbors assumed public positions based on their ostensibly private roles as dueñas de casa, organizing as women who sought to restore normalcy to their home lives. In her testimonial, Ana discusses her public work in terms of leaving the private sphere of the house. She did so in order to respond to a higher calling of solidarity and empathy; in order to continue "fighting for [her] pueblo." In describing why she and others created the new organizations, Ana said, "We went out to organize with the other compañeros in order to see how we could fix up the economic situation, how we could get together to help the people who didn't have anything to eat."

Ana also took part in the initial, public protests against the dictatorship's human rights abuses. As she pointed out, "It was us, the women, who were the first ones to go out into the streets and protest." Mobilizing the image of suffering mothers who had lost their loved ones, they found a particularly powerful, gendered voice with which to criticize the military regime. They also benefited, once again, from the support afforded by the Catholic church, taking full advantage of the seemingly apolitical and moral authority that the church offered. Within their protests, the women contradicted the image that regime officials extolled of a peaceful, normalizing country. They pointed instead to the ways in which their expectations for well-constituted homes and proper sociability had been torn asunder.[68]

In her activism, Ana's position as a woman and her work with the Catholic church granted her a degree of protection from the dictatorship.[69] But the threat posed by the security forces was still very real. In some of the first open women's protests against the regime that Ana attended in 1976, the military police teargassed the crowd and sprayed the protestors with water cannons. According to Ana and other sources, regime agents set fire to the local parish where she worked, causing significant damage. A number of fellow activists had disappeared or had been detained. Such acts raised unavoidable and disturbing questions. Were former activists who had been tortured and released now informants? Were there spies in the human rights groups or in the community organizations? Would more people disappear? But even amid such troubling uncertainty, Ana's life as an activist and neighborhood planner continued. Acting in solidarity with her party and her neighborhood, she worked with others to, in her words, "watch our own backs." The crises of the period demanded nothing less.

Locating States of Emergency

Writing from Paris in the late 1930s, Walter Benjamin (1988, 257) reflected on how the immediacy and horrors of the rise of fascism and economic depression blinded analysts to other structures of hierarchy and violence. In one of his "theses on history," Benjamin argues that "the tradition of the oppressed teaches us that the 'state of emergency' in which we live is not the exception but the rule. We must attain to a conception of history that is in keeping with this insight." In arguing this, Benjamin points to the intense political work that recognizing a "state of emergency" does. Through the declaration of a state of emergency, certain conditions receive attention while other dynamics and crises remain hidden. In pointing this out, Benjamin does not eschew the framework of a state of emergency but rather calls for awareness of the effects that declaring one can have. He further hopes to open up the framework by which states of emergency are understood.

The Chilean dictatorship was able to justify extreme forms of violence in establishing a state of siege and states of emergency. At the same time, the dictatorship built on preexisting understandings of abnormal and inappropriate conditions in the campamentos in order to mobilize particular resources and overcome a condition understood as aberrant and morally reprehensible. There was thus a logic behind the declarations of states of emergency in dictatorial Chile. Benjamin's thesis, however, emphasizes that understanding such a logic should be only a first step. It is also necessary to explore the effects that these declarations have and reveal emergency conditions that do not receive widespread recognition. For the oppressed in campamentos and poblaciones, states of emergency have been an ongoing historical presence, whether or not they have been recognized by the state or broader public audiences.

The conditions in Chile following the military coup were extraordinary, and the individuals who were tortured, mutilated, and killed by regime agents lived through an exceptional state of crisis. Numerous Chilean workers and homebuilders, moreover, suffered the horrors of the economic depression of the mid-1970s. But the difficulties that pobladores had to face were not entirely new, taking place instead in a social landscape already fractured by hierarchies, insecurity, segregation, and violence. Locating states of emergency that lay beyond the declarations made by regime officials makes it possible to discover the wounds from everyday forms of violence and deprivation that were present but not entirely specific to the dictatorship.[70] Such a perspective exposes the intolerable forms of power that lie both within and beyond the specific modes of horror implemented by the military regime. This both helps to explain the specific situation during the first years of the military dictatorship and aids in placing these years in a broader context.

The politics of declaring a state of exception also demonstrates a persistent, if also dynamic and contested, element of Chilean political culture. For planners in the military government, establishing a state of emergency helped to justify and consolidate the dictatorship. Yet a state of emergency framework also demonstrated some of the obvious contradictions of dictatorial rule. For many Chileans, and particularly for pobladores, the dictatorship did not normalize conditions, especially in the home. Many felt the wide gap between the expectations of an appropriate home life and the lived experience of violent repression and economic hardship. The politics of propriety thus continued to matter as pobladores suffered through crises. Despite its powers, the military regime could not control how sectors of society would respond to the exceptional conditions that many had to suffer through. Eventually, although after a very long and difficult wait that would include an economic boom and a series of efforts to further institutionalize the regime, this would expose the dictatorship to fatal weaknesses.

CHAPTER 6

AESTHETICS OF ORDER
Forging Spaces of Distinction amid Neoliberal Expansion

IN JANUARY 1979, THE CHIEF of the presidential staff, "on instructions from the señor Presidente de la República," General Augusto Pinochet, sent a memorandum to the minister of housing and urbanism. The president, the chief wrote, wanted to improve the "environmental and aesthetic quality" of the western section of the Alameda, Santiago's main thoroughfare. Providing access to the capital city from the airport and the country's principal port, the avenue was the first area that international visitors observed when they entered the country. The dictator was concerned that the neighborhood's low-income housing, abandoned buildings, sprawling market areas, heavy pedestrian traffic, graffiti, and littered streets provided a misleading impression. The chief wrote that the area did not "afford an image that was in accordance with the quality and rank of the capital city and the country" and ordered the minister of housing and urbanism to oversee the renovation of the western Alameda.[1]

With a budget of nearly US$11 million, the renovation plan would unfold on a number of fronts. In the words of the MINVU official who wrote it, the government would "eradicate 546 families" from their "unhealthy, dangerous, and overcrowded conventillos." These families would move to subsidized housing at a safe remove from the city center, beyond the view of tourists, foreign dignitaries, and business travelers. In addition, the Ministry of Public Works and Transportation was to oversee a number of infrastructure and beautification projects in the western Alameda, including the remodeling of the late nineteenth-century railway station. Typical of the regime's neoliberal policies that provided a means for public–private cooperation, government agencies would establish contacts with developers, bankers, and business owners, offering tax breaks and subsidies to lure investment and foment private initiatives. If all went according to plan, the process would produce a more attractive and vibrant area.[2]

The dictator would thus be able to drive by in his motorcade and view another area of his country undergoing perceived processes of modernization. As Pinochet often pointed out in his speeches, by 1979 Chile was entering its third year of unprecedented growth in GNP, rates that were among the highest in the world.[3] The dictator also boasted that international lending institutions and development bureaucracies praised Chile's fiscal "health" and that this had led to unparalleled levels of investment. Various industries were growing at record rates, including copper mining and "nontraditional" exports such as fresh fruit, forestry products, and fish, in addition to the financial and construction sectors.[4] Parts of Santiago were undergoing rapid and frenetic construction: new shopping malls, supermarkets, apartment buildings, and skyscrapers dotted the landscape, while the state-of-the-art metro subway system transported passengers throughout the city's downtown. Military regime officials interpreted these changes with optimism. In 1980, José Piñera, the minister of labor, claimed that Chile would be a "developed country" by 1990.[5]

The rapid changes pointed to the achievement of a kind of capitalist modernity in Chile. As they sought to attain this goal, the dictatorship's planners had a strong sense of how such modern development should appear and be measured. In assessing the urban landscape, they hoped to observe orderly and well-maintained areas of the city that were prosperous, dynamic, clean, and secure. For officials, the substandard conditions in the conventillos and the hundreds of campamentos in Santiago were a glaring problem. As centers of disorder, subversion, and poverty, they represented not only danger but also Chile's backward and chaotic past.

The celebration of growth, health, security, and cleanliness by the dictatorship's planners—and the corresponding concern and anxiety about realizing these conditions—has a familiar ring to it, reflecting what I term a modern aesthetics of order. This sense of aesthetics includes a normalizing, if at times contested, conception about the nature of appropriate living spaces, social interaction, and governance. It rests, to a certain degree, on a set of oppositions, in which categories of health and disease, cleanliness and dirt, order and disorder, growth and stagnation, and the future and the past frame understandings of what is desirable and attractive.[6] Such structures of feeling have been important in governing relations and in the evolution of segregation in Santiago throughout the period analyzed in this study. They have connected conceptions of modernity with civic consciousness and the management of populations and boundaries. Importantly, such understandings include the assumption that proper citizens deserve to inhabit "dignified" domestic spaces commensurate with their social standing.

The specific role of such aesthetic understandings of order, however, was particularly relevant during the establishment and eventual consolidation of neoliberalism. The reactionary ideology of the dictatorship granted these understandings a particular charge and brought them to the forefront. Aesthetics took on special importance under a regime that had much to hide and did not recognize how sociopolitical and economic relations contributed to inequality and class antagonisms. They also played a significant role in reinvigorating socioeconomic distinctions. The effects that capitalist expansion had on the built environment, moreover, became an important sign of growth and development, a welcome change for a regime that had been mostly reactive and repressive in its early years.

In the spaces of Santiago, regime officials implemented aggressive plans designed to create modern, distinct city spaces. They sought to *sanear* the campamentos, including the provision of property titles and infrastructure services considered basic. The dictatorship implemented a massive slum removal program in which they "eradicated" hundreds of campamentos in Santiago. This program turned tens of thousands into homeowners at the same time that it helped to lay the groundwork for a real estate boom and significantly increased residential segregation in the city.

Though these programs were often controversial, they nevertheless helped Pinochet in his quest to establish a long-term governing project. During the late 1970s the dictatorship consolidated its position. It lifted the state of siege, held a dubious national referendum in 1978, and drafted a new constitution ostensibly approved by voters on September 11, 1980.[7] The programs of urban renewal were an important part of the dictatorship's efforts to build legitimacy. Not coincidentally, these programs tapped into three far-reaching elements of the urban politics of propriety. First, the assumption remained that citizens who behaved in ways considered proper should live in legally sectioned properties. Second, residents should inhabit distinctive places appropriate to their social position and financial situation. Finally, the city should evolve in an orderly, efficient, and vibrant manner. Such suppositions—and their very problematic and partial fulfillment during periods of the dictatorship—helped the regime, for a time at least, to receive not only the backing of an important segment of the citizenry but also the support of major financial interests and international development institutions. For many, such phenomena as macroeconomic growth, real estate construction, slum removal, the "eradication of extreme poverty," and the development of infrastructure were worthy of celebration.

The consolidation of neoliberalism did not come easily, however, and constant strains lay beneath the surface. Dictatorial rule was contradictory, starting with the ongoing dislocations produced by state-sponsored repression and neoliberal restructuring. While these tensions remained largely out of the public discourse during the economic boom from 1977 to 1981, they nevertheless presented constant difficulties for both regime planners and citizens. It was an ongoing struggle to produce a desirable urban landscape; for many, developing homes considered proper was an elusive task. Eventually, opposition groups would point to these contradictions and help to undermine the regime by exposing the superficiality of the regime's aesthetic of order.

Governing Market Practices and the Role of Distinction

In ordering the renovation of the western Alameda, Pinochet assumed that visitors would evaluate Chile and its citizens through their impressions of the cityscape. In making this assumption, Pinochet was hardly unique in his thinking. Political leaders the world over have often sought to construct an impressive urban landscape in an effort to improve national status, build sociopolitical legitimacy, and attract investment. Urban aesthetics have long been a bulwark of nation-building and state formation. Not surprisingly, they thus informed the implementation of many of the Chilean dictatorship's most publicized and influential urban social programs. They became codified in law and in the categories of governance.

At the same time, such aesthetics were also structures of feeling that had deep cultural resonance. The notion that there was a link between the "quality and rank" of spatial forms and the city's inhabitants was widespread, weighing on the actions and decisions of government bureaucracies, private businesses, and citizens alike. As Santiago underwent tumultuous changes in the late 1970s, the idea that the appearance of neighborhoods in the city distinguished their residents worked its way into both how government planners sought to administer their programs and how consumers and citizens attempted to find a home. This idea had varied forms of expression and operated differently within the domain of state bureaucracies and in the private dealings of business and banking institutions. Aesthetic notions of order operate in distinct ways according to setting. But no matter the situation, aesthetics still carried weight as officials administered the city and citizens and consumers sought to find a home in it.

Officials in the dictatorship unambiguously supported a hierarchical vision of the city's spatial development. They implemented housing legislation and urban programs that sought to achieve "social homogeneity" in the city's municipalities. Officials explicitly divided "residential" neighborhoods of the city into different types, including those of "good quality" (*buena categoria*), others of "a middle category," and, at the bottom, those who lived in "social housing."[8] In a law passed in 1981, regime planners created sixteen new municipalities in Santiago as part of an effort to decentralize the administration of state services. The dictatorship split a number of mixed-income municipalities in two, separating distinct socioeconomic groups from each other. They thus facilitated the "social homogeneity" of the city's neighborhoods and reinforced class distinctions (Morales et al. 1990, 3). Officials justified these policies, in addition to the slum removal programs, by claiming that this process would allow municipal governments to focus on problems unique to particular socioeconomic groups. But the policy also produced further inequalities in the provision of services. The military regime mandated that the different municipalities pay for a larger percentage of welfare programs through their own tax bases. The difference in social spending per inhabitant between municipalities subsequently grew (Morales and Rojas 1987, 99–100).

As officials acted on the assumption that residential living spaces should be segregated by class, developers, real estate agents, prospective buyers, landlords, tenants, and homeowners did much the same. Through their practices, expectations, and limited options, these social actors contributed to the spatial stratification of the city. Decrees and policies were set, claims for housing were made, and developers and consumers chose their housing projects with notions of safety, cleanliness, order, and distinction in mind. Such decisions were made within a governing economy of reason, one which inexorably included aesthetic sensibilities of order.[9] For many, hierarchy was a natural part of this. It is possible to see this in the ways that members of the lower-middle and middle class sought to obtain homes of their own in government programs. They looked for houses that would be not only attractive and practical but also befitting their social status.

Consider, for example, the case of Juan Valenzuela Paredes, a low-level functionary in the Ministry of Public Works and Transportation. In a letter written in 1977 to the undersecretary of housing and urbanism, Valenzuela sought to convince the undersecretary that he lived in a neighborhood inappropriate to his place in society. Emphasizing that he was an employee in good standing, Valenzuela included a letter of support from his boss, a colonel in the army. While Valenzuela had received an apartment in 1975 through the "emergency housing plan," he wrote that a number of "marginal pobladores occupied" his neighborhood, making it a "real den of delinquency." On more than one occasion, his home had been vandalized, and in the month before he wrote the letter, a few men had tried to break into it. Given his problems, Valenzuela requested a new house, where he "would be able to live in a dignified way, in accordance with his social level."

A government-appointed social worker visited Valenzuela in his home and supported his claim. In her report, she wrote that Valenzuela was clearly of a "much higher social level" than his neighbors. She observed that there were many people of "bad living habits, including delinquents" in Valenzuela's población. The dangerous environment, the social worker concluded, had affected the health of Valenzuela's wife and children, disrupting the "harmony of the family." But given an improved home, Valenzuela would be able to assume a lifestyle more appropriate to his social position.[10]

Chileans like Valenzuela often went to great lengths to ensure that they would live in neighborhoods that they considered appropriate to their status. Beyond the employment and savings that they had to secure, they tended to spend much time working through slow-moving government bureaucracies and banking institutions in order to find a more desirable residence. This was particularly true in the late 1970s, when applicants for state-subsidized housing programs outnumbered recipients by as much as seven to one.[11] In facing a housing stock that fell far short of demand, Chileans with midlevel incomes often struggled to find homes (Kusnetzoff 1987, 167).[12] Finding an appropriate and attractive home tended to be hard work.

Mario Hugo Beltran's experience was fairly typical. A "subofficial" in the Army Engineering Command, Beltran wrote a letter to the undersecretary of housing and urbanism in the hope that he could live in a better home. Having already served for twenty-five years in the army, Beltran argued that he was now at the "height of his career." He noted, furthermore, that his responsibilities were many: his salary supported a family of seven, including his father who lived as an allegado. With "much effort and sacrifice," he had been saving his money since 1960 to buy a house. In December 1973 he had accumulated what he needed to enter a subsidized housing program, but it wasn't until late 1975 that he saw the announcement in the newspaper that he had been accepted for housing the following year.[13]

Unfortunately for Beltran, his wait had not ended. It took another sixteen months for MINVU to assign him an apartment. But it ended up being a bitter disappointment. The apartment had only two bedrooms and thus was not big enough to properly house his family. In legal terms, it failed to live up to the stipulations of the subsidy program Beltran was in. When Beltran went to MINVU's central offices to complain, he was informed that he could see three-bedroom houses in another area of the city. But this only ended up being another letdown. The homes were in complete disarray: the bedrooms and bathrooms lacked doors, vandals had broken windows, and looters had stolen the sinks and toilets. To make matters worse, Beltran wrote, the neighborhood was right next to "dangerous, marginal poblaciones." As a military man with a large family to look after, Beltran asserted that it was "just" for him to live in an area of "physical security." He deserved a neighborhood appropriate to his station, where he could have "dignified housing."

On the strength of these arguments, Beltran returned to MINVU's central offices to look for another house. He was subsequently pleased with what he saw: "beautiful houses" with three bedrooms, a living and dining room area, and space for a garden and outdoor entertaining. They were also well maintained and safe. Yet Beltran was once again left disappointed. Officials had reserved these houses for applicants who lived in the municipality where the homes were located, but Beltran lived elsewhere. Beltran found his search for housing infuriating, time-consuming, and full of bureaucratic red tape. Still, he believed that an appropriate solution could be found. There were too many factors in his favor: he had sufficient savings, a deserving family, and the support of his commanding officer, a brigadier general. Moreover, as Beltran put it, "just like [his] other comrades in arms, [he] had supported with his little grain of sand the memorable 9/11/73, [the day that] permitted our *patria* to find liberty and sovereignty." The weight of Beltran's claims ultimately proved successful: he finally received an apartment with all of the conditions he asked for in 1977.[14]

As the letters from Beltran and Valenzuela indicate, many Chileans identified themselves with distinct social strata and believed that this identification gave them the right to live in places that corresponded to their status.[15] Several housing applicants could hardly imagine themselves living in a población or a campamento. One woman, describing herself as a newly married professional from the "middle class," expressed her concern about the lack of affordable housing for people like herself. "Where are we going to live?" she asked. "We can't live in a room [in a conventillo or in a *cité*] because we are decent people, nor can we go to a población." Seeing herself as respectable and middle-class, this woman would not even consider living in certain areas.[16] Expectations such as this reflect how deeply seated stigmatizations of the pobladores and the spaces they lived in could be, an everyday dynamic that the dictatorship's policies reinforced.

The (Ir)Relevance of the Past in Present Spaces

In each of the above cases, the supposition that residents should live in areas commensurate with their social status rests on an understanding of individual merit. These claimants identify themselves as middle-class professionals and responsible parents. They have worked hard to have homes of their own. Given their actions and comportment, they deserve an appropriate house. In this conception, becoming a homeowner depends on personal agency. To a certain degree, of course, this is the case. In Chile and elsewhere, homebuyers typically spend time and effort in acquiring their homes and in developing and maintaining them. Beyond the remunerated labor that most have to undertake to afford a house, it is also necessary to find a suitable location, negotiate real estate and financial bureaucracies, furnish the house, keep it up, and become indebted. Yet the focus on this type of homeowning agency, as widespread and as consequential as it is, offers a partial and ideologically charged rendering of the making of a home. Significant forces tend to remain mystified, seemingly irrelevant to the ways that people go about their everyday lives. It is, on balance, not necessary for modern urban residents to be aware of how actions and dynamics from the past have shaped their living conditions. Amnesia and lack of awareness permeate the spaces of the present.

I observed the disconnection between how the past forces of history shape living spaces and how social actors simultaneously produce them during a moment when my archival work bumped into my own experiences in an unplanned way.[17] In August 2002, my wife Christina and I attended an opening for a clothing store in one of Chile's wealthiest municipalities, Las Condes. We did not spend much time in this area of the city, but we had come after receiving an invitation from an investor in the store, a Spanish acquaintance of ours named Patricia. Patricia was a trade negotiator for the European Union whom we had met through a Chilean friend, Miguel. Miguel had grown up with and remained very close to Patricia's husband, Gustavo.[18] Miguel and Gustavo often reminisced about their time together at the University of Chile in Valparaíso during the early to mid-1980s. They particularly enjoyed recalling their experiences in protesting against the dictatorship, as they were members of a student movement that was an important base of opposition to the regime, especially during the national protests that began in 1983.[19] Miguel and Gustavo remembered the protests as intense and occasionally thrilling events that united students. They would excitedly trade stories about the sit-ins and demonstrations that they had taken part in, the confrontations that had occurred between the students and the "security forces," and the general atmosphere of solidarity. For Miguel and Gustavo, the protests were a moment of activist awakening, a time in which the Chileans who opposed Pinochet asserted themselves. They had worked together, often at personal risk, to defeat a dictatorial, brutal regime that terrorized much of the citizenry and abused democracy.

Such memories of activism, solidarity, hardship, and eventual triumph seemed far removed from the lavish opening for the clothing store. Caterers worked their way through the crowd with trays of wine and champagne; an impressive array of hors d'oeuvres was spread out on two large tables draped in white cloth; and a few professional photographers snapped photos of the fashion models and the well-connected in attendance. It was an opulent, flashy, and exclusive scene, befitting a store that was to carry expensive brands of clothing imported from Europe. With an address on the trendy Avenida Alonso de Córdoba, the store was to take its place among some of the most expensive boutiques and shops in all of Chile.

It was hard to imagine that a little more than two decades before, a campamento had stood in the same location. Yet this was the case, as I had recently discovered. In fact, much of the shopping district in Alonso de Córdoba, now so marked by the distinctive trappings of conspicuous consumption, had once been Campamento San Luis. Known before the coup as Campamento Ho Chi Minh, the neighborhood had first been established through a land seizure in early 1972, sponsored by MIR militants and sympathetic workers from the municipality of Las Condes.[20] In June 1982, however, the government removed the campamento, placing the pobladores in a new settlement more than an hour away by bus, on the outskirts of Santiago's south side.[21] The opulent shopping scene at Alonso de Córdoba had thus been made possible, in no small measure, by the policies of the dictatorship.

The changes in this particular area were stark. In place of the narrow, pedestrian-friendly paths of a campamento were wide thoroughfares that served automobile traffic. Rather than poorly constructed small homes fashioned from cardboard, wood, tin, and concrete cinderblocks, manicured, gated apartment buildings and office buildings of steel and glass dominated the landscape. Where pobladores had once walked through Campamento San Luis with a general degree of familiarity with their neighbors, the residents of the barrio alto now used the public spaces of Alonso de Córdoba in a much more anonymous fashion. Whereas the only stores in the area had once been small-scale businesses that carried a rather limited supply of goods for immediate consumption, now there were stores with impressive showcases of exclusive luxury items. In place of an "anachronistic," "underdeveloped," and "shameful" area—as one journalist had described the campamentos in Las Condes in 1976—now stood "modern," new, and opulent developments.[22]

The nature of these changes made it possible to open the clothing store some twenty years later; it would have been unthinkable to open such a place in a campamento or even next to a low-income población or villa. The district was now attractive enough to bring in investment, new construction, and high-end shoppers. To an important degree, the policies of the dictatorship—not to mention its violent repression—had made that possible. If there were Chileans who recognized this, that was largely irrelevant to how the city continued to expand and grow in places like the shopping district of Alonso de Córdoba. Such growth was, at least in part, a legacy from the dictatorship that appeared to fit seamlessly and imperceptibly into the contemporary spaces of the city.

From 1977 to 1982, the dictatorship removed twenty-one campamentos from Las Condes as part of their plans to "eradicate extreme poverty" (Benavides, Morales, and Rojas 1983, 24). The removal of the campamentos contributed to a major transformation in the appearance of Las Condes and the other wealthy municipalities of Santiago's east side. In the areas where the campamentos had been removed, real estate values surged (Ducci, Fernández, and Agüero 1989). The cityscape underwent intoxicating and vertiginous changes: office buildings designed by world-renowned architectural firms shot skyward; apartment complexes with private security services and beautiful views of the Andes proliferated; retail outlets that mimicked malls in the United States opened; and a number of supermarkets, boutiques, and restaurants arrived.

All of this occurred in conjunction with the deepening of neoliberal reforms, including loosening financial, real estate, and credit regulations. In 1979 the regime passed a law that abolished limits on urban expansion and abrogated a number of zoning ordinances (see Morales and Rojas 1987; Arellano 1983; Hidalgo Dattwyer 2005, 366–75). These policies, in addition to the unprecedented surge in capitalist investment in Chile during the late 1970s, led to a speculative boom in construction and housing starts, particularly in the wealthier areas of Santiago. Eventually, this boom would collapse during the major economic crisis that engulfed Chile from late 1981 to 1985.[23] The crisis itself formed a crucial backdrop for the national protests, in which popular pressure forced the dictatorship to back off of some of its more extreme policies. This included contributing to the 1985 decision to repeal the law that permitted unchecked urban expansion (Bruey 2012).

Yet even as the dictatorship's policies led to an economic crisis, sociopolitical upheaval, and policy reversals, they would still continue to have long-lasting effects. This is especially true of the programs in urban renewal. Throughout both the economic boom and bust, real estate development in Santiago remained concentrated in Las Condes and a few neighboring municipalities. In 1986 these areas received more than 60 percent of the investment in housing starts and construction in Santiago while having only 12 percent of the city's population (Kusnetzoff 1987, 165–66). At the same time, the "eradication"

Figure 6.1. High-rises of the building boom in Santiago. The US embassy is in the foreground to the left. This picture and the one in figure 6.2 are taken from the same hill. They depict an area that had squatters removed and one that received them (photo by author).

programs directly facilitated the dictatorship's goal of creating the "social homogeneity" of Santiago's municipalities and neighborhoods. According to official statistics, between 1977 and 1986 the military regime removed approximately forty thousand "families" living in Santiago's campamentos, more than two hundred thousand people.[24] The dictatorship removed the vast majority of the campamentos in Santiago's wealthiest municipalities in the eastern and central sections of the city, sending the pobladores from these areas to outlying areas. Between 1979 and 1984, for example, the municipalities of Las Condes and Santiago "eradicated" more than thirty-five thousand pobladores, while the low-income municipalities of Renca and La Pintana, on the city's outskirts, received approximately fifty thousand new residents (Morales et al. 1990, 21). As a result, some of the most obvious signs of urban poverty are no longer present in the wealthier areas of the city. Today it is possible to travel east from the center of Santiago to where the city ends at the base of the Andes—a distance of some fifteen kilometers—without seeing campamentos or poblaciones.

The tumultuous resettling of Santiago in the late 1960s and the early 1970s and the lack of affordable housing for middle-income sectors in the first decade of the dictatorship caused many to express their alarm at the erosion of clearly demarcated residential spaces between the social classes. In the end, however, the dictatorship ensured that Santiago's segregation would remain pervasive. Today, most who believe themselves to be of different social strata

Figure 6.2. Panorama of an area of Santiago that received the "eradicated" from slum removal programs (photo by author).

than pobladores can generally stay away from where pobladores live. Santiago's fractured geography generally makes it possible for these Chileans and the typical foreign visitor to avoid these less valued areas. For many, the campamentos and the poblaciones are out of sight, understood in only the most fragmentary and piecemeal of ways.

The Interventions and Retreats of the Neoliberal State

The eradication programs illustrate the ambitious scope of the dictatorship's efforts to transform Chilean society, pointing to the forceful role that government agencies took in establishing what have come to be known as neoliberal policies. As the regime dismantled numerous state-directed welfare structures—ostensibly in the name of a hands-off, laissez-faire approach to economic relations—it made significant interventions in the market. The regime implemented programs such as the eradications that were large in scale and broad in effect. Through impunity and violence, officials pursued policies that would not have been possible before the coup. Officials dismantled pillars of the welfare state with great zeal, scaling back the state's social spending and privatizing the provision of social security, health care, housing, and education. Such changes are hallmarks of neoliberal regimes, yet they were made possible by bloody and expansive interventions in social life, underscoring how the state played a pivotal and direct role in the institution of neoliberalism in Chile. Cast as part of the regime's efforts to modernize state administration and target social spending, these programs received significant support from international development and financial institutions, lending legitimacy and crucial backing to the dictatorship.

State-sponsored repression dealt a significant blow to unions, decimating the leadership of the more radical organizations and sowing an environment of fear and mistrust among the rank and file. There was a significant decline in the number of unionized workers, as their numbers fell from 855,000 in 1972 to 320,000 a decade later (Constable and Valenzuela 1991, 227). New legal barriers made it much more difficult for organized workers to take part in work stoppages and strikes.[25] The restructuring of the workforce further undermined labor's position, as the lowering of tariff walls and the cutting of subsidies to domestic industries debilitated businesses where unions had once been powerful. According to one estimate, employment in industry dropped from 25.8 percent of the economically active population in 1971 to 13.1 percent in 1995 (Salazar and Pinto 2002, 218). In Santiago, work generally became less secure for low- and lower-middle-income wage earners, and an increasing number labored in the informal market, the service industry, and seasonal employment in fruit exports. One study found that the percentage of people working in the informal sector rose from thirteen to thirty-four between 1972 and 1984, making it the single largest labor sector in Santiago (Portes 1989, 34). Over the same period, the number of people working in services increased from forty to fifty percent (Rodriguez 1987, 30). This restructuring did not generate sufficient employment to make up for the lost jobs, however. Unemployment rates remained high at 17.1 percent throughout the dictatorship, nearly triple what they had averaged between 1960 and 1973 (INE 1999, 56).[26]

As the dictatorship dismantled much of the state sector and undermined the power of organized labor, it simultaneously implemented social welfare programs designed to target "extreme poverty." Officials predicted that their approach would lead to a fundamental break with the past. Miguel Kast told foreign dignitaries in a 1980 conference in Santiago that "in eight years there won't be any more children in extreme poverty in Chile."[27] Through the implementation of high-profile programs that would win the "battle against misery," officials such as Kast promised to "combat extreme poverty."[28]

A number of international development organizations found the dictatorship's plans to realize this goal attractive and worthy of support, especially in housing and so-called urban renewal. These organizations, such as the World Bank, USAID, and the Inter-American Development Bank, provided substantial loans and technical expertise for the dictatorship's slum removal and property titling policies.[29] These programs fit within the general prescriptions that development agencies offered for achieving fiscal "health," as they limited redistribution policies to a few targeted areas and streamlined government. Officials could wax rhapsodic about their new governing aesthetic. In reviewing the results of a four-year IDB loan and grant program to MINVU, a housing official wrote that Chile had "acquired an efficient economic and administrative structure that . . . created the integrated and harmonious development of the country" (MINVU n.d.[b], 9). Evidently, an appreciation for the beauty of order was not solely about interpretations of the built environment; it also spread to the prosaic tasks of state administration.

For international development institutions, efforts to reduce poverty through the provision of infrastructure services and property titles would strengthen this "integrated and harmonious development." By legalizing the land tenure status of a substantial segment of the population, planners sought to integrate the beneficiaries into financial and state institutions, just as Christian Democratic reformers had sought to do in the 1960s.[30] This, in turn, would supposedly contribute to improved forms of governance, as state bodies would be better able to regulate citizens and the spaces they lived in. Among Chilean state planners and their supporters in international development and finance, links between property holding and ideas of a proper order maintained a powerful hold.

Close links also remained between the Chilean Chamber of Construction and MINVU: beginning in the 1980s, every minister of housing and urbanism through the early 2000s was an executive that came from, as Ana Sugranyes (2005, 29) points out, "business circles that the Chamber of Construction leads."[31] Ultimately, the dictatorship's "eradication" policies were not solely about making the city more attractive and creating homeowners. They were also big business, in which MINVU and international agencies ensured that low-income housing development would be profitable for financial and real estate institutions. In a shift, MINVU began in the late 1970s to grant subsidies directly to housing beneficiaries, rather than to the construction companies themselves (see Sugranyes 2005; Kusnetzoff 1987). They also guaranteed loans to low-income households. Whereas private developers had previously benefited from the subsidies they had directly received from the government, they now could profit from the subsidies the government granted to housing recipients. They could do so, moreover, without assuming much risk. At the same time, the developers who agreed to build low-income housing for pobladores who had been removed from campamentos received the property rights to the vacated land.[32] Quite often, this was extremely valuable real estate, especially in municipalities such as Las Condes. The government, in other words, played a leading role in facilitating sweetheart deals in high-end real estate projects.

These projects proliferated as foreign capital investment rose to unprecedented heights in the late 1970s. With the dramatic rise in the price of oil, European and North American financial institutions were awash in so-called petrodollars. Banks, lending agencies, and investment firms redirected capital to countries such as Chile that were experiencing commodity booms. These institutions found Chile especially attractive because of its seeming stability, the selling off of state-led industries, and the liberalization and deregulation of the country's capital and real estate markets. In 1977, $572 million flowed into Chile through direct capital investment, while in 1981 that number stood at more than $3.3 billion (Foxley 1986, 14). Concentrated in the financial and real estate sectors, this investment made credit cheap and directly contributed to the speculative boom. It also helped to insulate the dictatorship from the pressure it faced on its human rights and democratic reform record (Arriagada 1988, 35).

Before the economic crash, the backing of foreign investors and development experts made it possible for regime planners to design increasingly bold projects in housing, poverty reduction, and urban development. In his presidential address in 1979, Pinochet announced that his government would spur development in the private sector in order to construct nine hundred thousand housing units in the following decade, a number far beyond any that the country had been able to build over a ten-year period. Through this action, Pinochet pledged to resolve the chronic housing shortage (Kusnetzoff 1987, 170). But Pinochet's numbers proved to be wildly optimistic. Initially there was a significant increase in new housing starts, as they rose from 19,437 in 1978 to 54,550 in 1981. They fell precipitously, however, during the economic crisis from 1982 to 1984, before there was a substantial increase again between 1985 and 1989 (Banco Central 2001, 265–66).

In their urban development policies, officials promised to fundamentally transform the campamentos. According to MINVU estimates, at the end of 1973 more than 270,000 Chilean "families" lived in "irregular" urban neighborhoods that lacked property titles and infrastructure services considered basic, including running water, electricity, access to public transportation, police patrols, and schools. This meant that in a country of only slightly more than eleven million people, well beyond one million lived-in areas that government agencies would have to *sanear* through property titling and the provision of infrastructure and services.[33] In Santiago, according to a 1978 survey, there were more than 25,065 "families" who had illegally seized lands before September 11, 1973, and still did not possess legal titles.[34] As large as this figure was—representing as many as 125,000 pobladores—it omitted those who had quietly set up homes during the dictatorship on the outskirts of established campamentos, in the alleyways of poblaciones, or in lands that had largely fallen into disuse. In addition, there were several pobladores who occupied legally established areas before the coup but lived in officially declared "irregular" or "emergency" campamentos, including a number of neighborhoods established through Operación Sitio and cooperatives.

In 1981, MINVU and the Ministry of the Interior began a massive program to legalize the land tenure status of these pobladores. As one MINVU official wrote, "Policy consists in making [beneficiaries] property owners."[35] Between 1981 and 1986, the government provided more than one hundred thousand property titles in the metropolitan area of Santiago alone (Kusnetzoff 1987, 165). This process, however, did not go smoothly, as government agencies confronted a tense social environment and a number of logistical challenges. In order to "regularize" neighborhoods, officials would need to create uniform lot sizes, provide certain infrastructure services, and document the land tenure status of pobladores. Yet the polarized, volatile, inequitable, and repressive atmosphere of the time ultimately provided a fundamental challenge to efforts to create a well-ordered and attractive city that would include a secure home life.

Patronage, Fairness, and (Dis)Order in the Administration of Housing Programs

The dictatorship's plans to eradicate extreme poverty in the late 1970s underscore the ways in which officials sought to construct forms of development in Chile. For officials, the programs would transform society, as home owning, disciplined citizens would live in manageable, modern city spaces. This vision, however, never matched conditions in the city. It depended, in the first instance, on continued economic growth, something that the speculative boom of the late 1970s and early 1980s could not sustain. The availability of easy money, the selling off of state industries, and the high price of copper would not last. Just as important, the poor labor conditions that pobladores confronted made many of them unable to meet the debt obligations that homeownership entailed. Instead of homeownership, many of these pobladores, like others in the city, faced dispossession. To make matters worse, officials often granted housing benefits and urban services through networks of patronage and favoritism.[36] Corruption, as the later discovery of Pinochet's secret bank accounts would poignantly illustrate, was a part of how the dictatorship operated. Ultimately, hundreds of thousands would remain without homes that they considered appropriate, a situation that undermined the dictatorship's claims to be modernizing the country.

Still, principles of fairness and propriety mattered in government housing programs. In administering their programs, MINVU officials claimed that they followed the "strict justice" of the law and treated citizens with "impartial, rational, and fair" criteria. As a part of this, they emphasized making transparent the basic requirements for subsidized housing. In general, they followed the standard precepts that had long been a part of state housing programs. To begin, applicants had to be part of a family, defined as a "legally constituted home," and they received extra points based on the number of family members they had.[37] In order to be able to make a down payment and demonstrate an ability to pay off loans, applicants had to accumulate savings through monthly payments. They received extra points for each year they were in the program. They also received priority if, as one MINVU resolution described it, they lived in "overcrowded, promiscuous, unhealthy, and poor housing conditions."[38] Finally, applicants had to demonstrate further discipline by being clean and orderly. The criteria were seemingly straightforward, and, according to officials, just. As Arthur Clarke, the undersecretary of housing and urbanism liked to put it in responding to requests for housing, the stipulations for state-sponsored housing programs "are based in objective, impersonal norms that don't allow for any exceptions."[39]

This principle often stood in stark contrast to the ways that applicants cast their claims. Citizens tended to evoke ideals of home and justice in their efforts to receive housing. In one fairly typical case, a group of "homeless" women appealed directly to Lucía Hiriart de Pinochet, the first lady. They chose to write to "Señora Lucía" because, as they described it at the beginning of their letter, "[We are] aware of your great spirit of service, of your decency, and, above all, of your qualities as a woman and as a mother." At the time that this letter was written in 1981, Hiriart had spent eight years as the most visible face of the regime's programs in charities and poverty reduction. Making appearances in the poblaciones and joining her husband at groundbreaking ceremonies for new housing developments, Señora Lucía had often made the case that the government's programs in homeownership and urban development strengthened families, particularly ones that demonstrated discipline and fortitude.

In their letter, the women asked Señora Lucía to help them receive housing. They had joined a housing cooperative that had been established in 1968. In spite of the passing of more than a decade, the members of the cooperative had not been able to achieve "the desire of every human being . . . a home of one's own." The women and their families had joined the cooperative with the understanding that they would soon be granted property titles, infrastructure services, and housing materials. They had believed that they were going to receive a subsidy in 1979, but that had not worked out. Eighteen members subsequently left the cooperative, leaving those who remained unable to assume the debt burdens demanded of them.

Two years later, the members of the cooperative remained without homes

Figure 6.3. "The desire of every human being . . . a home of one's own." Augusto Pinochet and Lucía Hiriart handing out property titles (*Amiga* 33, 10; image courtesy of the Biblioteca Nacional de Chile).

of their own, and they feared that despite all of their "effort, sacrifice, and savings," they would have to disband. The situation was unacceptable: they wrote that the attitude of the officials they had spoken to was contrary to the "true spirit of our governors, especially our president who has always wanted to grant subsidies to those people who, with great sacrifice, save and are deserving." But the members of the cooperative would be rejected one more time. Writing in response for the first lady, Undersecretary Clarke informed the cooperative members that they could not receive a subsidy since they did not have sufficient points. The "Supreme Government," the undersecretary explained, followed "impartial and fair" criteria and had to treat all applicants in the same way, without exception.[40]

MINVU planners argued that their strict adherence to procedure was in stark contrast to the process of favoritism in place before the coup. Officials were thus moving the country beyond "politics" and the unfair system of patronage and clientelism practiced before the coup.[41] They were creating a just and impersonal state administration that encompassed all citizens equally and fairly. Applicants would receive state benefits solely on the basis of their individual merits, and the state, acting in a rational and impartial manner, would not be swayed by other interests. The result would be a smoothly functioning bureaucracy that promoted a responsible citizenry and a well-organized, efficient, and just society. The modernizing spaces of Santiago would be one impressive example of this attractive new order.

Yet this fetishized understanding of the state belied how governing institutions actually tended to grant benefits and protections. The state was not a unified, singular entity that dispensed its benefits equally. Even within the formal operations of the state, bureaucrats sanctioned certain forms of patronage and favoritism. Official policy granted preferred status to the armed forces. The budget for the military nearly doubled in real terms between 1973 and 1981.[42] In housing programs, the government reserved 10 percent of the available housing stock for police officers and soldiers. They further granted retirees from these institutions more starting points than other applicants.[43] The dictatorship also reserved a percentage of the available housing subsidies for workers in the central government.[44]

Connections and influence also played a role in the administration of state programs. Many claimants called on military officials in order to access benefits. Where once politicians had interceded on behalf of citizens who sought housing, now officials in the dictatorship did so. In one example, a navy captain wrote a message to MINVU on behalf of Germán Zapata, one of the captain's employees in the Treasury General of the Republic. Characterizing Zapata as an "honorable person with a good record," the captain arranged for a social worker to assess Zapata's home situation. In her report, the social worker noted that Zapata had a "legally constituted family" of four, including two "legitimate" young children. But the family occupied a "deplorable situation of overcrowding": they lived in a five-by-five-meter *mediagua* that did not have potable water or sewer services. Despite the poor conditions, the social worker wrote that the family maintained a "clean and well-maintained home."[45] They were disciplined and well-behaved, leading the social worker to conclude that they should live in a larger, more established house. But Zapata did not have the savings required by the subsidized housing program. In responding, a MINVU official informed Zapata that the ministry had used up the available housing stock for the year, but that he could receive housing when new units became available. Despite Zapata's lack of savings, he would ultimately be able to access state benefits.[46]

If personal connections and patronage networks mattered in dispensing state benefits, Zapata's case also demonstrates that they were not the sole determinants. Even in an authoritarian context of favoritism and impunity, the politics of propriety continued to matter in the application of state programs. Military officials were not always successful in intervening on behalf of applicants, at times receiving the response that reiterated the goal of the "Supreme Government" to preserve fairness and objectivity in state projects.[47] The criteria were not completely hollow. On a more general level, certain fundamental assumptions remained about the roles that both government bureaucracies and citizens were supposed to play when state services were granted.

Officially, government agencies were to play a crucial but limited role in making impoverished Chileans property holders. These bodies were to strictly enforce regulations, but they would only help citizens to the extent that they could become responsible for themselves in the market economy.[48] As Clarke described the housing programs, "it is the responsibility of the head of the family to provide housing . . . the State acts to subsidize the neediest sectors of the community when they can't get housing on their own, recognizing the efforts they make to save."[49] The zeal with which planners sought to apply free-market fundamentals led them to define housing as a "good" rather than a "right" in the late 1970s, a significant shift. Ultimately, however, popular pressure during the national protests led officials to once again define housing as a right.[50] But even when it was defined as a right, it was one that, as a MINVU policy formulation stated, could only be "acquired through effort and savings, in which the family and the state contribute their share of responsibility" (MINVU 1975, 2).

Planners argued that inculcating this "share of responsibility" in the pobladores was central to developing them into new kinds of citizens. For officials, the actions of the pobladores in the land seizures had demonstrated that they lacked proper discipline. In a speech to the beneficiaries of an eradication program, Minister of the Interior César Raúl Benavides argued that pobladores had fallen into a "spiritual and moral rut" because they "had been tricked by those sectors that were responsible for offering them moral guidance."[51] But in moving into a new house, the pobladores would become aware of both "their rights and their obligations" as they cared for their new homes. "Houses," the minister explained, "don't make themselves, especially for those who don't have an interest in improving themselves [*superarse*] and who don't accept living with dignity."[52] In this view, "replacing an unhealthy callampa with a model villa" was about "a new way of life for a new family." For the minister, this meant the pobladores would "assume their responsibility in the national reconstruction" and understand that the "state is no longer the one responsible for the future of Chile."[53]

As the minister's condescending attitude suggests, the military regime took seriously efforts to educate pobladores. In the eradication programs, the regime used the mothers' centers and the neighborhood councils to instruct pobladores on how to be homeowners and disciplined citizens. The regime developed a network of more than twenty thousand female volunteers to staff these programs, featuring the wives of military officers and regime officials. Headed by First Lady Hiriart in the National Women's Secretariat, the mothers' centers concentrated on restoring the values of "family and fatherland [*patria*]." In attempting to teach pobladores the skills they would need to be homeowners, the mothers' centers set up programs designed to teach dueñas de casa how to maintain their houses through cleaning, upkeep, and the use of a monthly budget.

Antifeminist and ardently pro-regime, the classes sought to reinforce an apolitical notion of the family, in which mothers would dedicate themselves to homemaking. According to the program's basic principles, women needed to develop "a national consciousness and a correct understanding of the dignity of their mission inside the family" (*Mensaje Presidencial* 1977, 118). The volunteers prohibited discussion of "political" issues, including any talk of the social circumstances that may have contributed to the problems experienced by individual families (Valdés and Weinstein 1993, 115). For their participation in the mothers' centers, members were rewarded by the regime with important benefits such as food discounts and subsidized medical attention. Members were expected, however, to be present at meetings, not be involved in any neighborhood organizations outside of official channels, pay certain dues, and attend pro-regime rallies.[54]

The extent to which these programs succeeded in their goals is impossible to gauge. Some women who attended were undoubtedly Pinochetistas and shared some of the values of nationalism and militarism espoused by the volunteers. As Verónica Valdivia Ortiz de Zárate (2008) has demonstrated, the right-wing Independent Democratic Union (UDI) political party owes much of it success among pobladores in the 1990s and 2000s to the organizations and patronage networks that it established during the dictatorship. (Several mayors from the UDI, in fact, have been elected to low-income municipalities in Santiago following the end of the dictatorship, including in Renca.) But many women used the programs for their own purposes, while chafing under the repressive conditions and keeping their thoughts to themselves as they attended carefully staged official events.[55] Still others refused to take part, particularly those who had been active with Leftist political parties, often joining instead the numerous nongovernmental organizations that became active during the dictatorship, particularly in the 1980s. (This was, for example, how Eliana Parra and Ana Valdés reacted.) The dictatorship's rather heavy-handed efforts to build support did not necessarily meet with success.

Yet while many rejected elements of the dictatorship's ideological project and condemned the actions taken by the regime, they nevertheless could generally agree with a few of the assumptions embedded in the dictatorship's policies. In spite of the claims of officials like the minister of the interior that housing activists before the coup had led pobladores into a "spiritual and moral rut," it had always been important for pobladores who had taken part in the land seizures to demonstrate that they were proper citizens. The dictatorship's efforts to inculcate discipline in first-time homeowners was not new, but rather tapped into a moral register of state, in which hardworking and well-behaved citizens deserved an appropriate home. As one pobladora wrote in a letter to the First Lady, "I don't know what to do anymore in order to have housing so that I can live in a dignified way. My husband and I are working people, who have saved what we have with much sacrifice and we don't believe it is just that after battling so hard that we still don't have any chance [to receive housing]."[56]

The Underside of Order

As they sought to reorder Santiago and administer the often tumultuous re-settling of the city, planners struggled to achieve their governing aesthetic of order in a volatile social context marked by inequity, favoritism, and polarization. Within this precarious and contradictory atmosphere, developing homes considered proper was not possible for many, a phenomenon that would come to haunt officials. The appearance of order and tight control sat uncomfortably with a more troubled, insecure, and uncertain reality.

In the everyday administration of housing and urban programs, the presence of allegados and overcrowding often exposed the gap between living conditions and the expectations that residents had of how they should inhabit the city. Allegados, of course, had long been an important issue. By all accounts, however, the number of allegados increased dramatically during the dictatorship. In 1987, one broad estimate placed the number of allegados at 135,000 "families" in Santiago, more than 15 percent of the city's population (Kusnetzoff 1987, 168). Given such conditions, the possibilities for developing the "well-constituted homes" that pobladores had sought in the land seizures were remote.

In their reports, social workers pointed to the tense underside of home life and to the fact that government programs often could not develop adequate responses. In one typical case, a social worker reviewed the housing application of Jaime Palacios, a low-level functionary in the Treasury Department. Palacios lived with his pregnant wife and six-year-old son in a mediagua that was under twenty square meters in size, behind the house owned by Palacios' in-laws. Shared by six family members, the main house consisted of two bedrooms, a cramped living and dining room area, a kitchen, and a bathroom. The social worker expressed concern for the welfare of everyone living there. "The housing situation is extremely serious," she wrote. "Due to the overcrowding, there have been grave problems in family relations, having an impact on the nervous system of all of the members of the family group." The entire situation, the social worker wrote, was "uncomfortable" and "harmful." In replying to Palacios, a MINVU official indicated that he understood "the magnitude of the problem" that affected him, but that there wasn't any housing available. The government would follow the "fair" and "impartial" system of "strict justice" in assigning housing.[57]

Ultimately, government programs did very little to ameliorate overcrowding, in spite of the fact that there was a general agreement that the existence of so many allegados was undesirable. Allegados such as Palacios did receive extra points in housing subsidy programs if a social worker defined their living conditions as abnormal. Beyond that, however, they generally did not end up being the focus of plans in urban housing and poverty reduction. Instead, officials primarily targeted the "irregular" campamentos, following the precepts of the Map of Extreme Poverty and, more broadly, a governing aesthetic that emphasized spatial appearances. Allegados largely remained outside of the diagnoses made by poverty experts. This occurred even as housing officials recognized what numerous social worker reports described as "the neuroses" that cramped living conditions could engender.[58]

But while officials could distance themselves from allegados, they could not help but encounter problems in their efforts to reorder the city according to the principles of "social homogeneity," "regularization," and homeownership. The polarized atmosphere and the desire on the part of many to maintain segregation directly contributed to confrontations between neighborhoods. In a 1980 letter to the minister of housing and urbanism, a brigadier general described how such conflicts could take place. Writing on behalf of a group of police officers who lived in a cooperative, the general claimed that the officers had a number of disputes with an adjacent campamento. Having lived in the cooperative since 1968, the officers still had not yet received certain infrastructure services and property titles. During the Popular Unity government, a group of forty squatters had seized an area of land next to the police officers' campamento. As the years passed, new squatters had continued to arrive. By 1980 the campamento had more than two hundred shacks, having gone through the kind of quiet expansion then common.

In his letter, the general expressed how deeply troubled the police officers were by the squatters. The officers had not been able to receive paved roads and sewer services, since the existence of an "irregular" campamento meant that the area did not comply with regulatory standards. Moreover, the cooperative's residents had to put up with "provocations of all kinds, especially during the recent [1980] plebiscite, [including] ill treatments, insults, deterioration in the closest housing units, assaults against the children and insults to the women." The conditions in the campamento were also a problem, presenting the cooperative members with "difficulties encountered by sources of disease due to the outhouses and the lack of sewer services." According to the leaders of the cooperative, "this government has always shown concern for the problem," and it even eradicated a group from the campamento, but more had arrived. Despite all of their difficulties, the members of the cooperative patiently sought to find a legal resolution, "in order to protect the sanctity of their families" and not cause "any damage to the Supreme Government." The housing minister responded that his ministry planned to *sanear* the police officers' lots.[59]

Like many claimants, the members of this cooperative had to wait for a long time to "regularize" their housing situation. Creating a city that would conform to the precepts of a legally sanctioned urban domain was a long and arduous, even unending, process. Resolving the administrative and spatial problems presented by squatters was particularly difficult. Officials conceded that the landowners of properties that had been squatted on before the coup should either have their lands restored to them or receive restitution. Yet they had a hard time realizing these goals. They did not have adequate housing available for squatters and they expressed concern that general evictions would lead to a worsening housing situation and potential instability.[60] In one response to a landowner who had asked for evictions, a MINVU official argued that the issue of illegal squatters was a problem that the military regime had inherited. The official added that eviction of the squatters was a "complex issue . . . requiring the adoption of measures . . . at a national level" in order to find a "dignified solution for the pobladores."[61]

As the policies of slum removal and neighborhood "regularization" gained steam, officials began to give more latitude to government bodies to remove pobladores from campamentos, grant property titles, and pay indemnities to former landowners.[62] But even with more aggressive policies, a "dignified solution" was often beyond the means of government institutions. Officials scrambled to resolve the contradictions. In property titling programs, for example, officials had to ensure that pobladores would come to occupy neighborhoods in which property lots were of a minimum and uniform size. Following the land seizures, neighborhood councils had often organized their campamentos with this in mind, designing them so that they conformed to official standards. Yet there were a number of cases in which the settlement of the campamentos had occurred in a less systematic fashion, particularly in cases where squatters continued to arrive after the coup. In order to gain legal status, numerous neighborhoods needed to be reorganized, especially in cases where the "regulating plans" called for the creation of parks, community centers, and wider streets. In such cases, there often was insufficient space to fit all of the residents from a campamento. MINVU planners responded by passing a decree in 1981 that decreased the minimum size of housing lots from thirty-six to twenty-five square meters.[63] In government programs, a proper home could now be an extremely small one. This underscores how the dictatorship whittled down rights, services, and understandings of minimally acceptable conditions.

Yet even with this new lot size, many neighborhoods could not fit all of the pobladores who had been living in the campamentos. Neighborhood councils had some ability to exclude pobladores based on their personal antecedents, although less than they had had before the coup.[64] Generally speaking, the pobladores who left were those who were not able to maintain their debt burdens. In some cases, these burdens could be quite onerous, as MINVU officials appraised the lands according to local market rates.[65] In response to the difficulties that many pobladores had in buying their houses, MINVU stipulated that these applicants should not pay more than twenty percent of their incomes on dividend payments. But loans were readjustable based on the rate of inflation, forcing many pobladores to move once the higher rates set in.[66] At the same time, many of those who stayed often did not yet have fully constructed houses or access to urban services. In such conditions, they could not legally sell their houses, even if they now had to assume debt burdens. Foreclosure rates, particularly following the economic implosion, soared.[67] By

1982 and 1983, dispossession, rather than homeownership, was taking place, with devastating consequences. This not only contributed to tens of thousands of pobladores becoming allegados or returning to campamentos, but also to the mounting financial crisis and widespread protests.

Contradictions of the Dictatorial State

Between 1976 and 1981, the dictatorship consolidated its position. In passing the "Seven Modernizations" and a constitutional plebiscite, the regime demonstrated its intention to rule for a long time, however contrived its legal mechanisms were. Officials began to focus on the long term, in which, they evidently presumed, orthodox free-market policies would transform Chile into a country of growth and modern development. Yet Chile's capitalist transformation was far from free of the state's guiding hand, as the "eradication" programs, the repression of organized labor, and support for private development companies demonstrate. These interventions helped to make Chile into an alluring location for international investment. Changes in Santiago's built environment symbolized economic expansion and opportunity, while Chile's flexible, underpaid, and repressed workforce meant cheap costs for business. The dictatorship also touted its extreme poverty reduction programs. Some two hundred thousand pobladores became homeowners in Santiago during this period, coming to live in neighborhoods that symbolized the eradication of poverty. Many of the neighborhoods they left behind became sites of luxury, opulence, and investment, a seeming testament to the possibilities of urban expansion under the dictatorship's neoliberal reforms. Many of these reforms would remain in place well after the end of the dictatorship.

Yet despite all of these seemingly attractive accomplishments, the regime could not realize its vision for development. The situation was tense and contradictory, in which there was a dialectical relationship between the forms of development that the dictatorship sought to implement and breakdowns in order.[68] The dictatorship's own policies, from human rights abuses to neoliberal restructuring, created dislocation, inequality, and need. Celebratory images of the dictatorship and urban renewal papered over political violence and socioeconomic insecurity. The insecurity was evident in everyday efforts to occupy homes considered proper and secure. Chileans of numerous classes struggled to find a domestic life that respected their sense of propriety and social standing via citizenship. The regime faced constant breakdowns and tensions within its governing aesthetic of order. Such contradictions would deepen and spread into widespread dissent during the 1980s, a period of crisis when more and more Chileans would have the opportunity to denounce the legitimacy of the regime.

PART FOUR

DOMESTICATED PERIPHERIES

CHAPTER 7

CONTAINING PROTEST IN THE TRANSITION TO DEMOCRACY

IN LATE 1981 THE RAPID ECONOMIC GROWTH of the preceding four years quickly lost steam. The subsequent depression was even more devastating than the contraction of the mid-1970s. In certain fundamental ways, the harshness of the downturn exposed the dilemmas and contradictions of Chile's capitalist state formation under dictatorship. As the recession painfully deepened, opposition to the regime strengthened and found a powerful forum for critique in the national protests that began in May 1983. Activists questioned the order of the dictatorship with a boldness and openness previously unimaginable. Bringing together a diverse cross section of society, the protestors included not only labor unions and groups of pobladores but also middle- and upper-class sectors.

The national protests, however, ultimately lost momentum, as the numerous groups that had supported them splintered. An opposition movement eventually emerged that political party elites dominated, including the Christian Democrats and a "renovated" Socialist Party that had foresworn much of its previous radicalism and come to support free-market policies. These elites adopted a less confrontational stance as they agreed to use the channels available under the 1980 constitution. One significant reason for the split in the initial protest movement is that the mobilizations themselves became more associated with the forms that they took in certain poblaciones and campamentos. Many would come to see protests among pobladores as the actions of an undisciplined, criminal, and subversive population. Though these protests may have initially expressed, in E. P. Thompson's (1971) classic phrase, a "moral economy of the crowd," they were eventually cast in a very different light. The fear of an ugly disorder in the urban periphery—often linked to concerns over a return to the polarization and breakdown of the Allende years—ultimately contributed to the formation of an opposition coalition that marginalized the mobilization of pobladores.

During the last decade of dictatorship, pobladores were involved in varied types of protests. Many took part in relatively obscure moments of resistance, as when they mobilized over such issues as housing lot sizes and access to public transportation. Remarkably, a number of pobladores once again took part in land seizures. As they mobilized, many suffered intense forms of repression. Even so, pobladores achieved a degree of success in their activism, particularly as they sought to protect and develop their homes. Their protests, moreover, provided an opening that helped to lay the groundwork for an end to the dictatorship.

There were thus important possibilities and limits to protest, the boundaries of which include several crucial, intertwined dynamics in the urban politics of propriety. The protests brought very basic themes to the surface. They were impassioned, public outbursts over fundamental questions of rights, justice, and sociopolitical legitimacy. An analysis of the protests reveals the emotionally charged and often contested expectations that Chileans had about everyday living conditions, the constitution of home, and the obligations of the state. It also illuminates what actions citizens could appropriately take and what demands they could legitimately make as they sought change.

These issues held a particularly potent charge for pobladores, as they occupied a very specific place within the national imagination. If pobladores had long carried the burden of such stigmas as being lazy, dangerous, dirty, and criminal, they had also been a symbol of injustice and of the need for social transformation and activism. During the protests of the 1980s, each of these understandings came to the surface. Broader reactions to the protests that pobladores took part in often swung radically from sympathy to condemnation.[1] While officials at times responded harshly, they could accede to the demands that pobladores had. A close look at the trajectory of the activism in which pobladores took part thus helps to expose the fraught boundaries within which legitimate forms of protest could take place in the margins of urban Chile. It also reveals certain fissures and contradictions at the heart of state formation and national identity.[2] By the end of the dictatorship, a moderate, constrained opposition led a slow-moving transition to democracy. Not coincidentally, pobladores active in protests receded from the national spotlight and had fewer means to take part in successful mobilizations. This happened as pobladores increasingly had homes of their own. Pobladores would come to live in domesticated peripheries, domesticated in both their homes and the polity.

Transforming Campamentos into Poblaciones

By the early 1980s there was a broad gap between the kinds of city spaces that officials promised to develop and actual living conditions. Hundreds of thousands of pobladores in Santiago had endured a decade or more of living either in campamentos or as allegados, phenomena that only increased with the economic crisis. Given this, many would begin to more publicly express their anger. Implicit promises of citizenship had been left unfulfilled. This could occur even when government bodies took a proactive role in transforming campamentos into poblaciones, as in Las Palmeras, the former Campamento Lenin.

Since the military coup, Las Palmeras had continued to grow illegally, despite the threat posed by the dictatorship. The original leaders of the campamento had disappeared, either killed or cast into internal exile. For the most part, the remaining residents knew little of what specifically had happened to their former leaders, an uncertainty that heightened fear and distrust. Several pobladores from Las Palmeras remember how officials harassed and intimidated them. One figure, in particular, stands out: Renca's mayor in the late 1970s, Lieutenant Colonel Patricio Muñoz Vargas. In the words of one resident, Gustavo Retamales, Colonel Muñoz often came to Las Palmeras to "sow terror." Dressed in a military uniform with a gun holstered around his leg, the mayor would work his way through the campamento with a retinue of soldiers and police officers. According to Gustavo, the Colonel insulted residents, peppering his language with epithets. In one of our conversations, Gustavo imitated the mayor: "'And you, what are you doing here? . . . And you slackers [*vagos*] and you women, with your stinking garbage, you don't do anything at all. Do you want us to give you things while you don't have to do anything at all?" (Murphy 2004a, 130). In these recollections, the mayor is condescending, dismissive of the possibility that residents were hardworking, proper citizens who deserved respect and state services.

Residents in Las Palmeras also lived with uncertainty about the future of their neighborhood. Following the coup, a group of residents from more established neighborhoods in Renca claimed to be the rightful owners of Las Palmeras. They demanded that officials restore their properties. Gustavo Retamales had been one of these claimants (Murphy 2004a, 127–30). By the second half of the 1970s, however, Gustavo and the others had increasingly lost hope that they would recover their lands. Following the 1975 Map of Extreme Poverty, officials at MINVU and ODEPLAN identified Las Palmeras as a campamento that would need to be "regulated," "sanitized," and "made well" (Morales et al. 1990, 14). In doing this, the regime indicated that it was committed to transforming the neighborhood through the provision of property titles and basic services.

Some three years into the dictatorship, Gustavo came to the conclusion that the dictatorship would not raze the campamento. There was thus little chance that he would again be recognized as a legitimate property holder in Las Palmeras. At that point, Gustavo decided to move to the campamento, as many others continued to do. In his testimonial, Gustavo justified this decision by claiming first that he and his wife could no longer live as allegados with his parents and that his mother-in-law lived in Las Palmeras. His mother-in-law was also, Gustavo noted, married to the man who became the president of the neighborhood council after the coup. This gave them a connection to someone who would be important in making decisions about the neighborhood's fate. But Gustavo's family members, particularly his cousins, reacted angrily to his decision. Gustavo recalls them as saying, "How is it possible that you, *hombre*, could [take part in this]? These lands also belong to you." For the cousins, moving to Las Palmeras was not only illegal but also a betrayal that undermined their family's claims to property (Murphy 2004a, 127–30).

Officials, however, showed no indication of changing course and they continued to state that they had plans to transform Las Palmeras into a población. Yet during the late 1970s and early 1980s, there was only intermittent progress toward this goal. Residents continued to live in a neighborhood on the borders of legality. By the beginning of the 1980s, residents had received potable water in their homes, but they had only outhouses for toilets and a few paved streets. In order to have electricity, pobladores had unlawfully connected to the power grid. They also lacked uniform lot sizes. A number of houses spilled over into areas that, in an officially sanctioned neighborhood, would have been designated for roads or parks. If residents wanted to own their own homes, they would need to reorder the neighborhood.[3] And since there were so many pobladores, some would have to leave the campamento.

Officials attempted to create the proper lot sizes in Las Palmeras by force, following a frequently used policy that had been put in place to "regularize" urban neighborhoods.[4] Erika Cereño recalls that the municipality of Renca sent a number of workers to Las Palmeras to evict residents, raze certain houses, and reduce the size of some lots. But a number of pobladores put up a spirited resistance, as they blocked the entryways to the campamento with burning tires and makeshift barricades. Following a tense standoff with officials and soldiers, a group of residents met with representatives from the mayor's office. In Erika's recollections, the pobladores spoke sharply to regime officials, saying, "You all have no reason to come here and order us around or to take us away; we might be very modest, but this house is mine and we're going to stay here and no one is going to butt in here" (Murphy 2004a, 106–7). In this recollection, Erika has a clear sense of her rights as a proprietor; officials had no right to touch her home. The authorities, in fact, eventually relented, ordering the municipal workers to leave. From Erika's standpoint, the pobladores of Las Palmeras were thus able to successfully negotiate the protection of their homes.

Yet the campamento remained in limbo, as it was still legally defined as an "irregular" neighborhood. It had, moreover, competing claims for ownership. Because of this, officials from both the municipality and MINVU, in addition to neighborhood leaders, sought to find a more permanent solution. Eventually, the central government, working in conjunction with the municipality and transnational development institutions, changed course and decided to have residents join the hundreds of thousands of pobladores who were part of the "eradication" of campamentos. After they entered a state-sponsored savings plan, the vast majority of Las Palmeras's residents moved into a subsidized housing project. Las Palmeras itself became a park, extolled by municipal officials as a model of how the regime had made the city more attractive and livable.[5] The eradication took place in late 1983, as most of the pobladores from Las Palmeras moved into Lo Velásquez, a neighborhood that had been built on the edge of the municipality of Renca.[6] Like many neighborhoods in the dictatorship's slum removal programs, the new población was at the outermost edge of Santiago, where the city's boundary met the countryside.

The move to Lo Velásquez held a number of attractions for officials and citizens alike. By becoming homeowners in a legally sanctioned area with city services considered basic, the pobladores would have the opportunity to live, as many of them described it, a decent and dignified life. Regime planners, meanwhile, would achieve their goal of producing a developed neighborhood. Yet if the process held out the intertwined promises of homeownership and urban development, it would not necessarily end on happy terms for residents. For them, the process would illustrate the extent to which gaining access to property did not necessarily hold the key to the creation of a secure home life. Within this context, certain spaces for protest would be possible, while others would not.

As a state-planned neighborhood that received funding from the IDB, Lo Velásquez unsurprisingly offered its residents uniform housing with a precise street grid pattern. Residents received a thirty-two-square-meter basic house that included a kitchen, living room area, and bathroom, in addition to potable water, electricity, and sewer services.[7] Residents had the opportunity to build on to their new houses, and many brought parts of their shacks from Las Palmeras with them so as to construct additional rooms. Today, the initial

Figure 7.1. Houses in Lo Velásquez, 2002 (photo by author).

uniformity of the neighborhood's houses has given way to a panoply of styles and shapes, as residents have built additions, torn down walls, painted façades and interiors, laid down tiles, planted gardens, and added fences and security. To a certain degree, the process of ownership has thus included forms of individual distinction and agency.

In order to take part in the eradication, the pobladores had to save money, needing a sufficient amount to pay an initial down payment. Eventually, they would have to assume a fifteen-year loan. Some, however, were not able to afford this. As in relocation programs elsewhere, these pobladores moved to other parts of the city, while others squatted once again in campamentos or went to live as allegados. Some from Las Palmeras would move into cheaper housing in La Pintana, one of the lowest-income municipalities in Santiago. For family and friends, the distance was quite onerous: La Pintana is about an hour and a half away from Renca by bus.[8] The process served to further splinter the cohesiveness and unity of Las Palmeras as it broke up crucial ties of compadrazgo and neighborly support. This phenomenon was rather common in the eradication programs, reinforcing the ethos of individualism and atomization that the dictatorship fostered.

Still, many pobladores who moved to Lo Velásquez remember becoming a homeowner as an intense moment of pride. For Rosa Cancino, the effort to make the down payment was, as she described it, a "great sacrifice," one that "made her cry tears of blood." She remembers what she felt when she first saw her new house:

> When we came to see the completed house, I was very happy and gave thanks to God that he had given me the strength to do the savings . . . all of the sacrifice that I had undertaken was worth it in order to have the house. It was a house made of brick, with a little fence, with a kitchen, water, electricity, and toilets. It was a house, as they say, to live decently. Not like living in a campamento; in the campamento one only has a fountain and you don't have toilets or showers. (Murphy 2004a, 116)

As Rosa's recollection suggests, pobladores could find the benefits of the eradication programs attractive. Beyond granting residents access to solid housing and infrastructure services, the move from a campamento into a población could fulfill their long-held desire to acquire a legal home of their own. It validated the work that pobladores had undertaken, confirming their status and individual accomplishments. They had seemingly become agents in their own destiny, as they received a proper home that matched their sacrifices and social standing.

But social standing and living conditions are transient, shifting according to context and circumstance. For many in Lo Velásquez, the neighborhood did not initially fulfill the expectations that they had of a población. As was typical of many of the poblaciones built for the eradications, the location of Lo Velásquez was at first quite isolated, unconnected to the rest of Santiago by paved roads. Such isolation made many practical, daily tasks time-consuming and onerous. For those pobladores who had work, they generally had to commute long hours to central Santiago or the wealthier areas of the city. Everyone had to spend a great deal of time doing such things as going to market, paying bills, commuting to school, or visiting government bureaucracies. Most residents had to walk at least twenty-five minutes to even have access to public transportation.

As an urban neighborhood, many in Lo Velásquez felt that this isolation was an injustice. A group of dueñas de casa organized a petition to the mayor of the municipality, asking him to provide bus services and to pave the streets. Officials in the municipality initially promised to comply, but months went by and nothing happened. The group eventually decided on a more drastic action as they invited all of the dueñas de casa in the neighborhood to take part in a protest. For the participants, it was a nerve-racking and intense moment of activism. As Rosa remembered it, "All of the *mamás* went to make war on the mayor; we went to make war so that he would provide transportation, because that was his obligation. . . . There were a lot of threats and stuff like that . . .

but when they saw that all of the *mamás* were coming, it was something else. The mayor came out and talked to us" (Murphy 2004a, 117–18). The talks ended well for the pobladoras, as the mayor agreed to provide them with public transportation. Shortly after the protest, the municipality established a bus stop close to the neighborhood.[9]

As in their earlier confrontation in Las Palmeras, pobladores followed their sense of what a proper home and neighborhood should be like in negotiating with authorities. In relenting, officials tacitly agreed with the pobladores' assumptions, recognizing their right to inhabit what bureaucrats referred to as a "fully urbanized neighborhood." As they protested, women from Lo Velásquez assumed the familiar role of demonstrating in public in order to properly fulfill their roles as dueñas de casa. It was the *mamás*, Rosa emphatically states, who went to make war on the mayor. As in the past, Chileans more easily interpreted this kind of mobilization as apolitical. The protest, in fact, united a number of neighbors in Lo Velásquez who held disparate political views. During this period, Rosa had been involved in a human rights committee in Renca, but few women from Lo Velásquez joined her, because, as she put it, "there [were] many Pinochetistas" (supporters of Pinochet) in the neighborhood. Yet in the protest Rosa, a Christian Democrat, and Erika, a Communist Party sympathizer, joined the Pinochetistas. The cause of developing their neighborhoods and establishing proper homes superseded political affiliations. The seemingly apolitical nature of the protests quite naturally gained authority by drawing on the needs of dueñas de casa.

While protestors had to organize in particular ways in order to be successful, they also faced constraints in what they could demand. After residents resolved the issues of public transportation and paved streets, they did not subsequently take part in collective organization at the neighborhood level. For Rosa, the reasons for the subsequent lack of activism are fairly simple: "Now we don't have any needs [to fulfill] and we don't get together to organize or fight for anything else" (Murphy 2004a, 118). With property titles and "basic" infrastructure services, pobladores in Lo Velásquez have ostensibly had their housing and neighborhood needs met. In a certain sense, the neighborhood stands as a testament to successful development. Within state and international aid institutions, it is a sign of successful efforts to "eradicate extreme poverty." The campamento has become a población. Squatters have become homeowners. Another area of the city has become legally sanctioned.

These changes have had important effects. Clearly, pobladores in Lo Velásquez have greater security in their land tenancy and they have also enjoyed some specific improvements in their living conditions. Yet since residents are no longer a governing problem, they are left largely on their own. Any problems that the neighborhood would now experience were less the concern of state and international development institutions. Echoing a complaint made by many pobladores who had taken part in the eradication programs, Gustavo Retamales claimed, "After the move, we were once again forgotten" (Murphy 2004a, 131).

In Lo Velásquez, this new invisibility would make it much more difficult for citizens to criticize the conditions that they would come to live in. Other issues of intense, shared concern to neighborhood residents did not lead to renewed forms of activism. In the years following the completion of the neighborhood, the military regime established a number of new poblaciones and villas in the surrounding area through slum removal and subsidized housing programs. According to many in Lo Velásquez, conditions became significantly less secure. Rivalries and intimidation marked the relations between the residents of Lo Velásquez and the new arrivals. Drug trafficking and street violence increased.

Unsurprisingly in such a context, suspicion among pobladores in the new neighborhoods rose, further undermining a broader sense of solidarity. Residents particularly recall how groups of young men from distinct poblaciones led assaults on other neighborhoods, including robberies. These rival gangs had themselves come from different areas of the city as a part of the eradications.[10] But pobladores in Lo Velásquez were unable to do much to confront these new circumstances collectively. The situation was thus very different from how neighborhood leaders had dealt with similar issues when Campamento Lenin was first established. The decline in neighborhood organizations, the rise in criminality, and the fact that Lo Velásquez represented a successful form of poverty reduction meant that pobladores now had little public voice to denounce their concerns. Given this transformed context, some pobladores nostalgically look back on their lives in the campamentos. Rosa even expressed a desire to return to Las Palmeras: "I'd like to go back . . . it was a different environment" (Murphy 2004a, 118). This was not an altogether uncommon sentiment as certain pobladores longed for a period of collective action, greater social cohesion, and hope in future transformation.

There were even cases in which pobladores moved from established poblaciones to campamentos, especially when debt burdens became too great. Such actions not only defied the logic of state programs, but they also pointed to a gap between the promise of homeownership and social conditions that remained inequitable, insecure, and fractious. Building a safe and desirable home was an ongoing and complex social process, often burdened by setbacks and uncertainty. The government's housing programs did not assure such a home.

In 1985, Eli Cofré moved with her family into a newly built subsidized apartment block close to Lo Velásquez called La Maule (see figure 7.2). The IDB's loan project that had supported Lo Velásquez also helped to fund the construction of La Maule.[11] Like many other new homeowners, Eli described the initial move in positive terms:

> My mom was pleased because it was her house; it was the house that she had always dreamed of for her family. We found the apartment to be beautiful. It was nicely painted, it had playing fields in front, it was full of parks, trees, and a plaza. For us it was something beautiful. We were going to have our bath and everything . . . we could shower with hot water whenever we wanted to. So it was spectacular. . . . La Maule was a villa, a great población and it was the most beautiful thing that could have happened to us. (Murphy 2004a, 155)

The apartment, however, had only two bedrooms, and Eli lived there with her parents and eight siblings. Beyond the cramped quarters, conditions in La Maule were often harsh. The villa became a center of drug trafficking. Police raids and armed confrontations became common. In response to the escalating danger, Eli's parents often forbade the children to go outside. "We lived shut inside the apartment," Eli related. "We couldn't go out to the street because my mom and my dad were afraid that someone might hit us or that we would become involved in the fights that were going on." Eli remembers seeing a poblador knifed; one of her neighbors was shot.

For Eli, the times were tough, full of tense and compromising situations. Eli's parents concluded that living in La Maule was not tenable, ultimately deciding to leave the villa after one particularly unsettling experience. Early on a New Year's morning, a gang of some fifteen youths who were known for their involvement in drug dealing confronted a rival gang outside of Eli's apartment. As Eli recalled it, the young men had knives, metal poles, and rocks; a few had guns. During the ensuing melee, Eli's parents ordered the children to keep away from the window. Yet Eli's mother looked out and one of the young men noticed her and threw a rock at the window. The police arrived later, asking Eli's mother to testify against the people she had seen.

But rather than do that and risk reprisals, Eli's mother and father decided to move their family to Campamento Lo Boza.[12] Giving up on homeownership, basic infrastructure services, and debt, the family searched out a neighborhood that they believed would be more secure. For Eli's family, modern and developed housing had not provided the foundation for a proper

Figure 7.2. La Maule in 2009 (photo by author).

and secure home. Yet the family did not publicly protest the conditions they lived in. Generally speaking, pobladores neither collectively denounced nor rallied around such issues as overcrowding in a legally sanctioned home or neighborhood violence and criminal activity. The latter issue, in particular, was too morally compromising.

There was thus a particular space within which collective action and protest for pobladores in the establishment of legally sanctioned homes was possible. For occupants of neighborhoods such as Lo Velásquez, these areas had become domesticated peripheries. While residents lived in homes that symbolized successful development, they had fewer opportunities for protest and dissent. Through the policies of slum removal and property titling, the creation of domesticated peripheries would become ever more widespread. An increasing number of pobladores would have legal homes of their own. Yet this phenomenon is an important reason why there has been less mobilization in the low-income areas of Santiago both in the final years of the dictatorship and in the ensuing democracy.

Crisis and Mass Mobilization

With the onset of the depression in the early 1980s, the opportunities for establishing a stable home life considered appropriate became increasingly difficult. Chile's long dependence on exporting primary products for its economic health and the speculative, short-term capital flows that streamed in during the boom years were the two most important, intertwined reasons for the crisis. In each case, Chile's need for foreign markets and trade became painfully clear. Beginning in 1981, the unprecedented amount of money and credit that had circulated in Chile in the late 1970s began to rapidly decline. A precipitous drop in foreign direct investment, a contraction in the markets for Chile's exports, and a corresponding decline in the price of such goods as copper, wood products, salmon, and fresh fruit had devastating consequences. Tightening monetary policies in the United States and Great Britain contributed to a rise in interest rates in Chile, causing many banks to readjust their loans upward. A number of businesses failed, while many Chileans lost their homes. This was particularly true of homeowners who faced declining values in their properties. Rising foreclosure rates only worsened the availability of credit and loans.[13]

The crisis spread deep and wide, definitively undermining the façade of progress cultivated by regime officials. In 1982, per capita GNP fell nearly 15 percent, while the number of unemployed rose to 36 percent of the economically active population.[14] Not surprisingly, new construction and housing starts fell precipitously. This dealt a fatal blow to the ambitious housing programs that Pinochet had announced only two years before.[15] Public and private sector debt grew to 143 percent of the GNP by 1985, a particularly prominent example of the debt crisis that began to envelop Latin America generally (Collier and Sater 2004, 372).

In response to the situation, the military regime softened some of its orthodox neoliberal policies as it intervened in the country's largest financial institutions. It also began to use both fiscal and monetary policy to bolster liquidity in the economy. Yet this second option had major limitations, as the primary means of gaining access to international credit was now through the International Monetary Fund (IMF). As happened throughout Latin America and much of the global South, the IMF would demand austerity from Chilean officials in return for loans. The dictatorship—once a pioneer in strict free-market policies—would now reluctantly join numerous countries compelled to accept the prescriptions of neoliberal fiscal health.[16]

The crisis had major effects on urban living conditions and spatial development. In the poblaciones and the campamentos, conditions were particularly dire. According to one survey, close to two-thirds of pobladores in Santiago were undernourished (Schkolnik 1986). While unemployment rates had always been high in these areas during the dictatorship, they rose to unparalleled levels from 1982 to 1986. One survey of the poblaciones and campamentos in

1984 indicated that only 33 percent of those seeking employment had stable jobs. Nearly 25 percent of low-income wage earners took part in government work programs, in which they received 40 to 67 percent of the minimum wage for full-time employment (Oxhorn 1995, 73–74). In Santiago, the military regime used this reserve of cheap labor—totaling more than 13 percent of the employed in 1983—to work primarily on projects to beautify the city. Workers picked up trash, planted trees and flowers, built city parks, and paved streets.[17]

The crisis conditions made it increasingly difficult to establish a home considered appropriate and desirable. Many pobladores responded with levels of activism not seen since Allende's presidency. Organizations that had developed in the poblaciones during the first period of the dictatorship were reinvigorated, while a number of new ones that addressed issues of human rights, housing, nutrition, health care, and labor became active. Most of these organizations concentrated on attempting to ameliorate the crises impacting people's lives. They tended to focus on women, with an emphasis on helping dueñas de casa find the means to provide for their families. Organizations such as *ollas comunas*, food cooperatives, and supplemental income workshops proliferated. According to one survey, of the 120,000 pobladores involved in popular organizations in Santiago in 1983, 80 percent were women (Baldez 2002, 137).[18]

It was not easy to create this level of participation. Taking part in public activities not sanctioned by the regime was still extremely dangerous; many remained understandably fearful. Pobladores, moreover, also had to overcome the feelings of stigma and shame often associated with admitting that one did not have a job and could not provide for one's household. Many interpreted such a situation as a profound individual failure, calling into question one's moral worth. Organizers thus had to convince potential participants to take part. They did so by arguing that pobladores faced intolerable conditions that were not of their own making and they stressed that extreme circumstances justified exceptional forms of organizing and individual action.[19]

In her recollections of this period, Ana Valdés stressed this moral logic. Ana, it will be recalled, was a longtime leader in Población Primero de Mayo (now officially named Huamachuco I). Following the economic crisis of the early 1980s, Ana had to give up much of her work as a community organizer and began to take part in the government-sponsored manual labor programs. Her husband had lost his construction job, one of the hundreds of thousands of positions eliminated during this period. Ana stressed the difficulties her family went through as they passed weeks with little more than a diet of bread, cheese, tea, and sugar. Years later, Ana maintained both a sense of pride and a critical perspective toward the military regime because of the activities she took part in. "I wasn't ashamed of the work," she said. "With all of the misery created by the dictatorship, I did what I had to do to support my family" (Murphy 2004a, 49, 51).[20] For many, the fact that women took part in these programs underscored just how extraordinary and troubling circumstances had become. "It was painful to see the complete poverty," Erika Cereño commented. "The worst was to see women come to the extreme of digging in the dirt [in the work programs], just like the men" (Murphy 2004a, 104).

The emerging sense of crisis and the new channels for participation that became available in the early 1980s opened possibilities for public dissent. The Left became somewhat reenergized, labor unions once again became combative, liberation theology gained a greater foothold in the Catholic church, and student associations blossomed. Feminist organizations began to emerge that challenged both the dictatorship and patriarchy, often moving well beyond the public mobilization of women based solely on their roles as mothers (Pieper Mooney 2009, 134–62). All of these movements benefited from the democratic opening of the early 1980s and from the increasing presence of international solidarity networks, nongovernmental organizations, and the foreign press.[21] On the public stage, political parties also reappeared and certain media provided a forum for more direct and open criticism of the regime.

If many organizations in the poblaciones felt emboldened and began to adopt a more confrontational and militant posture, they nevertheless still had a difficult game to play. As before, these organizations had to ostensibly be dedicated to apolitical tasks, such as the rights of homeownership or the provision of basic forms of sustenance. Demanding more or adopting tactics that crossed the boundaries of presumed propriety exposed these groups to reprisals from the dictatorship. They also risked losing the support of the broader public and their links to international NGOs and the Catholic church. Activists thus had to tread through a very specific sociopolitical field, one fraught with risk and danger. The heightened possibilities and hazardous peril of the time period became particularly difficult for pobladores who took part in urban land seizures during the early 1980s.

The Return of Organized Squatters

At first, officials not surprisingly adopted a firm stance against urban land seizures, warning that they would lead to a chaotic disorder, one they tended to associate with the Popular Unity years. Brigadier General Roberto Guillard, the Governor of Santiago, argued, "If we permit people to not have respect for private property, then we're permitting a society in which the law of the jungle reigns, [one] that permits killing, robbing, and usurping."[22] Land seizures, once again, became a wild frontier, marking civilization from barbarism. Security personnel violently broke up the vast majority of land seizures. MINVU officials, moreover, passed a decree law in 1980 that permitted the government to revoke the right to housing subsidies for pobladores who took part in land seizures.[23]

Yet there was a surprising number of occasions when the military regime permitted squatters to remain on seized land. In September 1983, nearly fifteen thousand pobladores took part in the largest seizure in Santiago's history. They formed two campamentos that they named after Raúl Silva Henríquez and Juan Francisco Fresno, a cardinal and an archbishop, respectively, in the Chilean Catholic church. Throughout the dictatorship, the church had played a particularly visible role in supporting such causes as human rights, affordable housing, and public health. In naming the campamentos after Silva Henríquez and Fresno, the squatters attached themselves to the moral authority that the church granted. Catholic social service organizations, moreover, provided crucial logistical support to the squatters, providing them with food and building materials and acting as intermediaries between officials and the leaders of the squatters.[24]

In the days following the seizure, a number of arguments circulated about whether or not the actions taken by the squatters were appropriate. Officials claimed that Leftist political interests had instigated the seizure, seeking to embarrass the regime on the very day that the General Assembly of the United Nations was meeting to discuss a censure proposal against the dictatorship. Ominously, officials claimed that they had recently discovered a Communist Party "subversive plan" to destabilize the government, of which the land seizure was a part.[25] For their part, pobladores publicly denied any connections to politics or subversion. They argued instead that they were proper citizens who had suffered injustices and intolerable living conditions. The vast majority of the squatters, these pobladores pointed out, could find work only in government-sponsored labor programs, which did not provide an income sufficient to afford housing subsidies. Yet the squatters had nevertheless saved money and they offered to pay what they could in order to receive land titles. As in the past, they also stressed that they had been well organized and disciplined in establishing the new neighborhoods. One of the land seizure's leaders declared that "in the campamento, everything is in order and there aren't any fights, scandals, or robberies, nor is anyone allowed to drink."[26]

Eventually, the dictatorship granted the vast majority of the pobladores the right to remain on the lands that they had seized. Officials thus tacitly conceded that the squatters' demands for housing were legitimate and proper. This was an important concession, contradicting the dictatorship's efforts to define housing as merely a good and not as a right.[27] The activism of pobladores, set within the context of the urban politics of propriety, constrained the neoliberal fundamentalism of the dictatorship. While pobladores would still

Figure 7.3. Campamento Cardenal Juan Francisco Fresno, Santiago, July 1984 (photo by Marco Ugarte).

have to prove their worth as legitimate citizens, they would nevertheless retain a right to housing. This right ultimately allowed them to stay in Campamentos Cardenal Raúl Silva Henríquez and Juan Francisco Fresno.

By the following year, the number of pobladores in the two campamentos grew close to thirty thousand people. Yet officials continued to press their case that left-wing agitators had organized the seizure. In November 1984, they ordered a raid of the neighborhood, carried out by units from the army, the air force, special police forces, and a secretive, "antisubversive" agency, the National Center of Information (CNI). Arriving at four in the morning, the "security forces" employed more than one hundred armored personnel carriers and buses, ten tanks, two helicopters, and a number of police cars. Surrounding the campamentos and initiating a house-to-house search, they forced all males over fourteen into an open field. The process was violent and intimidating: state agents destroyed nearly one hundred shacks and detained more than four hundred. At least one hundred of the detainees, including all of the leaders of the seizure, were sent to Pisagua, a concentration camp in the Atacama Desert, where they were tortured.[28]

Clearly, the dictatorship remained willing to use its most coercive methods. Not surprisingly, such repression had a chilling effect on housing activists. Yet in permitting the campamentos to remain and in helping residents to gain services and property titles, officials also recognized the moral claims that these pobladores had made for housing. They could argue that the seizure itself was illegitimate and that pobladores had been led astray by Marxist provocateurs, but they could not deny that many deserving citizens lived in inappropriate conditions. Between 1980 and 1985, a surprising number of squatters would take advantage of this disjuncture. According to one source, 51,447 would seize land, most of whom would eventually become homeowners (Morales and Rojas 1987, 96). As they took part in these processes, squatters tested the boundaries of activism, discovering both the extreme dangers and the potential rewards afforded by collective mobilization in times of dictatorship.

The Fractious Unity of the National Protests

The question of what legitimate actions activists could take also became a central dynamic in what came to be known as the "days of national protests." The Chilean Copper Miners' Confederation (CTC) organized the first protest day on May 11, 1983.[29] The success that the CTC had in tapping into general levels of discontent led to a sustained protest movement during the next three years. Made up of a diverse cross section of society, the protestors came from labor unions, human-rights groups, certain church organizations, university student associations, the resurgent political parties of the Left and Center, small businesses, and trade associations. Particular neighborhoods and organizations in the poblaciones and campamentos became crucial centers of activism. Yet though the movement was powerful and diverse, it also suffered

Figure 7.4. Street graffiti, mid-1980s, that reads: "For the right to dignified housing" (photo by Kena Lorenzini, 2010, from Kena Lorenzini, *Marcas crónicas: rayados y panfletos de los 80* [Santiago: Ocho Libros, 2010], 82).

from internal schisms, a dynamic underscored by the ways in which the protests played out in Santiago.

In mobilizing, protest organizers called for demonstrations that would make strategic use of the home. Those who took part in the protests kept their children out of school, refrained from shopping and going to work, and boycotted public transportation. At particular moments, protestors banged empty pots, co-opting the symbol used by right-wing opponents of Allende's government. Expressive of deprivation in home life, the banging of empty pots stood as a unifying sign of need. It emphasized how important the protection of home was to the legitimacy of public governance. This kind of protest also mattered strategically: Chileans could make a public statement from the relative safety of their homes. Hearing others banging pots in neighborhoods and apartment blocks confirmed the sense that one was fighting a collective struggle.[30]

Following the first round of protests, the government ordered a number of radio stations closed, brought suit against the protest organizers, and conducted a series of large-scale raids in several poblaciones and campamentos. Military officials, however, found neither major caches of weapons nor activists who had played a central role in the planning of the protests. In anticipation of success in the raids, pro-government media had closely followed them. The failure to find incriminating evidence undercut official arguments about subversives based in the poblaciones and the possibility of a wider insurrection. This subsequently contributed to an increase in support for the mobilizations, and each of the next three protests was bigger than the last. By August 1983, the protests enjoyed broad support among different social organizations and classes (Martínez 1992, 155).

Officials responded in varied ways. They instituted curfews, arrested political party and opposition leaders, ordered raids of neighborhoods and the offices of opponents, and targeted individuals for detention and torture. Eighteen thousand soldiers occupied Santiago for the fourth day of protest in September 1983. The repression was severe: twenty-nine were killed, one hundred wounded, and more than a thousand detained. Casualties were, once again, disproportionately high in the poblaciones and campamentos.[31] But officials also reacted with certain moves toward a political opening, as they attempted to maintain the sense that the regime was continuing to democratize and normalize relations in the country. In late 1983 and 1984 they permitted many exiles to return, lifted censorship on a number of books, and granted new opposition media limited license to function. While the emerging context was replete with danger for protestors, it also appeared to offer them possibilities for negotiation and transformation.

Yet if the protest movement was gaining in strength, it also still struggled to overcome the great differences between its social bases and find a common way to express its dissent. In Santiago, the protests took on distinct characteristics according to the spaces of the city within which they took place.[32] In the city center, protestors marched in the main thoroughfares and denounced the regime in front of symbolically important buildings and monuments. Including a cross section of Chileans, these demonstrations often began during the day in university campuses or in particular neighborhoods. They tended to end in confrontations with riot police that could last into the night. While these confrontations were often violent, they generally did not produce high casualty rates, due in no small measure to the fact that national and international media outlets closely followed these events. In the barrio alto, by contrast, demonstrators occupied the streets in their cars. They would honk their horns and drive slowly so as to stop traffic. In more densely populated areas, particularly in certain apartment buildings, residents banged empty pots. There were, however, certain neighborhoods in the wealthier sections of the city that remained quiet. Overall, confrontations were few in the barrio alto.

In the poblaciones and campamentos, the mobilizations tended to be concentrated in particular neighborhoods and were more violent. They also often lasted well into the night, much longer than the protests elsewhere. Neighborhoods with a history of Communist Party mobilization were the most active, although a small number of neighborhoods settled by the MIR and the Socialists were also active.[33] In Renca, for example, poblaciones and campamentos originally settled with Communist Party support, such as the Primero de Mayo, became centers in the protests. There was very little activity, however, in neighborhoods such as Las Palmeras (and later in Lo Velásquez), where the MIR had played a crucial role in its establishment.[34] The población Primero de Mayo, like other areas that retained a Communist Party presence, could build on a more cohesive, long-standing base of activists. This helped to facilitate organization and it made infiltration by regime agents and informants more difficult.[35]

Many protestors in the poblaciones and campamentos took part in peaceful marches and the banging of empty pots. Yet a number also developed more confrontational and militant methods, particularly when neighborhood protests elicited a strong response from regime agents. On the days of announced protests, demonstrators in poblaciones like Primero de Mayo often woke up early to begin to fortify their neighborhoods.[36] At entry points, protestors erected barricades made from tires, rocks, barbed wire, wood, and scrap metal. They armed themselves with Molotov cocktails, rocks, metal poles, and glass bottles. In the streets, some would place *miguelitos*, small, circular objects made from nails that could puncture the tires of police and military vehicles. There was often an air of camaraderie to the proceedings, even as all residents did not necessarily take part. Groups of women made meals and coffee for the protestors, while the music of banned artists might be heard. Residents listened to Radio Cooperativa to be informed about the nature of the marches and mobilizations throughout the country. Sometimes police officers would dismantle a particular barricade, initiating conflicts with young pobladores. Others might scramble to reinforce barricades in other sections of the neighborhood.

In their recollections today, many activists nostalgically recall the sense of unity, passion, and struggle that the protests facilitated, despite the repression and hardship (Parra, Valdés, and Soto in Murphy 2004a). Demonstrators publicly recovered long-suppressed forms of public expression and communal defiance. Common slogans from the Popular Unity years reemerged: "the people united will never be defeated" and "we shall overcome [*venceremos*]." Yet while protestors united over a sense of the past, they also looked to the present and the future. Los Prisioneros, a popular band with a working-class background, expressed this sentiment in one of their songs with the lyrics, "Here comes the voice of the '80s . . . leave behind the apathy of the '70s, open your eyes, get on your feet . . . realize that you're alive" (Los Prisioneros 1983).

Figure 7.5. Banging empty pots on the day of a national protest (photo titled "In the Family: Get Out, Pinochet Assassin, Sept. 8, 1983," by Kena Lorenzini, 2007, from Kena Lorenzini, *Fragmento fotográfico: arte, narración y memoria* [Santiago: Ocho Libros, 2007], n.p.).

The protests were intense, emotional, and often chaotic. In speaking of the events years later, participants would raise their voices as they passionately described their memories: the moment at which they threw a rock, the time when an armored personnel carrier plastered protestors with a water cannon, or the day when regime agents indiscriminately fired machine guns into a neighborhood. Memorable and cathartic, these experiences brought the protestors together in a shared struggle, further developing a sense of common identity and camaraderie. As the mobilizations stretched into the night, protestors often cut off electrical towers. The sky became clouded over with smoke from burning tires and the acrid smell of tear gas hung in the air, stinging the eyes and burning the throat.

While the protests could be frenzied, they did follow a certain moral logic. They represented a unique opportunity for pobladores to directly confront agents of the dictatorship and express their disgust. The construction of barricades and the pitched street battles with military and police forces enabled pobladores to protect themselves and their homes. These actions signaled a defiant, if fleeting, declaration of independence from the sovereign power of the dictatorship. Raúl Soto, one of the teenagers who played a role in the protests in Primero de Mayo, characterized the mobilization in these terms: "Inside Renca, the most combative sector was our población. For the protests and the strikes, the Primero de Mayo was a liberated zone. The repression didn't enter in here, and if it entered, there was a fight . . . When the cops [*pacos*] wanted to come in to repress us, we would cut off the principal streets. We'd be on the corners where we made barricades . . . and we'd hit them with rocks."[37]

Certain protestors also chose other targets with specific goals in mind. Groups of pobladores from Primero de Mayo set fire to the local offices of a mothers' center and the government-sponsored work programs. Protestors also attacked power centers and electricity wires, causing widespread blackouts and undermining the regime's efforts to claim that everything was normal and under control. Other actions, even including looting and kidnapping, carried similar justifications. As Soto indicated, "People didn't have anything to eat. There was looting in the bakeries. . . . All of the people took things: pork, cheese, soft drinks, everything in the bakeries. I also remember that the Manuel Rodríguez Patriotic Front [a left-wing rebel organization] kidnapped General Carreño, and the Front asked them to send goods here to our sector. So all of the trucks came here loaded with stuff, because our sector was known for its popular character" (Murphy 2004a, 69). For Raúl, acts of looting and kidnapping provided food for undernourished pobladores and thus legitimately responded to the extraordinary circumstances of the period.[38]

But such actions could also be controversial. Even in the neighborhoods that were the most active, there was not a consensus about what methods pobladores had a right to take part in. Different groups of pobladores sought their own paths through the protests. Local parish priests often negotiated between police officials and groups of pobladores to put an end to street conflicts, while groups of women might confront a military patrol that forcefully broke into a house.[39] During the crises of the early to mid-1980s, the limits delineating what actions could be taken legitimately by pobladores were more porous. For some, more violent and combative forms of protest seemed acceptable, given that the dictatorship maintained its grip on power, living conditions had worsened, and discontent had reached unprecedented levels. But given the hostile social field within which pobladores trod, taking part in these actions entailed major risk: repression, stigmatization, further exclusion, and the dismissal of their overall cause.

On the national scene, groups that advocated armed revolution began to play a larger role. The Communist Party asserted in 1980 that all forms of struggle against the dictatorship were acceptable, thereby renouncing the party's tradition of seeking peaceful change through institutional means.[40] Some Communists and former members of the MIR helped to found the Manuel Rodríguez Patriotic Front in late 1983. In addition to the targeted kidnappings that Raúl mentioned, the Front also took part in assassinations, bank robberies, and the bombings of bus and train stations. While such actions were not widespread, they received considerable media attention and contributed to the sense on the part of many that Chile was heading toward polarization and a violent breakdown. This was particularly the case when the dictatorship took on a more belligerent and aggressive stance in late 1983.

These reactions contributed to setbacks within the protest movement, as many groups expressed their fears that the mobilizations had become counterproductive and dangerous to stability. For many, the climate evoked the polarized conflicts of the period before the coup. This general attitude cast more militant forms of protest as illegitimate.[41] Between November 1983 and March 1984, the opposition did not stage any national protests, as the different factions failed to agree on the effectiveness of the mobilizations and the methods that they should use. When the protests did reemerge, they often struggled to achieve the levels of unity that they had initially enjoyed. During some of the protests in 1984, activism among the middle- and upper-income sectors barely materialized. As a result, the protests in Santiago became more concentrated and sustained in the combative poblaciones and campamentos.

Not surprisingly, officials linked the violence in these poblaciones to subversion and crime. In the series of raids following the first protests labeled Operación Limpieza (operation cleanup), military and police officials defined their primary objective as "identifying and detaining subversive and/or delinquent elements."[42] The use of such a familiar discursive register signaled the return of more aggressive tactics. During the next three years, the number of raids in these areas would reach levels not seen since the period immediately following the military coup, with a subsequent rise in the number of those detained and tortured.[43]

For their part, many opposition leaders insisted that the protests in the poblaciones were an appropriate response to the degradation caused by the dictatorship, but they strongly condemned anyone who took part in violence, theft, or vandalism. In a declaration to the public, the archbishop's office in Santiago argued that "the inhabitants of the poblaciones and the campamentos have demonstrated their dissatisfaction [in the protests]. They ask for work, dignity and participation." However, the statement continued, there was "a danger of isolated acts of vandalism promoted by criminals [*antisociales*] who don't represent the feelings of the people."[44] Leaders of the Democratic Alliance, an increasingly influential coalition that united the political parties of the Center and the moderate Left, expressed a similar sensibility. In a communiqué issued on September 3, 1984, one day before another scheduled mobilization, the coalition stated:

> The Democratic Alliance, in anticipation of the success that the days of protest on September 4 and 5 will have, reaffirm their peaceful character and condemn in advance any violent act that occurs, no matter who provokes it. . . . The Chilean people will not use violence or crime, in spite of the provocations that it might be subjected to. We ask Chileans . . . to protest in strictly nonviolent ways. Whoever acts differently doesn't represent the spirit of the call made by the Alliance, assists the regime, and only creates a pretext for strong and excessive repression.[45]

In each of these declarations, the writers argued that there was a unified, peaceful protest movement that expressed the true will of *el pueblo chileno*, the Chilean people. Anyone who committed violence or acts of vandalism was not a part of the movement. Ultimately, they did not deserve a legitimate and proper place in the nation. Just like regime officials who committed human rights abuses and had overseen the degradation of Chilean social life, these antisociales violated the moral sentiments of the nation and its aesthetic of order. Such declarations were part of efforts that sought to unite the opposition and reassert the basic underpinnings for resistance to military rule.

Women's organizations began to play an increasingly prominent role in this task. Importantly, many of these organizations adopted strands of feminism, as they stressed how women suffered from both exploitative domestic relationships and constrained horizons, in which their social roles and practices were limited. These organizations emphasized, moreover, that women deserved basic rights of equality, irrespective of their status as mothers or as being dependents of men. One of the basic premises of many of these activists was that women suffered from the double burden of dictatorship and patriarchy.[46]

Yet despite the importance of this emerging feminism, women who took part in public forms of mobilization also claimed a privileged moral position in their roles as women. They maintained that they rose above the political fray and served the interests of their families and of the nation. As such, they argued that they could overcome the internal divisions and political party rivalries in the opposition. In a series of demonstrations and meetings, the most famous of which was held in the Caupolicán Theater in Santiago on December 29, 1983, they sought to call attention to the ways in which the dictatorship had provided a troubling incursion into the domestic sphere. Delivered by women of the Left and Center, this message helped to bridge the differences and rivalries in the opposition, including the many organizations dedicated to labor, human rights, feminism, and poblador issues (Baldez 2002, 146–67).

While this message of unity brought the movement together, it left little room for some of the tactics practiced in the more militant poblaciones and campamentos. Many in the opposition cast actions such as violent confrontations with riot police, looting, the blocking of roads, the cutting of electricity wires, and the burning of government buildings as the acts of terrorists and criminals. Raising fears of social breakdown, these actions evoked for many the Popular Unity years and the dangers associated with an unbridled mobilization among pobladores. Such attitudes seemed to tap a general sensibility, at least as it took shape in public debates and in polling data. In a survey performed in 1985, 80 percent disapproved of such tactics as spraying graffiti, erecting barricades, and throwing stones.[47] While this survey is probably overstated given the context of repression, it—and others like it—were nevertheless taken seriously by leaders of the opposition as they developed their political strategies.[48] In other polls, most stressed their desire for an immediate return to democracy, but they also expressed support for granting the government a strong hand in reinstating order. A majority, in fact, backed the institution of states of siege between 1984 and 1986 (Martínez 1992, 143). The last state of siege was put in place in July 1986 and lasted for several months, facilitating a severe crackdown that undermined the cohesiveness of the protestors. Yet again, activists among pobladores would suffer disproportionately from the dictatorship's repression.[49]

Legacies in the Transition to Democracy

Repression, internal division, and an improving economic situation ultimately led to the overall exhaustion of the national protests in 1986. Protests continued after that, but generally not on a national scale. The Democratic Alliance increasingly came to dominate the opposition and it sought the end of the dictatorship through institutional means. The Alliance became the Concertación, the group of political parties that led the campaign in the 1988 plebiscite against the continuation of Pinochet's rule, following the dictates of the 1980 constitution. In its campaign, the Concertación distanced itself from the street demonstrations, specifically seeking to minimize mobilization among groups of pobladores. Concentrating on an upbeat image of order, the Concertación adopted the mottoes "Happiness is Coming" and "Democracy in the Country and in the Home." The political campaign held out the promise that the hardships and conflicts of the recent past would come to an end.[50] The home was, not surprisingly, a part of this.

Following its victories in the 1988 plebiscite and in the 1989 presidential campaign, the coalition led the country through a transition from dictatorship to democracy, receiving widespread praise as it consolidated neoliberal policies. In housing and urban development, planners in the Concertación sought to create a technical and well-ordered government administration that would produce manageable populations and attractive landscapes. In certain cases they followed practices put in place by technocrats in the military regime. They sought to "combat extreme poverty," for example, by carrying out a series of eradications and providing property titles and certain infrastructure services for pobladores on an unprecedented scale. Certain elements of the governing order that planners in the dictatorship sought to instill thus continue to have relevance and efficacy in the present. In the waning years of the dictatorship and in the years that followed, a diverse group of social actors, including planning officials, international investors, development experts, and even many of Santiago's residents and visitors to the city, found elements of the neoliberal order attractive.

Clearly, the protests and the ultimate success of the opposition movement demonstrated a general rejection of the dictatorship. Yet certain elements of the dictatorship's approach have remained, a sometimes imperceptible part of the contemporary social fabric. Pobladores were most effective in their protests when they were seen as taking the proper steps to express their moral outrage at the abnormal and inappropriate level of need in their home lives. Such a register tapped into an understanding of the responsibilities of the Chilean state and of the rights of citizens. At the same time, it also fits well with the neoliberal notion that technocrats should target spending policies and focus resources on the circumstances of "extreme poverty." Such a register has helped more pobladores to have homes of their own. But many pobladores still live in a context of inequity, violence, and insecurity.

In the more open and tolerant environment of the post-dictatorship, pobladores have struggled in less visible and more atomized ways to produce homes that they consider desirable and appropriate. In general, they have come to live in domesticated peripheries. They occupy homes of their own on the margins of Chilean society and yet have little recourse to take part in the kinds of activism that they did before the military coup and during the national protests. Instead, they "participate" in very particular kinds of poverty reduction programs. Such programs eventually became a model of success for social reform within neoliberal democracies. Yet celebrants of these programs fail to recognize the crucial contributions that pobladores who adopted more combative forms of activism have made to current conditions. Despite their current marginalization, they contributed to both making Chile's return to democracy possible and ensuring that low-income Chileans would have an ongoing right to urban housing.

CHAPTER 8

FRACTURES OF HOME AND NATION
Property Titling after the Dictatorship

IT WAS A GREY, COOL DAY in early winter. It was threatening to rain but it had held off—fortunately, as it was moving day for the residents of the campamento. After more than six years of organizing and many false starts, these pobladores had finally become beneficiaries of MINVU's latest "eradication" program, Chile Barrio. They were leaving behind a densely packed neighborhood of some 650 residents, a campamento largely hidden behind eight-foot concrete walls. Residents in two neighboring poblaciones and a villa could not see the campamento from their homes. With only a small opening to the street, the campamento was hardly even noticeable to passing traffic. Like most of the remaining campamentos in Santiago by the early 2000s, this neighborhood was generally hidden from view for most residents of the city. Yet people who lived nearby certainly knew about it, as did those outsiders who came to the neighborhood looking for drugs.

Residents from the campamento—such as Roberto and Carmen—were moving to their brand-new apartment building, Villa Topocalma. Many had come to lend a hand in the move: government social workers, employees from NGOs, and volunteers from Catholic charities. For the heavy lifting, soldiers from an army regiment arrived with three military buses and four trucks. (To the consternation of everyone involved, however, the regiment turned up more than two hours late.) With a cameraman in tow, the mayor of Renca, Vicky Barahona, made a brief appearance, filming a few conversations with pobladores who expressed their excitement about the move. The regional governor of the metropolitan area of Santiago, Marcelo Trivelli, helped various pobladores with their personal items, something he often did in the eradications. Wearing one of the fashionable suits he's known for, the minister of housing and urbanism, Jaime Ravinet, showed up in the afternoon at the new villa. In a brief ceremony, he congratulated the residents on becoming homeowners and praised the sacrifices they had made. It was a day to enjoy, he claimed, and a demonstration of how pobladores, NGOs, and government institutions could work together to "overcome poverty" (*superar la pobreza*) and "end misery."

The eradication was a symbol of the state's efforts in the area of "extreme poverty" reduction. Governor Trivelli and Minister Ravinet, two officials from the Center-Left Concertación government, and Mayor Barahona, a leader of the right-wing Independent Democratic Union Party, all wanted to take part in the event, knowing that becoming property owners signaled a profound transformation in the lives of pobladores. Reporters and camerapersons from one of the major television networks and a few newspapers recorded scenes of smiling residents as they first stepped into their new apartments.

Events such as this one were relatively common throughout the 1990s and early 2000s. In the media, such moments projected an image of triumph and unity. Joaquín Lavín and Ricardo Lagos, adversaries in the 1999 presidential campaign, appeared together at what reporters and government officials touted as the last eradication of a campamento in the municipality of Santiago. Coverage depicted the occasion as historic, and, in an important sense, it was. Municipal authorities and central government planners had, after all, been removing slums from downtown Santiago since the time of Benjamín Vicuña Mackenna's reforms in the 1870s. But it now appeared as if that was all over.[1] In central Santiago, the campamentos, such visible signs of poverty and underdevelopment, were gone. Just as importantly, the land seizures were also largely a phenomenon of the past. Carefully designed property titling and eradication programs stood in their place. Collaboration and unity, rather than confrontation and discord, supposedly held sway. Even political adversaries could come together in these efforts to overcome poverty and transcend the past.

For celebrants of Chile's post-dictatorship democracy in the 1990s and early 2000s, the eradications and low-income housing programs were an indication that the country was entering an era of stability, development, and reconciliation. In promising dignified housing for the urban poor, these programs offered redemption for a nation battered by dictatorship, social schisms, and crises. The nation, moreover, gained international prestige from the programs, as influential observers in development institutions, financial organizations, and the media lauded the programs as a technocratic model for how to reduce poverty while maintaining fiscal discipline. This image was particularly powerful in the 1990s, when proponents of unfettered free markets viewed the spread of neoliberal governing projects as an epochal, ideological victory for American-style democracy. Chile was a poster child for this shift. As the story went, the governments of the Concertación were capable, democratic, and forward-looking. Achieving key reforms and embracing global capitalism, they had set the stage for an unprecedented period of growth, development, and stability.

A number of analysts have astutely criticized this celebratory image. They have examined how the country still lived in the shadow of the Pinochet regime. Debates raged about how to both remember the repression and democratize the country's governing institutions.² The country's labor regimes, consumptive practices, extreme levels of inequality, and dependence on primary products for export all point to continuities with the political economy put in place by the Chicago Boys. In exploring these phenomena, the critics have tended to focus on the silences and poorly recognized effects of Chilean neoliberalism, including its many victims. They have revealed, moreover, how the myth of a successful Chile has supported neoliberal forms of state making in the post-dictatorship.³

For all of the insights that the critics have made, they have tended to adopt a historical scale of analysis that works between the dictatorship and the present. Many describe the "Chilean miracle" as simply a thin veneer over a project irrevocably stained by the legacies of Pinochet. Others, in a more sympathetic vein, interpret the rule of the Concertación as one that made progress, even as it confronted ongoing dilemmas and obstacles. Yet few view the governments of the Concertación as the result of the neoliberal context of the 1990s and 2000s, continuities with the dictatorship, and longer-term legacies in state formation. In terms of the present context, not many have explored just how simultaneously destructive and creative the capitalist expansion since the late 1980s has been, transforming the social and spatial landscapes that Chileans inhabit.

I seek to provide these perspectives here by analyzing the eradication and property titling programs of the post-dictatorship, both a part of the massive construction boom that has taken place in the city. These programs have been enormously productive. Through the unprecedented construction of subsidized housing complexes, they have changed the face of low-income Santiago. The campamentos are practically gone; villas and poblaciones stand in their place. In providing housing on a massive scale, the post-dictatorship governments have implemented programs that are ambitious and expensive. They have, moreover, responded to long-standing demands for homeownership. Yet attempts at building homes for pobladores have been fragmentary and partial, based on particular understandings of poverty, in which there has been an emphasis on ridding the country of campamentos and homelessness. State bodies, citizen organizations, NGOs, charities, and development organizations have taken part in these efforts in well-publicized national campaigns. As such, eradication and property titling programs have been a part of efforts to build national unity. Placing these programs within the context of the resulting homes on the urban periphery, however, points to some of the nation's most prominent fissures, underscoring ongoing tensions within Chile's urban politics of propriety.

"To Be Defined as a Campamento"

In early 2002, I began spending time with Cecilia Castro and Ana Lamilla, the president and vice president, respectively, of the neighborhood council in Lo Boza, a neighborhood that a 1997 government-contracted "Survey of Precarious Settlements" had legally defined as a campamento (INVI 1997). (The survey was a rough equivalent to the Maps of Extreme Poverty overseen by the dictatorship.) Nestled at the base of the Cerro Colorado, one of the numerous "hills" in Santiago that form a part of the Andes mountain range, Lo Boza maintained its image as a rural settlement, even though recently constructed neighborhoods had pushed the outer limits of Santiago past the campamento. Some of these new neighborhoods were decidedly middle and lower-middle class. Protected behind iron gates and concrete walls, they had two-story homes with small backyards and driveways. These neighborhoods stood in stark contrast to Lo Boza and another campamento that remained in that section of Renca. They were also quite different from the many poblaciones and villas that had been established in the sector since the 1980s, including three low-income housing projects built in the late 1990s and early 2000s.

The majority of Lo Boza's residents were squatters on municipal lands, although some illegally occupied privately owned properties and others rented on either a formal or informal basis. Many tended to have a partial claim to the lands they inhabited: some held contested land titles sold to them by swindlers, while others had lived in their homes for nearly two decades and had put the land to productive use, thus theoretically allowing them rights to the land through adverse possession.[4] In relation to the tightly packed neighborhoods and apartment complexes that most in Renca had come to inhabit, the housing lots in Lo Boza were fairly large and many residents were able to maintain livestock and gardens. The houses were generally of different sizes, but they were almost entirely of a poor quality. Since the neighborhood's founding in the early 1980s, most residents had fashioned their dwellings from wood, concrete blocks, cardboard, and tin. The cheap construction of the houses came at a cost: during the winter wet season, storms often caused flooding and damage. Since the mid-1990s, both MINVU and charity organizations had

Figure 8.1. Sector of Campamento Lo Boza, 2002 (photo by author).

supported projects to improve Lo Boza's housing stock, primarily through the provision of mediaguas—one- and two-room, solidly built wooden structures.

As neighborhood council leaders, Cecilia and Ana had a busy schedule. They spent much of their time in the council building, an unassuming brick structure. They administered Lo Boza's health care and day care centers, worked on grants and reports for funding institutions, and oversaw the council's budget. They also helped residents take part in nutrition and microenterprise programs sponsored by government entities and NGOs. Most importantly, they were organizing a "committee of the homeless" so that most of Lo Boza's residents could move to a newly built subsidized housing project. In all of these projects, the neighborhood council had worked with an extraordinary number of institutions: six national government bodies, three administrative units in the municipality of Renca, four Chilean social service organizations; NGOs from the United States, Germany, Spain, and Luxemburg; architects from Harvard University; the embassies of Australia and Norway; one of Chile's oldest and most prominent banks, the Banco Edwards; and the Chilean Chamber of Construction.[5]

In receiving such support, the council had achieved a number of accomplishments. Beyond improving the neighborhood's overall housing stock and establishing the health clinic and day care center, the council had provided residents with access to potable water, ensured access to regular public transportation, and initiated a number of workshop training sessions and support groups. It was also laying the foundation for many residents to become homeowners. These initiatives had granted Ana and Cecilia certain clout and prestige among both their neighbors and social service and development organizations.

Even so, Ana and Cecilia could be very critical of their situation and the work they undertook. According to Cecilia, much of the success that the neighborhood council had achieved hinged on the fact that Lo Boza fit the definition of being a campamento. As she said: "It makes me very angry. . . . The concept of poverty is really poorly focused in this country. . . . To be defined as a campamento is humiliating, but it also means that we can receive help. If you're considered a campamento, you receive more help. The institutions will come to help you. If we weren't a campamento, we wouldn't be able to get this help. No one would notice us" (Murphy 2004a, 154).

In making this argument, Cecilia underscores a central limitation to how both the urban politics of propriety has generally operated in Chile and reductionist understandings of poverty and need. For state officials, private donors, and development organizations, the definition of *campamentos* as being in a state of "extreme poverty" helps to target resources to the "neediest," a key part of Chile's celebrated policies in poverty reduction. Yet this definition entails a horizon for the redistribution of resources, limiting what citizens can demand and receive. While cast as an objective measure that impartially identifies the "extreme poor," such a definition can also be "humiliating," acting counter to how neighborhood organizers such as Cecilia seek respect and dignity. Cecilia's critique underscores how the provision of housing, property titles, and infrastructure services in poverty reduction programs provide an important boundary in claims-making for low-income residents. It also points to how meanings of "extreme poverty" operate within a social field that produces stigmas and distinctions.

In post-dictatorship Chile, development work in the campamentos taps into a long-standing and widely shared belief that these kinds of neighborhoods should not exist. Still legally defined as being in a state of emergency, campamentos remain abnormal spaces in need of interdiction. To a lesser extent, low-income Chileans who live as allegados also continue to be "homeless" and worthy of support.[6] Pobladores are expected to live in legally sanctioned homes with property titles. Given this, campamentos have active neighborhood councils that work with governmental bodies, international NGOs, and charities. This kind of organization is a profound and ongoing effect of the urban politics of propriety and of state power. It ran against an important trend in the first sixteen years of the post-dictatorship, in which the popular sectors tended not to mobilize as they once had (Paley 2001; Delamaza 2005).[7]

Even with a return to popular activism in 2006, established poblaciones have continued to experience declines in participation and mobilization. Yet pobladores in campamentos can organize, as they have a ready platform from which to denounce their conditions. Still, the space for this organization has been a particular one. From her perspective as a neighborhood leader and pobladora, Cecilia underscores how the Concertación had a reformist agenda that was piecemeal and fragmentary, targeted at objectives that could paper over a hostile landscape of exclusion and insecurity, in which legacies from the past often troubled the present.

The Chilean Model and Its Discontents

Since the late 1990s, three recessions, the reemergence of popular protests, and a turn to the Left across much of Latin America have taken the luster off of the Chilean neoliberal model. But there had already been discontent, signs of which publicly surfaced at the end of the twelve-year economic boom in 1998. During that year, Pinochet's arrest in London sparked acrimonious debate about how to come to terms with the legacies of dictatorship, especially in the fields of human rights and constitutional reform. Widely publicized poll numbers indicated that a majority had a negative assessment of public institutions and believed that the economic expansion had served the interests of the national elite and foreign investors (Programa de las Naciones Unidas para el Desarrollo 1998, 2004). Schisms within the Concertación appeared.[8] The recession, meanwhile, had significant consequences. Unemployment in Santiago rose from just above 6 percent to 15 percent between 1998 and 2001 (Winn 2004c, 55).

Popular forms of mobilization started to surface, though on a relatively small scale compared to the protests of the 1980s and the activism before the military coup. In Santiago, some pobladores once again took part in land seizures. In 1999, a group of some five thousand famously seized land in the municipality of Peñalolén, next to a middle-class community known for its environmental ethos (Equipo Político SurDA 1999; Salcedo 2010). There were other seizures, including some occupations of newly built subsidized housing projects. With the exception of the seizure in Peñalolén, however, the Ministry of the Interior responded harshly, ordering the police to violently dislodge the squatters.[9] Officials also made it clear that pobladores who took part in seizures would not subsequently be able to enter subsidized housing programs.[10] The government sought to protect private property and low-income housing, seeing the latter as a crucial market that it wished to develop.

In response to both the signs of discontent and Pinochet's loss of influence, the Lagos administration (2000–2006) expanded certain reforms and moved forward in seeking to expose and prosecute the dictatorship's human rights violations. Still, despite some internal debate, the administration continued to embrace a neoliberal development model, which often garnered them praise from abroad. Heraldo Muñoz, the secretary general under President Lagos, wrote in an op-ed piece in 2002 that "the world looks at us as a reliable, trustworthy, and stable country that is progressing" (Muñoz 2002). Muñoz cited all of the countries and trading blocs that the government had recently signed or would soon sign free trade agreements with: the European Union, Canada, Mexico, the United States, China, Japan, Australia, and Switzerland, among others. For Muñoz, the country was becoming more cosmopolitan and open, leaving behind the international stigma that it suffered from during the dictatorship and the isolation that it felt under Allende.

It was also generating crucial foreign investments, the likes of which supported a boom in infrastructure, financial services, and real estate. This translated into a whirlwind of frenetic building, including major changes in Santiago's landscape. Since the late 1980s, construction in the city has taken place on an unprecedented scale. The two tallest buildings in South America now highlight the skyline, part of a general boom in high-rise building that has led Chileans to dub the commercial and residential district in the eastern part of the city "Sanhattan." MINVU and the Ministry of Public Works have refurbished parks and constructed a number of new ones. From its original two, the metro subway system has been extended to five lines. Three new major highways that serve Santiago have been built since 1990, in addition to countless byways and overpasses, and even a throughway under the Mapocho River in the city center. The well-off residents of Santiago's east side can now drive to the airport or the coast without having to work their way through stop-and-go traffic in Estación Central, the neighborhood that once so troubled Pinochet as being out of sync with Chile's "quality and rank." In this case, at least, different social classes barely see each other and they need not touch.[11]

The building has been particularly noteworthy in housing. According to one source, since 1990 there has been more housing construction per capita in Chile than in any other country (Salcedo 2010, 91). Through 1998, housing starts approved and initiated in the country grew to unprecedented rates of well beyond one hundred thousand per year, reaching a high of 143,813 in 1996. Such numbers far surpassed the levels of building construction from the 1960s to the mid-1980s, when total construction stayed annually under fifty thousand. The one exception to this, however, is the first year of Allende's presidency (Banco Central 2001, 264). In Santiago, housing starts climbed to nearly 62,151 in 1997, also an all-time record. Since 1998, housing construction has been considerably more volatile, following the overall ups and downs of the broader economy, as recessions in 2001–2002 and 2008–2009 followed the contraction of the late 1990s. Housing construction did, however, once again approach the levels of the mid-1990s from 2003 to 2008.[12]

Officials in the Concertación unambiguously celebrated such construction. For Secretary General Muñoz, it was an indication that the Concertación had facilitated an attractive climate of growth and investment that permitted the country to become more modern. Even so, Muñoz conceded that the government had work to do: the nation's poverty rates had to come down, the income gap remained intolerably high, and there was a need for more meaningful forms of citizen participation and social integration. Ultimately, however, Muñoz dismissed any criticisms and downplayed any tensions that might exist. He urged Chileans to overcome their divisions, look beyond parochial interests, and "believe the story" about Chile. In the end, this would "move forward a national agenda."

Muñoz's view represented a dominant one within the Concertación. Not only would the government achieve market growth and development, it would also build consensus. The coalition's name reflected this latter goal: *concertación* includes a sense of reconciliation, harmony, and coordination. Officials thus ostensibly sought to work in concert with the citizenry to both overcome the legacies of the dictatorship and achieve an alternative future. Beyond developing types of citizen participation and decreasing poverty, this included reforming the 1980 constitution, reducing the power of the military, and permitting the prosecution of human rights violators from the dictatorship. In assessing these changes, officials in the Concertación argued that they were leaving the past behind. In his annual address to the nation in 2005, President Lagos asserted that the transition to democracy had been completed (Gobierno de Chile, *Mensaje Presidencial* 2005, v–xxvii).

Such an assertion, however, failed to account for the many legacies that remained. It also assumed that a technocratic and neoliberal form of governance should be the standard through which to assess both the transition and the kind of democracy that Chileans should aspire to have. This view, moreover, did not engage with how Chile's continued embrace of global capitalism had produced a volatile mix of spectacular growth, labor insecurity, periodic contractions, and unequal distribution. Neoliberal policies contributed to the making of these phenomena, ultimately troubling governance and the smooth implementation of programs in poverty reduction and housing.[13]

Putting the Model in Its Place

Two brute statistics have supported the story of Chile as a neoliberal governing success. Between 1986 and 1998, the country averaged more than 7 percent growth in annual GNP as the size of its economy more than doubled (Banco Central 2001, 50). During the same period, government statistics indicate that the percentage of Chileans living below the poverty line decreased from a little more than 40 percent to about 20 percent (MIDEPLAN 2000, 333). Rates of economic growth and poverty reduction have subsequently slowed, due largely to the three recessions. Between 1999 and 2010, growth rates averaged 2.4 percent.[14] At the end of 2010, poverty rates stood at 19.7 percent, just about where they had been in 1998, after having declined to 13.7 percent in 2006.[15] Still, according to these statistics, Chile's growth and poverty reduction rates have been the best in Latin America over the past quarter century. Defenders of Chilean neoliberalism view this as evidence of successful modernization and humane social policies.

These statistics, however, should not be understood without either qualification or contextualization. Some argue that the "family basket" of goods that delineates the baseline of poverty is out of date; raising it to reflect contemporary consumption patterns would double the number of people currently defined as being poor.[16] Chile, moreover, emerged from its worst recession since the 1930s in 1986, when poverty rates had risen substantially. In 1970, they had been, according to one estimate, as low as 17 percent.[17] Overall, neoliberal policies have been at the root of a host of intense and even epochal changes. Yet major forms of poverty reduction have not been one of them.

An important reason for this is that the low-end labor market remains tenuous. Ongoing processes of deindustrialization and new modes of production have meant that the decline in the number of industrial workers has continued. As production has become more diffuse, employers have taken advantage of their ability to subcontract labor, hiring workers with lower wages, fewer protections, and reduced benefits. The number of laborers who have temporary contracts has risen notably. One study claims that in 1965 there was one temporary worker for every two permanent workers in Chile. In 2006, however, 71.8 percent of Chilean workers had indefinite contracts.[18] Employment today is flexible, an important part of the push toward building a competitive economy that attracts international investment. Laborers have continued their move into the service sector, while more are self-employed (Portes and Roberts 2005, 48, table two; Salazar and Pinto 2002; Soto, Espinoza, and Gómez 2008). Overall, these processes have made collective bargaining and labor mobilization more difficult, especially since parts of the dictatorship's restrictive labor code remain in place. Ultimately, work tends to be insecure, sporadic, and poorly remunerated for many pobladores. Pobladores often depend on having more than one wage earner in order to maintain their households. Most cover their expenses through rising indebtedness (Paley 2001, 64; Salazar and Pinto 2002, 218–19; Han 2011 and 2012).

As the nature of the labor force has changed, there is now an even stronger correlation between personal economic success and educational background. Most pobladores, however, have attended poorly funded and overcrowded public schools. Local municipalities run these schools, an administrative legacy from the dictatorship's move to decentralize services. Given the vastly different tax bases of Santiago's municipalities, public schools in low-income areas have few resources relative to their wealthier counterparts. Test scores for entrance to college are significantly lower in poorer municipal schools. They also have dropout rates of close to 35 percent. Unemployment rates for Santiago residents in their twenties without a high school diploma have been consistently higher than 20 percent since the 1980s, while most who do work hold temporary or part-time positions.[19] The conditions in low-income schools have helped to reproduce inequality and limit the life chances of their students, consequences that fueled the student protest movements that began in 2006 and expanded in 2011.

Significantly, average wages for laborers in the legal market have generally increased since the late 1980s. Low tariff walls have also made a number of goods cheaper. This, in addition to the increased availability of credit, has led to heightened opportunities for consumption. Yet Chileans carry unprecedented levels of debt, especially middle- and lower-income sectors. Indebted workers tend to work longer hours and seek overtime pay. This further undermines the solidarity of organized laborers (Stillerman 2004). Even without overtime, there are onerous time demands placed on workers. Chileans average some of the longest labor hours in the world, with a legally defined workweek of forty-five hours, reduced from forty-eight in 2005.[20]

The income inequality that sharply increased under the military dictatorship has, despite efforts to "grow with equity," not been redressed. In 2005, levels of inequality were greater than they were in 1981, making them among the highest in Latin America. This development underscores how the neoliberal period has heightened rates of inequality overall: in 1972, Chile had the second-*lowest* rate in Latin America (Winn 2004b, 56). Rates of inequality are even greater in Santiago. In 1997, in the final year of the economic boom, the three wealthiest municipalities in Santiago—Providencia, Vitacura, and Las Condes—had an average rate of "poverty" of 1.0 percent and a rate of "indigence" of 0.1 percent. The comparable figures for Lampa, Pudahual, and Renca, three of the poorest municipalities, were 38.7 percent and 10.1 percent (MIDEPLAN 1997). Such inequity interactively constitutes the built environment. During the 1990s, more than 50 percent of residential and commercial building in the country took place in four out of the thirty-two municipalities in the metropolitan area of Santiago; Las Condes alone accounted for nearly 20 percent (Rodríguez 2001, 3; Cámara Chilena de la Construcción 2005). The dictatorship's slum removal programs continue to influence this pattern of construction, having hardened residential segregation and created clearly defined areas of affluence and impoverishment.

Still, capital investment in urban real estate has not been exclusive to the high end. Certain middle- and low-income municipalities have taken advantage of state subsidies and incentives that seek to make building in Santiago denser (Lopez-Morales 2011). This has led to high-rise and commercial development in these municipalities. Neighborhoods with single, detached homes tend to surround these areas, as it is the still the dominant form of residence in Santiago (a style of home, it should be noted, that pobladores fought for in the land seizures). With prominent malls, massive supermarkets that successfully compete with Wal-Mart, and close access to metro lines and highways, these neighborhoods are the urban environment of mostly middle-income sectors, although they also include low-income groups. Pedro Lemebel (1998, 189), an astute urban chronicler, has quipped that these areas are places where "one can feel rich, if only in miniature."

Since the mid-1990s, this kind of development has extended to a certain degree to other low-income municipalities, where land is relatively cheap. New subdivisions have consequently sprouted up on the edge of the metropolitan area. Homogeneous in design, they tend not to facilitate foot traffic and public socializing. As on the outskirts of Renca near Lo Boza, these developments are gated communities. They have not integrated themselves into existing neighborhoods, even if they have tended to improve the local municipal tax base and thus contribute to the improved provision of certain services. Overall, Santiago's landscape remains fractured and segregated. Certain low-income municipalities are still fairly uniform, without significant new middle-income developments. But even in these places, the Concertación undertook extensive building programs and focused much attention on poverty reduction through the eradication of campamentos.

The Building Boom in Low-Income Santiago

Government support for housing programs has represented an important exception to unfettered free-market policies in Chile. Both government subsidies and foreign investment have been crucial to Santiago's housing boom. Through 2005, the governments of the post-dictatorship had provided subsidies for between 65 and 73 percent of annual housing starts.[21] This extraordinary figure underscores just how significant the relationship between governance and housing remains. The state has provided subsidies on a tiered basis, generally providing a greater percentage of the financing for housing the lower the income level of beneficiaries. Following the land and building seizures and the recession of the late 1990s, the Lagos administration even began to provide housing without debt for the lowest-income sectors, an astonishing new policy for a government still committed to neoliberal policies. Such a policy was born from the long-term struggles of the lower classes to have a right to their own homes.

In overall housing built, the results of state programs have been impressive. Between 1986 and 2005, the state contributed to subsidies for an average of twenty thousand housing units per year in Santiago for the lowest 40 percent in income, a figure that urban planners in earlier governments could have only dreamed about. A million or so people, close to a sixth of the city's population, thus received housing (Rodríguez and Sugranayes 2005, 63). According to government statistics, the country's overall "housing deficit"—defined in terms of quality of housing and access to infrastructure—decreased by 50 percent between 1990 and 1999 (Hidalgo 2004, 235). It has continued to decline subsequently, although at a slower rate. In Santiago, the level of housing understood as "irregular" has decreased substantially, from about 20 percent to near 3 percent by 2005 (Cámara Chilena de la Construcción 2005, 45; MIDEPLAN 2002, chart 8.1). If the general and immense construction boom since the late 1980s has been concentrated in the most expensive real estate markets, it has nonetheless also been significant for low-income residents. Their homes and neighborhoods look quite different today than they did in the 1980s.

For officials, building on this scale has responded to long-held demands for housing and has also reduced the risk of mobilization and polarization. Housing policies, moreover, have generally fit with how the Concertación has sought to govern. These policies have, for example, facilitated capital investment in real estate and the built environment, often with the kind of derivative credit default swap financing that was a part of the US housing boom of the 1990s and 2000s. Unlike in the United States, however, Chile has generally avoided a crash, because of both the level of government spending in the area and a generally propitious environment for Chilean exports.[22] The government, however, has had to intervene when certain financial institutions have fallen, at the same that it has increased spending in real estate financing in the wake of economic recessions and the overextension of housing investment.[23]

In addition to financing, a relatively small number of private developers have built Santiago's subsidized housing, often receiving favored treatment from state organizations. The close relationship that has historically existed between state institutions, building interests, and the Chilean Chamber of

Construction has not dissipated. But unlike before the coup, private interests have not undermined programs in low-income subsidized housing. They have instead tended to support subsidies for the low-income housing sector, as it has generally been a lucrative business that receives the full backing and assurance of the government.[24] As has continued to be the case since the late 1970s, individuals have received subsidies to buy housing, while private developers, who build standardized, often monotonous housing blocs, profit from these subsidies (Sugranyes 2005, 27). They also remain largely insulated from risk, as the government either guarantees loans or directly subsidizes the housing for those relative few who are in programs without mortgages.

In 1997, a highly publicized case involved a recently built low-income apartment block villa that had significant damage following a two-day winter storm. The construction company—Casas COPEVA—failed to follow building regulations, leaving residents in nearly destroyed apartment buildings. The owner of the company, Francisco Pérez Yoma, was the brother of the minister of defense, Edmundo Pérez Yoma. For a moment, the public dialogue focused on just how much economic and political interests overlapped, leading in this case to lax regulation and a sweetheart deal. Oversight has subsequently been tightened, but business interests within real estate still maintain important connections at both the national and municipal level to officials in charge of housing policies.

Beyond the subsidies, development companies have been able to lower the cost of housing construction. Imported building materials are cheaper than they were before the coup, given low overall tariff walls. The cost of labor, moreover, has declined in real terms. Like other employment sectors, construction workers are not organized like they once were and temporary contracts are more common. About 90 percent of formal construction workers have indefinite contracts, with 57.9 percent working for only the duration of individual projects.[25] Subcontractors make use of laborers from neighboring countries such as Peru, who often work illegally.[26] Housing developments, furthermore, are mostly on the outskirts of the city, in low-income sectors with the cheapest real estate. During the 1990s, when the price of land rose in these areas, more subsidized housing took place in municipalities that had previously not been a part of greater Santiago. This development has, once again, pushed concentrated pockets of poverty farther from the city center (Rodríguez and Sugranayes 2005).

Despite the flaws in subsidized housing programs, officials celebrated them as examples of how to develop "neoliberalism with a human face." The campamentos continued to be a sign of underdevelopment, inappropriate for a modern city that would be a global attraction for foreign businesses and tourists. At the same time, urban land seizures represented the polarization and sociopolitical breakdown of recent history, while squatters evoked a sense of dangerous mobilization. Given such conceptions, the seizures and the campamentos have evoked fear, serving as a kind of specter that has haunted post-dictatorship governments.[27] The eradication of the campamentos and the mass provision of housing, on the other hand, would help keep these ghosts at bay, serving as a way to maintain stability and avoid popular mobilization. Technocrats would carefully oversee the implementation of housing programs and maintain fiscal discipline. Finally, pobladores would take part in the housing programs, not as adversaries, but as participants, a welcome change from the land seizures.

In their public campaigns, the governments of the Concertación quite naturally linked the provision of housing with the eradication of extreme poverty and the end of the campamentos. Under President Eduardo Frei Ruíz-Tagle (1994–2000), the government, with much fanfare, released the 1997 "Survey of Precarious Settlements." It identified 972 campamentos in the country, including more than 107,000 households (INVI 1997). In the course of eight years, officials promised, these campamentos would be a phenomenon of the past. In his 2002 presidential address, Ricardo Lagos promised that his government would "win the battle against extreme poverty" and provide "dignified housing" to all Chileans by the year 2005. Lagos asserted that there had been significant progress in the program, claiming that the government had "eradicated 17,472 families" in the past year (Gobierno de Chile, *Mensaje Presidencial* 2002, xviii). If the general promise to provide housing to all Chileans was similar to many heard before, it came much closer to being realized than had any in the past. Within the contours of the post-dictatorship, pobladores continued to gain access to homes of their own. Many also mobilized in the campamentos to make sure this was the case.

Lo Boza: Organizing as the Face of Poverty

In signifying need and extreme poverty, campamentos still hold a broad symbolic significance. As the president and vice president of Lo Boza's neighborhood council, Cecilia Castro and Ana Lamilla were conscious of the fact that they had to negotiate this symbolism. They did this in their administrative responsibilities and in their public appearances as they sought services for their neighborhood. As they did so, they moved back and forth between two registers. On the one hand, they made use of constricted categories that fit the techniques of governance, in which categories such as extreme poverty, campamentos, and social housing were paramount. Yet they also articulated broader ideals about how the eradication of poverty and the provision of housing could be a part of the ideals of citizenship, guided by a vision of social justice, dignity, and propriety.

In much of their work, Cecilia and Ana played the role of state-like administrators. In a sense, they acted as the leaders of the land seizures had done. They helped survey residents and make them legible to state institutions, producing a paper trail that demonstrated Lo Boza's needs. These documents indicated that poverty rates in their neighborhood were over 70 percent; 95 percent of residents suffered from overcrowding; neighborhood adults had an average of five years of schooling; and a majority of the children suffered from malnutrition and inadequate health care.[28] If such statistics underscore harsh conditions, they were also invariably included in the documents Ana and Cecilia presented to development organizations and state institutions. In organizing and marshaling demands, Ana and Cecilia had to demonstrate that their neighborhood was a deserving and exceptional space.

In contradistinction to the period before the coup, Ana and Cecilia operated in a decentralized and diffuse neoliberal environment. To access funding and support, they had to negotiate the practical workings of numerous organizations. As Ana indicated to me one day over coffee, she and Cecilia knew better than they ever could have imagined how to work within government bodies and international donor organizations. They had held countless meetings, written dozens of grants, filled out innumerable forms, and taken various surveys of their neighbors. "We're experts in bureaucratic procedures [*trámites*]," Ana had said, chuckling. The bureaucratic skill that Ana and Cecilia have needed is a hallmark of the neoliberal era, although not entirely exclusive to it.[29]

As a part of efforts to work in concert with citizens, officials designed state programs with the explicit purpose of fomenting participation. Such participation was supposed to achieve a democratic process in which pobladores would have the opportunity to take control of planning their own neighborhoods. A publication for Chile Barrio, the official "eradication" program under the Lagos administration, put it thus: "If [participants in the program] don't generate and fortify organization in the campamentos and create leaders, it won't be possible for them to take part in their own development" (Chile Barrio 2000, 39). In practice, this has often meant that neighborhood leaders, who work either on a volunteer basis or with relatively little remuneration, contribute substantial labor to the administration of state programs. This fits into certain logics of neoliberal governance. It keeps the price of state programs down, while neighborhood leaders facilitate public and private partnerships.[30] Once again, however, this framework is not unique to the neoliberal period, as pobladores had long worked with outside institutions and contributed labor to develop their homes and neighborhoods.

Still, the number of organizations has increased and the importance of state bureaucracies has declined. Neighborhood organizers have to navigate different expectations and paradigms while competing for a limited pool of resources. Despite all of this, however, there is a prevailing framework at play in the dispensation of resources, as both public and private organizations share the goal of transforming the campamentos. Residents of these neighborhoods should live in legally sanctioned homes with property titles, preferably as homeowners.

Through determination, skill, and circumstance, Ana and Cecilia worked within this politics to become the public faces of Lo Boza. On more than one occasion, Cecilia had appeared on television. In one appearance, she was one of the featured personalities on a news spot that told the story of how a social service organization, Un Techo para Chile (literally, "a roof for Chile"), had provided a number of residents in campamentos like Lo Boza with mediaguas.[31] Simple and solidly constructed, these mediaguas were one-room huts that protected residents from the elements. Residents of Lo Boza used mediaguas as their living and dining room areas, often adding bedrooms to them. Among larger families and allegados, residents could use several mediaguas to house their families.

In its coverage of Lo Boza, the news report rather typically blurred the lines between journalism and charity fund-raising, providing a glorified narrative of the work that Un Techo para Chile does. The report begins with a close-up of the general director of Un Techo para Chile in his office. "A mediagua," he states, "is a wooden hut. But the truth is that for people who don't have anything, it's a palace." The scene changes and Cecilia is shown walking in front of Lo Boza. She begins to speak, saying, "More than building us a mediagua, they are helping us to have a sense of dignity as people, to make us feel that—just because we are poor or just because we live in a campamento—that we aren't any different than anybody else."

The story then shifts back to the reporter who says, "Un Techo para Chile has played a central role in many stories like this one." After citing statistics about how many campamentos remain in Chile (912) and the number of mediaguas that Un Techo para Chile has built (more than twelve thousand), the report concludes with a montage. As the music builds to a crescendo, a series of images cross the screen: campamentos that have new mediaguas; volunteers who help smiling pobladores move their personal items into a new house; a recently built wooden community center, brightly painted, including the clearly displayed words "Un Techo para Chile." Throughout, the telephone number to call to make donations flashes. Give money; help squatters; provide a home for all Chileans; end misery. Charity, social uplift, national integration, and the provision of homes all come together.

For Cecilia, as she suggests in the spot, such a vision includes the provision of dignity. Much of her work at the neighborhood council was about this possibility. Her work thus unfolded on a number of fronts, including childcare, health services, counseling, and neighborhood outreach. Such programs have largely become a female domain, as with Cecilia and Ana. To a degree, this represents an extension of the kind of female participation that has taken place in the campamentos and poblaciones since the 1960s. This dynamic continues to rest on two assumptions: that neighborhood organization is an extension of the home and that it is apolitical. At the national level, poverty reduction programs have specifically targeted women, part of a broader global trend.[32] Working with women in this way fits well with how officials in the postdictatorship have sought to move beyond the political conflicts of the past.

If neighborhood development and poverty reduction programs have thus operated under particular constraints, they have also been productive. Women, for example, could use these forums to expand their horizons and confront troubling domestic situations. Cecilia cast her activism as part of a personal journey that had fundamentally changed her life. Before being involved, she had dedicated herself primarily to household tasks, both in her work as a nanny and as a dueña de casa. "My life was inside the four walls of the home," she said, echoing a phrase that I had heard other women use to characterize how community organizations had transformed them (see also Rosa Cancino in Murphy 2004a, 119; Valdés and Weinstein 1993, 180; Franceschet 2005). For many women in Lo Boza, it was not easy to become a part of neighborhood organizations. Women often had to deal with the complaints and jealousy of their husbands for taking part; some had even been beaten (see the comments of Eli Cofré in Murphy 2004a; Paley 2001, 101). But being active allowed women to confront these dynamics and share them with others.

It also permitted participants to develop forms of solidarity and support. Consider, for example, the case of Rosa Carvajal, a pobladora from another campamento in Renca. When I first met Rosa in 2002 she was in her early thirties and had struggled with an intense drug addiction. In our conversations she said that she had taken part in robberies and sold off items from her home in order to support her habit. She had, however, hoped to change her ways and leave behind what she called "vices." She specifically wanted to bring her family back together, as the father of her two children and his *pareja* had taken custody of their children. For Rosa, gaining a legally sanctioned home of her own was a crucial part of this effort. In her legal custody battles, being a homeowner would demonstrate that she had assumed responsibility and could care for her children as a proper mother. She thus jumped at the opportunity to join a homeless committee in her campamento. In joining the committee, Rosa needed to develop a savings ledger, in which she would make monthly payments toward an eventual down payment on her new home. But having relatively large amounts of money on her person each month and in a savings account that she could access proved to be an irresistible temptation. On two separate occasions, she recalled, she depleted her savings in order to get high.

Rosa's problems were compounded by the fact that the first homeless committee in the campamento, according to Rosa and others, was corrupt, having embezzled funds from the savings ledgers of members.[33] The next homeless committee, however, proved to be much better, even helping people like Rosa with their savings. The treasurer worked with Rosa to set up a savings account from which she could only withdraw money when they both authorized it. He also allowed her to bring small amounts of money to him throughout the month so that he could make sure she made her monthly payment. Rosa eventually saved the money she needed. She described this achievement with great pride and mentioned how her neighbors reacted: "*Ay flaca*, it's so good what you've done" (Carvajal in Murphy 2004a, 179).

Rosa's case demonstrates that there can be a creative element to neighborhood organizing and involvement. The irony, however, is that once pobladores move to villas they receive less outside support for organizing. Making the move can be a celebrated event. Pobladores, moreover, achieve the much-sought-after goal of becoming homeowners, and they can gain a security of land tenure that they would not have had before. But the move to villas and poblaciones has other effects that temper the celebratory images of the eradication of campamentos.

From Campamento to Villa

In 2008, most of the residents of Lo Boza moved to Villa Antumalal. Planned by architects from Harvard University and Santiago's Catholic University, designers claimed that the development would be a prototype for what "social housing" could become in Chile and beyond. Those pobladores who moved to the villa have become homeowners. While they received funding from the Spanish embassy, Un Techo para Chile, and the European Union as a part of the process, they had to work with central bureaucracies within the national government to receive property titles. When it comes to homeownership and the establishment of a legally sanctioned neighborhood, the sovereign power of the national state is still supreme.

As in the past, the pobladores of Lo Boza had to demonstrate that they were deserving of state resources. While some of these requirements have changed quite significantly, questions of discipline and proper behavior nevertheless remain of paramount importance. Pobladores who took part in the move no longer had to be a part of a nuclear family, as state housing programs by the late 1990s finally recognized single mothers as legitimate heads of households (something that had previously only happened in a de facto manner, particularly under Allende's government). Also of great significance, pobladores taking part in the move only had to make a down payment in order to access their new housing, as they did not have to assume debt burdens, part of the new policy that the Lagos administration put in place for the lowest-income earners.

Yet all that was solid did not melt into air. Neighborhood leaders and social workers did make assessments about the behavior of pobladores. They explored whether or not applicants had criminal records, if they had been involved in neighborhood organizations, and whether or not they had shown themselves

Figure 8.2. Villa Antumalal, 2009 (photo by author).

to be good workers. Pobladores had to sign a pledge to either remain legally employed or enter into state-sanctioned job training programs, in addition to keeping any children younger than the age of sixteen in school.[34] Finally, they had to remain in Lo Boza for a minimum of five years.

As of this writing, I know of a few households that have left Villa Antumalal since they could either no longer afford to pay for utilities or they did not uphold the contractual agreements they had signed to have homes of their own. Given this, sensibilities about proper behavior continue to animate claims about a right to housing. At the same time, debt and financing also matter, even in cases where residents do not have to pay mortgage payments. The politics of propriety still have an important weight in the present, guiding state housing programs and redistributive policies.

These politics continue to matter when pobladores gain access to housing, property titles, and infrastructure services. Once pobladores live in established poblaciones and villas, they are generally no longer cast as a development problem. The concerns that they face tend not to be issues that state institutions are expected to address. In Villa Antumalal, for example, the only state and nongovernmental organizations still active at the neighborhood level are a government-sponsored day care center and a microenterprise program. Both Ana and Cecilia have used their experiences in Lo Boza to find work as consultants for homeless committees elsewhere. They do very little work in Villa Antumalal. Ultimately, pobladores in the villa have joined Santiago's domesticated periphery. They have homes of their own, but less recourse to organize and denounce the conditions they confront than they did in the campamento. The same is true of Villa Topocalma.

The Unresolved Housing Question

Housing programs in the post-dictatorship have been enormously productive. The extent to which state entities have intervened in the housing market represents an important exception to the unfettered forms of free-market capitalism generally associated with neoliberal policy prescriptions. Yet if housing is exceptional, it is also a testament to the unfolding of Chilean neoliberalism. Housing programs are a part of social policies that produce what Verónica Schild (2000, 2007) describes as "market citizens." In taking part in such programs and receiving benefits, citizens must be disciplined and develop the tools needed to fend for themselves in the marketplace without further assistance from the state. This overall framework, and the kind of state subject that it creates, is part and parcel of the general extension of market relations in Chile. It is not, however, entirely exclusive to the neoliberal era. In housing, at least, this framework also fits with how the urban politics of propriety has operated throughout the period analyzed in this book. Gaining access to homes and ending the campamentos is a process of "regularization" and *saneamiento*, in which exceptional circumstances are overcome and the spaces and subjects of the city conform to presumed norms and forms. In practical terms, finding a way to live within these norms and forms has been the end game of both state programs and citizen mobilization.

Citizens who gain housing and services considered basic subsequently have less recourse to mobilize publicly as pobladores against the conditions they face. The period between 1990 and 2006 was defined largely by a lack of activism among pobladores in established neighborhoods, a time of political withdrawal and social atomization. Rather than being a time of national solidarity and political belonging in Santiago's margins, it was an era that consolidated a domesticated periphery. The city went through an unprecedented building boom, from skyscrapers to villas and mediaguas. By and large, pobladores stopped living in the remaining campamentos (even if the occasional new one did pop up). Yet even as most pobladores now have homes of their own, they live in an insecure, segregated, and inequitable environment, in which dislocations of the past and present cast enduring shadows. Pobladores remain in marginal and precarious socioeconomic positions. As they continue to negotiate the often tense and insecure place that they inhabit, they can still find it difficult to occupy a home life that they would consider to be dignified and proper.

Within this context, protests over student debt loads and unequal access to education have gained considerable traction, first in 2006 and then with greater intensity in 2011. Yet pobladores and housing rights activists have not stepped into the fray like they did during previous periods of intense popular mobilization. They do not have the clear-cut issue of homelessness to rally around as they once did. A few housing organizations have become active. They have made demands for better-quality housing, safer neighborhoods, and the extension of credits and the forgiveness of debt. Many of these organizations have emphasized that their struggle is not just about gaining access to a house. As the First Congress of the Movement of Pobladores Ukamau put it, "We have always said and we have always proposed that we are fighting for much more than a house, our fight is to gain a dignified life, to recover our rights . . . and develop our own neighborhood."[35]

These activists put the question of dignity front and center, making it part of an ongoing challenge and struggle, the kind of "cry and demand" that Henri Lefebvre (1996) argues is a central part of struggles to gain "a right to the city." This cry and demand for dignity—repeated throughout the histories I've explored in this book—still haunts the acquisition of housing rights and the making of home in low-income Santiago. The question of dignity thus leaves the link between property and propriety unfulfilled for many. Ultimately, the urban politics of propriety has remained unsettled in the present, making the mass provision of housing under the Concertación less the realization of national integration and more a demonstration of the ongoing fractures that remain.

CHAPTER 9
THE INDIGNITIES OF HOME IN THE MARGINS OF MODERN URBAN LIFE

For many of the pobladores with whom I worked on this study, the question of dignity complicates their reflections on the trajectory of their neighborhoods. This question makes the connection between the past and the present a troubled one. This is especially the case for those who took part in the land seizures before the coup. In general, these pobladores have a security of land tenure and a degree of neighborhood development that once would have been difficult to imagine. Yet the years between the land seizures and the present have been tumultuous and unstable—shattered by dictatorial repression, punctuated by economic crises, and generally marked by a climate of insecurity. The kinds of solidarities that once existed among pobladores in these neighborhoods have declined. Social fragmentation has reinforced a sense of both atomization and opportunities lost. Fissures of home, city, and nation fracture the landscape.

Emilio Pastenes, the leader from Campamento Lenin, conveyed a particularly trenchant criticism of the fate of the poblaciones. Having fled his campamento in fear of the dictatorship, Emilio was not a part of the efforts to transform the neighborhood into a población. Nor did he take part in the move to Lo Velásquez, when most of his former neighbors finally became homeowners in 1983 during the dictatorship's "eradication" programs. Emilio does, however, still have friends and acquaintances in Lo Velásquez and he holds strong opinions about the neighborhood's fate in the current environment. As he said to me:

> I don't like that part of Renca; [there are] a lot of drugs. There's a lot of overcrowding [that] brings with it a lot of other things: crime, drug addiction, prostitution. It's our ugly side. . . . As a leader I never thought that there would be so much

overcrowding. . . . Had I known, I never would have been involved. I was a young man who fought for certain ideals of dignity, such as a home, such as a well-constituted family. I never thought that the neighborhoods would turn into the kinds of ghettos that they are now. (Pastenes in Murphy 2004a, 96)

Emilio's perspective is similar to those expressed to me by several other pobladores of his generation, especially community and housing activists who had ties to the Left. For many of these Chileans, nostalgia seeps into their memories of the past, while rueful disappointment and pointed criticisms mark their reflections of the present.[1] Conditions today do not live up to "certain ideals of dignity" that helped lead pobladores to organize, seize land, and establish their homes. Yet the question of dignity somehow persists, a kind of promise that having a home of one's own has left unfulfilled. This gap between the potential of the past and the perception of the present is a kind of specter that haunts the urban politics of propriety. The idea of having "a well-constituted home" stands in contrast to current conditions. Many parts of low-income Santiago—although far from all—have the look and feel of what Emilio refers to as "ghettos." Making a home in such areas tends to be a disproportionately fraught and troubled process.

In housing mobilization in Chile, having a home of dignity has always been interwoven with the claims of citizenship. Siba N. Grovogui (2009), in an illuminating essay, discusses the question of dignity as it relates to sociopolitical imaginaries in the modern era, broadly construed. As he argues, "the modern human has been imagined constitutionally as duty-bearing citizens, rights-bearing individuals, and dignity-bearing persons" (273). The differences between these conceptions are a matter of degree. They can also overlap and feed off of each other, as they have for pobladores. In order to access property, pobladores have had to assume the responsibilities of duty-bearing citizens who can demonstrate discipline and propriety. They have thus been able to properly assert their rights as individuals, including a right to housing. Yet this right has only been made possible because of the understanding that there is a dignity to personhood that should be respected. Repeatedly, both officials and citizens have described homeownership as an opportunity to live in a place of dignity and decency (if often from varied perspectives).

For pobladores, then, the duties of citizenship, the rights of the individual, and the dignities of personhood have overlapped in the ways they have accessed housing. Yet as Grovogui argues, it is also useful to separate these characteristics, at least heuristically. They all stress different dynamics and point to varied horizons and possibilities. This is particularly true of the category that Grovogui argues is the most expansive: dignity-bearing persons. Yet while Grovogui asserts that this category is the broadest, he also states that under present circumstances "the requirements of life-in-dignity have been forgotten. They are indeed constitutionally unclaimed nearly everywhere" (273). Grovogui's claim is provocative, and he overreaches in making such a broad statement. Yet he does point to an important tension, one that the current situation among homeowning pobladores underscores.

For pobladores who now have homes of their own, finding a dignified life is largely a private affair, not forming a part of public, constitutional claims. If pobladores have generally (and increasingly) come to live in legally sanctioned homes, the promise of a life in dignity has been far more elusive. The gap between property holding and the realization of a dignified existence underscores a limit to what pobladores have been able to accomplish within the urban politics of propriety. Pobladores have established communities and homes during the past half century, carving out an important space for themselves in the city and in the polity. They have gained a right to housing. Yet they have not generally realized the more expansive promises of dignity embedded in their struggles.

Pobladores have undertaken such struggles within a liberal, Chilean register of citizenship and personhood. To an important degree, this register has historically facilitated activism and social consciousness. Many have pointed to the gap between expectations of a proper home life and actually existing conditions in order to mobilize and condemn elements of the sociopolitical order. Yet despite its historical contribution to collective action and forms of critique, this liberal register invariably falls back on notions of individual rights and propriety. It has also played out within particular understandings of need, poverty reduction, and minimally acceptable living conditions. Once in homes of their own, pobladores have less recourse to mobilize publicly. The forms of marginality and insecurity that many of them have continued to suffer have tended not to form the basis for a criticism of governance.

For groups such as pobladores in Chile, the hostile, inequitable, and volatile urban environment they disproportionately confront makes maintaining a home life considered appropriate often fraught and troubled. In building their homes, pobladores generally encounter greater challenges in achieving the forms of self-possession, propriety, and dignity that homeownership or other forms of legally sanctioned housing is supposed to bring with it. The result can be volatile and conflictive, as pobladores work through the constrained choices they have and the troubled contexts they face.

In exploring these dynamics, I return here to cases that came to light primarily through my lived experiences in Renca and the particular kinds of participant observation I undertook. I focus on a few moments when modes of self-possession and notions of propriety oriented aspirations, practices, and conflicts in the making of home life, in which two young parents—a mother and a father from two separate households—confronted agonizing circumstances in the making of their families and homes. Their choices and situations underscore the ongoing hold that the urban politics of propriety has, as it remains embedded in property relations and the making of home life. These cases point to how questions of what is proper intimately influence relationships and personhood, if in at times problematic and particular ways, especially when such questions play out within a context of insecurity, duress, and heightened atomization.

As I have asserted throughout this book, notions of propriety, dignity, respect, and self-possession carry weight in the making of home, having a subtle yet pervasive hold over both behavior and desire. Such notions help to orient how pobladores (and others) practice their everyday lives, negotiate work and debt, and develop their family relations and their ties of compadrazgo. These social actors do not necessarily blindly accept links between property and notions of what is proper. There is room for contestation, play, individual style, and change. This can lead not only to compromised choices but also to conflict and violence. Such outcomes are often far from the "ideals of dignity" that can undergird ideas of having a "well-constituted family." In the struggles to lead home lives of dignity that certain pobladores related to me, they negotiated some of the most haunted spaces of modern urban life. Pobladores live in ongoing histories of property and propriety, perhaps in no greater way than in their daily struggles to develop and maintain their homes.

An Allegado in Lo Velásquez

When I first met Alexi Martínez, he was an allegado and one of many young men between the ages of eighteen and thirty-two who disproportionately filled out the ranks of Santiago's unemployed. Like many of the men close in age to me who became informants, friends, and acquaintances (the lines of which were often blurred), I tended to speak with Alexi privately, in places where we could carve out a moment to ourselves: a street corner, the edge of a concrete soccer field, the small courtyard space between the house he lived in and the property's fence, or in the house's cramped, walled-in backyard. These were the kinds of spaces that were appropriate for men like us in order to have more intimate and private conversations.[2]

Alexi was from Lo Velásquez I in Renca, the villa built in 1983 during the dictatorship's "eradication" programs that Emilio Pastenes described as a "ghetto." A father of two young children, Alexi lived with his wife and her family, in circumstances that were fairly typical of allegados. He shared a small bedroom with his nuclear family. In the room, the family had managed to pile in a black-and-white television set, a bunk bed, a dresser, an old armchair, a transistor radio, and a portable closet, overflowing with clothes, shoes, and other items. The room included a small stove and refrigerator, allowing them to occasionally eat meals and snacks together, apart from the others. Several years before, when Alexi had first moved into the house, he had built the room with help from his brother-in-law. "The room," Alexi had told me, "was supposedly a temporary solution. . . . One day, we'll have our own home, where all our things can go." If the room granted the family a measure of privacy, it was far from the kind of domestic space that Alexi thought he should have as a father of two.

The rest of the house was also crowded, as there were six people who shared two other bedrooms, a kitchen, a bathroom, and a dining-living room area. Alexi and his in-laws were in the process of building on to the house, the kind of *auto-construcción* (self construction) that many pobladores have taken part in and have contributed to the multiple sizes and styles of houses in the poblaciones (see figure 9.1). They had started adding a second-floor bedroom the year before, although they had not yet completed it. The common room, like the rest of the house, was rather Spartan. It had a concrete floor and cinder block walls. Its adornments were fairly typical: a calendar that included scenes

Figure 9.1. A panorama of a section of the municipality of Renca, showing the different styles of housing (photo by author).

of alpine mountains and glaciers from southern Chile, a poster image of the Virgin Mary in a blue-and-white robe, a plaque of one of Pablo Neruda's love poems, a small Chilean flag, a clock, and a banner for Colo Colo, a soccer team with a passionate following in the poblaciones. The furniture included a worn wooden dining room table that seated six, in addition to a couch and matching armchair with fraying and faded red upholstery. A few plastic plants filled out the décor.

Dominating the front of the room was a flat-screen color television set and a new stereo system, recently bought on a three-year credit plan from a department store by Alexi's stepfather-in-law. By the early 2000s, the conspicuous display of televisions and stereos was an increasingly common practice in houses in the poblaciones and villas. Such a display acts as a demonstration of individual purchasing power, and it underscores the important role that the home plays in being a focal point for socializing and relaxation. This role is especially important for pobladores, given the dangers and insecurities that many of them disproportionately face in the streets. In poblaciones like Lo Velásquez, moreover, residents tend to frequent nightclubs, cafes, and restaurants less than other Chileans. Such locales are not only expensive, but generally concentrated in areas at a distance from the poblaciones.

Beyond the television and the stereo, there were other imported electrical items in the home, including a microwave, a blender, and a washing machine—goods that have become widely present in the households of pobladores. These items make it easier to finish certain domestic chores faster and more efficiently. This is especially important for women, who, as in Alexi's household, tend to shoulder a much greater percentage of household work. Women continue to do this in spite of the fact that they have come to work more and more in remunerated jobs outside of the home since the 1970s. The double duty they take on is often onerous. According to one study, women who hold jobs labor an average of seventy hours per week between domestic tasks and employment (Avendaño 2008, 226–29).

All of the electrical goods in Alexi's house are the kinds of imported commodities that became relatively cheaper and more accessible following the lowering of tariff walls during the dictatorship.[3] Most pobladores, moreover, have tended to buy these kinds of goods in the same way as Alexi's stepfather-in-law had, on credit. Such consumption is dependent on rising levels of indebtedness, a phenomenon that has increased exponentially since the 1970s. By the mid-1990s, more than 90 percent of households in Santiago made use of consumer credit.[4] As a percentage of income, debt was significantly higher among low-income populations than among other groups. In 2006, low-income Chileans who earned between $110 and $360 per month had come to pay an average of 36 percent of their monthly incomes on consumer debts. (The minimum wage at this time was approximately US$250 per month [MIDEPLAN 2010].)

For many, debt burdens have become onerous, often making basic forms of consumption precarious. Holding debt has become interwoven with the fulfillment of everyday needs. People go into debt, for example, to buy food and household supplies at the supermarket and clothes and personal goods from department stores. Most also pay their monthly bills for water, electricity, and cell phones in this way. Such debt, as Clara Han (2011 and 2012) points out, is fundamental to supporting the varied relations that constitute home. Not only does debt permit people to survive in precarious circumstances but it also helps them to maintain their kinship relations, fictive or otherwise, and their ties of compadrazgo. Without debt, Chileans could not maintain home lives considered proper, in which everyday forms of consumption, from food to bills, television, washing machines, and the internet, play important roles in responding to social needs and desires. But debt is also risky and misleading, as it can generate a veneer of wealth and ownership that may not be sustainable and can lead to long-term stresses.

At the level of individual households in the poblaciones, there is a good deal of anxiety about rising indebtedness. In certain parts of Renca, it was not uncommon to hear of security personnel from department stores coming to houses to take products back following missed payments. Neighbors and family members can respond to such circumstances by condemning the debt holder for failing to live up to ideals about personal responsibility and propriety. The one time that I saw two representatives of a department store come to a home to take back certain goods, a neighbor said, "They haven't paid anything; they're irresponsible." Beyond the opprobrium of others, Chileans who fail to pay off their debts have little recourse to cleanse their credit records through personal bankruptcy. Those who have defaulted and received bad credit scores not only have an extremely difficult time reentering the world of credit, they can be barred from jobs and political office.

Alexi had spoken to me about his own debt obligations. As he relayed it to me, he had bought a number of birthday and Christmas gifts, in addition to groceries, clothes, and a cell phone, on consumer credit. The vast majority of his purchases had involved links to his extended family and household. He also indicated that he had made a number of these purchases on credit in order to pay for school fees and supplies for his eldest child, while saving his cash to pay for school fees. (As he described all of this to me, he made a few pointed side comments about the large class sizes and the poor resources that the school offered.)

Alexi had first gone into this debt when he had held jobs as a landscaper and construction worker, sporadic jobs that occasionally left him short of money. The situation worsened after he had broken his wrist in an accident while bicycling home from a construction job. Lacking health care coverage, he had not had his wrist set properly and he now found it difficult to do manual labor.[5] His wife, who worked part time in an after-school program at a local NGO, had helped him to pay off his debts. She and Alexi had scrambled around, shifting debt burdens and borrowing from friends and family, afraid of what a permanent mark on Alexi's credit record would mean for future employment and borrowing options. In finally making his payments, Alexi and his wife had not only taken money from family members, but were subsequently unable to contribute anything to broader household expenses, something that Alexi indicated had contributed to arguments inside the house. These arguments had often spilled over to conflicts between Alexi and his wife; recriminations could fly, especially about being irresponsible or useless. Alexi's initial indebtedness had helped, for a time, to assuage such difficulties. But his debts eventually only made the problems worse.

Some acquaintances had once approached Alexi with an offer to help him out. Saying that they wanted to "look out for the people of the *pueblo*," they asked Alexi if he'd like to join them in robberies in the barrio alto. "They knew I was unemployed and fed up [*choreado*] and that I had two kids. They wanted to help me. They told me, 'You can make a lot of money and they're only the snobby rich [*cuicos*].'" Alexi's acquaintances sought to justify their actions by tapping into a moral register about need.[6] To a degree, their arguments were reminiscent of the reasons that pobladores had used in taking part in the land seizures. These men claimed that they were ultimately trying to support people from the neighborhood like Alexi, a young father who was struggling to provide for his family. According to these comments, Alexi could push on the boundaries of certain moral and legal frameworks, even transgressing them. He was, after all, unable to properly care for his family. Both Alexi and his acquaintances, moreover, were dismissive of the wealthy: they were the snobby rich who neither needed all their money nor cared for the poor. Robbing such people thus had its justifications.

For Alexi, however, his acquaintances' arguments crossed a line. "But no," he said to me, "I don't get involved in those kinds of things." A former soldier, Alexi had a firm sense of discipline and order, and he even defended some of the work that the dictatorship had done. As he claimed, the regime had "cleaned up the dirt [*la mugre*]. Most of the people who were killed or tortured deserved it." When I pressed him on this issue, he said, "Look, they committed crimes. They were trash." Given such a perspective, Alexi refused, at least as he related it to me, to take part in criminal activity in order to support his family. As an individual enmeshed in codes of propriety and forms of self-possession, Alexi defined for himself what an appropriate act would be and he reached his own conclusions about how he would seek to navigate his situation. But his options were few. In the end, Alexi would endure the indignities of being fed up in relative inactivity and silence, as he was unemployed and largely without the means to denounce his situation publicly. But the pressure to have a home more in keeping with desire and expectations of propriety remained a source of anguish and conflict, a haunting presence in Alexi's life.

Informal Activities and Neighborhood Insecurity

Alexi was not alone in facing moral questions about activities on the margins of the law or of social acceptability. For many pobladores, such activities are a part of life. More pobladores take part in informal and perhaps illegal practices than other sectors of the population, even as such practices invariably include relations with people from all walks of life. In Chile, as elsewhere, daily rhythms would not be possible without informal activities.

In seizing land and squatting on it, pobladores set up informal housing, in which they often confronted great risk and danger. Yet squatters also worked toward the formalization of their land tenure, in which they made explicit efforts to be included in the rights of citizenship by becoming property owners and formalizing their land tenure. Informality, in this case, was a necessity, but one that, under certain conditions, was acceptable and could open up to legal forms of inclusion. As in the case of housing, people need to take part in many of the informal practices that continue to exist. Most of these practices, however, do not serve as a basis for making a claim to citizenship. People who take part in these informal activities generally do not suppose they will become legal. Given their often tense location on the boundaries of the law and of social acceptability, many of these activities can contribute to a climate of distrust, insecurity, and stigmatization. As pobladores disproportionately depend on them, they suffer the brunt of their negative consequences, especially as informal activities more commonly take place in the neighborhoods that pobladores live in.

Still, numerous informal practices can be fairly out in the open and widely accepted. Employers tend to pay maids, gardeners, waiters, and a host of other service workers under the table, in unregulated relationships.[7] On the buses, in the metro, and in areas with a lot of pedestrians, musicians often play their songs as they seek pocket change, while itinerant salespeople sell soft drinks, ice cream, or chocolate bars. There is also a thriving business in pirated literature, music, movies, and software, the likes of which one can easily find in certain plazas, thoroughfares, or market squares. When police show up, a street hawker will whistle a warning, and the illegal merchandise will be quickly whisked away into backpacks and handbags.

Among pobladores, services and expertise can be offered as a form of support and solidarity. Pobladores with medical skills administer care to neighbors, friends, and family members, fictive or otherwise. They might do this for free, charge a reduced rate, barter, or ask for a favor. Local barbers often grant discounts on their haircuts to acquaintances in need, at times in exchange for handy work, goods from a storeowner, or groceries. Following a fire, car accident, or operation, neighbors often gather donations or hold a kind of charity event that includes food, music, and dancing in exchange for monetary contributions or other forms of support. Many women take part in *la polla*, a form of rotating credit in which groups of people, generally headed by a pobladora, contribute weekly sums to a shared pot of money. Members of *la polla* groups take weekly turns drawing from the pot, granting them access to a larger quantity of money than they would otherwise have. They can subsequently use this money to pay off debts and cover basic expenses (see Han 2012, 70–75). Such acts of solidarity hearken back to the struggles in the land seizures and the subsequent establishment of campamentos, when neighbors developed networks of support and organization in building houses, developing infrastructure, caring for children, and protecting the neighborhood and its residents. These activities form a part of what pobladores call acting in solidarity, a term that may refer to ideological support for a cause, but points more centrally to sharing burdens and offering personal support in times of need (see Adams 2014, 262).

While many informal activities receive social acceptance and even encouragement, others are more suspect, shrouded in secrecy and caution. Inside the home, electricians and television repairmen—legally employed or otherwise—often help people connect illegally to the electrical grid or cable and internet services. Storeowners might sell unauthorized alcohol, as municipal officials tend not to grant liquor permits in neighborhoods they view as dangerous or prone to crime.[8] People take part in numbers games and illegal betting practices. Prostitution is also practiced by a small, if still substantial, number. While a few prostitutes walk the streets and others develop their client base through pimps and personal contacts, most work out of massage parlors and strip clubs.[9] Others may be able to use the house of a friend or acquaintance, often in exchange for money or goods.

The sheer number of informal activities that exist is a testament to both the limits of the state's regulatory authority, the problematic low-end of the job market, and, for many, a moral economy that supersedes the legal one. In so many of these activities, the transgression of legal boundaries is common. In certain cases, these kinds of acts are given barely a second thought and receive little social sanction, legal or otherwise. They might also be perfectly understandable as they alleviate certain daily pressures and permit pobladores and others to support each other and their households. As with the land seizures, transgression is at times necessary and defensible. Yet as in Alexi's case, people can meet such activities with condemnation, as there is a troubled and often contested line between what is appropriate and what is reprehensible. Such questions are given a greater charge when they involve the legal frameworks and institutions of the state.

The presence, moreover, of certain informal activities that *are* dangerous and without widespread social approval tends to reinforce a level of distrust and uncertainty. In certain poblaciones, villas, and campamentos (but by no means all), it is not difficult to find illegal drugs, from a relatively accepted traffic in marijuana to more forcefully prohibited narcotics such as cocaine, forms of crack, and bags of glue and other inhalants. This was certainly the case for Lo Velásquez: many residents complained about what Rosa Cancino described as "the plague of drugs" in the neighborhood (Murphy 2004a, 118). I learned to avoid certain areas, especially at night, as dealers operate in specific parks and alleyways, and also out of particular households. Of course, people of all social classes both consume these drugs and condemn their use, including pobladores. But the presence of drug dealing was unmistakable in the neighborhood, reinforcing for many, especially parents of young children, a sense of danger and a desire to withdraw into the home.

Beyond territorial forms of stigmatization, activities such as drug dealing play a part in what Loïc Wacquänt (2007, 68) has called lateral denigration, in which heightened levels of suspicion exist among neighbors. If pobladores generally have poor relations with police and other state officials, many of them also tend to focus inward so as to avoid the entanglements of the street and relations with neighbors, especially after they stop being involved in collective forms of organizing. In neighborhoods with higher levels of drug running and street crime—such as Villa Topocalma and Lo Velásquez—one of the most common responses I received when I asked research participants to describe their relations with neighbors was, "I don't get involved with anyone." They said this in spite of the tradition of activism among pobladores and ongoing forms of solidarity. Nongovernmental organizations and church programs that work with women often have as one of their first goals to prevent "confinement in the house." Gender relations and expectations of domesticity obviously play a role in such a phenomenon, but so do criminality and insecurity. Many long-term neighborhood organizers complained to me about how it was more difficult to have neighbors work together in such an environment of suspicion and *desconfianza* (distrust).[10]

Walled-in homes underscore the sense of solitude and confinement in the area. Houses and apartments have imposing fences, exterior walls with shards of broken glass embedded in a top layer of concrete, windows fortified with iron bars, and securely locked doors. Beyond serving as a physical instantiation of Santiago's private property regime, such barricades reinforce a landscape of distrust and separation. Residents often discuss where and when it is safe to walk outside of their homes. They take care to chart a path where trusted acquaintances live and they generally know where drug dealing takes place, if only to avoid it. After a few hours of darkness, the streets and parks tend to become empty, although young men often roam around in groups.[11]

Some of these youths are armed with knives and a few with guns. The younger men I knew often shared stories about late-night conflicts, involving everything from attempted robbery and conflicts with police to arguments between variously defined groups. These groups might have loyalties based on being from a particular neighborhood or sharing a certain lifestyle choice, such as being *hip-hoperos*, *rockeros*, or *punkeros*.[12] More serious confrontations break out between rival drug dealers fighting for turf, although Santiago has

Figure 9.2. Memorial marking the spot of a murder victim, Renca, 2009 (photo by author).

never had the levels of drug violence that has beset cities in such countries as the United States, Mexico, Colombia, El Salvador, Guatemala, Honduras, Venezuela, Jamaica, and Brazil. Still, certain streets in the poblaciones and villas of Renca have small shrines called *animitas* that are about two feet high, memorializing the spot where a person was killed, often over drug conflicts, violence between members of different soccer clubs, or run-ins with police (see figure 9.2). In such an external environment of violence and distrust, many turn to the development of their homes as a site of relaxation and consumption. But these areas can also be troubled and conflicted, especially for pobladores.

For a Proper Family: Single Motherhood and the Ties of (Fictive) Kin

When I first came to know Angela Rivera, she was a thirty-two-year-old single mother who lived in a campamento.[13] As a part of a subsidized housing program, she would later move to Villa Topocalma. According to certain statistical indicators, single motherhood and other forms of "nontraditional" families had increased overall from 1972 to 2002 from close to 15 percent to more than 25 percent (Halpern 2002, 36). By 2011, that number had grown to 39 percent. In the case of households living below the poverty line, it stood at 51 percent.[14]

It is possible that the statistics behind this rise are exaggerated. Since the late 1960s, Chilean society has generally become more accepting of family forms beyond an idealized nuclear mold. This is a broad change in expectations that can be seen at the highest levels of state policy and governance. Divorce was made legal in 2004 and Michelle Bachelet became president as a single mother in 2006. Just as significantly, housing programs no longer privilege married couples and nuclear families in the dispensation of benefits. Given the changed environment, survey respondents are perhaps more willing to indicate that they live in non-nuclear family arrangements than they were in the past. Still, these statistics do point to a significant shift.

In conjunction with the rise in single motherhood, more women like Angela have become workers in the formal labor market. This has happened because of real gains in education for women and gender integration in the workplace. But it has also taken place because of the evolving nature of labor relations. Before the neoliberal era, workers in the formal sector tended to have contracts with clauses that were meant to support family and home, including stipulations about wages, health benefits, social security, vacations, and housing. But the flexible and insecure labor environment of the neoliberal era is quite different. Neither employers nor state institutions have to assume much responsibility in the development of home life. It is in this more atomized and flexible context that more women work today.[15]

Still, the labor that women engage in outside of the home has provided many of them with certain opportunities. Through their work, women have had the chance to expand their life experiences and escape abusive or troubled marriages they were once more likely to endure.[16] Angela, as I indicate below, is one of those women. But her experience also underscores how difficult it can be to become more independent as a single mother. The relationships of family life—fictive or otherwise—still carry with them important expectations and obligations, both of which play crucial roles in the formation of home and the making of personhood.

When I first met Angela she had been in the campamento for ten years. She had moved to the neighborhood because her sister and mother had lived there and they had enough land for Angela to build a shack in front of theirs. Some four years before I came to the campamento, however, her sister and mother had successfully entered a subsidized housing program and had moved to San Bernardo, a municipality about an hour and a half away on the other side of greater Santiago. Angela lived in a two-room wooden mediagua that she had received at a much-reduced price through a lottery from the Santiago chapter of the Bank of Boston. Compared to the shack that it replaced, the mediagua was, in Angela's words, "a luxury."

She shared her two-room home with three boys, two of whom were her biological children. The other was a sixteen-year-old named Pedro, who, according to Angela, had an absent father who was a drug addict and a mother who was overwhelmed in taking care of Pedro's four brothers and sisters. Pedro had been living mostly on the street, and Angela offered to let him live with her but only on the condition that he change his ways. He had been involved in what Angela described as "purely evil things," including robbing houses and selling *pitos* and *monos*, joints made from, respectively, marijuana and a mild version of crack. "I offered to help him and he said yes," Angela recalled. "He promised me that he would change." Angela thus accepted Pedro, but only if he would stop the "evil things," go to school, and help Angela to look after the two children. In the year since Pedro had come to live with Angela and her two sons, he had come to act more and more like he was a part of the family. He called Angela his *mamá*, and if the younger children misbehaved, he felt it was his right to discipline them.

The fictive or vernacular kin relationship between Angela and Pedro is a relatively common practice among pobladores, yet census figures generally do not track them.[17] These relationships are crucial for survival: they help people have certain choices in times of labor insecurity and domestic uncertainty. For pobladores, bouts of unemployment or addiction can lead to calamitous consequences, as many do not have the financial resources that more privileged Chileans can draw on in order to make it through such circumstances. Given this, domestic relations are often under greater strain, as it is relatively common for someone who previously provided crucial income or labor for a household to no longer be able to do so. In response, individuals move on at greater rates and establish new kinds of familial relationships. Domestic relations thus tend to be more fluid, although it is crucial to note that this is a tendency, not a destiny.[18] As in Pedro's case, this can leave children or young adults largely on their own, with few resources to draw on. Developing an informal kind of kin relation is an important means of survival. It can also be, as with Angela, a form of solidarity and support.

In whatever case, such relations entail expectations about reciprocity, obligation, and propriety. These expectations can vary, yet they are of considerable importance, perhaps particularly since they are not based on ties of blood and are, as in Angela's case, dependent on the goodwill of a parent. In my experience, it was the dueñas de casa, the housewives, who made the decision to invite an extended family member or someone unrelated into the home. In broad terms, women generally play crucial rules in establishing such familial ties and those of compadrazgo (see also Han 2012).

That was how it had been for Erika Cereño, the dueña de casa from Lo Velásquez. In one of our conversations, she told me about having "rehabilitated" Julián, a young drug user from her población. When he was fourteen, Julián had come to Erika's house on several occasions. He had begged for food from the fruit and vegetable stand that Erika and her husband operated in their small front courtyard. As Erika recounted it to me, Julián was lost and a bit wild, dirty and with torn clothes. He was, in her words, a "thrown-out kid," with parents who were alcoholics and failed to take care of him. In her testimonial, Erika offered Julián the chance to be looked after, saying the following:

> From today onwards I am going to take care of you. I don't want you to get high anymore, because I'm going to take care of you and give you food and all of your things. All you're going to do is sleep in your house, and I'm going to provide you with all that you need, but I'm not going to give you anything. You're going to work and you're going to pay me for what I give you to eat, so that you learn how to make a living and that you don't walk around here high all the time, like some piece of trash. (Murphy 2004a, 108)

For the next few years, Julián spent his days with Erika and her family, and he even began to sleep over on occasion. According to Erika, however, Julián eventually returned to drug use. Erika subsequently disowned him, refusing to let him in the house. Julián disappeared for several weeks. When he returned,

Erika recalled, he begged her, as his *mamá*, to forgive him. But Erika said that she responded sharply: "I am not your *mamá* and I don't ever want to see you again." He persisted, however, and Erika finally relented and agreed to take him back after he entered a drug treatment program. From Erika's perspective, she had made sure that Julián's needs were met and that he would be able to "learn values." Either he had to act accordingly or she would no longer open up her home to him. Years later when she related this to me, Erika indicated how proud she was that Julián eventually came to have a job as a mechanic, in addition to a family of four and a home of his own. Through the support and ties of fictive kin, Julián had learned responsibility and self-possession. From Erika's perspective, the fruits of this learning lay in his family and in his own home.

Of course, expectations in domestic and family relations include spouses, children, parents, and in-laws. Angela, for her part, structured much of her life history around the ultimate failure of her marriage and the improprieties of her husband, Carlos. She had, in fact, originally come to the campamento after leaving him. When they were first together, Angela had lived as an allegada with her in-laws for two years. Angela said that the couple had little privacy in the house. Such an impropriety contributed to arguments over money and Carlos's family. During this time, Carlos found only sporadic work as an electrician. According to Angela, Carlos's siblings and parents often fought, and Carlos became physically abusive with Angela. "There was a lot of resentment between everyone," she said, "It was a tense and difficult situation."

After giving birth to the couple's first child, Angela convinced Carlos that it would be best for them to move. She found a job as a waitress and they rented a room in Población Primero de Mayo where Angela had grown up with one of her aunts. But Angela did not find a desirable home life. According to Angela, Carlos often stayed out late at night, leaving Angela alone in the house. Despite her work schedule, Angela also assumed most of the household chores, something she described as onerous and unending. She thus assumed the common forms of double work duty that working women take part in. Worse, Carlos was often jealous of her activities outside of the house, leading to arguments if she sought to leave home for companionship or entertainment.

Beyond remembering her solitude and work, Angela also complained about Carlos's spending habits. While Angela stated that Carlos was a good worker, she said, "We never advanced much, or, we only had a few things. What happened is that [Carlos] really liked nice clothes. He'd buy really expensive clothes, designer pants and shoes. . . . But I'd always go buy the cheap stuff at the outdoor market." For Angela, then, questions of consumption weighed heavily on the relationship. From Angela's point of view, Carlos had misplaced priorities: he spent too much on fashion and he did not save enough for the family.

The situation became worse when Angela discovered that Carlos was having an affair. For Angela, Carlos's behavior had become intolerable, inappropriate for a committed relationship. Carlos's lover lived in the campamento where Angela's mother and sister lived, and Carlos had often forbidden Angela from going there. Angela found this unacceptable: "He didn't let me see my family, but he would go and hang out and smoke pot in the campamento, and he got involved with someone else. So I decided to leave him and I left him with all of our things. I didn't care; one can get material things later, but it's the sentimental that really matters."

When she left Carlos, Angela went to the campamento. To an extent, the move freed Angela from the weight of her entangled relationship with Carlos. Once again, however, a secure and desirable home would prove elusive. The new neighborhood brought a host of new challenges. "It was almost impossible to live," Angela recalled, "because people would come from other poblaciones and there would be shots in the air, and these guys would pull out knives and daggers and there would be these big fights." Angela described this time as a "black period." She did make a few friends and gained a level of trust and support among her neighbors. Generally, however, she felt isolated, uncertain of how to proceed.

To make matters worse, Carlos sought to gain custody of their youngest son, Emilio. A social worker came to the campamento to assess Angela's capacity to take care of her child. Since Angela had to support herself, she often left Emilio alone or in the care of a neighbor when she went to work in a cafeteria, where she served food and cleaned. In her recollections, Angela claimed that she told the social worker about her job and the difficulty she sometimes had in making sure she had someone to look after her son. The social worker responded by convincing Angela that she was not providing appropriate care for him. As Angela relayed it to me, she thus agreed to let Carlos take Emilio back, and the child went to live first with Carlos's parents and then later in the home that Carlos began to establish with another woman.

The loss of her child led Angela into what she describes as her most difficult period, as she suffered the pain of personal loss and began to doubt her capacity as a mother and as a dueña de casa. She became a self-described drug addict: "I have realized now that one is never justified in doing what one does, but in that moment, it was like a great big push when they took my child away. I suffered because I adored my child and I fell into depression. I spent three years using *pasta base* [a relatively mild form of crack]." Throughout,

Angela kept working, but she sold many personal items to support her habit. Eventually, she found the fortitude to stop using. As she put it, "I love myself a lot and I have to treat myself well and I wasn't well . . . I fought, and I was able to move forward and improve myself." Angela describes her ability to quit drugs as a triumph of individual responsibility and sacrifice. This conception of personhood is a pervasive one, circulating through the drug rehabilitation programs Angela attended and structuring the way Chileans often narrate how they have developed their personal lives, achieved difficult objectives, and established their friendships and kinship networks. Pobladores, for example, regularly adopt this narrative in explaining how they came to have a home. It encapsulates the strength, fortitude, and self-possession that one is able to marshal to properly move forward.

Shortly after what Angela describes as becoming "clean" (*sana*), she began to have Emilio stay with her during the weekends. According to Angela's testimonial, at the end of the weekend Emilio wouldn't want to leave, because he was treated unfairly at his father's house. Carlos's girlfriend refused to wash his clothes and scolded him a lot, even hitting him at times. Angela claimed that the girlfriend was jealous of Emilio and unwilling to treat him as a family member.[19] From Angela's perspective, the situation was unacceptable. At the end of one weekend, Angela refused to let Emilio go back with Carlos. After a heated argument, Carlos finally left, leaving their son with her.

Despite the general bitterness in their relationship, Angela tried to reconcile with Carlos a few years later, after she had successfully moved into subsidized housing. For Angela, this effort was about trying to build a proper family. As she put it, "I wanted to have another child, but I always promised that the other child would have the same father, because I don't like it when they have different last names, it doesn't appear right to me." Largely because of this attitude, Angela invited Carlos to live with her again. The couple stayed together for several months and Angela became pregnant. But the relationship deteriorated again, and the only support Carlos offered to the second child was helping to pay for some of the medical costs when Angela went in to labor. They have only seen each other sporadically since. Angela now has children with the same last names, but her struggle to live in a home she considers appropriate continues.

The Persistent, Flexible Nature of the Politics of Propriety

As forms and expectations of propriety extend into varied, interconnected domains, they are often subtle and pervasive. They can include common practices and assumptions, such as the respect and importance that social actors grant to the privacy of the home. Certain acts and interactions, for example, are appropriate in a bedroom while others are not. If this is a simple point, it underscores how there are naturalized norms and conceptions that form a part of the politics of propriety and the making of home, serving as important foundations for behavior and social practice.

At the same time, however, individuals can challenge how ideas of possession and propriety might orient social relations. Raúl Soto, the poblador from Población Primero de Mayo, indicated in one of our conversations that he would never refer to Giovanna, his domestic partner, as *"mi señora* [my wife], as if I had bought her." Raúl was acutely aware of how notions of possession could problematically weigh on interpersonal relations, including the gendered bonds of marriage. Nonetheless, Raúl's understanding was not part of a wholesale rejection of the connection between individual property and personhood. Later in the same conversation, Raúl discussed how when he received subsidized housing in the early 1990s, he looked after his home like it was "a holy bone." He underscored how happy he was to have his own property, adding, "When a human being feels like the possessor of something, that person feels untouchable" (Murphy 2004a, 72). For Soto, having a home of his own was an empowering instantiation of his self-worth. Links between property, propriety, self-possession, and personhood were of vital importance.

Ubiquitous and complex, such links also entail individual expression and style, a point that can be lost if the focus remains exclusively on the disciplinary and normalizing elements of the urban politics of propriety. Consider, for example, Emilio Pastenes, who claimed that the "ideals of dignity" for which he had fought in taking part in establishing Campamento Lenin were at a far remove from present conditions in Lo Velásquez. Judging from his appearance, Emilio's comments on fighting "for ideals of dignity, such as a home, such as a well-constituted family" might seem out of place. Emilio has thick, long, greying hair that he pulls back in a ponytail. He wears leather bracelets and a silver necklace; multiple tattoos visibly stand out on his arms and neck. He delights in brash and uncouth talk, often poking fun at pretense and conventions. He occasionally makes sexually suggestive jokes, the kind that can make me blanch, upsetting both my feminist point of view and my white, North American, middle-class sensibilities.

On certain occasions, Emilio has invited me to his home for gatherings with friends and family. By all appearances, Emilio relishes boisterous gatherings and he is particularly fond of playing loud music (from classic hard rock bands like Deep Purple to contemporary Chilean hip hop acts). Attending these kinds of events is not something I take lightly: Chileans, and especially pobladores, tend to have a fairly tight circle of friends, family, and fictive kin who come to gatherings inside the home. As with Emilio, hosts generally seek to ensure that there is plenty to enjoy, as generous forms of sharing are a part of maintaining connections to extended family and close friends. Developing this circle of relations entails commitment, obligation, and reciprocity, including repeated attendance at gatherings for birthday parties, holidays, and other celebrations. It also involves support and solidarity in times of need. As an outsider, I was not always expected to act in these kinds of ways, but the fact that Emilio hosted me in his home for this type of get-together was nevertheless significant.

In important respects, Emilio is an heir to many countercultural movements in Chilean history. He initially assumed the look of a hippie during the late 1960s and early 1970s, subsequently adapting that style to fit with more contemporary trends.[20] His male swagger, working-class origins, and combative attitude recall the characteristics that fed the militancy of labor movements and other forms of popular activism before the military coup.[21] Emilio, it will be remembered, directly participated in this activism: he was a leader in a campamento known for its ties to the MIR and he subsequently took part in the street protests against the dictatorship during the 1980s. Through his appearance and attitude, Emilio expresses his disdain for conservative comportment and his support for alternative forms of bodily expression.

Given this, one might expect him to dismiss comments about dignity, home, and a well-constituted family. But the defense of such ideas has never been entirely antithetical to lower-class identities, countercultural styles, or popular forms of protest. To the contrary, such ideas have been woven into the fabric of both everyday life and public activism. There have been intense disagreements about what kind of behavior should be considered proper. Emilio would condemn, in no uncertain terms, the strict forms of personal discipline that the dictatorship enforced in hair styles and clothing, not to mention its harsher forms of violence and repression. He also is accepting, like many other pobladores, of varied kinds of family relationships, including those of fictive kin and single motherhood. His preference for tattoos, long hair, and jewelry are expressions of personal choice and style, an instantiation of the control he has over his body and the kind of lifestyles he chooses to take part in and celebrate. If, as I have argued, the links between property and propriety entail elements of personhood and forms of self-possession, they naturally lead to varied lifestyle choices as long as they are set within certain forms of discipline and comportment.

As a leader of Campamento Lenin in 1973, Emilio had helped to ensure that the pobladores in the neighborhood followed what he termed "moral requirements." This included relative abstinence from alcohol and drugs, not making "scandals" in which neighbors would be disturbed by domestic arguments or street conflicts, and a general willingness to act in solidarity (Murphy 2004a, 88–89). These requirements helped to create a more secure and communal neighborhood. For example, residents could depend on their neighborhood organization for support in building their homes and security at a time when they had neither locks nor security fences (see Cereño, Valdés, and Cancino in Murphy 2004a). The neighborhood was also, as in the case of Rosa Cancino, a relative sanctuary for single mothers. Rosa would have had little chance to access state-sanctioned housing without the land seizures. Given greater forms of tolerance for single motherhood in the campamento, she was able to establish a home of her own, finding a place in which her particular domestic situation was accepted. The neighborhood council, moreover, helped to make sure that Rosa's children were looked after when she was at her work as a maid, a rather different situation from what Angela described in the campamento she lived in during the 1990s and early 2000s. For pobladoras such as Rosa, collective action and neighborhood solidarity operated as a powerful form of support.

Such forms of neighborhood solidarity and support are not entirely gone. As discussed earlier, neighbors casually help each other out, providing a buffer against the pressures of commodified social relations. But such activities are much less common in the present environment: neighborhood organizations have declined; pobladores have withdrawn further into barricaded homes; suspicion and insecurity are more pronounced. The neoliberal environment places a greater emphasis on individual mobility and success, and pobladores have less ability to mobilize *as a group* around the conditions they face today than they once did. As Greg Grandin (2004, xv) argues more broadly for Latin America as a whole from the mid-twentieth century through the early 2000s, the link "between individual dignity and social solidarity" has, in important respects, been severed. Both dictatorial repression and neoliberal restructuring has helped to make this happen.

Though most pobladores have homes of their own, including access to urban services considered basic, they still struggle to create a home life of dignity and propriety, the ideals that inspired pobladores in the land seizures. An insecure and hostile urban environment adversely shapes the making of home. In such a context, pobladores confront a series of obstacles that can lead to difficult choices and strained domestic relations. They also find it more difficult to achieve the forms of self-possession and propriety that animate Chile's liberal property regime. The expectations of a proper, well-constituted, and desirable home that remain haunt the making of actually existing domestic spaces in the margins of urban life.

In a discussion of housing conditions in Mumbai, Arjun Appadurai (2000, 647) argues that the scarcity of housing in that city has a spectral quality to it, "haunt[ing] many conversations about resources, plans, hopes, and desires among all of its citizens." In Santiago today, housing is not nearly as scarce as it is in Mumbai. It is not nearly as scarce, for that matter, as it was fifty years ago in Santiago itself. Certain key processes analyzed in this book—the land seizures, urban renewal projects, subsidized housing programs, and building booms (and busts)—have changed the housing stock and, to a lesser extent, sociospatial relations in the city. The vast majority of pobladores today live in legally sanctioned homes. But housing, or, more to the point, the making of home, still haunts and vexes, especially for many pobladores. In Santiago's periphery, plans and hopes for home are entwined with evaluations of what is proper and the experience of a hostile urban environment, often leading to outcomes at odds with notions of a dignified life.

CONCLUSION

An y reader of this book, I suspect, has a strong point of view on the processes of reform, revolution, and reaction that pobladores have been embroiled within as they have struggled to gain a right to housing since the 1950s. Internationally, Chile stands as a poignant example of some of the new possibilities, destructive polarization, and imperial relations that were an integral part of Cold War conflicts in the Americas and the transition to neoliberalism. In a similar vein, I also suspect that the dynamics of urban marginality discussed provoke impassioned reactions. Few tend to remain neutral when considering such phenomena as the widespread existence of squatters, mass mobilizations on the part of the urban poor, and the implementation of far-reaching state policies in low-income housing.

Generally speaking, these are issues of broad concern for a number of publics in the world today. As such, people from across the globe have powerful and often conflicting interpretations that they can draw on in order to assess their significance. Strident and unambiguous language forms a part of these interpretations. Consider many of the terms that have been integral to the histories developed in this book: "state of emergency," "underdeveloped," "modernization," "national security," "land seizures," "slums," and "extreme poverty." There is an urgency here; such terms elicit a pervasive sense of insecurity and crisis. Violence, instability, chaos, and misery loom. Certain societies and populations seem destined to languish in poverty and backwardness. Exceptional measures must be taken in order to deal with the crises. Such categories are hardly neutral: they frame analysis and interpretation, often in the service of state power or imperial relations.

In researching and writing this book, I have not been immune to a sense of urgency. I have at times wanted—in keeping with a long line of urban and political chroniclers—to write an exposé of the conditions and dynamics I have come across, one that could perhaps mobilize a sense of shock and indignation. In many instances, my conversations with research participants unfolded in this vein, as we—and especially the interviewees—adopted a tone of righteous anger and denounced certain circumstances, relationships, and interests. As I spoke with them, they often formulated critical and caustic reflections about their place in the unfolding of Chilean history, from the nature of popular activism to social stigmatizations, governing structures, and living conditions in the campamentos and poblaciones. Such conversations could lead to significant insights, such as when Cecilia Castro criticized how definitions of poverty and campamentos delimit political action and community organizing.

Other kinds of conversations could also leave me with a sense of indignation and anger, but in a different way. Participants in the research for this book often shared painful recollections, filled with grief, anger, and loss. In one particularly emotional conversation, Ana Valdés related to me how in 1986 she suffered some of the very worst of the dictatorship's human rights abuses: kidnapping, secret detention, extreme torture, sexual violation, and eventual exile. The dictatorship's agents from the National Center of Information (CNI) targeted her for her past as a Communist Party leader of the May Day land seizure and subsequent activities as a community organizer and political activist. In 1998, she returned from having lived for more than ten years in Australia to Población Primero de Mayo, a place that was much changed for her. She found it difficult, at least as she related it to me, to find her footing in the shadow of past traumas and violations. There were, moreover, fewer opportunities to take part in the kinds of political organizing that had once been such a central part of her life. To make matters more complicated, only two of her four children had gone with her into exile. Upon returning, Ana indicated that it had not always been easy to bring the members of her family back together.[1]

There were, then, very specific histories and points of view that led me to a sense of urgency and indignation. At various moments when I engaged in conversation with the participants in my research project and prepared their testimonials for the public record, they seemed to expect that this would be the case, and that I would relay this response. I have not, however, ultimately written a singularly focused exposé. Instead, I have asked, why have struggles over property and propriety in the margins of urban Chile provoked repeated invocations to crises and states of emergency? Why would the mass presence of squatters have often been such an anxious point of contention, even as squatters themselves have been a part of a relatively disempowered underclass, often ignored and stigmatized? Why would observers from across the political spectrum have viewed mass numbers of squatters as an urgent problem? Why, alternatively, would it be more difficult, once former squatters have homes of their own, to denounce their present conditions and mobilize against them?

In apparently occupying a place outside of property relations, urban squatters have called attention to the tensions and weaknesses within the overall private property regime and even the liberal sociopolitical order. Squatters, in fact, have represented failings in that order. Reformists, revolutionaries, and reactionaries have each responded differently to these perceived failings. In the 1960s, Christian Democratic reformers sought programs that could integrate the urban poor more fully into political and economic structures, including loans and homeownership. Certain Leftists, for their part, viewed squatters who seized land as potential revolutionaries who could help build a socialist society. Reactionaries, on the other hand, tended to see squatters themselves as the problem: they were barbaric and subversive outsiders who needed to be disciplined and controlled. Eventually, as part of a dialectical response to the insurgent challenge posed by housing rights activism and a criticism of the existing state-sponsored housing projects for the urban poor, certain neoliberals would come to look at squatters in a more positive light. They began to argue that squatters had shown ingenious adaptive practices and entrepreneurial spirit in establishing their homes and communities. If squatters were granted the "freedom to build" through property titling programs, not only would they be more secure, they would also contribute to economic growth and a more integrated social order.[2]

Such interpretations are quite distinct and resonate far beyond Chile's borders. They have served as the foundation, moreover, for very different kinds of policies and approaches toward squatters. Nonetheless, they share the assumption that their existence demonstrates that something is fundamentally amiss or out of order. Throughout this book, I have sought to encapsulate this sense of something being out of order by exploring the multiple links between property and propriety, that nexus that I have referred to as the urban politics of propriety. Squatters have occupied a liminal, often dangerous space on the margins of this politics. Through the process of insurgent ownership, however, they have come in from the margins and gained a right to housing through their activism, a historic achievement. Yet in a tragic twist, they have not come to occupy conditions that certain links between property and propriety—such as a home life of dignity—were supposed to entail.

In the mid-twentieth century in Chile, squatting and low-income urban housing received unprecedented attention. There were a number of reasons for this. Santiago was growing at an unprecedented rate, part of a trend in major cities throughout Latin America and much of the global South. "Development" became a key term through which to understand Chile's trajectory and the status of its inhabitants, with particularly important consequences for groups like the urban poor. The political parties of the Left and Center worked more closely with pobladores than they ever had before. The central government, in collaboration with transnational development institutions, put in place housing projects that were unparalleled in scale. If such projects generally fell short of their promises, they underscored the wide gap between expectations of modern, "well-constituted homes" and actually existing conditions.[3] In a novel form of activism, pobladores began to establish housing and neighborhoods through well-publicized, organized land seizures, generally with the sponsorship of Leftists.

Yet though all of this was new, squatting and being *sin casa* in Santiago had long been problems. These conditions not only underscored the troubling circumstances that the urban poor had suffered, they also stood as an affront to the dignity and the sociopolitical status of the urban poor, presenting fundamental dilemmas for governance and citizenship. Since the colonial period, residential property holding in the city was part and parcel of exclusive forms of political belonging. With independence and the promises of liberal rule, more and more Chileans came to expect legal residence in the city as a right of citizenship. By the late nineteenth century, it became a basic norm of governance that the state would provide certain infrastructure services and minimally acceptable homes to citizens residing legally in the city. If this expectation reinforced a long-term bias that validated officially sanctioned urban residence, it also permitted low-income groups to demand specific rights within the city.

By the twentieth century, the "homeless" increasingly made a public claim that they were proper, urban citizens who deserved legally sanctioned homes and a certain range of services. Given prevailing attitudes toward the urban poor, successfully making this claim was never easy. Low-income residents had to demonstrate discipline as hardworking, responsible neighbors with the right kind of domestic relations. In the first half of the twentieth century, "homeless" pobladores also faced difficult conditions: a rapidly expanding yet ill-equipped city, a volatile and often corrupt urban real estate market, high levels of unemployment and underemployment, and forms of stigmatization and exclusion. Many could profit from the existence of illegal settlements, including politicians, welfare institutions, and land speculators. There was a great deal of confusion over the status of land titling in the city, a phenomenon that various actors could manipulate for their own ends.

Within this troubled and murky context, both officials and citizens increasingly recognized a crisis in urban housing. Beginning in the 1930s, the government passed a series of decrees and laws declaring that the callampas and campamentos were in a state of emergency. Such governing relations with squatters have been far from exclusive to Chile. Partha Chatterjee (2004), for example, explores how squatters in India live in extralegal conditions governed by emergency rule. Because of this situation, Chatterjee claims, these squatters cannot take part in the dynamics of "proper citizenship." Instead, they are a "governed" population, unable to act as members of civil society and make demands in the name of popular sovereignty. Their space for maneuver takes place within constricted notions of social well-being and formative categories that define how certain populations, such as squatters, can be a part of governing relations.

Chatterjee's analysis astutely points to some of the dangers and limits faced by squatters. When state bodies define squatters as being outside of the boundaries of proper citizenship, they can harshly repress and discipline them. Squatters, moreover, do tend to have a constricted horizon of demands they can make for housing. Yet Chatterjee's analysis is also too rigid; there can be a creative element to the ways in which squatters interact with the field of governing relations.[4] As happened in the Chilean case, squatters can act on the logic of a state of emergency in order to take part, as citizens, in such bold actions as the land seizures and occupy lands illegally. In Chile, homeless pobladores have argued that they were suffering in exceptional circumstances in which the extraordinary step of seizing land was a necessary one.

This was an assertion of popular sovereignty and part of a broader insurgent challenge to business as usual in the city. Squatters demanded that the forms of justice, fairness, and regulation that the state is supposed to ensure be made real. In taking part in the land seizures, homeless activists and pobladores adopted a new and more transgressive form of popular mobilization. They thus would stretch what was achievable within state frameworks, pushing the limits of property relations. They ultimately acted as insurgent owners, as they extended the boundaries of the possible within Chile's liberal property regime by ensuring that they would come to have homes of their own. Housing became a right of citizenship. The overall property regime became more inclusive. Yet as it was broadened, it was simultaneously strengthened.

Through both the intense activism of pobladores and programs of property titling and subsidized housing, the vast majority of low-income residents in Santiago have come to live in homes with undisputed property titles. This result makes the Chilean case rather distinct relative to the many cities that have had large numbers of squatters through the twentieth century. In a number of other cases, squatters have carved out a space for themselves in the city on murkier terms. This is, for example, the situation in Rio de Janeiro, as Brodwyn Fischer (2008, 305–15) demonstrates (see also McCann 2014). In Rio, *favelados* have generally gained access to their homes by taking advantage of the fact that their land titles are disputed. Over the years, squatters have bolstered their claims to their homes by, among other things, tending to their houses, receiving certain infrastructure services, and working within the legal system. As in the Chilean case, they have had show that they are citizens properly deserving of housing. Still, their situation is insecure as they ultimately have a disputed claim to their lands. Given this outcome, Fischer argues that favelados suffer from "a poverty of rights," in which they have not been able to fully claim their properties and the protections and benefits that citizenship is supposed to offer.

Such insecure and de facto forms of land tenure are a relatively common outcome for squatters in the global South. Given this, the Chilean case lies on one end of a continuum for squatters and former squatters, ranging from those who have no legal claim to their lands at all to those who have clear and free property titles. Pobladores in Chile do have a security of land tenure that many other squatters do not. They have also gained a right to housing. Still, they struggle to build their homes in an insecure, inequitable, and often hostile urban environment. Given this particular outcome, the Chilean case is less one of a poverty of rights, in which squatters are unable to gain full rights in the polity, than it is the fulfillment of an impoverished set of rights. Such rights can perhaps be broadened, as has happened in Chile, but the present context underscores their limits, especially in the wake of reactionary violence and neoliberal restructuring.

In any case, residential property has become even more embedded in the making of the city, a process that is particularly pronounced in Chile, but one that is also generally happening in much of the global South. In Chile, homeownership and the extension of residential forms of property have generally expanded across multiple centuries, but particularly so since the mid-twentieth century. Legally sanctioned residential properties have become so central to the social landscape today that they have played significant roles in shaping the built geographies of the city, the making of personhood, elements of citizenship, political economic relations, and the formation of the state. Yet while homeownership—and the broader private property regime of which it is a part—has been a crucial, enduring, and generally expanding part of the urban landscape, it has also been volatile, conflictive, and inequitable. Home has been a site of social reproduction and, undoubtedly, a source of comfort and joy for many. But it has simultaneously been a domain of struggle and unfulfilled desire, in which inequality and lack have been all too present.

Ultimately, the Chilean experience with the urban politics of propriety opens a window to the historically embedded, expansive, and consequential nature of private property regimes and the making of home within modern urban social relations and liberal forms of governance. The significance of this politics across projects of reform, revolution, and reaction underscores its centrality. Such an observation need not diminish the importance of ideological conflicts and radical political changes. In seizing land, pobladores took part in a general democratic insurgency that granted them greater rights and legal residence in the city. In repressing housing activists, reactionaries in the dictatorship contained the more radical and expansive strands that went into the mobilization of pobladores. In their social policies, these reactionaries responded only to the demand for minimally acceptable housing, not to broader efforts to build homes of dignity and a more inclusive, democratic society. Still, whether reformist, revolutionary, or reactionary, each of Chile's presidencies has acted within a field of governing relations in which links between property and propriety have invariably carried weight. Over the long run, moreover, these presidencies have also each contributed to the fact that pobladores now generally live in legally sanctioned housing.

The kinds of mass mobilizations, intense conflicts, and ambitious development projects that have hinged on efforts to make legally recognized homes point to the urgent and pervasive nature of the urban politics of propriety. This politics has given meaning and substance to many of the profound crises and spectacular transformations that Chileans have gone through during this period. In the end, the urban politics of propriety has provided an ongoing, if evolving, grounding for the formation of the state and sociospatial relations.

Within this politics, pobladores have earned a basic right as citizens to housing. Yet while such a change is of profound importance, it has not necessarily provided the means for a home life of security, comfort, and dignity. For the period covered in this study, pobladores have generally ended up being constrained in their gains by both the achievement of homeownership and bounded notions of poverty reduction. The uneasy outcome has been circumscribed and troubled forms of housing in which political activism has become more difficult for pobladores. As Engels (1872) argued in a polemic long ago, "the housing question" can be a limited one, especially in the ways that it is approached and answered in terms of charity and state policy.

Engels, however, paid scant attention to how practices, expectations, and desires have a pervasive hold on the making of home and residential property.

I have sought throughout this book to take such phenomena into account, embedding housing debates and the acquisition of property within an interpretation that weaves together elements of market dynamics, gender practices and ideologies, state formation, the production of space, and citizen relations. When contextualized in this way, the housing question remains an open and often unsettled one, an elemental part of modern spatial relations within liberal polities. Questions about how to make a proper home life endure, forming an ongoing part of everyday life.

In one of his earlier writings, Raymond Williams (1989 [1958], 4) claimed that "the making of a society is the finding of common meanings and directions, and its growth is an active debate and amendment under the pressures of experience, contact, and discovery, writing themselves into the land." In seizing land and establishing homes of their own, pobladores have "written themselves into the land." They now generally have legally sanctioned residence. They have changed their living conditions and ensured that housing is a right of citizenship. Intense mobilization made these transformations possible, struggles that often included a revolutionary component.

In making their homes, pobladores have contributed to the making of their city and society. In doing so, they have also played a role in the extension of private property regimes, the unfolding of state power and citizenship, and the production of space in the city. In spite of such contributions, their efforts to build a home life considered appropriate continue, as they live in a city marked by unmet desires and fractured social and spatial relations. The problematic circumstances that pobladores often face today provide an unsettled conclusion to a half century of struggles over housing. To paraphrase Marx, pobladores have homes of their own, but not necessarily under conditions of their choosing. Their efforts to build home lives of dignity continue. As Dipesh Chakrabarty (2001, 123–24) insists, "To be at home in modernity . . . is an ongoing and ceaseless process."

David Harvey (2012, 4) has written that "the question of what kind of city we want cannot be divorced from the question of what kind of people we want to be, what kind of social relations we seek, what relations to nature we cherish, what style of life we desire, what aesthetic values we hold." Life in the city entails a host of interconnected elements, including comportment, tastes, consumptive practices, forms of production, the making of the state, and the built environment. Throughout this book, I have sought to recognize how these elements have come together in the making of homes on Santiago's urban periphery. I have thus attempted to contextualize the kinds of claims to housing that pobladores have been able to make. Limited, governing visions and techniques of housing have done insufficient justice to the multiple elements that go into the constitution of home. Yet home and private property remain intractably tied to how so many humans inhabit their dwellings, in Chile and globally. In certain ways, home can provide a vision of peace, security, and belonging in a hostile and fractured world, in which crises are all too present. As such, people will continue struggling to create and maintain homes they consider to be appropriate. Activism will surely be a part of this. In these struggles to come, efforts to build proper homes might be freed from the shackles and emergencies of the past, but cognizant of the critical place that home occupies in any movement for forms of social justice.

NOTES

Introduction

1. Working in the early 1970s in Mexico City, Lomnitz describes networks of *compadrazgo* that were more central to the lives of the groups that she studied than they were for low-income urban Chileans in the early 2000s. In the Chilean case, the urban poor lived in a more individualistic context, brought on by decades of neoliberal policies and the fact that most lived in generally established and physically secure neighborhoods. Still, most of the urban poor in Santiago depended, to one degree or another, on ties of compadrazgo.

2. I discuss the labor market at greater length in chapter eight. The country saw a rise in the official unemployment rate from about 7.5 percent in 2008 to near 11 percent in mid-2009. See INE (2010).

3. For 1960, I have determined this number based on data in the second national census of housing, available in INE (1960). See also Astica and Vergara (1958). For 2002, see MIDEPLAN (2002, chart 8.1). Note that these statistics refer only to the fact that the dwellings are legally owned. The occupants themselves are, in many cases, renters and do not own the properties they dwell in. While these statistics illustrate trends, for several reasons they should not be taken as precise. Shifts in housing, particularly in precarious squatting settlements, have often occurred quickly in Chile's urban periphery. Surveys often miss this fluidity. Moreover, respondents may not be forthcoming about their situation due to the stigma associated with squatting and its illegality.

4. Eley (1994) and Calhoun (1992), among others, develop the idea that public legitimacy depends on certain levels of well-being within the private sphere of the home. For a synthetic discussion of the public and the private, see Warner (2005, 21–64).

5. Engels (1872) first noted the constrained nature of "the housing question," something I explore at greater length in Murphy (2013a).

6. There are other analysts who also avoid reifying the home, especially among feminist Marxists.

7. As part of a long-running literature in anthropology, Janet Carsten (2004, 83–108; Carsten and Hugh-Jones 1995) discusses how both the house and kinship act as an extension of personhood.

8. Paley (2001), Salazar (2005), and Bengoa (2009), among others, explore the effects of neoliberal restructuring in Santiago.

9. Bruey (2012) insightfully raises this point while examining housing mobilization during the dictatorship. The best general literature on neoliberalism emphasizes not only

its extensive reach but also its limits and the need to contextualize it within specific historical trajectories. See Brenner and Theodor (2002), Harvey (2005, 2012), and especially Kingfisher and Maskovsky (2008).

10. See, for example, Haber (2009). Gilbert (2002) traces Chile's rise as a model for neoliberal housing policies.

11. Critics can also propagate this myopia, as in the otherwise excellent contributions in Rodríguez and Sugranyes (2005).

12. Among others, Gay (2005), Holston (2008), and Goldstein (2004) have noted how legal land tenure can help squatters have more security and thus commit more resources and effort to improving their housing.

13. I discuss these points further in chapter three.

14. There are also cases where the state subsidized only the development and demarcation of empty lots with infrastructure surfaces, a particularly important approach to housing during the 1960s, as I discuss in chapter three.

15. As these developments have become more common, the stigma associated with them has slowly loosened its grip, especially in areas, as Salcedo (n.d.) notes, in which there are a number of middle- and lower-income neighborhoods.

16. On this general perspective, see, among others, Williams (1973) and Harvey (2003).

17. Rodríguez and Sugranayes (2005) emphasize the importance of these programs since the 1970s and argue that the urban poor today confront difficulties that move beyond issues of basic housing. While agreeing with their conclusion, I date the importance of state housing programs to earlier periods and discuss how popular forms of mobilization also helped to shape contemporary low-income housing conditions.

18. Close male friends in Chile also often call each other *compadres* informally, without necessarily establishing the reciprocal ties of compadrazgo that I am referring to here.

19. Gandolfo (2009, 187) insightfully raises these points.

Chapter 1. The Urban Politics of Propriety through Revolution and Reaction

1. Westad (2007) adopts the term "global cold war."

2. On human rights, see, among others, Lowden (1996) and Wright (2007).

3. Among others, see Grandin (2004, 2006), Harvey (2005), and Coronil (2007).

4. Stern (1999) argues that time plays particular "tricks" in Latin America, as elements of the colonial past weigh heavily on the conditions and sensibilities of the present. From a very different perspective, Massey (1993) argues that analysts need to account for space and time simultaneously, as physicists since Einstein have done (see also Coronil 1997).

5. On gender for recent periods, see Kirkwood (1990), Rosemblatt (2001), Frazier (2007), Pieper Mooney (2009), and Thomas (2011). On looking beyond the dictatorship as a singular aberration in an otherwise peaceful, democratic history, see Frazier (2007), Mallon (2001, 2005), and Loveman and Lira (2000).

6. Latin American historians of gender are one example of this trend, generally stressing that the ideologies and dynamics of gender simultaneously change and operate through long-term legacies. Adelman (1999) discusses the importance and difficulty of accounting for persistence in Latin American history.

7. After several decades of interdisciplinary work produced in anthropology and history, I cannot provide a review of this rich and varied scholarship here. For recent assessments, however, see Willfred and Tagliacozzo (2009) and Murphy et al. (2011). In the latter volume, I developed, in conjunction with a team of co-editors and contributors, the kind of critically reflexive, socially engaged, and transdisciplinary approach to scholarship that I have sought to practice in working on this book.

8. There is a vast literature on limits and liminality, beyond what I can cite here, although three works have been particularly instructive to my approach. Das and Poole (2004) emphasize how analyzing the state's margins offers an insightful vantage point from which to explore the shape and boundaries of state power itself. In a literary analysis of the Pinochet dictatorship, Lazarra (2006) explores how the regime created "limit experiences" that took place at the very boundaries of discursive expression, producing liminal subjects. In a historically suggestive ethnography, Gandolfo (2009) shows how the tense unfolding of order, hierarchy, and urban renewal efforts in Lima can best be understood by exploring taboos and transgressions.

9. For important overviews in this vein, see Verdery (2003, 1–32) and Verdery and Humphrey (2004).

10. Appadurai (1986) develops the notion of the "social lives of things," while Blomley (2003, 122) makes the general observation that one's standing in relation to property is a critical factor in "evaluations of one's political and moral worth."

11. I have loosely drawn inspiration here from Latour (2005, 145), who insists on the importance of "going back to the object."

12. For other discussions of the link between property and propriety, see Sturman (2005), Verdery (2003, 15–20), Scott (2001), and Collins (2011).

13. Holston (2008, 114) notes that the idea that individuals need to *earn* self-possession (being the proprietors of their own persons) through labor and merit is a Hegelian concept, different from that of John Locke, who saw self-possession as inherent in nature. The Hegelian concept has informed jurisprudence in Brazil, as it also has done in Chile.

14. In an overview of anthropological approaches to the home, Miller (2001b) points out that there has been an increasingly ubiquitous split between the private and public in home life on a global level. For a statement on the broader relevance of the characteristics I list for modernity, see Chakrabarty (2001).

15. The Right to the City Movement is an important organization seeking housing rights in the United States. Samara (2013) provides a discussion.

16. This dominant ideology elides how the US federal government has played a crucial role in developing homeownership since the 1930s and how restrictive neighborhood covenants and redlining practices have shaped the segregated geographies of homeownership. See, among others, Sugrue (1996).

17. Davis (2006, 25–26), drawing from UN HABITAT (2005, 13–14), makes this credible estimate. The use of the term "slum" is problematic, failing to account for the heterogeneity of urban poverty.

18. Dawdy (2008) develops this point in examining eighteenth century French colonization in New Orleans. For historical perspectives from Latin America, see Milanich (2009),

Picatto (2001), and especially Chazkel (2011). Roy and AlSayyad (2004), Portes and Haller (2005), and Roy (2011), among others, develop contemporary, global analyses in this vein.

19. On these general dynamics, see Fischer (2014a), in addition to Skrabut (2013) and Roy (2003).

20. For examples of laws and ordinances that refer to *poblaciones de emergencia* in order to implement specific state policies, see Ley 11211 (1953), Ley 14670 (1961), Ley 16955 (1968), and Resolución 3717 (1991), all available at the Biblioteca del Congreso. Espinoza (1988) and Hidalgo (2005) note that governments in the 1930s initiated emergency housing legislation. The Argentine state developed similar legislation, as Benmergui (2013) and Healey (2011) discuss. On the importance of a state of emergency framework for squatters in India and Colombia, see Chatterjee (2004) and Ziederman (2008), respectively.

21. Martland (2007) analyzes how responses to the 1906 earthquake in Valparaíso contributed to an expansion in the size of the state bureaucracy, something that also happened following an earthquake in the south in 1938. For a similar process in Peronist Argentina, see Healey (2011).

22. My wording in this sentence follows Rabinow's (1989) in assessing the "norms and forms" of the social environment.

23. Given this, Buck-Morss (2007) persuasively argues that Gramscian perspectives on consensual forms of hegemony need to be modified in order to account for these kinds of state mechanisms.

24. In an analogous register, Goldstein (2004) analyzes how low-income residents in Cochabamba, Bolivia, claim a right to take part in such actions as land seizures and lynchings since state institutions have failed to provide housing and security.

25. See my discussion in chapter two, in addition to Holston (2008), Fischer (2008), Benmergui (2009, 2013), Healey (2011), and Way (2012). In Chile, Klubock (1998, 2004a), Rosemblatt (2000), Espinoza (1988), and Garcés (2002a) discuss how organized workers in Chile generally came to access housing by the mid-twentieth century.

26. For examples, see Holston (2008), Goldstein (2004), Perlman (2010), Murphy (2004b), and Rodgers (2014). Gilbert (2004, 57–59) observes that the neoliberal property titling policies in vogue in international development circles since the early 1990s extended legally sanctioned property holding. It is far from inevitable, however, that new squatter neighborhoods will not appear. In examining a squatter settlement in greater Buenos Aires, Auyero and Swistun (2009) develop how the economic crises of the late 1990s and early 2000s played an important role in the formation of this settlement and others.

27. See Fischer (2008), Skrabut (2013), and McCann (2014). Dahua (2014) and Fischer (2014a, 2014b) each caution that land tenancy patterns are variable in Latin American squatter settlements and develop in grudgingly accepted ways. Neuwirth (2005) places this point in a global perspective.

28. Holston (2008) and Fischer (2008) discuss the prevalence of corruption in the Brazilian case, while Skrabut (2013) analyzes similar dynamics in contemporary Peru.

29. Thomas (2011) analyzes the importance of normative ideals of family in debates about the legitimacy of Chile's governing order between 1970 and 1990. Frazier (2007, 161) astutely analyzes how suffering motherhood is a part of a "hierarchy of deserving victimhood" crucial to politics in Chile and beyond.

30. Teresa Valdés (2010, 255), a presidential adviser to Bachelet, is remarkably forthcoming on this point.

31. In Chile, for the period from the 1960s to the present, see Kirkwood (1990), Baldez (2002), Power (2002, 2004), Franceschet (2005), Tinsman (2002), Pieper Mooney (2009), and Thomas (2011). For elsewhere in Latin America, see Schirmer (1989), Randall (1992), and Gandolfo (2009, 208–13).

32. See Taylor (1997) and Grandin (2004, 133–68) for the opposite poles in this debate.

33. On state fetishism, see, among others, Taussig (1993), Coronil (1997), and Gupta and Ferguson (2002).

34. Holston and Appadurai (1999) call these kinds of performances "dramas of citizenship," a term that Goldstein (2004) also uses and elaborates on.

35. I first developed a similar argument in examining the consolidation of a squatter community in the Guatemalan context. In that case, I used the ironic title "sustainable periphery." See Murphy (2004b).

36. Although less explicit about it, Stern (2004, 2006, and 2010) and Holston (2008) also refer to how ideas of dignity are entwined with the claims of citizenship.

Chapter 2. Property, Governance, and the City: A *Longue Durée* Perspective

1. Like the Annales School from which it takes its inspiration, this chapter is a bit schematic and generally reliant on other social histories. If these are shortcomings (which I'm not convinced they are), they have nonetheless permitted me to take a long-term view that reveals how it became possible for a disjuncture to develop between expectations of an appropriate home life and actually existing living conditions. This provided a means for low-income urban citizens to claim a right to housing. This perspective reorients the conjunctures described in later chapters.

2. I identify these two impulses based first on the kinds of Marxist interpretations of urbanization that Berman (1982) and Harvey (2003) develop and second on the perspectives of Michel Foucault (1975, 1991).

3. Also of note, the civil wars of 1851 and 1859 undermined regionalism, fortifying Santiago as the dominant metropolitan center in Chile.

4. Cariola and Sunkel (1982, 89, 141) observe that the number of national public functionaries increased from 3,048 in 1880 to 27,469 in 1919, reaching 47,193 by 1930.

5. For Vicuña Mackenna's use of these terms, see Hidalgo (2005, 33). Illanes (1993) discusses the relationship between Chilean public health projects and efforts to order urban space and society. For comparative perspectives, see, among others, Armus (2011, 307–44), Rodríguez (2006), and Picatto (2001).

6. For overviews on policía in the colonial period, see Kagan and Marías (2000), Fraser (1990), and Lechner (1981). Staples (1994) explores a national period use of the term in Mexico, while Goldstein (2014) and Gandolfo (2009) analyze its legacies in urban Peru.

7. This grid design had Roman precedents. De Solano (1996) provides a compilation of laws and decrees that developed how the layout of the city should appear.

8. For specifics in Santiago, see de Ramón (2007). De Solano (1996) and Kinsbruner (2005) provide Latin American overviews.

9. The extent to which the ideas entailed in policía extended into the consciousness of the lower classes is an open question. As Spanish American historiography makes clear, the colonial project was quite diverse and leaky, with several groups, especially in outlying areas, practicing a great deal of autonomy. My concern in this brief overview, however, is to identify those elements of policía that endured into the national period and worked in conjunction with new factors to produce the politics I analyze more fully in later periods.

10. Intendencia de Santiago, Plan Regulador 1872, as cited in Espinoza (1988, 20).

11. I use the term "popular" to refer generally to the lower classes, as this is the term used both in Chile and Chilean historiography. It has a more particular valence in Chilean Spanish than in English, as it points to how lower-class experiences and struggles point to what many interpret as general phenomena.

12. For the original uses of these terms, see de Ramón (2007, 146).

13. The city's percentage of the national population increased from 7.1 percent to 12.7 percent.

14. For the statistic on female industrial labor, see Hutchison (2001, 44). See also Vicuña (2001, 129–234).

15. Salazar (1992 and 2000) makes this error, in work that often otherwise brilliantly exposes the alternative practices of the popular sectors in Chile. Salazar conceives of the popular classes as both too autonomous and too singular in their formation, misconceptions that often bedevil studies of marginal urban populations.

16. Chazkel (2011, 264) notes the importance of "resisting resistance" narratives in describing people who take part in informal activities.

17. The literature on the formation of labor unions in this period is too vast to cite here, but see DeShazo (1983), Salazar (2000), and Klubock (1998).

18. Arrate and Rojas (2003), Frazier (2007), and Pavilack (2011), among others, analyze Leftist imaginaries.

19. Orlove (1997), Espinoza (1988, 24–32), and Garcés (2003) also provide overviews of the riots.

20. See, for example, the communiqué issued by the Democratic Party, as cited in Espinoza (1988, 31).

21. On these general dynamics, see Hidalgo (2005). Hidalgo (2005, 4) also notes that certain Catholic groups and some of Chile's larger industries, such as the Compañía de Gas, began to build houses for married workers with the idea of promoting indebted, if also subsidized forms of homeownership.

22. Espinoza (1988, 35) provides the quote, in addition to a number of similar ones.

23. On this general point outside of Chile, see, among others, Armus (2011, 316–17) and Burnett (1986).

24. Espinoza (1988, 39–45) and Hidalgo (2005, 53–98) provide overviews of the law.

25. Hidalgo (2005, 56) notes that the law provided the basis for the 1910 formation of the Caja Nacional de Ahorros, a state body that helped to foment and regulate mortgages.

26. On soccer clubs and fields, see Elsey (2011). Armus (2011, 334–44) discusses the importance of the "hygienic house" in Buenos Aires.

27. Walter (2005, 35) notes that official oversight of the conventillos was also poor, especially given the limited resources municipalities had.

28. *El Mercurio*, July 9, 1914.

29. *La vivienda*, Apr. 24, 1927, 1.

30. See capítulo 3, artículo 10, punto 10 of the 1925 constitution, available at the Biblioteca del Congreso. For a discussion of the clauses about private property, see Gómez Leyton (2004, 109).

31. Espinoza (1988), Hidalgo (2005), and Walter (2005) all discuss the 1906 legislation, but do not mention how this included implicit promises about urban services and legally sanctioned residence.

32. See, for example, the earlier advertisement in *El Mercurio*, Aug. 19, 1914.

33. Fischer (2008) details similar processes in Rio de Janeiro.

34. To my knowledge, a survey of these neighborhoods does not exist. There is some general data in the documentation that accompanies the 1968 law designed to clean up the "ghost subdivisions." See Biblioteca del Congreso, Historia de la Ley 16.741, and Espinoza (1988, 125–29).

35. Contemporaries, Walter (2005, 145–65) writes, described a "fever of construction."

36. See, for example, the testimonial in Garcés (2002a, 35–41).

37. Hidalgo (2005, 147) notes the precedent set in this regard in laws established in 1931 and 1935.

38. See, for example, the quotes in Espinoza (1988, 96).

39. Fischer (2008) and Holston (2008) examine how important long-term occupation of land, in which residents developed their own homes, was to the legal claims that squatters made in Brazil during this period.

40. See *Vivir*, publication of Vista Hermosa Población, June 1927, as cited in Espinoza (1988, 137).

41. I have determined the change by doing a general electronic search of certain newspapers and publications from the late nineteenth century through the 1920s.

42. On these terms, see Milanich (2009, 16–17) and Salazar (1992).

43. Valdés (1987, 266) provides these statistics, which should be taken as general trends; there are discrepancies among sources. Compare, for example, Instituto Nacional de Estadísticas (INE) (2005, 36).

44. For the 1940 figure, see INE (1952) and for 1970, MIDEPLAN (1996a).

45. Meller (1996) provides an insightful overview of these developments of the role of copper in Chile.

46. Three important recent studies in this vein are Tinsman (2014), Elena (2011), and Karush and Chamosa (2010).

47. See, among others, Zeitlin and Ratcliff (1988) and Winn (1986, 13–31).

48. On the rise of the middle class from the late nineteenth century onward, see Barr-Melej (2001) and Salazar and Pinto (2002, 65–92).

49. Klubock (1998), Vergara (2008), Rosemblatt (2000), Frazier (2007), Arrate and

Rojas (2003), Pinto, Candina, and Lira (2001), and Pavilack (2011) analyze the evolution of Leftist political parties and popular forms of mobilization.

50. I date the end of the Popular Front to the year in which the governing coalition outlawed the Communist Party.

51. Klubock (1998 and 2004b) pioneered this analysis.

52. For two examples, see Winn (1986) and Sabatini (1995). Sabatini details how the Hirmas textile conglomerate built three neighborhoods for their workers in Renca: Hirmas 1, 2, and 3.

53. See Besse (1996) and Caulfield (2000), among others. For Chile, Rosemblatt (2000) insightfully discusses the "gendered compromises" of the Popular Front. See also Pieper Mooney (2009) and Tinsman (2002).

54. On the general importance of housing and family relations to issues of labor and governance in Latin America at this time, see Farnsworth-Alvear (2000), Weinstein (1996, 219–50), and Elena (2011).

55. On the Pereira Law, see Hidalgo (2005, 180–82); on the 1959 legislation, see Biblioteca del Congreso, Historia del Decreto con Fuerza de Ley 2, Cleaves (1974, 245–48), and Hidalgo (2005, 227–66).

56. Maltes, Bessone, and Cabala (1970, 36), compiled the survey data.

57. On the importance of housing initiatives in the Americas in the 1950s and 1960s, see Benmergui (2009, 2013).

58. Among others, see Espinoza (1988, 250–70) and Garcés (2002a, 121–66).

59. Engels (1872) provides the classic Marxist perspective.

60. Fischer (2008, 2014c) discusses Communist Party involvement in the favelas of Rio de Janeiro.

61. Garcés (1998, 2002a), Educación y Comunicaciones (1994), and Espinoza (1988, 185–386) analyze the PC's sponsorship of Santiago's most famous land invasions between 1947 and 1970 and their increasing importance to the national imagination.

62. For illuminating analyses of the role of the political parties, see Moulian (1993) and Valenzuela (1978).

Chapter 3. A Place in the State: Housing Activism and the Seizure of Land, May Day, 1969

1. For the edited testimonial on which I base this reconstruction, see Murphy (2004a, 39–65).

2. In developing her analysis, Rosemblatt (1995 and 2000) draws on the term "well-constituted home." This expression overlaps with Ana's phrase, although it points more centrally to the material reality of a house.

3. These events, called *peñas*, became more and more common in the poblaciones throughout the 1960s. The political parties of the Left often, but by no means exclusively, hosted the peñas. For contemporary descriptions of peñas, see the accounts in neighborhood and municipal presses, such as *El Cordillerano*, *El Vocero*, and *Adelante Poblador*, in addition to Gustavo Retamales in Murphy (2004a, 122–26).

4. According to Cleaves (1974, 288), there were seventy-four urban land seizures in

Chile between 1955 and 1969, the vast majority of which the police broke up. See also Garcés (2002b, 4) and Goldrich (1970, 194).

5. This figure is an estimate. Duque and Pastrana (1972, 259) note that 54,710 "families" took part in the land seizures. The use of *families* is problematic, however, since it uncritically asserts that families were the basic unit in household organization. Despite this shortcoming, I estimated the total number of people based on combining Duque and Pastrana's figure with a contemporary survey that determined that the average household size in low-income Santiago was 5.1. See Maltes, Bessone, and Cabala (1970, 28).

6. The increase in urban land seizures follows a similar trajectory as the takeovers of agricultural estates and the increased strike activity in the factories and mines. See Tinsman (2002, 195) and Valenzuela (1978, 29–31), respectively.

7. *El Diario Ilustrado*, May 5, 1969.

8. Salazar (1998) and Valenzuela (1977) provide perspectives on the historical preeminence of the Chilean central government from the late nineteenth century until the military coup.

9. Poole (2004) usefully analyzes how state bureaucracies offer both "threats" and "guarantees" to citizens.

10. *El Siglo*, April 29, 1969, 9. Silvia Contreras and Eliana Parra in Murphy (2004a) also remembered Marín's involvement. On a daily basis, Humberto Fuentes, a *concejal* from Renca, played a much greater role in the lives of the pobladores.

11. Valenzuela (1978, 9) makes this general point.

12. For but one of dozens of examples of elected officials writing to MINVU officials on behalf of neighborhood organizations, see the letter from Eugenio Ballesteros Reyes, the president of the Chamber of Deputies to the Minister of Housing and Urbanism, Modesto Collados, Jan. 18, 1966, in the Archivo de la Administración (hereafter ADA), Ministerio de Vivienda y Urbanismo, Oficios con Antecedentes (hereafter MINVU OA), Feb./Mar. 1966. See also Equipo de Estudios Poblacionales (1972, 57).

13. One example is in ADA, MINVU OA, July, Aug., and Sept. 1966.

14. There were other mottoes that rhetorically linked the land seizures to revolutionary socialism, including "Home or death, we shall overcome" (Casa o muerte, venceremos), a saying that echoed the "Socialism or death, we shall overcome" motto of the Cuban Revolution.

15. Goldrich (1970, 194), Cleaves (1974, 292), and Garcés (2002a, 358) provide estimates of the number of pobladores involved.

16. See *Las Noticias de Última Hora*, Mar. 16, 1967, 16, and Equipo de Estudios Poblacionales, CIDU (1972, 57). *El Siglo*, Mar. 17, 1967, 7, a Communist daily, reports that thirty-eight were arrested, while *El Mercurio*, Mar. 17, 1967, 23, Chile's conservative newspaper of record, puts the number at fourteen. Discrepancies of this kind occurred often in the press, a reflection of the polarized ideological positions held by Chile's mass media.

17. *El Siglo*, Mar. 17, 1967, 1, covers Marín's involvement and *El Mercurio*, Mar. 17, 1967, 23, Allende's.

18. Details of the survey are in *El Siglo*, Apr. 20, 1967, and Cleaves (1974, 293).

19. For this description of Herminda de la Victoria, in addition to the sources cited

above, I have also relied on Moulián and de Wolf (1993), Espinoza (1988, 282–89), Muñoz Tamayo and Madrid Herrera (2005), and press reports.

20. Jara released the album for the Seventh National Congress of the National Command of the Homeless in September 1971. See *El Siglo*, Sept. 19, 1971, 5, and *La Prensa*, Sept. 26, 1971, 6.

21. Marín's claims that the Renca homeless committee all had met savings quotas was a contentious point, as I discuss below. Her speech is in *El Siglo*, Apr. 29, 1969, 4.

22. Murphy (2004a, 34). Eliana told me this story on a cold, rainy day in July 2002 as we shared cups of Nescafé and reruns of Chilean *telenovelas* played in the background. I have no way to verify the extent to which Eliana's recollections follow the precise conversations that occurred. But Eliana and other research participants often recalled situations in which they could denounce government officials. Such recurrent narrative forms (Passerini 1987) suggest how important it is for pobladores to create a space in which they demand and receive the respect of government representatives. See also chapter five, note 14.

23. On the Alliance for Progress and the Christian Democratic platform, see, among others, Sigmund (1993, 11–47), Pieper Mooney (2009, 74–101), Tinsman (2002, 82–127), and Moulián and Guerra (2000, 145–212).

24. Frazier (2007) argues that a "desire for the working class" was important in both Leftist activism and reform efforts.

25. Grandin (2004), Joseph (2008), and Grandin and Joseph (2010) provide this interpretation of the Cold War, decentering the understanding of the conflict away from an overemphasis on the United States and the Soviet Union.

26. Cámara de Diputados, *Sesiones Ordinarias*, June 25, 1969, 969.

27. Benmergui (2009, 2013) analyzes the transnational dimensions of such experts in Argentina and Brazil.

28. Oficio 7763 in ADA MINVU 1966, in addition to Cleaves (1969, 55) and Cleaves (1974, 201).

29. *La Nación*, Dec. 6, 1964, 15.

30. See, for example, Orlando Millas's intervention in the Chamber of Deputies in Cámara de Diputados, *Sesiones Ordinarias*, June 16, 1965, 1073–74.

31. In fact, the most Chile had built in a year was 36,961 units in 1962. See Bravo Heitmann (1993, 45).

32. *El Diario Ilustrado*, Nov. 4, 1964, 35.

33. See ADA, MINVU OA, Jan. 1968, letter from J. Eduardo Truyol Díaz to the president of the Directorate of Población Canihuante, Ovalle, Jan. 5, 1968.

34. By the 1970s and 1980s, the term *callampa* had largely fallen into disuse.

35. In his analysis of modern understandings of health, Conguilhem (1989) argues that conceptions of what is normal presume the existence of pathology, reflecting a normative stance about what is a proper state of being. See also Sontag (1990).

36. Cámara de Diputados, *Sesiones Ordinarias*, June 16, 1965, 1068.

37. Cámara de Diputados, *Sesiones Ordinarias*, June 16, 1965, 1069.

38. Tinsman (2002, 186), has analyzed similar assumptions in the land reform programs, while Benmergui (2009) uncovers them in urban housing projects in Argentina and Brazil.

39. Academics working at the think tank DESAL (el Centro de Desarrollo Social de América Latina) developed the intellectual arguments at the heart of Popular Promotion and the marginality school in Chile. For a widely read, synthetic statement on the assumptions and goals of Popular Promotion, see Vekemans and Venegas (1966).

40. Valenzuela (1978, 33) points out that these government figures are probably overstated, but there was nevertheless a significant increase.

41. Maltes, Bessone, and Cabala (1970, vol. 1, 117), reported that close to 30 percent of pobladores were migrants. Herrick (1965, 46 and 97) places the number at 37 percent, a number equal to the overall immigration for all sectors in Santiago.

42. Power (2002, 96 and 140) provides statistics on the voting results in seven low-income municipalities in Santiago in the 1964 and 1970 elections. In the 1970 elections, for example, Allende won the national election with 36 percent of the vote while his support in the poblaciones ran at 42 percent. See also Urzúa Valenzuela (1992, 641–43).

43. Perlman (1976) makes this case for Brazil, Portes (1971 and 1976) for Chile.

44. For a synthetic critique of the marginality school along these lines, see Castells (1983, 175–212).

45. There is a vast literature on modernization theory. Latham (2000) criticizes its teleological assumptions. Ferguson (1991), Escobar (1995), and especially Saldaña-Portillo (2003) underscore the hierarchical sensibilities and forms of subjectivity embedded in discourses of development more broadly.

46. Perlman (2010) and González de la Rocha et al. (2004) provide current reflections on the Marginality School and its critics.

47. It should be noted that this is also what Oscar Lewis (1970) believed as he developed his thesis of a "culture of poverty." The Marginality School drew on Lewis, as did policymakers in the United States. As Rosemblatt (2009) discusses, different audiences took varied lessons from Lewis's work; some focused more on the pathologies of the urban poor than others.

48. ADA, MINVU OA, Feb. 1969, César Díaz Muñoz to Eduardo Toledo Mora, Feb. 2, 1969.

49. Cleaves (1974, 234–73) demonstrates that this process was not necessarily legally corrupt but that the Chilean Chamber of Commerce and MINVU were interdependent. These bodies had shared interests, in which 80 percent of housing contracts originated in the public sphere. Pastrana and Threlfall (1974, 62), note that, by law, the state could spend only 20 percent of its budget on public sector housing programs—the remaining 80 percent that MINVU spent went to private construction companies.

50. See Equipo de Estudios Poblacionales CIDU (1972, 55) and, on the increase in rent, at least until 1966, the letter dated Sept. 28, 1966, in ADA, MINVU OA, Oct.–Dec. 1966. The increase in the price of housing was actually less than the average increase of all goods and services for consumers, but only by a little (Banco Central 2001, 309).

51. The "sanitary huts" provided a bathroom, kitchen, and small living/dining room area.

52. The amount of labor that pobladores were willing to expend was often an important negotiating point between neighborhood committees and MINVU officials. For one

typical case, see the Oct. 31, 1969, Act regarding Campamento Laura Allende in ADA, MINVU Antecedentes/Providencias, Oct. 1969. In their official platforms, the Socialists and the Communists opposed using the labor of pobladores in the construction of neighborhoods, although party activists were willing to offer it in exchange for state recognition and services.

53. Volunteers from outside the poblaciones often helped with these projects, viewing this kind of labor as an act of revolutionary solidarity and redemption. Consult Dorfman (1999, 163–66, 191) and Carmen Gloria Aguayo's testimonial, as related in Shayne (2004, 75).

54. ADA, MINVU OA, July 1969.

55. Homeless committees often complained about this tendency, as one did in a letter dated Mar. 8, 1967, in ADA, MINVU OA, Apr. 1967.

56. On the massacre in Puerto Montt and the ensuing scandal, I have relied on Garcés (2002a, 370–81), Loveman and Lira (2000, 294–302), and contemporary press accounts. The divisions created by reactions to the massacre eventually contributed to Allende's election, as they provided the impetus for dissident Christian Democrats to form the Movement for Unitary Popular Action (MAPU), a party that joined the Popular Unity in 1970.

57. In a 1967 letter, Minister of Housing and Urbanism Juan Hamilton states this policy. See ADA, MINVU OA, Apr. 1967.

58. See the stipulations outlined in Oficio 345, ADA, MINVU OA, Apr. 1967.

59. For the legislation that established the neighborhood councils, see Biblioteca del Congreso, *Historia de la Ley 16.880, Ley sobre Juntas de Vecinos y demás Organizaciones Comunitarias*, 10–21.

60. For similar statements, see the comments of a pobladora in the testimonial provided by Garcés (1998, 90), Juan Araya's point of view in Garcés (2002a, 354), and Muñoz Tamayo and Madrid Herrera (2005, 21).

61. This point was made clear to me after I received reactions to my book of oral histories. Several pobladores criticized the testimonials in the first chapter of the book since they focused on PC leaders from the May Day land seizure. One woman asked me why I had focused on PC militants. Didn't I know, she asked, that there were many people who took part in the land seizures who didn't do politics? All that they wanted, she insisted, was a place to live. Of course, as Eliana Parra's comments demonstrate, PC leaders said much the same thing.

62. The extent to which women assumed leadership in the homeless committees is relative. In relationship to the political parties and unions, women's activism in housing was substantial, and several women held important positions of authority.

63. Women's activism during this era often followed this logic. See Tinsman (2002), Power (2002), Baldez (2002), Barr-Melej (2006), and Pieper Mooney (2009).

64. Goldrich (1970, 194–95), notes that this was common.

65. The general stipulations of the Christian Democratic housing programs are in Oficio 27206, ADA, MINVU OA, Jan. 1966. The specific requirements of the Frei Montalva government differed in degree, rather than in kind, to those in place before and after Frei Montalva's presidency. For the stipulations under Allende, see Oficio 6865, ADA, MINVU OA, Dec. 1970. For statements on the policy that favored families over individuals, see Minister Juan Hamilton's letter in ADA, MINVU OA, 1967.

66. See, for example, ADA, MINVU OA, June 1972, letter from the undersecretary of housing and urbanism to Humberto Vergara.

67. *El Siglo*, Apr. 29, 1969, 4.

68. *El Siglo*, May 2, 1969, 3.

69. *El Siglo,* May 2, 1969, 7.

70. *El Siglo*, May 2, 1969, 3.

71. *El Diario Ilustrado*, May 3, 1969, 6.

72. *El Diario Ilustrado*, May 3, 1969, 3.

73. *El Siglo*, 2 May 1969, 3. Homeless committees often asked that surveys be taken. See, for example, the letter dated September 22, 1970, in ADA, MINVU OA, September/October 1970.

74. Homeless committees often asked that surveys be taken. See, for example, the letter dated Sept. 22, 1970, in ADA, MINVU OA, Sept./Oct. 1970.

75. On the "golden ledgers," see also the interview of a pobladora involved in the land seizure in *El Siglo*, May 2, 1969, 3.

76. *La Tarde*, May 5, 1969, 3.

77. See *El Siglo*, May 6, 1969, 7. Infant deaths often spurred negotiations, as in Oficio 5530, ADA, MINVU OA, Aug. 1970.

78. Behind the scenes, the housing minister had reached an agreement with the landowners to buy their land.

79. *La Nación*, Aug. 30, 1969, 2, and the June 17, 1969, letter in ADA, MINVU OA, Mar. 1970.

80. A letter from Mar. 3, 1970, in ADA, MINVU OA, Mar. 1970, indicates that MINVU completed the acquisition of this property on Jan. 30, 1970.

81. See Oficio 2262 in ADA, MINVU OA, Mar. 1970. In this letter, a MINVU official explains how MINVU had removed "the most serious cases" from the Primero de Mayo campamento.

82. Housing officials explain this policy in Oficio 859, ADA, MINVU OA, Sept. 1967, and Oficio Interno 485, ADA, MINVU OA, July 1967.

83. I explored these issues in interviews with Ana Valdés, Eliana Parra, Emilio Pastenes, Ericka Cereño, and Rosa Cancino.

84. For other examples, see the testimonial in Pastrana and Threlfall (1974, 74–76) and my discussion in chapter four. Rosemblatt (1995 and 2000) describes how activists from the Socialist and Communist parties sought strikingly similar goals in the 1930s and 1940s.

85. Following the agreement they made with neighborhood representatives, government officials made arrangements to lay down the streets, build curbs, provide for sewers, place water spigots on each block, post street signs, and ensure the division of individual properties. See the report from the Construction Department in the Municipalidad de Renca, Dirección de Obras, Antecedentes de Huamachuco I.

86. Valdés's memory recalls the way critics of the Christian Democratic government often dismissed Operación Sitio as "Operation Chalk."

87. Distributors of bottled water often took advantage of the desperate situation that pobladores in campamentos faced by overcharging, as discussed in the Oficio dated Mar. 26, 1970, in ADA, MINVU OA, May 1970.

88. *El Siglo*, Mar. 21, 1967, 7. For similar descriptions in other campamentos, both in the city and in the countryside, see Castells (1983, 202) and Tinsman (2002, 186).

89. *El Siglo*, Mar. 21, 1967, 7. For a similar case that describes tensions between Communist ideals and the establishment of a campamento, see the description in Equipo de Estudios Poblacionales CIDU (1972, 64).

90. Despite the deal reached between the pobladores and the government, Christian Democratic officials continued to insist that the May Day land seizure was illegal and that the majority of the squatters illegitimately held their land. See the Oct. 3, 1969, letter in ADA, MINVU OA, Oct. 1969.

91. *La Tercera de la Hora*, May 15, 1970, 12; *El Siglo*, May 15, 1970, 6.

92. At the time of the coup, the residents of Primero de Mayo had received "sanitary huts" from Operación Sitio, the division of streets into a grid pattern, a number of water fountains, outhouses, and electricity. The neighborhood slowly gained the pavement of streets, sewer systems, potable water, and undisputed property titles during the dictatorship, not receiving all of these services until 1981. The IDB provided many of the funds for this process. See Municipalidad de Renca, Dirección de Obras, "Antecedentes de Huamachuco I."

93. For the term "seizing their place," see Garcés (2002a). Salazar (1990, 311–31) provides a similar narrative assessment.

Chapter 4. Specters in the Revolution: Dilemmas of Home during the Chilean Path to Socialism

1. In conversations, several Chileans who supported Allende fondly remembered the spectacle and excitement of the street demonstrations. See, for example, Ana Lamilla's comments in Murphy (2004a, 139).

2. Nationalization of the copper mines occurred in July 1971. The statistics are in INE (1999, 122 and 124).

3. In casting the revolutionary subject as male, Chilean Marxists reflected a gender bias common to the Latin American Left of this time period, as Shayne (2004) and Saldaña-Portillo (2003), among others, point out. In the Chilean case, this ideal revolutionary subject was also a hardworking father and husband, although militants could also tap into a swaggering male identity that disdained and even subverted idealized family roles (Mallon 2003). See also Klubock (1998) and Tinsman (2002).

4. Allende made these pledges on several occasions. See, for example, Martner (1992, 281–86).

5. The literature on this point is voluminous, although my general approach draws on Marx ([1857] 2009b) and Mauss ([1950] 1990). Some more recent anthropological literature, as in Miller (2001a, 2005), provides great insight into the powers and new realities of "consumption" and "materiality," but nevertheless fails to adequately account for the interrelationship between production and consumption, ultimately fetishizing the consuming process.

6. This analysis largely draws on Stern (2004, 21–27) and Valenzuela (1978).

7. UP candidates won 48.6 percent of the vote during the 1971 municipal elections and

43.9 percent in the 1973 congressional ones. For analysis of voting patterns during the UP, see Valenzuela (1978) and Urzúa Valenzuela (1992).

8. Winn (1986) has shown brilliantly how this occurred in the first nationalized factory. See also Gaudichard (2004).

9. Relatively speaking, copper prices were still fairly high, following increased demand in the 1960s, brought on in no small measure by the Vietnam War.

10. For Nixon's quote, see the declassified notes written by CIA director Richard Helms, "Meeting with the President on Chile at 1525," Sept. 15, 1970, reprinted in Kornbluh (2003, 36).

11. Valenzuela (1978, 57), provides statistics on the cutback in aid.

12. The literature is too voluminous to cite here, but see Sigmund (1977), Haslam (2005), and Qureshi (2009).

13. This refers to the plan to kidnap General René Schneider, the head of the army, and declare a state of emergency, suspend the Constitution, and hold new presidential elections in which Eduardo Frei Montalva would presumably have won, given his popularity. Conspirators, however, mistakenly killed the general in a shootout in downtown Santiago. In response, Chileans overwhelmingly rallied to defend the constitution and national sovereignty.

14. Grandin (2004) provides a superb analysis of these dynamics in Guatemala, demonstrating that they helped to initiate a broader process of polarization throughout Latin America.

15. The previous record high was 36,486 in 1965, the first year of Frei Montalva's presidency. In the end, the UP government initiated about seventy-three thousand units in 1971, but left many incomplete due to a lack of building materials (AUCA 1972, 43).

16. On the increase in fiscal spending, see Collier and Sater (2004, 331), and the reports provided by different bureaucratic institutions in Gobierno de Chile, *Mensaje Presidencial* (1971).

17. For Vuskovic's views, consult *Las Ultimas Noticias*, Nov. 13, 1970; *El Siglo*, May 25, 1971; and *El Siglo*, Sept. 11, 1971.

18. Collier and Sater (2004, 330), and Erika Cereño, Eliana Parra, Ana Valdés, and Cecilia Castro in Murphy (2004a).

19. For MINVU projects in this vein, see Sierra (1970) and AUCA (1972).

20. Consult Gobierno de Chile, *Mensaje Presidencial* (1971, 585), and Gobierno de Chile, *Mensaje Presidencial* (1972, 561). On the general sense of activity and celebration in the poblaciones, see Pastenes, Lamilla, and Valdés in Murphy (2004a).

21. For the importance of this to the UP, see Gladys Marín's speech, reproduced in *Principios* (1972), 29.

22. *Ercilla*, May 23, 1973, 19–20, and *El Siglo*, Feb. 24, 1972.

23. As discussed in the last chapter, this was the case for the pobladores of the May Day Campamento. A research team, Equipo de Estudios Poblaciones, CIDU (1972, 64), found that when government officials offered high-rise apartments to pobladores in twenty-five campamentos, residents rejected this offer in *every* case. See also Castells (1983, 202) and the correspondence about Los Guindos, Ñuñoa in ADA, MINVU OA, Feb. 1973.

24. *El Siglo*, Aug. 17, 1971, 6.

25. Leinaweaver (2008, 105–33) provides an insightful analysis of "overcoming" in the Peruvian context.

26. Many officials expected to confront difficult legacies from the past. They argued, however, that their maneuvers were part of a dialectical process that would ultimately be successful. For a useful overview of this view among specialists who worked in communications, see Fernández Labbé (2003).

27. Oficio 273, ADA, MINVU OA, Jan. 1971.

28. ADA, MINVU OA, Feb. 1971. Oficio 6348, in ADA, MINVU OA, Oct. 1970, contains further documentation on the case.

29. Oficio 285, ADA, MINVU OA, Oct. 1970. Although not clear from the archival records, it is also possible that Contreras received rent from the inhabitants of Green Valley. Though illegal, this was a common practice.

30. The ministry officials cited clauses from the 1967 Law 16,741, the Ley de Loteos Brujos, "Law of the Phantom Subdivisions."

31. Oficio 599, ADA, MINVU OA, Mar. 1971 and Oficio 722, ADA, MINVU OA, May 1972. A social worker's report, Oficio 411, ADA, MINVU OA, Mar.–Apr. 1972, is also revealing.

32. *El Mercurio*, Nov. 23, 1970, 23, and *El Siglo*, Nov. 23, 1970, 1.

33. Oficio 6699, ADA, MINVU OA, Nov. 1970.

34. On failed efforts to pass laws that would sanction the seizures, see ADA, MINVU OA, Oficio 1442, June 1971 and *La Tercera de la Hora*, Feb. 27, 1972, 12. Debates in the legislature are also revealing, such as Gobierno de Chile, *Boletín de Sesiones Ordinarias del Senado de 1971*, June 30, 1971, 1113–19, and Aug. 4, 1971, 2189–236.

35. Oficio 880, ADA, MINVU OA, May 1972.

36. Oficio 1108, ADA, MINVU OA, Aug. 1973.

37. MINVU officials took the strongest stance with seizures that might upset the circulation of goods. See Oficio 462, ADA, MINVU OA, Feb. 1971 and Oficio 353, ADA, MINVU OA, Jan. 1971.

38. DPDU 2643, ADA, MINVU OA, Nov. 1971. Many of MINVU's low-level workers seized land, causing considerable concern, as expressed in the memorandum dated Mar. 21, 1973, ADA, MINVU OA, Apr. 1973.

39. In fact, UP legislators sought to codify this policy into law. See Gobierno de Chile, *Cámara de Diputados, Boletín de Sesiones Ordinarias*, Sept. 9, 1971, 3170–79.

40. Oficio 689, ADA, MINVU OA, Mar. 1971. For similar cases, see Oficio 1112, ADA, MINVU OA, June 1972 and Oficio 121, ADA, MINVU OA, Jan. 1971.

41. MINVU sought to ensure a steady income stream by passing a law stating that squatters had to assume ownership responsibilities the moment they occupied their lands, not when they would acquire the actual property title. See Oficio 522, ADA, MINVU OA, Aug. 1972.

42. Oficio 2198, ADA, MINVU OA, Sept. 1971 and Oficio 599, ADA, MINVU OA, Mar. 1971.

43. There is a typical example in Oficio 725, ADA, MINVU OA, Mar. 1971.

44. Pastrana and Threlfall (1974, 61) also note this change.

45. Peter Winn (2010) points out that one reason these groups focused on urban land seizures is that they did not have the base of support that the Communists did in the labor unions.

46. For a detailed statement on the position of these groups, see the comments of the MIR housing activist Víctor Toro in *Punto Final*, Jan. 18, 1972, 20–23.

47. For contemporary press accounts of the MIR's involvement in land seizures in Las Condes, see *La Tribuna*, May 11, 1972, 12; *La Tercera de la Hora*, May 12, 1972, 5; *Puro Chile*, May 12, 1972, 11; *La Segunda*, May 12, 1972, 1c; and *El Mercurio*, May 12, 1972, 1.

48. On the disciplinary practices of the MIR, see my discussion below and the following sources: Pastrana and Threlfall (1974, 75–77); Castells (1983, 199–209); and the document "Los pobladores y el poder," written by the Movement of Revolutionary Pobladores (MPR), whose members helped to settle the famous Campamento Nueva la Habana. The document is available in the Princeton University Chile Ephemera Collection, "Unidad Popular: 1969–1972, Pamphlets."

49. Oficio 374, ADA, MINVU OA, Feb. 1971.

50. See, for examples, *La Tercera de la Hora*, Mar. 17, 1973, 18; *El Mercurio*, Mar. 17, 1973, 1; *El Siglo*, Mar. 17, 1973, 3; and *La Prensa*, Mar. 17, 1973, 8.

51. See Cantero (1972) and the comments of Housing Minister Canturias in *La Tercera de la Hora*, Feb. 27, 1972.

52. See ADA, MINVU OA Oficio 2887, Nov. 1971. CORVI agreed to offer services to this neighborhood, such as potable water in Oficio 1112 from June 1972, ADA, MINVU OA.

53. See the letter dated Dec. 7, 1970, in ADA, MINVU OA, Aug. 1972. In addressing Allende, the leader of the neighborhood council employs the familiar *tú* form. This is an important shift that occurs in much correspondence to Allende as citizens felt emboldened to write to the president informally and more as an equal.

54. Oficio 583, ADA, MINVU OA, Apr. 1973.

55. Oficio 850, ADA, MINVU OA, May 1972. In responding, a MINVU official said he would seek to provide the pobladores with larger houses, but wrote that this would be very difficult because of the increasing lack of building materials.

56. Cancino's edited testimonial appears in Murphy (2004a, 111–20).

57. Some landowners were able to reach better terms for themselves by entering into preemptive negotiations with homeless groups. For their part, squatters received assurances that they could regularize their neighborhoods.

58. See the announcement in *Puro Chile*, Dec. 25, 1971.

59. For the statutes, see ADA, Ministerio de Economía, Fomento, y Reconstrucción Nacional (MEFR), Dec. 1971.

60. On the specifics of the decree law passed in 1959, see Biblioteca del Congreso, *Historia de la Ley 16.742*. See also Bravo Heitmann (1993).

61. For the reasons why the committee decided to seize the land, see the letter written by Campamento Lenin's "Neighborhood Command" to *Chile Hoy*, Mar. 9, 1973, 2.

62. For more on disciplinary committees and practices during this period, see *El Siglo*, Mar. 10, 1972, 5.

63. For discussions of "youth culture" and its relationship to the Left, see Elsey (2011, 207–41), and Barr-Melej (2006).

64. On this phenomenon, see Tinsman (2002, 209–46); Elsey (2011, 210–16); Pieper Mooney (2009, 102–39); and Shayne (2004, 67–89).

65. Oficio 910, ADA, MINVU OA, May 1971. This was part of a larger effort on the part of UP officials to legalize divorce and abortion, two legislative initiatives that did not come to pass.

66. *El Siglo*, Mar. 10, 1972, 5.

67. A growing number of analysts have examined the feminine opposition to Popular Unity. Among others, and beyond the sources I cite in the text, see Baldez (2002) and Mattelart (1975).

68. Donoso's speech is cited in *El Mercurio*, Dec. 5, 1971, 4.

69. *La Segunda*, July 31, 1972, 1.

70. For a similar analysis of the Dominican Republic under Rafael Trujillo, see Derby (2009).

71. For examples, see *El Mercurio*, July 26, 1973, 21; *Chile Hoy*, no. 59, July 27, 1973, 3; and Eliana Parra's comments in Murphy (2004a, 34–35).

72. Stern (2004, 107) points out how common memories like Emilio's are.

Chapter 5. Locating States of Emergency: The Politics of "Normalization" after the Military Coup

1. Decree Law 5, issued on Sept. 12, 1973, in Gobierno de Chile (1973a, 16).

2. Moulian (1997) argues that the dictatorship initiated "revolutionary" transformations, despite its claims to be upholding tradition.

3. See Stern (2006, 33–128) and, for this shift among Christian Democrats, Moulián and Guerra (2000, 275–94) and Winn (2004a, 23–25).

4. See Decree 1367, ADA, MINVU OA, Sept.–Oct. 1973.

5. I spoke with many low-income Chileans who supported the military takeover. See also Power (2002) and Stern (2004, 7–34).

6. For two troubling cases, see the Comisión Nacional de Verdad y Reconciliación (hereafter the Rettig Commission) (1991, 228) and Stern (2004, 68–87).

7. See the Madrid daily, *ABC*, Oct. 10, 1973, 37, as cited in Moulián and Guerra (2000, 276).

8. Redfield (2005) calls attention to how efforts to resolve crises often include a humanitarian and medical understanding of emergency.

9. Decree Law 77, promulgated on Oct. 13, 1973.

10. Comisión Chilena de Derechos Humanos, Fundación Ideas (hereafter Comisión Chilena) (1999, 229). This number is a low estimate, as Stern (2004, 168–71) discusses at length. On the political party affiliation of the documented cases, see Comisión Chilena (1999, 231), and the Rettig Commission (1991, 885).

11. This number refers strictly to political exile. Estimates on the total number of Chileans who left the country are as high as one million, as Meade (2001, 138), asserts.

12. Decree Law 418 mandated these kinds of name changes. See the *Diario Oficial*, Apr. 19, 1974, 1.

13. See, among others, Constable and Valenzuela (1991, 91–99), Kornbluh (2003, 157–73), and the Rettig Commission (1991, 45–46).

14. The fact that the others waiting in line supported Ana and knew that soldiers had forced other women to stop wearing pants permitted Ana to speak collectively about her experience. Analyzing a number of Latin American testimonials, Sommer (1988) points out that the speakers often present their memories in these terms, allowing the narrators to speak on behalf of a larger public, granting greater urgency and weight to their claims.

15. Comisión Nacional sobre Prisión Política y Tortura (hereafter the Valech Commission) (2004, 223–58).

16. The statistic that the Valech Commission (2004) produced omits those who were killed after being tortured and those tortured in raids who were not detained, in addition to those tortured individuals who were unable or unwilling to present themselves to the commission.

17. For these general dynamics, consult Rettig Commission (1991, 124), Stern (2006, 33–76), and Constable and Valenzuela (1991, 15). Garcés and Leiva (2005) analyze the one población, La Legua, that offered armed resistance in the days and weeks immediately following the coup.

18. In a "White Book" (Gobierno de Chile 1973b), the regime outlined the details of a "Plan Z," a supposed plot by UP and MIR supporters to take armed control of the country. Spooner (1994, 89), Constable and Valenzuela (1991, 55), and the Valech Comission (2004, 235) all note how regime agents acted on the assumption that "Plan Z" actually existed.

19. More research needs to be done on this issue, particularly since much of the documentation remains inaccessible. Commanders, however, clearly expected to confront resistance in neighborhood raids. Earlier coup plots had included plans to subdue "Communist neighborhoods." See CIA, SECRET Cable from Santiago Station [Report on Plan to Kidnap Gen. René Schneider and Initiate a Military Coup], Oct. 19, 1970, in Kornbluh (2003, document 1.13). After the coup press reports, as in *Vea*, Oct. 26, 1973, 6–9, continued to claim that the Left controlled these neighborhoods through "domination" and "terror."

20. As a US State Department official observed, "Fear of civil war was an important factor in their decision to employ a heavy hand from the outset. Also present is a puritanical, crusading spirit—a determination to cleanse and rejuvenate Chile. " See Department of State, SECRET Memorandum for Henry Kissinger, "Chilean Executions," Nov. 27, 1973, in Kornbluh (2003, document 3.1).

21. The Rettig Commission (1991, 123–244, 886) identified 387 victims killed by military regime agents in Santiago from the coup through the end of 1973. The commission identified ninety-eight by their relationship to a specific población. This number, accounting for more than 25 percent of all cases, underrepresents the total, since the entries only describe the immediate surroundings of the arrest. The majority of the victims held the kind of low-income employment more common in the poblaciones (Rettig Commission 1991, 887). In an exhaustive study of military raids during the dictatorship, the Colectivo de Memoria Histórica (2005) demonstrates that the regime primarily targeted neighborhoods that were lower-class and had a history of Leftist activism.

22. On the independent nature of these raids, see Mallon (2003, 207–8, 215; and 2005, 136–47).

23. A soldier mentions this policy in Stern (2004, 136). For examples of such actions, see the testimonials in the Valech Commission (2004, 253), Ana Valdés in Murphy (2004a, 50), Garcés and Leiva (2005, 92), and the discussion below.

24. Cecilia Castro describes such a scene in her neighborhood on the night of a raid in Murphy (2004a, 147).

25. Consult the testimonial recorded in Garcés and Leiva (2005, 92).

26. For two examples, see the letter from the neighborhood council of La Victoria to Eduardo Frei Montalva, June 16, 1966, in ADA, MINVU OA, July, August, September 1966 and Oficio 692, ADA, MINVU OA, Mar. 1971.

27. In conversations with other pobladores from Campamento Lenin, I never heard of any weapons stockpiling, although it is possible that there was some. The subject of weapons stockpiling is difficult to track because it still provides a defense for the dictatorship's repression. See Mallon (2005, 142–47). It still remains the case, however, that the dictatorship never faced a substantial armed threat.

28. Emilio recalled that five other people were held with him and that two of them, also neighborhood leaders in Renca, were killed. The Rettig Commission (1991, 170–72), identifies nine pobladores from Conchalí and Renca who were killed on September 22 and 23, 1973. The *carabineros* and the same military regiment that raided Campamento Lenin were responsible for these executions.

29. For another example, see Álvarez (2003, 82–83).

30. For Pastenes's description of these events, see Murphy (2004a, 89–94). I supplemented the description provided in the book with a follow-up interview.

31. Nov. 17, 1976, UPI [Archivo de la Fundación de la Vicaría de la Solidaridad], as cited in Loveman and Lira (2000, 411–12).

32. Reconciliation was an official policy of the dictatorship, as Loveman and Lira (2000, 412) note.

33. Regime officials often claimed that their project was "apolitical." Loveman and Davies (1978) develop how a "politics of antipolitics" was a central justification for many contemporary Latin American dictatorships.

34. For a representative quote, see the speech by the leader of the National Women's Secretariat, Carmen Grez de Anrique, in *Amiga* 2 (28): 11. For a critical analysis of the evolution of this historical memory, see Valdivia Ortiz de Zarate (2003).

35. Many Chileans I spoke to somewhat sheepishly told me that they had remained largely unaware of the extent of the dictatorship's abuses. In addition, as Stern (2004, 88–101) argues, many did not wish to revisit potentially troubling and divisive memories.

36. For press coverage, see *El Mercurio*, Sept. 15, 1973, 2; *La Tercera de la Hora,* Sept. 15, 1973, 2; and *El Mercurio*, Sept. 17, 1973, 1.

37. Stern (2006, chapter two) provides an impressive analysis of the initial, majority support for the regime.

38. Letter, Oct. 23, 1973, ADA, MINVU OA, Sept.–Oct. 1973.

39. *Vea*, Oct. 25, 1973, 6–8. See also Constable and Valenzuela (1991, 142).

40. Oficio, Oct. 30, 1973, in ADA, MINVU OA, Oct. 1973. The undersecretary of housing and urbanism during the UP period laid out the government's opposition to "self-construction" efforts in Oficio 25, ADA, MINVU OA, Jan. 1971. Officials in the Frei Montalva government, on the other hand, had invested substantial resources in these kinds of programs.

41. Oct. 10, 1973, letter in ADA, MINVU OA, Nov. 1973.

42. Oficio 352, ADA, MINVU OA, Apr.–June 1974, letter dated Feb. 11, 1974.

43. On the rise of the Chicago Boys, see Constable and Valenzuela (1991, 166–98), Winn (2004a), and Silva (1991 and 2008). Huneeus (2000) demonstrates the close professional, ideological, and social links between the neoliberal Chicago Boys and the dictatorship's primary legal and political reformers, the "Gremialists."

44. For the statistic on the GNP, see Banco Central (2001, 32), and for unemployment, INE (1999, 56).

45. On these general changes, see Winn (2004c).

46. *La Segunda*, Nov. 12, 1973, 2.

47. Decree 1367, ADA, MINVU OA, Sept.–Oct., 1973 and the *Mensaje Presidencial* (1977, 23–26). The National Office of Emergencies, like many other bureaucratic structures created through emergency development legislation, had its genesis in responding to a "natural" disaster—in this case, flooding.

48. For an initial use of the term, see the *Instructivo* in ADA, MINVU OA, Dec. 1973.

49. *Qué Pasa*, Apr. 8, 1976, 31–32, and *Qué Pasa*, Apr. 19–25, 1979, 6–11.

50. Mujica Ateaga and Rojas Pinaud (1986) and INVI (1997). It is important to note that the 1997 map was simply a survey of campamentos and "irregular settlements," not a "map of extreme poverty." Nonetheless, certain connections between the campamentos and extreme poverty remained.

51. In 1980 the government began to use a survey, the Ficha CAS, in order to identify the poorest families and prioritize state services. This survey identified poverty levels through a number of indicators, including education levels and access to health care and basic services. Significantly, however, the single most important variable continued to be housing, including the general condition of the house, the number of rooms, and the availability of electricity and potable water. See Vergara (1990).

52. See, for example, Ordinance No. 1596, in ADA, MINVU OA, 1979.

53. Appadurai (1996), among others, analyzes how statistics gain legitimacy through their claims to an objective, rational framework

54. *La Tercera*, Sept. 28, 1973, 10.

55. Oficio 1929, ADA, MINVU OA, Nov. 1973.

56. Oficio 1890, ADA, MINVU OA, Nov. 1973. The harsh judgment of these tactics, however, did not always lead to official sanction, particularly as officials became more resigned to institutionalizing and legalizing campamentos by the mid-1970s. See for example, Oficio 598, ADA, MINVU OA, 1977.

57. The stipulations of housing programs come through in the hundreds of positions I reviewed, although they are not often explicitly cited.

58. ADA, MINVU OA, Apr.–July 1974, Subsecretario Etcheverry, July 9, 1974.
59. See ADA, MINVU OA, nos. 23–420, 1981, ordenanza no. 380.
60. *El Mercurio*, May 9, 1976, 1, and Gobierno de Chile, *Mensaje Presidencial*, 1974, 341.
61. See, for example, Oficio 1851, ADA, MINVU OA, Nov. 1973, and Oficio 483, ADA, MINVU OA, Apr.–June 1974.
62. The mayor of a Santiago municipality notes these phenomena in Ordinance 11880, ADA, MINVU OA, Apr.–July 1974. See also Oficio 3578, ADA, MINVU OA, 1977.
63. Ana Valdés, Eliana Parra, Erika Cereño, and Rosa Cancino, interviews in August 2004. On the "irregular" layout of Huamachuco and Las Palmeras, see Municipalidad de Renca, Antecedentes de Huamachuco and Las Palmeras, respectively.
64. Examples are in Oficio 1376, ADA, MINVU OA, 1977 and Oficio 1958, ADA, MINVU OA, 1977.
65. The *Informe* dated Oct. 19, 1973, in ADA, MINVU OA, Dec. 1973, outlines the policy.
66. For the general problematic, see the internal memorandum from the Executive Vice President of CORVI to the minister of housing and urbanism, Oficio 10888 in ADA, MINVU OA, Jan.–Mar. 1974. The minister asked for patience from landowners in *Las Ultimas Noticias*, Aug. 6, 1975, 8, and *El Mercurio*, Aug. 5, 1975, 3.
67. Valdés and Weinstein (1993), Baldez (2002, 136–40), and Hardy (1987) analyze these organizations.
68. Writing about the Argentine military dictatorship (1977–1983), Taylor (1997) argues that the protestors accentuated their roles as mothers, ultimately following a predetermined gender script. Baldez (2002, 125–67) downplays the extent to which Chilean protestors did the same. But her analysis demonstrates that Chilean women publicly framed their protests as the work of desperate dueñas de casa who had been forced to leave the domestic sphere in order to demonstrate.
69. On the role of the Catholic church in organizing human rights groups, shielding regime enemies, and establishing social service organizations, see Smith (1982), Frühling (1992), and Jordá (2001).
70. Skurski and Coronil (2006) warn against focusing exclusively on the "most extreme manifestations of violence" such as wars, genocide, or state-sponsored terror. See also Roitman (2014).

Chapter 6. Aesthetics of Order: Forging Spaces of Distinction amid Neoliberal Expansion

1. See the letter in ADA, MINVU OA, Gabinete Subsecretario, 1979, no. 6.
2. MINVU (n.d.[a]).
3. Official statistics indicate that between 1977 and 1981 the GNP grew 8 percent per annum, although economists outside of the regime claimed that the growth was closer to 6 percent (Constable and Valenzuela 1991, 341).
4. Despite the dictatorship's claims, the nontraditional export boom has roots in the subsidies put in place during the era of state-led development, as Klubock (2004b) and Tinsman (2014) demonstrate.
5. *El Mercurio*, Aug. 28, 1980, 1, 12.

6. This approach draws on what Chakrabarty (2002) terms the "ideals of public health." Chakrabarty himself builds on Mary Douglas ([1966] 1980). Chakrabarty recognizes that Douglas's structural approach can be ahistorical and fails to account for contradiction and contestation. Nevertheless, he effectively uses her framework in order to explore how the modern "citizens' gaze" affects governing practices and spatial relations.

7. In each of these "elections," the opposition had extremely limited access to the press, many voters were unable to register, and irregularities occurred in numerous polling stations.

8. Letter from the mayor of Ñuñoa in ADA, MINVU OA, Oficios 4374–868, 1977. See also Paley (2001, 70) and Morales et al. (1990, 3–4).

9. Eagleton (1990, 13–69) argues for a link between aesthetic sensibilities and rationalism, in what he terms an "ideology of the aesthetic." Stoler (2004 and 2009) underscores the complex interrelationship between affective sensibilities and governing orders of reason.

10. Oficio 4793 and the attached correspondence in ADA, MINVU OA, 1977.

11. See the data in Gobierno de Chile, *Mensaje Presidencial* (1976–1977, 598, 610; and 1977–1978, 514–15).

12. Many middle-class Chileans complained about this situation, as in *La Segunda*, Apr. 12, 1976, 6, and *El Mercurio*, Nov. 12, 1981, 2.

13. The subsidized housing programs were of three types: "social housing," type A and type B. Beltran was in the program for type B, the program that required the most savings and offered the largest dwellings. Critics of the dictatorship's subsidized housing programs often argued that cases like Beltran's demonstrated the inconsistencies in the regime's policies, as the dictatorship continued to support housing for middle-income sectors through their subsidies. (See, for example, the letter to the editor in *Mensaje*, June 1981, 299, 245.) These criticisms, particularly in the first decade of the dictatorship, often hit their mark. Of 12,947 housing units completed with government subsidies between September 1976 and September 1977, only 2,353 were built for "social housing" (Gobierno de Chile, *Mensaje Presidencial* 1977, 596). Also consult Vergara (1990, 205–44) and Kusnetzoff (1987).

14. Oficio 1993 and the attached correspondence in ADA, MINVU OA, 1977.

15. The fact that Beltran and Valenzuela worked in the army and in a state bureaucracy, respectively, is also significant, as I discuss below.

16. Oficio 354, ADA, MINVU OA, 1978. For other similar examples, see Ord. 838, ADA, MINVU OA, 1982 and Ord. 839, ADA, MINVU OA, 1982.

17. My interpretation here builds on Lefebvre's ([1991] 2004) concept of the production of space.

18. These names are pseudonyms.

19. I discuss the national protests at much greater length in chapter seven. On university student involvement in the protests, see Schneider (1995, 119–28) and Stern (2006, 179–95).

20. See *Puro Chile*, May 12, 1972, 11, and *El Mercurio*, May 12, 1972, 1.

21. The press celebrated these moves, as two headlines indicate: "*Pobladores* Will Have Their Own House[s]," and "Toward a New Life," in, respectively, *La Gaceta de Las Condes* 110, Aug. 8, 1981, and *La Gaceta de Las Condes* 129, June 5, 1982.

22. *La Gaceta de La Condes*, Apr. 28–May 4, 1976, 2.

23. Such boom and bust cycles, a pattern throughout Chilean history, have been particularly strong during the neoliberal period. Periods of great real estate growth from the late 1980s to the late 1990s, and then again from 2002 to 2008, have been followed by retrenchment.

24. I have totaled these statistics by analyzing the figures provided by Morales and Rojas (1987, 100), Hidalgo (2005, 375), and the *Mensaje Presidencial* (1977, 599). These statistics include only those who were actually listed in state housing forms and thus significantly understate the total. State programs did not include allegados or fictive kin in official forms, even though many pobladores who lived in these situations were part of these programs.

25. On these general changes, see the contributions in Winn (2004a), particularly Winn, Klubock, Stillerman, and Tinsman.

26. These official statistics most likely underreported the number of unemployed.

27. *Las Ultimas Noticias*, Nov. 4, 1980, c1.

28. The terms in quotes circulated widely during the dictatorship and continue to do so today. Agamben (2005, 21) observes how war metaphors mark the political vocabulary whenever "decisions considered to be of vital importance are being imposed."

29. On the specific support that these organizations offered to these programs, see, for the World Bank, Kusnetzoff (1987, 183), and for the IDB, Ord. No. 2042, ADA, MINVU OA, 1979, and MINVU (n.d.[b]). USAID provided financial backing to many of the dictatorship's first programs in housing and to subsidized food distribution. See the *Mensaje Presidencial* (1977, 598) and MINVU (n.d.[c]) for the details of a US$55 million loan and grant. The overall aid provided an important bulwark of support for the Pinochet regime, particularly during the period of "economic shock treatment" from 1974 to 1976 (Angell 1993, 182). The initial IDB investment in housing infrastructure was US$45.8 million from 1975–1979, although with the economic improvement of the late 1970s the Chilean government covered some of these costs (MINVU n.d.[b], 10). US development assistance decreased generally during the Carter administration and then increased during the first years of the Reagan administration.

30. See Oficio 3612 in ADA, MINVU OA, 1977, and Ord. no. 813, ADA, MINVU OA, 1977, both of which lay out the goals and stipulations of agreements between MINVU and the IDB.

31. This point underscores how there were often also close personal and financial connections between government officials, bankers, and real estate developers. More research, however, is needed on this point.

32. Publicly, officials claimed they made these concessions because Chilean banks tended not to lend to low-income sectors due to the risks involved. See the letter from the undersecretary of housing and urbanism, Peter Bromberg, to Sergio Molina, in ADA, MINVU OA, 1978, nos. 21–240. Financial institutions lobbied the government for these stipulations.

33. See MINVU (1990, 3). The population statistic comes from Valdés (1987, 266).

34. Resolution No. 880, ADA, MINVU OA, 1979. As in earlier periods, the term

"families" is not very precise, as it excludes allegados, fictive kin, and alternative living arrangements.

35. See Gobierno de Chile, *Mensaje Presidencial*, 1979–1980, 603, circular no. 81, ADA, MINVU OA, 1979, and "Programación Masiva de Otorgamiento de Títulos," Ord. No. 1361, ADA, MINVU Gabinete Ministro, 1981.

36. Loveman (1988, 321–22) notes the contradictions in the dictatorship's selective use of the law. See also Frazier (2007).

37. As in past administrations, single men complained that they could not enter subsidized housing programs, as in the letter from Héctor Aliaga Mera, in ADA, MINVU OA, 1983, no. 3014.

38. The quote is in Resolución Exenta 310, ADA, MINVU OA, 1977. On the general stipulations of the government's programs, see Oficio 354, ADA, MINVU OA, 1978, and circular no. 81, ADA, MINVU OA, 1979. For a critical perspective, consult the article in *Mensaje* 299, June 1981, 245.

39. See, for example, Ord. No. 528, ADA, MINVU OA, 1982.

40. See Ord. No. 231 and the attached correspondence in ADA, MINVU OA, 1981.

41. See, for example, *La Patria*, Jan. 25, 1975, 4.

42. The Chilean government, in fact, became one of the highest spenders on the military in Latin America, with nearly six percent of the GDP going to the armed forces in 1980. See Angell (1993, 188).

43. Oficio 354, ADA, MINVU OA, 1978, and Ord. No. 17, ADA, MINVU OA, 1979.

44. Resolución Exenta 310, ADA, MINVU OA, nos. 3846–4313, 1977.

45. Social workers often commented on cleanliness and house maintenance in their reports. See also Ord. No. 1181, ADA, MINVU OA, 1979 and Ord. No. 796, ADA, MINVU OA, 1983.

46. Ord. No. 1411 in ADA, MINVU OA, 1981. For other examples of military officials offering certain benefits to applicants, see Oficio 4793, ADA, MINVU OA, 1977; Oficio 1518, ADA, MINVU OA, 1981; Ord. No. 1376, ADA, MINVU Gabinete Ministro, 1981; and Ord. No. 1155, ADA, MINVU OA, 1983.

47. For some examples of hundreds of cases of rejections, see Ord. No. 1745, ADA, MINVU OA, 1978; Oficio 354, ADA, MINVU OA, 1978; and Ord. No. 1157, ADA, MINVU OA, 1979.

48. Verónica Schild (2000) argues that this has the effect of producing "market citizens." As I demonstrated in earlier chapters, this effect was also in place before the coup, although it became more pronounced during the dictatorship.

49. Ord. No. 528, ADA, MINVU OA, 1982.

50. See Bruey (2012) and my discussion in chapter seven.

51. *El Mercurio*, Apr. 29, 1977, 3.

52. *El Cronista*, July 21, 1977, 9.

53. *El Cronista*, Apr. 23, 1977, 9.

54. For more on the mothers' centers, see Valdés and Weinstein (1993, 89–128) and Franceschet (2005, 58–60).

55. See, for example, Constable and Valenzuela (1991, 162). During one of our conver-

sations, Gustavo Retamales mentioned that he attended pro-regime rallies as a member of a neighborhood council. He added, however, "We didn't go there out of our own free will. [They would say,] 'If you don't go, you're going to be put on a suspect list' . . . [At one rally,] Pinochet passed just a few meters in front of me. It really pissed me off, and I wanted to yell, I wanted to say something." See Murphy (2004a, 131).

56. See Ord. No. 1058, ADA, MINVU OA, 1982.

57. Ord. No. 1155, ADA, MINVU OA, 1983.

58. See Minuta Reserva No. 130, ADA, MINVU OA, 1983; Oficio 1958, ADA, MINVU OA, 1977; the Informe Social dated Dec. 13, 1979, in ADA, MINVU Gabinete Ministro, 1981; and Ord. No. 1920, ADA, MINVU OA, 1981.

59. Ord. No. 1376 ADA, MINVU OA, Gabinete Ministro, 1981.

60. MINVU, in fact, passed a decree law that postponed requirements to recover lands that illegal squatters occupied. See Decree Law 1560, as cited in Ord. No. 490, ADA, MINVU OA, 1978.

61. See Ord. No. 1974, ADA, MINVU OA, 1978, in addition to the discussion in chapters five and seven and Ord. No. 2563, ADA, MINVU OA, 1979.

62. See, for example, Decree Law 2698 from 1979.

63. For the 1981 stipulations, see Ord. No. 1132, ADA, MINVU OA, 1981. The earlier minimum size requirement is mentioned in passing in Ord. 1536, ADA, MINVU OA, 1978.

64. The decrease in the power of neighborhood organizations was due to the weakened role that they played during the dictatorship. See, however, the unnumbered Ordenanza in Gabinete Ministro, ADA, MINVU OA, 1981; Ord. No. 194, ADA, MINVU OA, 1982; and Rosa Cancino in Murphy (2004a).

65. Informe No. 28 in ADA, MINVU OA, 1978 and Ord. No. 682 in ADA, MINVU Antecedentes de Oficios, 1980.

66. See Ord. No. 380, ADA, MINVU OA, 1981.

67. Ord. No. 527, ADA, MINVU OA, 1983.

68. This formulation overlaps with J. T. Way's (2012, 41–66) analysis of the dialectic between chaos and rationality in the Guatemalan ghetto.

Chapter 7. Containing Protest in the Transition to Democracy

1. Coronil and Skurski (2006) discuss how reactions to anti-neoliberal protests among the popular sectors in Venezuela were similarly volatile.

2. I draw inspiration in this chapter from Sherry Ortner's (1995) approach to resistance, in which she argues that a "thick" analysis of resistance lays bare broader dynamics of power, underscoring the tensions and horizons in projects of resistance.

3. Some residents, such as Erika Cereño, had big lot sizes and stood to lose some of their land through the regularization of the neighborhood.

4. In addition to oral sources, a report included in Municipalidad de Renca, Sección de Obras, Antecedentes de Lo Velásquez, Sector I (hereafter MR SO, AV1), mentions this effort. On this general policy, see Ord. No. 1132, ADA, MINVU OA, 1981.

5. *La Presencia de Renca* 17, Mar. 1990, 10.

6. MR SO, AV1.

7. MR SO, AV1.

8. On the location of the move, see Morales et al. (1990, 14) and Raúl Soto in Murphy (2004a, 67). La Pintana was a new municipality in the southern section of Santiago.

9. On the provision of bus services and the pavement of roads in Lo Velásquez, see *La Presencia de Renca*, 1988, no. 5.

10. Paley (2001, 72–73) describes a similar dynamic in another area of the city.

11. *El Mercurio*, Aug. 8, 1983, 7c, and MR SO, Antecedentes de La Maule.

12. For Eli's description, see Murphy (2004a, 155–59).

13. Officials discuss the mounting problem of foreclosures in ADA, MINVU OA, 1981, no. 2631.

14. On per capita GNP, see Banco Central (2001, 32), and on unemployment see Martínez (1992, 157).

15. On the fall in construction and housing starts, see Banco Central (2001, 265–66). See Ord. No. 1201, ADA, MINVU OA, 1983, for the difficulties this caused MINVU officials.

16. Foxley (1983), Meller (1996), and Constable and Valenzuela (1991, 163–96) provide important overviews of the crisis.

17. *La Presencia de Renca*, the monthly periodical of the municipality of Renca, provided continual coverage of the projects that work programs undertook.

18. Other surveys placed the number of pobladores involved in base organizations even higher, such as Angell (1991, 202) and Valdés (1987, 43).

19. On this point, see the testimonials and interviews in Budnik (1986, 53–57).

20. In this quote, Ana casts her labor as one of necessity and sacrifice that would fulfill her maternal obligations. James (2000, 232–35) and Hutchison (2001, 9), two Latin American historians working in the mid- and early twentieth century, respectively, have observed that female workers often cast their work in manual, "manly" labor in similar terms.

21. On the role of international solidarity networks, see Lowden (1996) and Wright (2007). Smith (1982) develops the early role of the church in building opposition to the dictatorship, while Jordá Sureda (2001) and Aldunate (2000) provide firsthand accounts and reflections from church activists throughout the entire period.

22. *El Mercurio*, Sept. 28, 1983, 10.

23. *Diario Oficial*, Mar. 28, 1980, 1.

24. Religious figures often supported the housing claims made by pobladores. See, for examples, Ord. No. 2201, ADA, MINVU OA, 1979 and Ord. No. 2600, ADA, MINVU OA, 1979.

25. *Las Últimas Noticias*, Sept. 29, 1983, 36.

26. *La Tercera*, Sept. 27, 1983, 4.

27. On this general transformation, see Bruey (2012).

28. For the details of the raid and detentions, see AS, AVS, A.T. no. 1, "Operativo militar-policial en campamentos 'Cardenal Raúl Silva Henriquez' y 'Juan Francisco Fresno.'"

29. On the role of the CTC, see Klubock (2004b).

30. Martínez (1992) and Baldez (2002, 146–51) analyze the use that the protestors made of the private and public spheres.

31. De la Maza and Garcés (1985, 38). For contemporary reports about the violence from parishes and human rights organization, see AS, AVS, boxes 48 and 49, *Protestas* and AS, AVS, A.T. no. 349.

32. Much of the following analysis relies on Martínez (1992).

33. Cathy Schneider (1995) first developed the argument about the Communist Party. Certain iconic MIR neighborhoods, such as Nueva la Habana (now Nuevo Amanacer), did become centers of protest, as Olavarría (2009), among others, describes.

34. Summary reports from priests in Catholic parishes and human rights observers that detail the level of activism and violence are available in AS, AVS, A.T. no. 349.

35. See Eliana Parra and Ana Valdés in Murphy (2004a) and Schneider (1995, 139). Álvarez (2008) and Pinto and Leiva (2008) respectively cover the roles of the Communist Party and the MIR in the protests.

36. For descriptions of the activities in the more combative poblaciones on the days of national protests, see Parra, Valdés, and Soto in Murphy (2004a), Oxhorn (1995, 343–49), Schneider (1995), and de la Maza and Garcés (1985).

37. Murphy (2004a, 69). Ana Valdés expresses a similar sentiment in ibid., 51–52.

38. Many others expressed the sentiment that the difficult conditions of the time meant that exceptional measures were necessary. For another example, in which a truck driver gave the sausages in his delivery truck to impoverished pobladores, see Stillerman (2004, 189).

39. Oxhorn (1995, 345–47) describes these incidents in a protest he witnessed.

40. Álvarez (2003 and 2008) provides an excellent overview of the trajectory of the Left.

41. Stern (2006, 297–327) brilliantly tracks the public reception to the protest movement.

42. See the SECRET Order of May 12, 1983, in an appellate court dossier filed in San Miguel on May 26, 1983, available in AS, AVS, A.T. no. 1, "Allanamientos."

43. AS, AVS, boxes 48 and 49, "Protestas" and AS, AVS, A.T. no. 349.

44. AS, AVS, Caja "Protestas," A.T. no. 47.

45. The text is available in AS, AVS, Caja "Protestas," A.T. no. 47.

46. For an influential, contemporary perspective along these lines, see Kirkwood (1990). Pieper Mooney (2009, 134–62) provides an insightful review.

47. FLACSO (1986, 13), as cited in Constable and Valenzuela (1991, 163).

48. Paley (2001) discusses the general importance of this kind of polling data in the making of elite opinion.

49. AS, AVS, Caja "Protestas," A.T. no. 47.

50. On the campaign, see Hirmas (1993), Stern (2006, 344–79), and Thomas (2011, 203–39).

Chapter 8. Fractures of Home and Nation: Property Titling after the Dictatorship

1. This presumes, of course, that future crises would not lead to the creation of new slums in the municipality of Santiago. Strikingly, however, nobody mentioned this.

2. As part of an extensive literature, beyond what I can cite here, Stern (2010) provides a detailed account of memory struggles during the post-dictatorship.

3. For the perspectives in this paragraph, see, among others, Moulian (1997), Paley (2001), Winn (2004a), Salazar (2005), and Alexander (2009).

4. Interviews and documents available in the archive of the Junta de Vecinos, Lo Boza.

5. I identified these various organizations through ethnographic observation, interviews, and the documentation available in the archive at the Junta de Vecinos, Campamento Lo Boza.

6. According to the Ministry of National Planning, "progressive housing" programs "are fundamentally meant for families of scarce resources in emergency conditions with a lack of housing." See MIDEPLAN (1999, 18).

7. Drogus and Stewart-Gambino (2005) note the overall decline, yet they also point to new, less confrontational forms of organizing in the post-dictatorship, largely based in NGOs, state-sponsored programs, and religious organizations.

8. See, among others, Silva (2008, 192–217).

9. See, for examples, *El Mercurio*, May 7, 1998, C1, and *La Tercera*, Jan. 4, 2002, 10.

10. José Antonio Gómez, a MINVU official, articulates this policy in *La Tercera*, Jan. 9, 2002, 7.

11. This is not true, however, of the public transportation system, which the Lagos and Bachelet administrations overhauled by funneling users from throughout the city into a now often crowded metro system.

12. For the statistics on Santiago, see Cámara Chilena de Construcción (n.d.) and MINVU (2006, 9–10). In the recession years between 2000 and 2002, housing starts averaged twenty-two thousand in Santiago.

13. In a more general vein, Taylor (2006) argues that one of the central contradictions of the Concertación was the effort to support social welfare policies while broadening neoliberal policies of economic integration.

14. Banco Central, accessed Mar. 5, 2011, http://www.bcentral.cl/estadisticas-economicas/series-indicadores/index_aeg.htm.

15. MIDEPLAN (2010) and "Terremoto del 27-F dejó 500 mil nuevos pobres en Chile," Jan. 25, 2011, accessed Jan. 25, 2011, www.lanacion.cl. The rise between 2006 and 2010 occurred primarily because of the fallout from both the 2008 global financial crisis and the February 2010 earthquake.

16. *El Mercurio*, July 1, 2007, B11. Soto, Espinoza, and Gómez (2008, 21), also note that 46.1 percent of legally employed workers in Chile received less than a "family basket" in take-home pay in 2006 according to the criteria of the International Labor Organization of the United Nations.

17. For the statistics on poverty rates in 1970, see CEPAL (1990). PREALC (1990) provides an alternative, higher estimate that examines only greater Santiago. Taylor (2006, 139) makes a similar point to the one I do, although he cites statistics that are higher than the ones I use.

18. For the first statistic, see Díaz (1991), as cited in Salazar and Pinto (2002, 219), and for the second, Dirección del Trabajo, Chile (2009, 40).

19. For the statistics in this section, see Bengoa (2009, 67–68). It is important to note, however, that the number of students studying in universities overall *tripled* in size between 1990 and 2010.

20. Winn (2004a, 57) notes that Chileans work an average of 2,244 hours a year; Europeans, 1,600. For similar comparative data see also *La Nación*, Feb. 2, 2007, accessed Sept. 17, 2012, www.lanacion.cl/noticias/site/artic/20070207/pags/20070207204156.html.

21. See Cámara Chilena de la Construcción (2005, 20–23) and Sugranyes (2005, 37), who places the percentage for the 1990s at 75 percent.

22. In keeping the cost of subsidized housing low, the government has subsidized 24 percent of investment in housing (Cámara Chilena de la Construcción 2005, 23).

23. For example, the government-supported housing financing after Habitacoop, a housing cooperative, had to fold in the wake of the Asian financial crisis. See *El Mercurio*, Dec. 22, 2001, D1–2.

24. In an interview with former president Ricardo Lagos on May 4, 2011, I asked him if his administration had found it difficult to have housing developers build low-income housing. He indicated that it was exactly the opposite, provided that these companies could work in areas where the price of land was cheap and subsidies remained high.

25. Dirección del Trabajo, Chile (2009, 46).

26. It is an open secret that many illegal immigrants work in the construction sector. I base my assertion, however, on interviews with two longtime construction workers, Raúl Soto and Alexi Martínez. I do not know of a specific study that has tracked informal labor relations in the construction sector.

27. Andrés Palma, the executive director of Chile Barrio, in an interview in 2002, indicated that the Concertación had been aggressive in housing policies because of a fear of a return to land seizures. See also Paley (2001) and Sugranyes (2005, 43).

28. Junta de Vecinos Archive, Campamento Lo Boza.

29. Schild (2000) and Paley (2001) impressively criticize the technocratic characteristics of the post-dictatorship democracy, but overemphasize their neoliberal nature. Silva (2008) provides an important corrective.

30. Schild (2000), Paley (2001), and Leiva (2005) develop critical perspectives on popular participation programs.

31. Cecilia provided me with a tape of the report that originally aired on the Catholic University television station sometime in late 1999.

32. See Chile Barrio (2000), and *La Tercera*, May 23, 2002, 12.

33. See Murphy (2004a, 179, 195). This was a not altogether uncommon problem, raising concern among housing officials and NGO administrators (Chile Barrio 2000, 48).

34. For the stipulations of housing programs, see MIDEPLAN (1996b).

35. Accessed July 12, 2012. http://mp-ukamau.blogspot.com/2012/02/vecinos-vecinas-y-amigos-ya.html.

Chapter 9. The Indignities of Home in the Margins of Modern Urban Life

1. Frazier (2007, 190–241) examines how a nostalgic melancholia oriented the interpretations of the past and present for the activist Left in the 1990s and early 2000s. For a different demographic, Bengoa (2009, 99–128) provides an astute analysis of attitudes of anger and withdrawal among young pobladores via interviews, ethnography, and contemporary hip-hop lyrics.

2. Although I came to know Alexi well, I did not formally interview him and he does not appear in the book of oral histories I compiled. I have consequently used a pseudonym for him since he did not have the opportunity to prepare his testimonial for the public record. His quotes come from my field notes written shortly after our conversations between 2002 and 2004.

3. Tinsman (2014, 64–102) insightfully develops this dynamic, in addition to the points raised in the previous paragraph.

4. The statistic on the number of Santiago residents who have access to consumer credit comes from the Cámara de Comercio de Santiago (1995), as cited in Moulian (1997, 100–101).

5. In 2005, the Lagos administration passed important legislation that expanded health care coverage. For low-income groups, however, coverage can still be piecemeal and sporadic.

6. On other occasions, I had heard young men discuss the justice of robbing the rich, especially when I volunteered in 1994 and 1995 at a community center in Renca that worked with teenagers who had dropped out of school, many of whom had drug and alcohol addiction problems. One youth expresses a similar sentiment in an article in *El Mercurio*, June 25, 2000, D17. This justification could also move into drug dealing, although this was less common.

7. Maids have recently gained greater rights that have formalized, for many, their relationships with employers.

8. I observed this practice on a number of occasions and discussed it with two store owners who were in this situation.

9. Salazar and Pinto (2002, 207–39) provide an insightful discussion.

10. Goldstein (2004) notes the general importance of *desconfianza* among his interlocutors in a low-income area of Cochabamba, Bolivia.

11. Paley (2001, 86) notes similar dynamics. For general, comparative perspectives on the barricaded nature of contemporary urbanism, see, among others, Caldeira (2000), Holston (2008, 279–313), and Low (2003).

12. I heard some of these stories at parties and gatherings on the streets, where I at times joined predominantly male groups in conversation and drinking. They were also the type of recollection I heard when I worked at the youth center in Renca in the mid-1990s.

13. For Rivera's testimonial, see Murphy (2004a, 181–90).

14. *La Nación*, July 25, 2012, accessed July 25, 2012, http://www.lanacion.cl/preocupacion-en-el-gobierno-por-aumento-de-la-pobreza-con-rostro-de-mujer/noticias/2012-07-25/130321.html.

15. Tinsman (2014, 64–102) discusses the significance of this shift among grape workers in the Central Valley.

16. See Tinsman (1997, 2014), in addition to Avendaño (2008) and Salazar and Pinto (2002, 194–239).

17. In her study of child circulation and the state in late nineteenth- and early twentieth-century Chile, Milanich (2009) criticizes the use of the term "fictive kin," noting that kinships not based on a blood relationship were (and are) quite common and that they should not be measured against a presumed norm. Milanich's point about presuming that blood-kin relationships are the norm is well taken, but I persist in using the term since I have found Chileans themselves to treat these kinds of kinships as having a special status. The anthropological and historical use of "fictive kin" need not pathologize, but rather underscore the social importance of these particular relationships.

18. In a now-classic formulation, Carol Stack (1974) describes these kinds of relationships among African Americans as "domestic kin networks." See also, among others, Venkatesh (2006, 21–90).

19. Jealousy was a common theme in life histories and in descriptions of competition in kin relations, especially when it involved nonbiological relations, such as a stepmother or stepfather. Jealousy of this sort points to the powerful hold that expectations of possession have in familial relationships.

20. Barr-Melej (2006) and Elsey (2011) both explore the evolution of a youth counter-culture in the 1960s.

21. Mallon (2003) discusses these characteristics among MIR militants, while Klubock (1998) and Tinsman (2002) do so for industrial and agricultural workers, respectively.

Conclusion

1. Valdés's testimonial is in Murphy (2004a, 39–65). For documentation on her detention, court cases, and reports from human rights lawyers, see AS, AVS.

2. As part of an early wave of writers who celebrated the ingenuity of squatters, Turner and Fichter (1972) adopted the term "freedom to build." Turner, Fichter, and others astutely criticized state-led housing projects for their authoritarian and inflexible tendencies. Yet while Turner and Fichter made this criticism, they were not neoliberals. Neoliberals such as Hernando de Soto, however, would later adopt both these kinds of criticisms and celebrations of squatters in developing their policy recommendations.

3. My formulation here loosely draws from Ferguson's (1999) analysis of "expectations of modernity."

4. Das (2010) criticizes Chatterjee for the inflexibility of his approach.

GLOSSARY AND ACRONYMS

allegado, -a. A person living in the house of extended family, fictive kin, or friends.
arrabal. A shantytown, in use during the colonial period and into the nineteenth century, literally refers to a town or place of Arabs.
callampa. A shantytown, in use from approximately the 1920s through the 1970s, literally a type of mushroom that sprouts up during the night.
campamento. An "encampment," a reference to a squatter settlement, in use through most of the twentieth century and into the present.
CEMA. Mothers' centers, first created in 1954, specifically a part of state programs through the early 1990s.
Concertación. The coalition of center-left political parties that formed in the late 1980s and sent four consecutive candidates to the presidency from 1990–2010.
compadrazgo. Ties of kin or fictive kin, includes god-parentage and potentially close friends.
conventillos. Tenements that first appeared in the late nineteenth century.
CORVI. The Corporation of Housing, a government entity founded in 1953 dedicated primarily to low-income housing, real estate financing, and urban development.
CTC. The Chilean Workers' Federation.
DINAC. National Office of Supplies and Commercialization, a government body formed during Salvador Allende's presidency in charge of certain forms of commercial distribution and the provision of basic supplies, particularly food baskets.
dueñas de casa. Housewives, literally female masters of the house.
mediagua. A wooden housing hut, either built by squatter residents themselves or provided by charity organizations and government institutions.
MINVU. The Ministry of Housing and Urbanism, formed in 1965.
MIR. Movement of the Revolutionary Left, formed in 1967.
olla común. "A common pot," a neighborhood based organization that provides food, usually a meal, to neighbors.
Operación Sitio. "Operation Housing," a program in place from 1964 to 1970 that provided housing lots and certain urban services, generally with little or no housing.
PC. The Communist Party, founded in 1922.
PDC. The Christian Democratic Party, founded in 1957.
población. A low-income urban neighborhood.
poblador, -a. A resident of a low-income urban neighborhood.

Popular Promotion. Program in place between 1964 and 1970 that sought to foment the organizational capacity of low-income Chileans.

ranchería. A neighborhood of shacks.

rancho. A shack, generally associated with the countryside, although they are also often a part of urban squatter settlements.

sanear. Literally means to sanitize, to heal, and to regulate simultaneously; in the context of residences and neighborhoods, refers to the process of creating undisputed and legally sanctioned properties that have certain infrastructure services considered basic.

sin casa. Literally "without a home," refers to individuals who are a part of a loosely organized family unit who do not have their own house.

UDI. The Democratic Independent Union, a right-wing political party founded in 1983.

UP. Acronym for the Popular Unity, the coalition of parties that supported Salvador Allende's presidency.

villa. A housing complex.

REFERENCES

Archives

Archivo de la Administración (ADA):
- Ministerio de Vivienda y Urbanismo, Oficios con Antecedentes (MINVU OA)
- Ministerio de Vivienda y Urbanismo, Oficios Recibidos (MINVU OR)
- Ministerio de Vivienda y Urbanismo, Antecedentes/Providencias (MINVU AP)
- Ministerio del Interior (MI)
- Ministerio de Economía, Fomento, y Reconstrucción (MEFR)

Arzobispado de Santiago, Archivo de la Vicaría de la Solidaridad (AS, AVS)

Biblioteca del Congreso (Santiago):
- Gobierno de Chile, *Mensajes Presidenciales*, 1957, 1965–1974, 1976–2010
- Historias de las Leyes: 16.391, 16.392, 16.741, 16.880
- Historia del Decreto con Fuerza de Ley 2
- Laws and Resolutions: Ley 11211 (1953), Ley 14670 (1961), Ley 16955 (1968), and Resolución 3717 (1991).

Cámara Chilena de la Construcción

Comisión Nacional de Prisión Política y Tortura (Comisión Valech). 2004. *Informe de la Comisión Nacional de Prisión Política y Tortura*. Santiago: Ministerio Secretaría General de Gobierno.

Comisión Nacional de Verdad y Reconciliación (Informe Rettig). 1991. *Informe de la Comisión Nacional de Verdad y Reconciliación*. Santiago: Ministerio Secretaría General de Gobierno.

Junta de Vecinos, Campamento Lo Boza

Municipalidad de Renca (MR):
- Actas (A)
- Carpetas Comunales (CC)
- Dirección de Obras (DO)

Princeton University Library Pamphlet Collection, Chile

Sesiones ordinarias de la Cámara de Diputados, 1965–1973

Sesiones extraordinarias de la Cámara de Diputados, 1965–1973

Sesiones ordinarias del Senado, 1965–1973

Sesiones extraordinarias del Senado, 1965–1973

Secondary Sources

Adams, Jacqueline. 2012. *Surviving Dictatorship: A Work of Visual Sociology*. New York: Routledge.

Adelman, Jeremy. 1999. *Colonial Legacies: The Problem of Persistence in Latin American History*. New York: Routledge.

Agamben, Giorgio. 2005. *State of Exception*. Chicago: University of Chicago Press.

Aldunate Lyon, José. 2000. *Crónicas de una iglesia liberadora*. Santiago: Ediciones LOM.

Alexander, William, ed. 2009. *Lost in the Long Transition: Struggles for Social Justice in Neoliberal Chile*. Lanham, MD: Lexington Books.

Álvarez Vallejos, Rolando. 2003. *Desde las sombras: una historia de la clandestinidad comunista (1973–1980)*. Santiago: LOM.

Álvarez Vallejos, Rolando. 2008. "'Aún tenemos patria, ciudadanos': El Partido Comunista de Chile y la salida no pactada de la dictadura (1980–1988)." In *Su revolución contra nuestra revolución*, Vol. 2: *La pugna marxista-gremialista en los ochenta*, edited by Verónica Valdivia Ortiz de Zárate, 19–82. Santiago: LOM.

Anderson, Benedict. 1991. *Imagined Communities: Reflections on the Origin and Spread of Nationalism*. London: Verso.

Angel, Shlomo. 2000. *Housing Policy Matters: A Global Analysis*. Oxford: Oxford University Press.

Angell, Alan. 1991. "Unions and Workers in Chile during the 1980s." In *The Struggle for Democracy in Chile, 1982–1990*, edited by Paul Drake and Ivan Jaksic, 188–210. Lincoln: University of Nebraska Press.

Angell, Alan. 1993. "Chile since 1958." In *Chile since Independence*, edited by Leslie Bethell, 121–202. Cambridge: Cambridge University Press.

Appadurai, Arjun. 1986. *The Social Life of Things: Commodities in Cultural Perspective*. Cambridge: Cambridge University Press.

Appadurai, Arjun. 1996. *Modernity at Large: Cultural Dimensions of Globalization*. Minneapolis: University of Minnesota Press.

Appadurai, Arjun. 2000. "Spectral Housing and Urban Cleansing: Notes on Millennial Mumbai." *Public Culture* 12 (3): 627–51.

Appadurai, Arjun. 2002. "Deep Democracy: Urban Governmentality and the Horizon of Politics." *Public Culture* 14 (1): 21–47.

Arellano, José Pablo. 1976. *Elementos para una política de vivienda social*. Santiago: Corporación de Investigaciones Económicas para Latinoamérica.

Arellano, José Pablo. 1983. "Políticas de vivienda, 1975–1981: financiamiento y subsidios." *EURE* 10 (28): 9–24.

Armus, Diego. 2011. *The Ailing City: Health, Tuberculosis, and Culture in Buenos Aires, 1870–1950*. Durham, NC: Duke University Press.

Arrate, Jorge, and Eduardo Rojas. 2003. *Memoria de la izquierda Chilena: Tomo I (1850–1970)*. Santiago: Javier Vergara Editor.

Arriagada Herrera, Genaro. 1988. *Pinochet: The Politics of Power*. Boston: Unwin Hyman.

Astica, Juan, and Mario Vergara. 1958. "Antecedentes para la evaluación del problema de las poblaciones callampas en Chile." Informe de la delegación a la Segunda Reunión Interamericana de Vivienda y Planeamiento, Lima, Noviembre.

AUCA. 1972. "Plan de Emergencia, 1971: Advenimiento del Gobierno Popular." 43–53.

Auyero, Javier. 2001. "Researching the Urban Margins: What Can the United States Learn from Latin America and Vice Versa?" *City and Community* 10 (4): 431–36.

Auyero, Javier, and Débora A. Swistun. 2009. *Flammable: Environmental Suffering in an Argentine Shantytown*. Oxford: Oxford University Press.

Avendaño, Cecilia. 2008. "Conciliación trabajo-familia y mujeres: reflexiones en una perspectiva psicosocial." In *Flexibilidad laboral y subjetividades: hacía una comprensión psicosocial del empleo contemporáneo*, edited by Álvaro Soto, 221–35. Santiago: LOM Ediciones.

Baldez, Lisa. 2002. *Why Women Protest: Women's Movements in Chile*. Cambridge: Cambridge University Press.

Banco Central. 2001. *Indicadores económicas y sociales: 1960–2000*. Santiago: Banco Central.

Barahona, Pablo, and Olga Mercado Villar. 1970. "Comercialización y aspectos económicos en el sector Manuel Rodríguez." In *La marginalidad urbana: origen, proceso y modo: resultados de una encuesta en poblaciones marginales del Gran Santiago*. Santiago: DESAL.

Barr-Melej, Patrick. 2001. *Reforming Chile: Cultural Politics, Nationalism, and the Rise of the Middle Class*. Chapel Hill: University of North Carolina Press.

Barr-Melej, Patrick. 2006. "Siloismo and the Self in Allende's Chile: Youth, 'Total Revolution,' and the Roots of the Humanist Movement." *Hispanic American Historical Review* 86 (4): 747–84.

Benavides Zamora, Leopoldo, Edward Morales, and Sergio Rojas. 1983. *Campamentos y poblaciones de las comunas del Gran Santiago: una síntesis informativa*. Santiago: FLACSO.

Bengoa, José. 2009. *La comunidad fragmentada: nación y desigualdad en Chile*. Santiago: Catalonia.

Bengoa, José, Susana Aravena, and Francisca Márquez. 1999. *La desigualdad: testimonios de la sociedad Chilena en la última década del siglo XX*. Santiago: Ediciones SUR.

Benjamin, Walter. 1988. "Theses on the Philosophy of History." In *Illuminations: Essays and Reflections*, 253–64. New York: Schocken Books.

Benmergui, Leandro. 2009. "The Alliance for Progress and Housing Policy in Rio de Janeiro and Buenos Aires in the 1960s." *Urban History* 36 (2): 304–26.

Benmergui, Leandro. 2013. "The Transnationalization of the 'Housing Problem': Social Sciences and Developmentalism in Postwar Argentina." In *The Housing Question: Tensions, Continuities, and Contingencies in the Modern City*, edited by Edward Murphy and Najib Hourani, 35–56. London: Ashgate Press.

Berman, Marshall. 1982. *All That Is Solid Melts into Air: The Experience of Modernity*. New York: Simon and Schuster.

Besse, Susan K. 1996. *Restructuring Patriarchy: The Modernization of Gender Inequality in Brazil, 1914–1940*. Chapel Hill: University of North Carolina Press.

Blomley, Nicholas. 2003. "Law, Property, and the Geography of Violence: The Frontier, the Survey, and the Grid." *Annals of Association of American Geographers* 93 (1): 121–41.

Boorstein, Edward. 1977. *Allende's Chile: An Inside View*. New York: International Publishers.
Bourdieu, Pierre. 1999. "Effects of Place." In *The Weight of the World: Social Suffering in Contemporary Society*, 123–29. Cambridge: Polity Press. First published 1977.
Bravo Heitmann, Luis. 1993. "Retrospectiva de 50 años de vivienda social." In *Chile: 50 años de vivienda social, 1943–1993*, 3–72. Valparaíso, Chile: Universidad de Valparaíso Facultad de Arquitectura.
Brenner, Neil, and Nik Theodore. 2002. "Cities and the Geographies of 'Actually Existing Neoliberalism.'" In *Spaces of Neoliberalism: Urban Restructuring in North America and Western Europe*, 2–32. Malden: Blackwell.
Brito, Alejandra. 1995. "Del rancho al conventillo: transformaciones de la identidad popular femenina, 1850–1920." In *Disciplina y desacato: construcción de identidad en Chile, siglos XIX y XX*, edited by Lorena Godoy et al., 27–70. Santiago: Ediciones SUR, CEDEM.
Bruey, Alison. 2012. "Limitless Land and the Redefinition of Rights: Popular Mobilization and the Limits of Neoliberalism in Pinochet's Chile, 1973–1985." *Journal of Latin American Studies* 44: 523–52.
Buck-Morss, Susan. 2007. "Sovereign Right and the Global Left." *Rethinking Marxism* 19 (4): 432–51.
Budnik, Miguel. 1986. *Los marginados*. Santiago: Araucaria.
Burnett, John. 1986. *A Social History of Housing, 1815–1985*. London: Methuen.
Caldeira, Teresa. 2000. *City of Walls: Crime, Segregation, and Citizenship in São Paulo*. Berkeley: University of California Press.
Calhoun, Craig. 1992. *Habermas and the Public Sphere*. Cambridge: MIT Press.
Cámara Chilena de la Construcción. 2005. *Balance de la vivienda en Chile: análisis de la evolución sectorial, estimación de requerimientos habitacionales y proyectos en el mediano plazo*. Santiago: Cámara Chilena de la Construcción.
Cámara de Comercio de Santiago (Chile). 1995. *Deudas de consumo consolidadas por estrato socioeconómico en Chile: (antecedentes a Diciembre de 1995)*. Santiago: Cámara de Comercio de Santiago.
Canguilhem, Georges. 1989. *The Normal and the Pathological*. New York: Zone Books.
Cantero, Victor. 1972. "Vivienda: Trabajo de Masas." *Principios* (March, April): 92–103.
Cariola Sutter, Carmen, and Osvaldo Sunkel. 1982. *La historia económica de Chile, 1830 y 1930: dos ensayos y una bibliografía*. Madrid: Ediciones Cultura Hispánica del Instituto de Cooperación Iberoamericana.
Carsten, Janet. 2004. *After Kinship*. Cambridge, UK: Cambridge University Press.
Carsten, Janet, and Stephen Hugh-Jones. 1995. *About the House: Lévi-Strauss and Beyond*. Cambridge: Cambridge University Press.
Castells, Manuel. 1975. *La Lucha de Clases en Chile*. México: Siglo Veintiuno Editores.
Castells, Manuel. 1983. *The City and the Grassroots: A Cross-Cultural Theory of Urban Social Movements*. Berkeley: University of California Press.
Castillo, Carmen E. 1999. *Un día de octubre en Santiago*. Santiago: LOM Ediciones.

Caulfield, Sueann. 2000. *In Defense of Honor: Sexual Morality, Modernity, and Nation in Early Twentieth-Century Brazil*. Durham, NC: Duke University Press.

Cavallo, Ascanio. 2001. *La historia oculta del régimen militar Chile 1973–1988*. Santiago: Grupo Grijalbo-Mondadori.

CEPAL. 1990. *Magnitud de la pobreza en los años ochenta*. Santiago: CEPAL.

Chakrabarty, Dipesh. 2000. *Provincializing Europe: Postcolonial Thought and Historical Difference*. Princeton, NJ: Princeton University Press.

Chakrabarty, Dipesh. 2001. "Adda, Calcutta: Dwelling in Modernity." In *Alternative Modernities*, edited by Dilip Gaonkar, 123–64. Durham, NC: Duke University Press.

Chakrabarty, Dipesh. 2002. "Of Garbage, Modernity, and the Citizen's Gaze." In *Habitations of Modernity: Essays in the Wake of Subaltern Studies*, 65–79. Chicago: University of Chicago Press.

Chatterjee, Partha. 2004. *The Politics of the Governed: Reflections on Popular Politics in Most of the World*. New York: Columbia University Press.

Chazkel, Amy. 2011. *Laws of Chance: Brazil's Clandestine Lottery and the Making of Urban Public Life*. Durham, NC: Duke University Press.

Cheetham, Rosemond. 1971. "El sector privado de la construcción: patrón de dominación." *EURE* 1 (3): 125–48.

Chile Barrio, Ministerio de Vivienda y Urbanismo. 2000. *Voces de Chile Barrio*. Santiago: Chile Barrio.

Cleaves, Peter. 1969. *Developmental Processes in Chilean Local Government*. Berkeley: University of California Press.

Cleaves, Peter. 1974. *Bureaucratic Politics and Administration in Chile*. Berkeley: University of California Press.

Colectivo de Memoria Histórica. 2005. *Tortura en poblaciones del Gran Santiago*. Santiago: Corporación José Domingo Cañas.

Collier, Simon, and William F. Sater. 2004. *A History of Chile, 1808–2002*. Cambridge: Cambridge University Press.

Collins, John F. 2011. "Culture, Content, and the Enclosure of the Human Being: UNESCO's 'Intangible' Heritage in the New Millenium." *Radical History Review* 109 (winter): 121–35.

Collins, Joseph. 1995. *Chile's Free-Market Miracle: A Second Look*. Oakland: Food First.

Comaroff, Jean, and John Comaroff. 1992. "Homemade Hegemony." In *Ethnography and the Historical Imagination*, 265–96. Boulder, CO: Westview Press.

Comisión Chilena de Derechos Humanos, Fundación Ideas. 1999. *Nunca más en Chile. sintesis corregida y actualizada del "Informe Rettig."* Santiago: Ediciones LOM.

Conguilhem, Georges. 1989. *The Normal and the Pathological*. Translated by Carolyn R. Fawcett. New York: Zone Books.

Constable, Pamela, and Arturo Valenzuela. 1991. *A Nation of Enemies: Chile under Pinochet*. New York: Norton.

Cooper, Frederick. 2005. "Modernity." In *Colonialism in Question: Theory, Knowledge, History*, 113–52. Berkeley: University of California Press.

Cooper, Frederick, and Randall Packard. 1997. *International Development and the Social*

Sciences: Essays on the History and Politics of Knowledge. Berkeley: University of California Press.

Coronil, Fernando. 1994. "Listening to the Subaltern: The Poetics of Neocolonial States." *Poetics Today* 15 (4): 642–58.

Coronil, Fernando. 1997. *The Magical State: Nature, Money, and Modernity in Venezuela.* Chicago: University of Chicago Press.

Coronil, Fernando. 2004. "Latin American Postcolonial Studies and Global Decolonization." In *Postcolonial Literary Studies*, edited by Neal Lazarus, 221–40. Cambridge: Cambridge University Press.

Coronil, Fernando. 2007. "After Empire: Reflections on Imperialism from the Americas." In *Imperial Formations*, edited by Ann Stoler, Laura McGranahan, and Peter C. Perdue, 241–74. Santa Fe, NM: School of American Research.

Coronil, Fernando, and Julie Skurski. 2006. "Dismembering and Remembering the Nation: The Semantics of Political Violence in Venezuela." In *States of Violence*, 83–152. Ann Arbor: University of Michigan Press. First published 1991.

Corporación José Domingo Cañas and Laura Moya. 2005. *Tortura en poblaciones del Gran Santiago (1973–1990): Colectivo de Memoria Histórica.* Santiago: Corporación José Domingo Cañas.

Corradi, Juan, Patricia Weiss Fagen, and Manuel A. Garretón Merino. 1992. *Fear at the Edge: State Terror and Resistance in Latin America.* Berkeley: University of California Press.

Dahse, Fernando. 1979. *El mapa de la extrema riqueza: los grupos económicos y el proceso de concentración de capitales.* Santiago: Aconcagua.

Dahua, Emilio. 2014. "The Informal City: An Enduring Slum or a Progressive Habitat?" In *Cities from Scratch: Poverty and Informality in Urban Latin America*, edited by Brodwyn Fischer, Bryan McCann, and Javier Auyero, 150–69. Durham, NC: Duke University Press.

Das, Veena. 2010. "State, Citizenship, and the Urban Poor." Ambedkar Memorial Lecture, Ambedkar University, Delhi, India.

Das, Veena, and Deborah Poole. 2004. *Anthropology in the Margins of the State.* Santa Fe: School of American Research Press.

Davidoff, Leonore, and Catherine Hall. 1987. *Family Fortunes: Men and Women of the English Middle Class, 1780–1850.* Chicago: University of Chicago Press.

Davis, Mike. 2006. *Planet of Slums.* London: Verso.

Dawdy, Shannon. 2008. *Building the Devil's Empire: French Colonial New Orleans.* Chicago: University of Chicago Press.

de la Maza, Gonzalo. 2005. *Tan lejos tan cerca: políticas públicas y sociedad civil en Chile.* Santiago: LOM.

de la Maza, Gonzalo, and Mario Garcés. 1985. *La explosión de las mayorías: protesta nacional, 1983–1984.* Santiago: Educación y Comunicaciones.

de la Rocha, Mercedes, Janice Perlman, Helen Safa, Elizabeth Jelin, Bryan Roberts, and Peter Ward. 2004. "From the Marginality of the 1960s to the 'New Poverty' of Today: A LARR Research Forum." *Latin American Research Review* 39 (1): 183–203.

de Ramón, Armando. 2007. *Santiago de Chile: historia de una sociedad urbana*. Santiago: Catalonia. First published 1992.

Derby, Lauren. 2009. *The Dictator's Seduction: Politics and the Popular Imagination in the Era of Trujillo*. Durham, NC: Duke University Press.

DESAL. 1966. *Aportes para un programa de Promoción Popular*. Santiago: DESAL.

DeShazo, Peter. 1983. *Urban Workers and Labor Unions in Chile, 1902–1927*. Madison: University of Wisconsin Press.

de Solano, Francisco. 1996. "Estudio preliminar." In *Normas y leyes de la ciudad hispano-americana*, xxii–xl. Madrid: Consejo Superior de Investigaciones Científicas.

de Soto, Hernando. 1989. *The Other Path: The Invisible Revolution in the Third World*. New York: Harper & Row.

de Soto, Hernando. 2000. *The Mystery of Capital: Why Capitalism Triumphs in the West and Fails Everywhere Else*. New York: Basic Books.

de Soto, Hernando. 2004. "Foreword." In *A Possible Way Out: Formalizing Housing Informality in Egyptian Cities*, by Ahmed Soliman. Lanham, MD: University Press of America.

de Vylder, Stefan. 1976. *Allende's Chile: The Political Economy of the Rise and Fall of the Unidad Popular*. Cambridge: Cambridge University Press.

Díaz, Estrella. 1991. *Investigación participativa acerca de las trabajadoras termporeras de la fruta*. Santiago: Canelo de Nos.

Dirección del Trabajo, Chile. 2009. *ENCLA 2008: Resultados de la Sexta Encuesta Laboral*. Santiago, Chile: Dirección del Trabajo, Gobierno.

Dorfman, Ariel. 1999. *Heading South, Looking North: A Bilingual Journey*. New York: Penguin Books. First published 1998.

Douglas, Mary. (1966) 1980. *Purity and Danger: An Analysis of Concepts of Pollution and Taboo*. London: Routledge & Kegan Paul.

Drake, Paul. 1978. *Socialism and Populism in Chile, 1932–52*. Urbana: University of Illinois Press.

Drake, Paul. 1993. "Chile, 1930–1958." In *Chile since Independence*, edited by Leslie Bethell, 87–128. Cambridge: Cambridge University Press.

Drogus, Carol, and Hannah Stewart-Gambino. 2005. *Activist Faith: Grassroots Women in Democratic Brazil and Chile*. University Park: Pennsylvania State University Press.

Ducci, Eugenia T., Viviana Fernández, and Daisila Agüero. 1989. *Evaluación de las variaciones de la calidad de vida de la población erradicada en el Area Metropolitana de Santiago: un estudio de casos para el período 1979–1985*. Santiago: Pontificia Universidad Católica, Instituto de Estudios Urbanos.

Duque, Joaquin, and Ernesto Pastrana. 1972. "La movilización reivindicativa urbana de los sectores populares en Chile, 1964–1972." *Revista Latinomericana de Ciencias Sociales* 4: 259–94.

Eagleton, Terry. 1990. *The Ideology of the Aesthetic*. Oxford: Blackwell.

Educación y Comunicaciones (ECO). 1994. *Historias para un fin de siglo: primer concurso de historias locales y sus fuentes*. Santiago: ECO.

Elena, Eduardo. 2011. *Dignifying Argentina: Peronism, Citizenship, and Mass Consumption.* Pittsburgh, PA: University of Pittsburgh Press.

Eley, Geoff. 1994. "Nations, Publics, and Political Cultures: Placing Habermas in the Nineteenth Century." In *Culture/Power/History: A Reader in Contemporary Social Theory*, edited by Nicholas Dirks, Geoff Eley, and Sherry Ortner, 297–335. Princeton, NJ: Princeton University Press.

Elsey, Brenda. 2011. *Citizens and Sportsmen: Fútbol and Politics in Twentieth-Century Chile.* Austin: University of Texas Press.

Elyachar, Julia. 2005. *Markets of Dispossession: NGOs, Economic Development, and the State in Cairo.* Durham, NC: Duke University Press.

Engels, F. (1872) 1887. *The Housing Question.* Translation of 2nd German edition, marxists.org, 1995. Accessed January 3, 2012. http://www.marxists.org/archive/marx/works/1872/housing-question/index.htm.

Equipo de Estudios Poblacionales, Centro de Investigaciones del Desarrollo Urbano y Regional (CIDU). 1972. "Reivindicación urbana y lucha política: los campamentos de pobladores en Santiago." *EURE* 2 (6): 55–82.

Equipo Político SurDA. 1999. "Campamento Peñalolén: las claves de una toma que no afloja." *SurDa* 23: 20–25.

Escobar, Arturo. 1995. *Encountering Development: The Making and Unmaking of the Third World.* Princeton, NJ: Princeton University Press.

Espinoza, Vicente. 1988. *Para una historia de los pobres de la ciudad.* Santiago: Ediciones Sur.

Fanon, Frantz. 1963. *The Wretched of the Earth.* New York: Grove Weidenfeld.

Farnsworth-Alvear, Ann. 2000. *Dulcinea in the Factory: Myths, Morals, Men, and Women in Colombia's Industrial Experiment, 1905–1960.* Durham, NC: Duke University Press.

Fazio, Hugo. 1997. *Mapa actual de la extrema riqueza en Chile.* Santiago: LOM Ediciones.

Fazio, Hugo. 2005. *Mapa de la extrema riqueza en Chile.* Santiago: LOM Ediciones.

Ferguson, James. 1991. *The Anti-Politics Machine: "Development," Depoliticization, and Bureaucratic Power in Lesotho.* Minneapolis: University of Minnesota Press.

Ferguson, James. 1999. *Expectations of Modernity: Myths and Meanings of Urban Life on the Zambian Copperbelt.* Berkeley: University of California Press.

Fernández Labbé, Marcos. 2003. "Nuestra forma de alienación es simultáneamente nuestra única forma de expresión: debate intelectual, política cultural y compromiso político en la intelectualidad de la izquierda en Chile, 1970–1973." In *1973: La vida cotidiana de un año crucial*, edited by Claudio Rolle, César Albornoz, and Patricio Bernerdo Pinto, 97–136. Santiago: Editorial Planeta Chilena.

Fischer, Brodwyn. 2008. *A Poverty of Rights: Citizenship and Inequality in Twentieth-Century Rio De Janeiro.* Stanford, CA: Stanford University Press.

Fischer, Brodwyn. 2014a. "Introduction." In *Cities from Scratch: Informality and Poverty in Urban Latin America*, edited by Brodwyn Fischer, Bryan McCann, and Javier Auyero, 1–7. Durham, NC: Duke University Press.

Fischer, Brodwyn. 2014b. "A Century in the Present Tense: Crisis, Politics and the Intellectual History of Brazil's Informal Cities." In *Cities from Scratch: Informality and Poverty in Urban Latin America*, edited by Brodwyn Fischer, Bryan McCann, and

Javier Auyero, 9–67. Durham, NC: Duke University Press.

Fischer, Brodwyn. 2014c. "The Red Menace Reconsidered: A Forgotten History of Communist Mobilization in Rio de Janeiro's Favelas, 1945–1964." *Hispanic American Historical Review* 94 (1): 1–33.

FLACSO. 1986. *Encuesta sobre la realidad sociopolítica chilena: resultados preliminares.* Santiago: FLACSO.

Foucault, Michel. 1975. *The Birth of the Clinic: An Archaeology of Medical Perception.* New York: Vintage Books.

Foucault, Michel. 1991. "Governmentality." In *The Foucault Effect: Studies in Governmentality with Two Lectures by and Interview with Michel Foucault*, edited by G. Burchell, C. Gordon, and P. Miller, 87–104. Chicago: University of Chicago Press.

Foxley, Alejandro. 1983. *Latin American Experiments in Neoconservative Economics.* Berkeley: University of California Press.

Foxley, Alejandro. 1986. "The Neoconservative Economic Experiment in Chile." In *Military Rule in Chile: Dictatorship and Oppositions*, edited by Juan Valenzuela and Arturo Valenzuela, 13–50. Baltimore: Johns Hopkins University Press.

Franceschet, Susan. 2005. *Women and Politics in Chile.* Boulder, CO: Lynne Rienner Publishers.

Frank, Volker. 2004. "Politics without Policy: The Failure of Social Concertation in Democratic Chile, 1990–2000." In *Victims of the Chilean Miracle: Workers and Neoliberalism in the Pinochet Era, 1972–2002*, edited by Peter Winn, 71–124. Durham, NC: Duke University Press.

Fraser, Valerie. 1990. *The Architecture of Conquest: Building in the Viceroyalty of Peru, 1535–1635.* Cambridge: Cambridge University Press.

Frazier, Lessie Jo. 2002. "Forging Democracy and Locality: Democratization, Mental Health, and Reparations in Chile." In *Gender's Place: Feminist Anthropologies of Latin America*, edited by Rosario Montoya, Lessie Frazier, and Janise Hurtig, 91–114. New York: Palgrave Macmillan.

Frazier, Lessie Jo. 2007. *Salt in the Sand: Memory, Violence, and the Nation-state in Chile, 1890 to the Present.* Durham, NC: Duke University Press.

French, John, and Daniel James, eds. 1997. *The Gendered Worlds of Latin American Women Workers: From Household and Factory to the Union Hall and Ballot Box.* Durham, NC: Duke University Press.

Frühling, Hugo. 1992. "Resistance to Fear in Chile: The Experience of the Vicaría de la Solidaridad." In *Fear at the Edge: State Terror and Resistance in Latin America*, edited by Juan Corradi, Patricia Weiss Fagen, and Manuel A. Garretón Merino, 121–40. Berkeley: University of California Press.

Fundación Nacional para la Superación de la Pobreza. 2011. "Análisis comparativo de la incidencia de la pobreza en América Latina." Accessed June 4. http://www.fundacionpobreza.cl/info-pobreza-archivo/pobreza_y_desigualdad_en_la_region_y_el_mundo.pdf.

Gal, Susan, and Gail Kligman. 2000. *The Politics of Gender after Socialism: A Comparative-Historical Essay.* Princeton, NJ: Princeton University Press.

Gandolfo, Daniella. 2009. *The City at Its Limits: Taboo, Transgression, and Urban Renewal in Lima*. Chicago: University of Chicago Press.

Gaonkar, Dilip Parameshwar, ed. 2001. *Alternative Modernities*. Durham, NC: Duke University Press.

Garcés Durán, Mario. 1998. *Historia de la Comuna de Huechuraba: memoria y oralidad popular urbana*. Santiago: Educación y Comunicaciones.

Garcés Durán, Mario. 2001a. *Memorias de la dictadura en La Legua: relatos, historias, cuentos, poesía y canciones de su gente*. Santiago: Educación y Comunicaciones.

Garcés Durán, Mario. 2001b. "Introducción." In *Memorias de la dictadura en La Legua: relatos, historias, cuentos, poesía y canciones de su gente*, 1–25. Santiago: Educación y Comunicaciones.

Garcés Durán, Mario. 2002a. *Tomando su sitio: el movimiento de pobladores de Santiago, 1957–1970*. Santiago: LOM Ediciones.

Garcés Durán, Mario. 2002b. *Recreando el pasado: guía metodológica para la memoria y la historia local*. Santiago: Educación y Comunicaciones.

Garcés Durán, Mario. 2003. *Crisis social y motines populares en el 1900*. Santiago: LOM Ediciones.

Garcés Durán, Mario, and Sebastián Leiva. 2005. *El golpe en La Legua: los caminos de la historia y la memoria*. Santiago: LOM Ediciones.

Gatica Barros, Jaime. 1989. *Deindustrialization in Chile*. Boulder, CO: Westview Press.

Gaudichard, Franck. 2004. *Poder popular y cordones industriales: testimonios sobre el movimiento popular urbano, 1970–1973*. Santiago: LOM Ediciones.

Gay, Robert. 2005. *Lucia: Testimonies of a Brazilian Drug Dealer's Woman*. Philadelphia: Temple University Press.

Gilbert, A. 2002. "Power, Ideology, and the Washington Consensus: The Development and Spread of Chilean Housing Policy." *Housing Studies* 17 (2): 305–24.

Gilbert, A. 2004. "Love in the Time of Enhanced Capital Flows: Reflections on the Links between Liberalization and Informality." In *Urban Informality: Transnational Perspectives from the Middle East, Latin America, and South Asia*, edited by Ananya Roy and Nezar AlSayyad, 33–66. Lanham, MD: Lexington Books.

Gobierno de Chile. 1973a. *100 primeros decretos leyes dictados por la junta de Gobierno de la República*. Santiago: Editorial Jurídica.

Gobierno de Chile. 1973b. *Libro blanco del cambio del gobierno en Chile: 11 de Septiembre de 1973*. Santiago: Editorial Lord Cochrane.

Godoy Urzúa, Hernán. 1978. "La mujer chilena: Antecedentes históricos de su individualidad." *Amiga* 25 (February): 20–21.

Goffman, Erving. 1981. "Footing." In *Forms of Talk*, 124–59. Philadelphia: University of Pennsylvania Press.

Goldrich, Daniel. 1970. "Political Organization and the Politicization of the Poblador." *Comparative Political Studies* 3 (2): 176–202.

Goldstein, Daniel. 2004. *The Spectacular City: Violence and Performance in Urban Bolivia*. Durham, NC: Duke University Press.

Gómez Leyton, Juan Carlos. 2004. *La frontera de la democracia: el derecho de propiedad en Chile, 1925–1973*. Santiago: LOM Ediciones.

González de la Rocha, Mercedes, Janice Perlman, Helen Safa, et al. 2004. "From the Marginality of the 1960s to the 'New Poverty' of Today: A LARR Research Forum." *Latin American Research Review* 39 (1): 183–203.

Gonzalez Pino, Miguel. 1997. *Los mil días de Allende*. Santiago: Centro de Estudios Públicos.

Grandin, Greg. 2004. *The Last Colonial Massacre: Latin America in the Cold War*. Chicago: University of Chicago Press.

Grandin, Greg. 2006. *Empire's Workshop: Latin America, the United States, and the Rise of the New Imperialism*. New York: Metropolitan Books.

Grandin, Greg, and Gilbert M. Joseph, eds. 2010. *A Century of Revolution: Insurgent and Counterinsurgent Violence during Latin America's Long Cold War*. Durham, NC: Duke University Press.

Gross, Patricio. 1991. "Santiago de Chile (1925-1990): planificación urbana y modelos políticos." *Revista EURE* 17 (52): 27–52.

Grovogui, Siba N. 2009. "The Secret Lives of the Sovereign: Rethinking Sovereignty as International Morality." In *The State of Sovereignty: Territories, Laws, Populations*, edited by Douglas Howland and Luise White, 261–76. Bloomington: Indiana University Press.

Guarda, Gabriel. 1966. "Influencia miliar en las ciudades del reino." In *El proceso de urbanización en América desde sus orígenes hasta nuestros días*, edited by Jorge Enrique Hardoy and Richard P. Schaedel, 261–302. Buenos Aires: Editorial del Instituto.

Guillaudat, Patrick, and Pierre Mouterde. 1998. *Los movimientos sociales en Chile*. Santiago: LOM Ediciones.

Gupta, Akhil, and James Ferguson. 2002. "Spatializing States: Toward an Ethnography of Neoliberal Governmentality." *American Ethnologist* 29 (4): 981–1002.

Guy, Donna J. 2009. *Women Build the Welfare State: Performing Charity and Creating Rights in Argentina, 1880–1955*. Durham, NC: Duke University Press.

Haber, Stephen. 2009. "Latin America's Quiet Revolution." *Wall Street Journal*, January 30.

Halpern, Pablo. 2002. *Los nuevos Chilenos y la batalla por sus preferencias*. Santiago: Planeta.

Han, Clara. 2004. "The Work of Indebtedness: The Traumatic Present of Late Capitalist Chile." *Culture, Medicine and Psychiatry* 28 (2): 169–87.

Han, Clara. 2011. "Symptoms of Another Life: Time, Possibility, and Domestic Relations in Chile's Credit Economy." *Cultural Anthropology* 26 (1): 7–32.

Han, Clara. 2012. *Life in Debt: Times of Care and Violence in Neoliberal Chile*. Berkeley: University of California Press.

Hann, C. M. 1998. "Introduction: The Embeddedness of Property." In *Property Relations: Renewing the Anthropological Tradition*, edited by C. M. Hann, 1–47. Cambridge: Cambridge University Press.

Haramoto, Edwin. 1983. "Políticas de vivienda social: experiencia chilena de las tres últimas décadas." In *Vivienda social: reflexiones y experiencias*, edited by Joan MacDonald and Modesto Collados, 75–151. Santiago: Corporación de Promoción Universitaria.

Harding, David, Michèle Lamont, and Mario L. Small, eds. 2010. "Reconsidering Culture and Poverty." Special issue, *Annals of American Political and Social Science* 629 (May).

Hardy, Clarisa. 1987. *Organizarse para vivir: pobreza urbana y organización popular*. Santiago: Programa de Economía del Trabajo.
Harvey, David. 2003. *Paris: Capital of Modernity*. New York: Routledge.
Harvey, David. 2005. *A Brief History of Neoliberalism*. Oxford: Oxford University Press.
Harvey, David. 2012. *Rebel Cities: From the Right to the City to the Urban Revolution*. London: Verso.
Haslam, Jonathan. 2005. *The Nixon Administration and the Death of Allende's Chile: A Case of Assisted Suicide*. London: Verso.
Healey, Mark. 2011. *The Ruins of the New Argentina: Peronism and the Remaking of San Juan after the 1944 Earthquake*. Durham, NC: Duke University Press.
Herrick, Bruce. 1965. *Urban Migration and Economic Development in Chile*. Cambridge, MA: MIT Press.
Hidalgo Dattwyler, Rodrigo. 2004. "La vivienda social en Santiago en la segunda mitad del siglo XX: actores relevantes y tendencias espaciales." In *Santiago en la globalización: ¿una nueva ciudad?*, edited by María Ducci and Carlos De Mattos, 219–42. Santiago: Ediciones SUR.
Hidalgo Dattwyler, Rodrigo. 2005. *La vivienda social en Chile y la construcción del espacio urbano en el Santiago del siglo XX*. Santiago: Pontificia Universidad Católica.
Hirmas, María Eugenia. 1993. "The Chilean Case: Television in the 1988 Plebiscite." In *Television, Politics, and the Transition to Democracy in Latin America*, edited by Thomas Skidmore, 81–104. Washington, DC: Woodrow Wilson Center Press, Johns Hopkins University Press.
Hite, Katherine. 2000. *When the Romance Ended: Leaders of the Chilean Left, 1968–1998*. New York: Columbia University Press.
Hite, Katherine. 2003. "Resurrecting Allende." *NACLA Report on the Americas* 37 (1): 19–24.
Holston, James. 1999. "Spaces of Insurgent Citizenship." In *Cities and Citizenship*, 155–76. Durham, NC: Duke University Press.
Holston, James. 2008. *Insurgent Citizenship: Disjunctions of Democracy and Modernity in Brazil*. Princeton, NJ: Princeton University Press.
Holston, James. 2013. "Housing Crises, Right to the City, and Citizenship." In *The Housing Question: Tensions, Continuities, and Contingencies in the Modern City*, edited by Edward Murphy and Najib Hourani, 255–70. London: Ashgate.
Holston, James, and Arjun Appadurai. 1999. "Introduction: Cities and Citizenship." In *Cities and Citizenship*, edited by James Holston, 1–20. Durham, NC: Duke University Press.
Huneeus, Carlos. 2000. "Technocrats and Politicians in an Authoritarian Regime: The 'ODEPLAN Boys' and the 'Gremialists' in Pinochet's Chile." *Journal of Latin American Studies* 32 (2): 461.
Hurtado, Carlos R.-T. 1966. *Concentración de población y desarrollo económico: el caso chileno*. Santiago: Universidad de Chile, Instituto de Economía.
Hutchison, Elizabeth. 2001. *Labors Appropriate to Their Sex: Gender, Labor, and Politics in Urban Chile, 1900–1930*. Durham, NC: Duke University Press.
Hutchison, Elizabeth. 2011. "Shifting Solidarities: The Politics of Household Workers in Cold War Chile." *Hispanic American Historical Review* 91 (1): 129–62.

Huyssen, Andreas, ed. 2008. *Other Cities, Other Worlds: Urban Imaginaries in a Globalizing Age*. Durham, NC: Duke University Press.

Illanes, María. 1993. *"En el nombre del pueblo, del estado y de la ciencia": historia social de la salud pública Chile, 1880–1973: hacia una historia social del siglo XX*. Santiago: Colectivo de Atención Primaria.

Institucional Nacional de la Vivienda (INVI). 1997. *Catastro de campamentos y asentamientos irregulares: Cartografía nacional por región*. Santiago: Universidad.

Instituto Nacional de Estadísticas (INE). 1952a. *Primer Censo Nacional de Viviendas*. Santiago: INE.

Instituto Nacional de Estadísticas (INE). 1952b. *XII censo general de población y vivienda: Localidades y límites*. Santiago: INE.

Instituto Nacional de Estadísticas (INE). 1960. *II censo de vivienda: Resumen país*. Santiago: INE.

Instituto Nacional de Estadísticas (INE). 1970. *III censo de vivienda: Resumen país*. Santiago: INE.

Instituto Nacional de Estadísticas (INE). 1999. *Estadísticas en el Siglo XX*. Santiago: INE.

Instituto Nacional de Estadísticas (INE). 2002. *VI censo de vivienda: Resumen país*. Santiago: INE.

Instituto Nacional de Estadísticas (INE). 2005. *Ciudades, pueblos, aldeas, y caseríos*. Santiago: INE.

Instituto Nacional de Estadísticas (INE). 2010. "Situación de la fuerza del trabajo y tasas mensuales." Accessed August 26, 2010. http://www.ine.cl/canales/chile_estadistico/mercado_del_trabajo/empleo/series_estadisticas/cifra_desempleo_mensual.php.

James, Daniel. 2000. *Doña María's Story: Life History, Memory, and Political Identity*. Durham, NC: Duke University Press.

Jara, Joan. 1984. *An Unfinished Song: The Life of Victor Jara*. New York: Ticknor & Fields.

Jara, Víctor. 1972. *La población*. Copyright 1972, by DICAP. JJL 14, Compact Disc.

Jordá Sureda, Miguel. 2001. *Martirologio de la Iglesia Chilena: Juan Alsina y sacerdotes víctimas del terrorismo de Estado*. Santiago: LOM Ediciones.

Joseph, Gilbert. 2008. "What We Know and Should Know." In *In From the Cold: Latin America's New Encounter with the Cold War*, edited by Gilbert Joseph and Daniela Spenser, 3–46. Durham, NC: Duke University Press.

Joseph, Gilbert, and Daniel Nugent. 1994. *Everyday Forms of State Formation: Revolution and the Negotiation of Rule in Modern Mexico*. Durham, NC: Duke University Press.

Kagan, Richard L., and Fernando Marías. 2000. *Urban Images of the Hispanic World, 1493–1793*. New Haven, CT: Yale University Press.

Karush, Matthew B., and Oscar Chomosa, eds. 2010. *The New Cultural History of Peronism: Power and Identity in Mid-Twentieth Century Argentina*. Durham, NC: Duke University Press.

Kast, Miguel. 1976. *Política económica y desarrollo social en Chile*. Santiago: ODEPLAN.

Kast, Miguel, and Sergio Molina. 1975. *Mapa extrema pobreza*. Santiago: ODEPLAN y Instituto de Economía, Universidad Católica.

Kingfisher, Catherine, and Jeff Maskovsky. 2008. "Introduction: The Limits of Neoliberalism." *Critique of Anthropology* 28 (2): 115–26.

Kinsbruner, Jay. 2005. *The Colonial Spanish-American City: Urban Life in the Age of Atlantic Capitalism*. Austin: University of Texas Press.

Kirkwood, Julieta. 1990. *Ser política en Chile: los nudos de la sabiduría feminista*. 2nd ed. Santiago: Editorial Cuarto Propio. First published 1986.

Klein, Naomi. 2007. *The Shock Doctrine: The Rise of Disaster Capitalism*. New York: Metropolitan Books/Henry Holt.

Klubock, Thomas. 1998. *Contested Communities: Class, Gender, and Politics in Chile's El Teniente Copper Mine, 1904–1951*. Durham, NC: Duke University Press.

Klubock, Thomas. 2004a. "Class, Community and Neoliberalism in Chile: Copper Workers and the Labor Movement during the Military Dictatorship and the Restoration of Democracy." In *Victims of the Chilean Miracle: Workers and Neoliberalism in the Pinochet Era, 1972–2002*, edited by Peter Winn, 209–60. Durham, NC: Duke University Press.

Klubock, Thomas. 2004b. "Labor, Land, and Environmental Change in the Forestry Sector in Chile, 1973–1998." In *Victims of the Chilean Miracle: Workers and Neoliberalism in the Pinochet Era, 1972–2002*, edited by Peter Winn, 337–87. Durham, NC: Duke University Press.

Kornbluh, Peter. 2003. *The Pinochet File: A Declassified Dossier on Atrocity and Accountability*. New York: New Press.

Kouyoumdjian, Armen. 2008. "Chile y la crisis internacional: ¿cerca o lejos?" Accessed July 16, 2012. http://www.newropeans-magazine.org/content/view/8727/314.

Kusnetzoff, Fernando. 1987. "Urban and Housing Policies under Chile's Military Dictatorship: 1973–1985." *Latin American Perspectives* 14 (2): 157–86.

Latham, Michael. 2000. *Modernization as Ideology: American Social Science and "Nation Building" in the Kennedy Era*. Chapel Hill: University of North Carolina Press.

Latour, Bruno. 2005. *Reassembling the Social: An Introduction to Actor-Network-Theory*. Oxford: Oxford University Press.

Lavín Infante, Joaquín. 1986. *Miguel Kast: Pasión De Vivir*. Santiago: Zig-Zag.

Lavín Infante, Joaquín. 1988. *Chile: Revolución Silenciosa*. Santiago: Zig-Zag.

Lavrin, Asunción. 1995. *Women, Feminism, and Social Change in Argentina, Chile, and Uruguay, 1890–1940*. Lincoln: University of Nebraska Press.

Lazarra, Michael J. 2006. *Chile in Transition: The Poetics and Politics of Memory*. Gainesville: University of Florida Press.

Lechner, Juan. 1981. "El concepto de 'policía' y su presencia en los primeros historiadores de Indias." *Revista de Indias* 41: 390–404.

Leeds, Anthony, and Elizabeth Leeds. 1976. "Accounting for Behavioral Differences: Three Political Systems and the Responses of Squatters in Brazil, Peru, and Chile." In *The City in Comparative Perspective: Cross-national Research and New Directions in Theory*, edited by John Walton and Louis Masotti, 219–45. New York: Sage Publications.

Lefebvre, Henri. 1996. *Writings on Cities*. Malden, MA: Wiley Blackwell.

Lefebvre, Henri. (1991) 2004. *The Production of Space*. Translated by Donald Nicholson-Smith. Malden, MA: Blackwell.

Leinaweaver, Jessaca B. 2008. *The Circulation of Children: Kinship, Adoption, and Morality in Andean Peru*. Durham, NC: Duke University Press.

Leiva, Fernando. 2005. "From Pinochet's State Terrorism to the 'Politics of Participation.'"

In *Democracy in Chile: The Legacy of September 11, 1973*, edited by Silvia Nagy-Zekmi and Fernando Leiva, 73–87. Brighton: Sussex Academic Press.

Lemebel, Pedro. 1998. *De perlas y cicatrices*. Santiago: LOM Ediciones.

Lewis, Oscar. 1970. "The Culture of Poverty." In *Anthropological Essays*, 67–80. New York: Random House.

Locke, John. 1988. "Of Property." In *Two Treatises of Government*. Cambridge: Cambridge University Press. First published 1689.

Lomnitz, Larissa Adler de. 1977. *Networks and Marginality: Life in a Mexican Shantytown*. New York: Academic Press.

Lopez-Morales, Ernesto. 2011. "Gentrification by Ground Rent Dispossession: The Shadows Cast by Large Scale Urban Renewal in Santiago." *International Journal of Urban and Regional Research* 35 (2): 330–57.

Lorenzini, Kena. 2007. *Fragmento fotográfico: arte, narración y memoria*. Santiago: Ocho Libros.

Lorenzini, Kena. 2010. *Marcas crónicas: rayados y panfletos de los 80*. Santiago: Ocho Libros.

Los Prisioneros. 1983. *Grandes Éxitos*. EMI BMG 7 98186 2, 1991, compact disc.

Loveman, Brian. 1988. *Chile: The Legacy of Hispanic Capitalism*. New York: Oxford University Press. First published 1979.

Loveman, Brian, and Elizabeth Lira. 2000. *Las ardientes cenizas del olvido: vía Chilena de reconciliación política 1932–1994*. Santiago: LOM Ediciones and DIBAM.

Loveman, Brian, and Thomas Davies. 1978. "Introduction." In *The Politics of Antipolitics: The Military in Latin America*. Lincoln: University of Nebraska Press.

Low, Setha M. 2003. *Behind the Gates: Life, Security, and the Pursuit of Happiness in Fortress America*. New York: Routledge.

Lowden, Pamela. 1996. *Moral Opposition to Authoritarian Rule in Chile, 1973–90*. New York: St. Martin's Press.

Magnet, Alejandro. 1978. *El Padre Hurtado*. Santiago: Escuela Offset-Tipográfica Salesiana.

Mallon, Florencia. 2001. "Land, Morality and Exploitation in Southern Chile: Rural Conflict and the Discourses of Agrarian Reform in Cautín, 1928–1974." *Political Power and Social Theory* 14: 143–95.

Mallon, Florencia. 2003. "Barbudos, Warriors, and Rotos: The MIR, Masculinity, and Power in the Chilean Agrarian Reform, 1965–1974." In *Changing Men and Masculinities in Latin America*, edited by Matthew Gutmann, 179–215. Durham, NC: Duke University Press.

Mallon, Florencia. 2005. *Courage Tastes of Blood: The Mapuche Community of Nicholás Ailío and the Chilean State, 1906–2001*. Durham, NC: Duke University Press.

Maltes, Sergio, Santiago Bassone, and Angélica Cabala. 1970. *Hacia un diagnóstico de la marginalidad urbana: Tomo II, características socioeconómicas de las poblaciones marginales del Gran Santiago*. Santiago: Consejería Nacional de la Promoción Popular.

Martínez, Javier. 1992. "Fear of the State, Fear of Society: On the Opposition Protests in Chile." In *Fear at the Edge: State Terror and Resistance in Latin America*, edited by Juan Corradi, Patricia Weiss Fagen, and Manuel A. Garretón Merino, 142–60. Berkeley: University of California Press.

Martland, Samuel. 2007. "Reconstructing the City, Constructing the State: Government in Valparaiso after the Earthquake of 1906." *Hispanic American Historical Review* 87 (2): 221–54.

Martner, Gonzalo. 1992. *Salvador Allende 1908–1973: obras escogidas*. Santiago: Ed. Copesa.

Marx, Karl. (1852) 2009a. "The Eighteenth Brumaire of Louis Bonaparte." In *Marx: Later Political Writings*, edited by Terrell Carver, 21–127. Cambridge: Cambridge University Press.

Marx, Karl. (1857) 2009b. "'Introduction to the Grundrisse." In *Marx: Later Political Writings*, edited by Terrell Carver, 128–157. Cambridge: Cambridge University Press. First published.

Massey, Doreen. 1993. "Politics and Space/Time." In *Place and the Politics of Identity*, edited by Michael Keith and Steve Pile, 139–59. London: Routledge.

Massey, Doreen. 1994. *Space, Place and Gender*. Oxford: Polity Press.

Mattelart, Michèle. 1975. "The Feminine Side of the Coup, or When Bourgeois Women Take to the Streets." *NACLA* 9 (6): 14–25.

Mattelart, Michèle, and Armand Mattelart. 1990. *The Carnival of Images: Brazilian Television Fiction*. Translated by David Buxton. New York: Bergin & Garvey. First published 1977.

Mauss, Marcel. (1950) 1990. *The Gift: The Form and Reason for Exchange in Archaic Societies*. New York: Norton.

McCann, Bryan. 2014. *Hard Times in the Marvelous City: From Dictatorship to Democracy in the Favelas of Rio de Janeiro*. Durham, NC: Duke University Press.

Meade, Teresa. 2001. "Holding the Junta Accountable: Chile's 'Sitios de Memoria' and the History of Torture, Disappearance, and Death." *Radical History Review* 79: 123–39.

Meller, Patricio. 1996. *Un siglo de economía política Chilena (1890–1990)*. Santiago: Editorial Andrés Bello.

Meller, Patricio. 1999. "Pobreza y distribución del ingreso en Chile." In *El modelo chileno: democracia y desarrollo en los noventa*, edited by Paul Drake and Ivan Jaksic, 41–64. Santiago: LOM Ediciones.

MIDEPLAN. 1996a. *Diagnóstico región metropolitana*. Santiago: MIDEPLAN.

MIDEPLAN. 1996b. *Manual unificado Ficha CAS-2*. Santiago: MIDEPLAN.

MIDEPLAN. 1997. *Encuesta de caracterización socioeconómica nacional*. Santiago: MIDEPLAN.

MIDEPLAN. 1999. *Programas sociales de gobierno asignados por la Ficha CAS-2*. Santiago: MIDEPLAN.

MIDEPLAN. 2000. *CASEN 2000, Información estadística módulo comunal*. Santiago: MIDEPLAN.

MIDEPLAN. 2002. *CASEN 2001, Encuesta de caracterización socioeconómica nacional*. Santiago: MIDEPLAN.

MIDEPLAN. 2010. *CASEN 2009, Encuesta de caracterización socioeconómico nacional*. Accessed August 26, 2010. http://www.mideplan.cl/casen2009/RESULTADOS_CASEN_2009.pdf.

MIDEPLAN-FOSIS. 1991. *Ordenamiento y clasificación de comunas según su grado de 'po-

breza' de acuerdo a un índice compuesto por tres variables. Santiago: FOSIS.
Milanich, Nara. 2009. *Children of Fate: Childhood, Class, and the State in Chile, 1850–1930*. Durham, NC: Duke University Press.
Millas, Orlando. 1996. *Una digresión*. Santiago: CESOC.
Miller, Daniel, ed. 2001a. *Consumption: Critical Concepts in the Social Sciences*. 4 vols. London: Routledge.
Miller, Daniel. 2001b. "Behind Closed Doors." In *Home Possessions: Material Culture behind Closed Doors*, edited by Daniel Miller, 1–21. Oxford: Berg.
Miller, Daniel, ed. 2005. *Materiality*. Durham, NC: Duke University Press.
Milos, Pedro. 2007. *2 de abril de 1957: historia y memoria*. Santiago: LOM Ediciones.
Ministerio del Interior, Intendencia de Santiago, y SECPLAC Metropolitana. 1982. *Proyecto Saneamiento de Campamentos de la Región Metropolitana*. Santiago: Ministerio del Interior.
MINVU. 1972. *Política habitacional del Gobierno Popular, Programa 72*. Santiago: Editorial Universitaria.
MINVU. 1975. *Vivienda social para sectores de menores ingresos*. Santiago: MINVU.
MINVU. 1979. *Política nacional de desarrollo urbano*. Santiago: MINVU.
MINVU. 1990. *Memoria, 1973–1989*. Santiago: MINVU.
MINVU. 2004. *Chile: Un siglo de políticas en vivienda y barrio*. Santiago: MINVU.
MINVU. 2006. *Informativo estadístico No. 282*. Santiago: MINVU.
MINVU. n.d.(a). *Remodelación Sector Poniente Alameda*. Santiago: MINVU.
MINVU. n.d.(b). *Contrato de crédito con el Banco Interamericano de Desarrollo* Santiago: MINVU.
MINVU. n.d.(c). *Circulares: Coordinadora de Créditos Externos*. Santiago: MINVU.
Mitchell, Timothy. 2002. *Rule of Experts: Egypt, Techno-Politics, Modernity*. Berkeley: University of California Press.
Mitchell, Timothy. 2005. "The Work of Economics: How a Discipline Makes Its World." *Archives européennes de sociologie* 2: 297–322.
Moffett, Matt. 2009. "Prudent Chile Thrives amid Downturn." *Wall Street Journal*, May 27, A1 and A16.
Molina, Natacha. 1989. "Propuestas políticas y orientaciones de cambio en la situación de la mujer." In *Propuestas políticas y demandas sociales*, edited by Manuel Antonio Garretón, 33–71. Santiago: FLACSO.
Morales, Eduardo. 1983. *Algunos indicadores de niveles de vida en campamentos de las comunas del Gran Santiago*. Santiago: FLACSO.
Morales, Eduardo. 1990. "Políticas de segregación espacial: implementación autoritaria y respuesta popular." In *Erradicados en el régimen militar: una evaluación de los beneficiarios*, 22–37. Santiago: Facultad Latinoamericana de Ciencias Sociales.
Morales, Eduardo, Susana Levy, Adolfo Adunant, and Sergio Rojas. 1990. "Introducción." In *Erradicados en el régimen militar: una evaluación de los beneficiarios*, 1–21. Santiago: Facultad Latinoamericana de Ciencias Sociales.
Morales, Eduardo, and Sergio Rojas. 1987. "Relocalización socio-espacial de la pobreza: política estatal y presión popular, 1979–1985." In *Espacio y poder: los pobladores*, edited by Jorge Chateau, 77–120. Santiago: Facultad Latinoamericana de Ciencias Sociales.

Moran, Theodore. 1974. *Multinational Corporations and the Politics of Dependence: Copper in Chile*. Princeton, NJ: Princeton University Press.

Moreno, Albrecht. 1986. "Violeta Parra and la nueva canción Chilena." *Studies in Latin American Popular Culture* 5: 108–21.

Moulián, Luis, and Gloria Guerra. 2000. *Eduardo Frei M. (1911–1982): biografía de un estadista utópico*. Santiago: Editorial Sudamericana.

Moulián, Luis, and Lydia de Wolf. 1993. "Herminda de la Victoria: aspectos históricos." In *Historias locales y democratización docal*, edited by Ana Farías, 36–43. Santiago: ECO.

Moulian, Tomás. 1993. *La forja de ilusiones: el sistema de partidos, 1932–1973*. Santiago: Universidad ARCIS and FLACSO.

Moulian, Tomás. 1997. *Chile actual: anatomía de un mito*. Santiago: LOM Ediciones.

Moulian, Tomás. 1998. *El consumo me consume*. Santiago: LOM Ediciones.

Mujica Ateaga, Rodrigo, and Alejandro Rojas Pinaud. 1986. *Mapa de la extrema pobreza en Chile, 1982*. Santiago: Universidad Católica, Instituto de Economía (IEUC).

Muñoz, Heraldo. 2002. "Creerse 'el cuento del país.'" *La Tercera*, May 21, 7.

Muñoz Tamayo, Víctor, and Patricia Madrid Herrera. 2005. *Herminda de la Victoria: autobiografía de una población*. Santiago: Libros La Calebaza del Diablo.

Murphy, Edward. 2004a. *Historias poblacionales: hacia una memoria incluyente*. Santiago: CEDECO.

Murphy, Edward. 2004b. "Developing Sustainable Peripheries: The Limits of Citizenship in Guatemala City." *Latin American Perspectives* 31 (6): 48–68.

Murphy, Edward. 2013a. "Introduction: Housing Questions Past, Present, and Future." In *The Housing Question: Tensions, Continuities, and Contingencies in the Modern City*, edited by Edward Murphy and Najib Hourani, 1–21. London: Ashgate.

Murphy, Edward. 2013b. "Between Housing and Home: Property Titling and the Dilemmas of Citizenship in Santiago, Chile." In *The Housing Question: Tensions, Continuities, and Contingencies in the Modern City*, edited by Edward Murphy and Najib Hourani, 199–218. London: Ashgate.

Murphy, Edward, David William Cohen, Chandra D. Bhimull, et al. 2011. *Anthrohistory: Unsettling Knowledge, Questioning Discipline*. Ann Arbor: University of Michigan Press.

Neruda, Pablo. 1991. *Canto General*. Berkeley: University of California Press.

Neuwirth, Robert. 2005. *Shadow Cities: A Billion Squatters, A New Urban World*. New York: Routledge.

O'Connor, Alice. 2001. *Poverty Knowledge: Social Science, Social Policy, and the Poor in Twentieth-Century U.S. History*. Princeton, NJ: Princeton University Press.

ODEPLAN. 1975. *Avance de las políticas encaminadas a erradicar la extrema pobreza en Chile*. Santiago: ODEPLAN.

ODEPLAN. 1983. *FOAP (Fomento de Ahorro y Préstamo)*. Santiago: ODEPLAN.

Olavarría, Margot. 2009. "Builders of the City: *Pobladores* and the Territorialization of Class Identity in Chile." In *Lost in the Long Transition: Struggles for Social Justice in Neoliberal Chile*, edited by William Alexander, 153–68. Lanham, MD: Lexington Books.

Orlove, Benjamin. 1997. "Meat and Strength: The Moral Economy of a Chilean Food Riot." *Cultural Anthropology* 12 (2): 234–68.

Ortner, Sherry. 1995. "Resistance and the Problem of Ethnographic Refusal." *Comparative Studies in Society and History* 37 (1): 173–93.

Oxhorn, Philip. 1995. *Organizing Civil Society: The Popular Sectors and the Struggle for Democracy in Chile.* University Park: Pennsylvania State University Press.

Paley, Julia. 2001. *Marketing Democracy: Power and Social Movements in Post-Dictatorship Chile.* Berkeley: University of California Press.

Passerini, Luisa. 1987. *Fascism in Popular Memory: The Cultural Experience of the Turin Working Class.* Cambridge: Cambridge University Press.

Pastrana, Ernesto, and Monica Threlfall. 1974. *Pan, techo y poder: el movimiento de pobladores en Chile, 1970–1973.* Buenos Aires: Ediciones Siap-Planteos.

Pavilack, Jody. 2011. *Mining for the Nation: The Politics of Chile's Coal Communities from the Popular Front to the Cold War.* University Park: Pennsylvania State University Press.

Perlman, Janice. 1976. *The Myth of Marginality: Urban Poverty and Politics in Rio de Janeiro.* Berkeley: University of California Press.

Perlman, Janice. 2010. *Favela: Four Decades of Living on the Edge in Rio de Janeiro.* Oxford: Oxford University Press.

Petras, James, and Fernando Ignacio Leiva. 1994. *Democracy and Poverty in Chile: The Limits to Electoral Politics.* Boulder, CO: Westview Press.

Picatto, Pablo. 2001. *City of Suspects: Crime in Mexico City, 1900–1931.* Durham, NC: Duke University Press.

Pieper Mooney, Jadwiga. 2009. *The Politics of Motherhood: Maternity and Women's Rights in Twentieth-Century Chile.* Pittsburgh, PA: University of Pittsburgh Press.

Pinto Vallejos, Julio, Azun Candina, and Robinson Lira. 1999. *Historia contemporánea de Chile: actores, identidad y movimiento.* Santiago: LOM Ediciones.

Pinto Vallejos, Julio, and Sebastián Leiva Flores. 2008. "Punto de quiebre: el MIR en los ochenta." In *Su revolución contra nuestra revolución, Vol. 2: la pugna marxista-gremialista de los ochenta,* edited by Verónica Valdivia Ortiz de Zárate, 83–138. Santiago: LOM.

Poole, Deborah. 2004. "Between Threat and Guarantee: Justice and Community on the Margins of the Peruvian State." In *Anthropology in the Margins of the State,* edited by Veena Das and Deborah Poole, 35–66. Oxford: James Currey Publishers.

Portelli, Alessandro. 1997. *The Battle of Valle Giulia: Oral History and the Art of Dialogue.* Madison: University of Wisconsin Press.

Portes, Alejandro. 1971. "Urbanization and Politics in Latin America." *Social Science Quarterly* 52 (3): 697–720.

Portes, Alejandro. 1976. "Occupation and Lower Class Political Orientation in Chile," In *Chile: Politics and Society,* edited by Arturo Valenzuela and Samuel Valenzuela, 201–37. New Brunswick: Transaction Books.

Portes, Alejandro. 1989. "Latin American Urbanization during the Years of the Crisis." *Latin American Research Review* 24 (3): 7.

Portes, Alejandro, and William Haller. 2005. "The Informal Economy." In *The Handbook of Economic Sociology,* edited by Neil J. Smelser and Richard Swedberg, 403–25. Princeton, NJ: Princeton University Press.

Portes, Alejandro, and Bryan Roberts. 2005. "The Free-Market City: Latin American

Urbanization in the Years of the Neoliberal Experiment." *Studies in Comparative International Development* 40 (1): 43–82.

Power, Margaret. 2002. *Right-Wing Women in Chile: Feminine Power and the Struggle against Allende, 1964–1973*. University Park: Pennsylvania State University Press.

Power, Margaret. 2004. "More than Mere Pawns: Right-Wing Women in Chile." *Journal of Women's History* 16 (3): 138–51.

Prakash, Gyan. 2008. "Introduction." In *The Spaces of the Modern City: Imaginaries, Politics, and Everyday Life*, edited by Gyan Prakash and Kevin Kruse, 1–20. Princeton, NJ: Princeton University Press.

PREALC (Programa Regional de Empleo para América Latina y el Caríbe). 1990. "Pobreza y empleo: un análisis del periodo 1969–87 en el gran Santiago." Geneva: Working Paper 348, 1990.

Principios. 1972. "Hacía el séptimo congreso de las Juveniles Comunistas." January/February: 21–30.

Programa de las Naciones Unidas para el Desarrollo (PNUD). 1998. *Desarrollo humano en Chile 1998: las paradojas de la modernización*. Santiago: PNUD.

Programa de las Naciones Unidas para el Desarrollo (PNUD). 2004. *Desarrollo humano en Chile 2004: las paradojas de la modernización*. Santiago: PNUD.

Quintanilla, Rosa. 1988. *Yo soy pobladora*. Santiago: Taller Piret.

Qureshi, Lubna Z. 2009. *Nixon, Kissinger, and Allende: U.S. Involvement in the 1973 Coup in Chile*. Lanham, MD: Lexington Books.

Rabinow, Paul. 1989. *French Modern: Norms and Forms of the Social Environment*. Cambridge, MA: MIT Press.

Randall, Margaret. 1992. *Gathering Rage: The Failure of Twentieth-Century Revolutions to Develop a Feminist Agenda*. New York: Monthly Review Press.

Red de Organizaciones Sociales de La Legua. 1999. *Lo que se teje en La Legua*. Santiago: ECO.

Redfield, Peter. 2005. "Doctors, Borders, and Life in Crisis." *Cultural Anthropology* 20 (3): 328–61.

Reuque Paillalef, Rosa, and Florencia Mallon. 2002. *When a Flower Is Reborn: The Life and Times of a Mapuche Feminist*. Durham, NC: Duke University Press.

Rivera, Gustavo. 2013. "Reinventing *Favela* Aesthetics: From Shacks to Public Housing Buildings." In *The Housing Question: Tensions, Continuities, and Contingencies in the Modern City*, edited by Edward Murphy and Najib Hourani, 141–60. London: Ashgate.

Roberts, Kenneth. 1998. *Deepening Democracy? The Modern Left and Social Movements in Chile and Peru*. Stanford, CA: Stanford University Press.

Rodgers, Dennis. 2014. "*Compadres, Vecinos*, and *Bróderes* in the Barrio: Kinship, Politics, and Local Territorialization in Urban Nicaragua." In *Cities from Scratch: Poverty and Informality in Urban Latin America*, edited by Brodwyn Fischer, Bryan McCann, and Javier Auyero, 127–49. Durham, NC: Duke University Press.

Rodríguez, Alfredo. 2001. "La vivienda privada de ciudad." *Temas Sociales* 39 (August).

Rodríguez, Alfredo, and Ana Sugranayes. 2005. "El problema de vivienda de los 'con techo.'" In *Los con techo: un desafío para la política de vivienda social*, edited by Susana Aravena, Alfredo Rodríguez, and Ana Sugranayes, 59–78. Santiago: Ediciones SUR.

Rodríguez, Alfredo, and Lucy Winchester. 2005. "Santiago: una ciudad fragmentada." In *Santiago en la globalización: ¿Una nueva ciudad?*, edited by Carlos de Mattos et al., 115–36. Santiago: Sur Ediciones.

Rodríguez, Julia. 2006. *Civilizing Argentina: Science, Medicine, and the Modern State*. Chapel Hill: University of North Carolina Press.

Roitman, Janet. 2014. *Anti-Crisis*. Durham, NC: Duke University Press.

Ronald, R., and M. Elsinga. 2012. "Beyond Home Ownership: An Overview." In *Beyond Home Ownership: Housing, Welfare, and Society*, edited by R. Ronald and M. Elsinga, 1–28. London: Routledge.

Rose, Carol. 1994. "Takings and the Practices of Property: Property as Wealth, Property as Propriety." In *Property and Persuasion: Essays on the History, Theory, and Rhetoric of Ownership*, 49–70. Boulder, CO: Westview Press.

Roseberry, William. 1994. "Hegemony and the Language of Contention." In *Everyday Forms of State Formation: Revolution and the Negotiation of Rule in Modern Mexico*, edited by G. Joseph and Daniel Nugent, 355–66. Durham, NC: Duke University Press.

Rosemblatt, Karin. 1995. "Por un hogar bien constituido: el estado y su política familiar en los frentes populares." In *Disciplina y desacato: construcción de identidad en Chile, siglos XIX y XX*, edited by Lorena Godoy. Santiago: SUR/CEDEM.

Rosemblatt, Karin. 2000. *Gendered Compromises: Political Cultures and the State in Chile, 1920–1950*. Chapel Hill: University of North Carolina Press.

Rosemblatt, Karin. 2001. "What We Can Reclaim of the Old Values of the Past: Sexual Morality and Politics in Twentieth-Century Chile." *Comparative Studies in Society and History* 43 (1): 149–80.

Rosemblatt, Karin. 2009. "Other Americas: Transnationalism, Scholarship, and the Culture of Poverty in Mexico and the United States." *Hispanic American Historical Review* 89 (4): 603–41.

Roy, Ananya. 2003. *City Requiem, Calcutta: Gender and the Politics of Poverty*. Minneapolis: University of Minnesota Press.

Roy, Ananya. 2011. "Slumdog Cities: Rethinking Subaltern Urbanism." *International Journal of Urban and Regional Research* 35 (2): 223–38.

Roy, Ananya, and Nezar AlSayyad, eds. 2004. *Urban Informality: Transnational Perspectives from the Middle East, Latin America, and South Asia*. Lanham, MD: Lexington Books.

Sabatini, Francisco. 1982. "Santiago: sistemas de producción de vivienda, renta de la tierra y segregación urbana." In *CIDU-IPU Documento de Trabajo* 128. Santiago.

Sabatini, Francisco. 1995. *Barrio y participación: mujeres pobladoras de Santiago*. Santiago: Ediciones SUR.

Salazar, Gabriel. 1990. *Violencia política popular en las "Grandes Alamedas": Santiago 1947–1987: una perspectiva histórico-popular*. Santiago: Ediciones SUR.

Salazar, Gabriel. 1992. "La mujer de 'bajo pueblo': bosquejo histórico." *Proposiciones* 21 (December): 89–107.

Salazar, Gabriel. 1998. "'El municipio cercenado' (la lucha por la autonomía de la asociación municipal en Chile, 1914–1973)." In *Autonomía, espacio y gestión: el municipio cercenado*, edited by Gabriel Salazar and Jorge Benítez, 5–60. Santiago: Universidad ARCIS.

Salazar, Gabriel. 2000. *Labradores, peones, y proletarios: formación y crisis de la sociedad popular chilena del siglo XIX*. Santiago: LOM. First published 1985.

Salazar, Gabriel. 2005. "Ricardo Lagos, 2000–2005: perfil histórico, trasfondo popular." In *El gobierno de Lagos: balance crítico*, edited by Gabriel Salazar, 71–100. Santiago: LOM Ediciones.

Salazar, Gabriel, Arturo Mancilla, and Carlos Durán. 1999. *Historia contemporánea de Chile: Estado, legitimidad, ciudadanía*. Santiago: LOM Ediciones.

Salazar, Gabriel, and Julio Pinto. 2002. *Historia contemporánea de Chile IV: hombría y feminidad*. Santiago: LOM Ediciones.

Salcedo, Rodrigo. 2010. "The Last Slum: Moving from Illegal Settlements to Subsidized Housing in Chile." *Urban Affairs Review* 46 (1): 90–118.

Salcedo, Rodrigo. n.d. "The Heterogeneous Nature of Poor Urban Families." Unpublished manuscript.

Saldaña Portillo, María Josefina. 2003. *The Revolutionary Imagination in the Americas and the Age of Development*. Durham, NC: Duke University Press.

Samara, Tony. 2013. "Citizenship and the Urban Polity: Right to the City and the Meanings of Home." In *The Housing Question: Tensions, Continuities, and Contingencies in the Modern City*, edited by Edward Murphy and Najib Hourani, 219–37. London: Ashgate.

Schild, Verónica. 1997. "The Hidden Politics of Neighborhood Organizations: Women and Local Participation in the Poblaciones of Chile." In *Community Power and Grassroots Democracy: The Transformation of Social Life*, edited by Michael Kaufman and Alfonso Haroldo Dilla, 126–50. London: Zed Books.

Schild, Verónica. 2000. "Neo-liberalism's New Gendered Market Citizens: The 'Civilizing' Dimension of Social Programmes in Chile." *Citizenship Studies* 4 (3): 275–305.

Schild, Verónica. 2007. "Empowering 'Consumer-Citizens' or Governing Poor Female Subjects? The Institutionalization of 'Self-Development' in the Chilean Social Policy Field." *Journal of Consumer Culture* 7 (2): 179–203.

Schirmer, Jennifer G. 1989. "'Those Who Die for Life Cannot Be Called Dead': Women and Human Rights Protest in Latin America." *Feminist Review* 32: 3–29.

Schkolnik, Mariana. 1986. *Sobrevivir en la Población José M. Caro y en Lo Hermida*. Santiago: Programa de Economía del Trabajo.

Schneider, Cathy. 1995. *Shantytown Protest in Pinochet's Chile*. Philadelphia: Temple University Press.

Scott, James. 1998. *Seeing Like a State: How Certain Schemes to Improve the Human Condition Have Failed*. New Haven, CT: Yale University Press.

Scott, Rebecca. 2001. "Reclaiming Gregoria's Mule: The Meanings of Freedom in the Arimao and Caunao Valleys, Cienfuegos, Cuba, 1880–1899." *Past and Present* 170: 181–216.

Scott, Rebecca. 2013. "*Dignité/Dignidade*: Organizing to Threats against Dignity in Societies after Slavery." *Proceedings of the British Academy* 192: 61–77.

Shayne, Julie. 2004. *The Revolution Question: Feminisms in El Salvador, Chile, and Cuba.* New Brunswick, NJ: Rutgers University Press.
Sierra, Malú. 1970. "El Arte Debe Ser Para Todos." *Paula* (October): 84–88.
Sigmund, Paul. 1977. *The Overthrow of Allende and the Politics of Chile, 1964–1976.* Pittsburgh, PA: University of Pittsburgh Press.
Sigmund, Paul. 1993. *The United States and Democracy in Chile.* Baltimore: Johns Hopkins University Press.
Silva, Patricio. 1991. "Technocrats and Politics in Chile: From the Chicago Boys to the CIEPLAN Monks." *Journal of Latin American Studies* 23 (2): 385–410.
Silva, Patricio. 2008. *In the Name of Reason: Technocrats and Politics in Chile.* University Park: Pennsylvania State University Press.
Skrabut, Kristin. 2013. "Recognizing (Dis)Order: Topographies of Power and Property in Lima's Periphery." In *The Housing Question: Tensions, Continuities, and Contingencies in the Modern City*, edited by Edward Murphy and Najib Hourani, 183–98. London: Ashgate.
Skuban, William E. 2007. *Lines in the Sand: Nationalism and Identity on the Peruvian-Chilean Frontier.* Albuquerque: University of New Mexico Press.
Skurski, Julie, and Fernando Coronil. 2006. "Introduction: States of Violence and the Violence of States." In *States of Violence*, edited by Fernando Coronil and Julie Skurski, 1–32. Ann Arbor: University of Michigan Press. First published 1991.
Smith, Brian. 1982. *The Church and Politics in Chile: Challenges to Modern Catholicism.* Princeton, NJ: Princeton University Press.
Smith, Neil. 1992. "Contours of a Spatialized Politics: Homeless Vehicles and the Production of Geographical Scale." *Social Text* 33: 54–81.
Smith, Neil. 1996. *The New Urban Frontier: Gentrification and the Revanchist City.* London: Routledge.
Soliman, Ahmed. 2004. *A Possible Way Out: Formalizing Housing Informality in Egyptian Cities.* Lanham, MD: University Press of America.
Sommer, Doris. 1988. "Not Just a Personal Story: Women's Testimonios and the Plural Self." In *Life Lines: Theorizing Women's Autobiography*, edited by Bella Brodzki and Celeste Schenck, 107–30. Ithaca, NY: Cornell University Press.
Sontag, Susan. 1990. *Illness as Metaphor.* New York: Doubleday.
Soto, Álvaro, Gabriela Espinoza, and Javiera Gómez. 2008. "Aspectos subjetivos vinculados a la flexibilidad laboral." In *Flexibilidad laboral y subjetividades: hacia una comprensión psicosocial del empleo contemporáneo*, edited by Álvaro Soto, 11–37. Santiago: LOM Ediciones.
Spooner, Mary. 1994. *Soldiers in a Narrow Land: The Pinochet Regime in Chile.* Berkeley: University of California Press.
Stack, Carol B. 1974. *All Our Kin: Strategies for Survival in a Black Community.* New York: Harper & Row.
Staples, Anne. 1994. "Policía y Buen Gobierno: Municipal Efforts to Regulate Public Behavior, 1821–1857." In *Rituals of Rule, Rituals of Resistance: Public Celebrations and Popular Culture in Mexico*, edited by William H. Beezley, Cheryl English Martin, and William E. French, 115–26. Wilmington: Scholarly Resources, Inc.

Stern, Steve J. 1999. "The Tricks of Time: Colonial Legacies and Historical Sensibilities in Latin America." In *Colonial Legacies: The Problem of Persistence in Latin American History*, edited by Jeremy Adelman, 135–50. New York: Routledge.

Stern, Steve J. 2004. *Remembering Pinochet's Chile: On the Eve of London, 1998*. Durham, NC: Duke University Press.

Stern, Steve J. 2006. *Battling for Hearts and Minds: Memory Struggles in Pinochet's Chile, 1973–1988*. Durham, NC: Duke University Press.

Stern, Steve J. 2010. *Reckoning with Pinochet: The Memory Question in Democratic Chile, 1989–2006*. Durham, NC: Duke University Press.

Stillerman, Joel. 2004. "Disciplined Workers and Avid Consumers: Neoliberal Policy and the Transformation of Work and Identity among Chilean Metalworkers." In *Victims of the Chilean Miracle: Workers and Neoliberalism in the Pinochet Era, 1972–2002*, edited by Peter Winn, 164–208. Durham, NC: Duke University Press.

Stoler, Ann Laura. 2004. "Affective States." In *A Companion to the Anthropology of Politics*, edited by David Nugent, 4–20. Malden, MA: Blackwell.

Stoler, Ann Laura. 2009. *Along the Archival Grain: Epistemic Anxieties and Colonial Common Sense*. Princeton, NJ: Princeton University Press.

Sturman, Rachel. 2005. "Property and Attachments: Defining Autonomy and the Claims of Family in Nineteenth-Century Western India." *Comparative Studies in Society and History* 47 (3): 611–37.

Sugranyes, Ana. 2005. "La política habitacional en Chile, 1980–2000: un éxito liberal para dar techo a los pobres." In *Los con techo: un desafío para la política de vivienda social*, edited by Alfredo Rodríguez and Ana Sugranyes, 23–58. Santiago: Sur Ediciones.

Sugrue, Thomas J. 1996. *The Origins of the Urban Crisis: Race and Inequality in Postwar Detroit*. Princeton, NJ: Princeton University Press.

Taussig, Michael. 1993. "Maleficium: State Fetishism." In *Fetishism as Cultural Discourse*, edited by Emily Apter and William Pietz, 217–47. Ithaca, NY: Cornell University Press.

Taylor, Diana. 1997. *Disappearing Acts: Spectacles of Gender and Nationalism in Argentina's "Dirty War."* Durham, NC: Duke University Press.

Taylor, Marcus. 2006. *From Pinochet to the 'Third Way': Neoliberalism and Social Transformation in Chile*. London: Pluto Press.

Thomas, Gwynn. 2011. *Contesting Legitimacy in Chile: Familial Ideals, Citizenship, and Political Struggle, 1970–1990*. University Park: Pennsylvania State University Press.

Thompson, E. P. 1971. "The Moral Economy of the English Crowd in the Eighteenth Century." *Past and Present* 50: 76–136.

Tinsman, Heidi. 1997. "Household *Patrones*: Wife-Beating and Sexual Control in Rural Chile, 1964–1988." In *The Gendered Worlds of Latin American Women Workers: From Household and Factory to the Union Hall and Ballot Box*, edited by John French and Daniel James, 264–96. Durham, NC: Duke University Press.

Tinsman, Heidi. 2002. *Partners in Conflict: The Politics of Gender, Sexuality, and Labor in the Chilean Agrarian Reform, 1950–1973*. Durham, NC: Duke University Press.

Tinsman, Heidi. 2004. "More than Mere Victims: Women Agricultural Workers and Sociocultural Change in Rural Chile." In *Victims of the Chilean Miracle: Workers and Neoliberalism in the Pinochet Era, 1972–2002*, edited by Peter Winn, 261–97. Durham, NC: Duke University Press.

Tinsman, Heidi. 2014. *Buying into the Regime: Grapes and Consumption in Cold War Chile and the United States*. Durham, NC: Duke University Press.

Trouillot, Michel-Rolph. 1995. *Silencing the Past: Power and the Production of History*. Boston: Beacon Press.

Trouillot, Michel-Rolph. 2001. "The Anthropology of the State in the Age of Globalization: Close Encounters of the Deceptive Kind." *Current Anthropology* 42 (1): 125–38.

Tsing, Ana Lowenhaupt. 2005. *Friction: An Ethnography of Global Connection*. Princeton, NJ: Princeton University Press.

Turner, John F. C., and Robert Fichter, eds. 1972. *Freedom to Build: Dweller Control of the Building Process*. New York: Macmillan.

UN Habitat. 2005. *Financing Urban Shelter: Global Reports on Human Settlements*. London: Earthscan.

Urzúa Valenzuela, Germán. 1992. *Historia política y su evolución electoral desde 1810 a 1992*. Santiago: Editorial Jurídica.

Valdebenito Acosta, Francisca. 2009. *Tinta papel ingenio: panfletos politicos en Chile, 1973–1990*. Santiago: OchoLibros.

Valdés, Hernán. 1975. *Diary of a Chilean Concentration Camp*. London: Gollancz.

Valdés, Teresa. 1987. "El movimiento de pobladores, 1973–1985: la recomposición de las solidaridades sociales." In *Decentralización del estado: movimiento social y gestión local*, edited by Jordi Borja, 263–320. Santiago: FLACSO.

Valdés, Teresa. 2010. "El Chile de Michelle Bachelet: ¿Género en el poder?" *Latin American Research Review* 48 (Special Issue): 248–73.

Valdés, Teresa, and Marisa Weinstein. 1993. *Mujeres que sueñan: las organizaciones de pobladoras en Chile, 1973–1989*. Santiago: FLACSO.

Valdivia Ortiz de Zarate, Verónica. 2003. "Terrorism and Political Violence during the Pinochet Years: Chile, 1973–1989." *Radical History Review* 85 (1): 182–90.

Valdivia Ortiz de Zarate, Verónica. 2008. "'Cristianos por el gremailismo': la UDI en el mundo poblacional, 1980–1989." In *Su revolución contra nuestra revolución*. Vol. 2, edited by Verónica Valdivia Ortiz de Zarate et al., 181–230. Santiago: LOM Ediciones.

Valenzuela, Arturo. 1977. *Political Brokers in Chile: Local Government in a Centralized Polity*. Durham, NC: Duke University Press.

Valenzuela, Arturo. 1978. *The Breakdown of Democratic Regimes: Chile*. Baltimore: Johns Hopkins University Press.

Vekemans, Roger, and Ramón Venegas. 1966. "Marginalidad y promoción popular." *Mensaje* 149 (June): 218–22.

Venkatesh, Sudhir. 2006. *Off the Books: The Underground Economy of the Urban Poor*. Cambridge, MA: Harvard University Press.

Verdery, Katherine. 2003. *The Vanishing Hectare: Property and Value in Postsocialist Transylvania*. Ithaca, NY: Cornell University Press.

Verdery, Katherine, and Caroline Humphrey. 2004. "Introduction: Raising Questions about Property." In *Property in Question: Value Transformation in the Global Economy*, 1–25. Oxford: Berg.

Verdugo, Patricia. 2001. *Chile, Pinochet, and the Caravan of Death*. Translated by Marcelo Montecino. Coral Gables, FL: North-South Center Press.

Vergara, Angela. 2008. *Copper Workers, International Business, and Domestic Politics in Cold War Chile*. University Park: Pennsylvania State University Press.

Vergara, Pilar. 1990. *Políticas hacia la extrema pobreza en Chile: 1973–1988*. Santiago: FLACSO.

Vicuña Urrutía, Manuel. 2001. *La belle époque chilena: alta sociedad y mujeres de elite en el cambio de siglo*. Santiago: Editorial Sudamericana.

Villar, Olga Mercado, Patricio De la Puente, and Francisco Uribe-Echevarría. 1970. *La marginalidad urbana: origen, proceso y modo: resultados de una encuesta en poblaciones marginales del Gran Santiago*. Santiago: DESAL.

Wacquänt, Loïc J. D. 1996. "The Rise of Advanced Marginality: Notes on Its Nature and Implications." *Acta Sociologica* 39 (2): 121–39.

Wacquänt, Loïc J. D. 2007. "Territorial Stigmatization in the Age of Advanced Marginality." *Thesis Eleven* 91 (1): 66–77.

Wacquänt, Loïc J. D. 2008. *Urban Outcasts: A Comparative Sociology of Advanced Marginality*. Malden, MA: Polity.

Walter, Richard J. 2005. *Politics and Urban Growth in Santiago, Chile, 1891–1941*. Stanford, CA: Stanford University Press.

Ward, Peter. 2004. "Introduction and Overview: Marginality Then and Now." *Latin American Research Review* 39 (1): 183–203.

Warner, Michael. 2002. *Publics and Counterpublics*. New York: Zone Books.

Way, J. T. 2012. *The Mayan in the Mall: Globalization, Development, and the Making of Modern Guatemala*. Durham, NC: Duke University Press.

Weber, Max. 1946. "Politics as a Vocation." In *Max Weber: Essays in Sociology*, edited by H. H. Gerth, 77–128. Chicago: University of Chicago Press.

Weinstein, Barbara. 1996. *For Social Peace in Brazil: Industrialists and the Remaking of the Working Class in São Paulo, 1920–1964*. Chapel Hill: University of North Carolina Press.

Westad, Odd Arne. 2005. *The Global Cold War: Third World Interventions and the Making of Our Times*. Cambridge: Cambridge University Press.

Weyland, Kurt. 1999. "La política economía en la nueva democracia Chilena." In *El modelo Chileno: democracia y desarrollo en los noventa*, edited by Paul Drake and Ivan Jaksic, 65–92. Santiago: LOM Ediciones.

Wilde, Alexander. 1999. "Irruptions of Memory: Expressive Politics in Chile's Transition to Democracy." *Journal of Latin American Studies* 31 (2): 471–500.

Willford, Andrew C., and Eric Tagliacozzo, eds. 2009. *Clio/anthropos: Exploring the Boundaries between History and Anthropology*. Stanford, CA: Stanford University Press.

Williams, Raymond. 1973. *The Country and the City*. New York: Oxford University Press.
Williams, Raymond. 1989. "Culture is Ordinary." In *Resources of Hope: Culture, Democracy, Socialism*, 3–18. London: Verso.
Winn, Peter. 1986. *Weavers of Revolution: The Yarur Workers and Chile's Road to Socialism*. Oxford: Oxford University Press.
Winn, Peter, ed. 2004a. *Victims of the Chilean Miracle: Workers and Neoliberalism in the Pinochet Era, 1973–2002*. Durham, NC: Duke University Press.
Winn, Peter. 2004b. "'No Miracle for Us': The Textile Industry in the Pinochet Era, 1973–1998." In *Victims of the Chilean Miracle: Workers and Neoliberalism in the Pinochet Era, 1973–2002*, 125–63. Durham, NC: Duke University Press.
Winn, Peter. 2004c. "The Pinochet Era." In *Victims of the Chilean Miracle: Workers and Neoliberalism in the Pinochet Era, 1973–2002*, 14–70. Durham, NC: Duke University Press.
Winn, Peter. 2010. "The Furies of the Andes: Violence and Terror in the Chilean Revolution and Counterrevolution." In *A Century of Revolution: Insurgent and Counterinsurgent Violence during Latin America's Long Cold War*, edited by Greg Grandin and Gilbert M. Joseph, 240–75. Durham, NC: Duke University Press.
Wong, Jorge, Miguel Lawner, and Fernando Cortés. 1971. "Una nueva 'CORMU.'" *AUCA* 21 (1): 1.
Wright, Thomas. 2007. *State Terrorism in Latin America: Chile, Argentina, and International Human Rights*. Lanham, MD: Rowman & Littlefield.
Wright, Thomas, and Rody Oñate. 1998. *Flight from Chile: Voices of Exile*. Albuquerque: University of New Mexico Press.
Zárate, Soledad. 1995. "Mujeres viciosas, mujeres virtuosas: la mujer delincuente y la casa correccional de Santiago , 1860–1900." In *Disciplina y desacato: construcción de identidad en Chile, siglos XIX y XX*, edited by Lorena Godoy and Corinne Antezana-Pernet, 149–80. Santiago: SUR/CEDEM.
Zeiderman, Austin. 2008. "Risk, Rights, and Resettlement: Biopolitical Dispossession in Bogotá, Colombia." *Anthropology News* 49 (9): 9–10.
Zeitlin, Maurice, and Richard Earl Ratcliff. 1988. *Landlords and Capitalists: The Dominant Class of Chile*. Princeton, NJ: Princeton University Press.

INDEX

Note: Page references in *italics* refer to figures and tables.

activism, 50, 64, 65, 66, 74, 79, 80–81, 98, 102, 149, 193, 194, 200, 205, 207, 214, 217, 218, 244, 252, 271; (a)political nature of, 91–92; female, 36, 129, 284n63; forms of, 31, 209; homeless, 87, 268; housing, 3–4, 6, 8, 10, 37, 71, 90–91, 100, 116, 185, 266, 268, 270; lack of, 240; land seizures and, 73, 99; leftist, 78, 81, 111, 143, 291n21; memories of, 172; MIR, 123–24; pobladore, 6, 74, 81; popular, 50, 52, 261, 265; renewed, 201, 225; revolutionary, 39, 75; social, 5, 12, 24; squatter, 75, 100
aesthetic, 110, 139, 164, 271; governing, 177, 185, 186, 189; ideology of, 295n9; sense of, 44, 165; urban, 43, 47, 167, 168
alcohol, 256, 262, 303n6
Alessandri, Arturo, 62, 113
allegados, 78, 92, 115, 158, 169, 185–87, 195, 198, 245–50; campamentos and, 189; described, 72–73; squatters and, 112
Allende, Salvador, 12, 23, 37, 77, 99, 101, 131, 152, 205, 210, 238; book publishing and, 108; bureaucracy and, 114; changes for, 102; citizens and, 289n53; on collective work, 104; consumer goods and, 107; death of, 137; difficulties for, 103, 104–5, 129; election of, 101, 105, 111, 116, 284n56; housing and, 119–20, 157, 158, 226; land seizures and, 73, 115, 121; letter to, 112; "maximalist" approach and, 105; overthrow of, 106–7, 126; personal interest and, 110; public debates and, 129; revenue sources and, 105; Román and, 113; social breakdown and, 194; speech by, 103, 112; vision of, 104
Alliance for Progress, 81, 82, 90, 282n23
animitas, 253, 254
Appadurai, Arjun, 263
Araya, Juan, 77–78, 98, 115

Arbenz, Jacobo, 24
arrabales, 46, 47, 55, 56; creation of, 48; improvement of, 45
atomization, 198, 215, 240, 242, 245, 254

Bachelet, Michelle, 36, 254, 301n11
Ballesteros Reyes, Eugenio, 281n12
Balmaceda, José Manual, 111
Barahona, Vicky, 219, 220
Barrancas, homeless in, 77, 78
behavior, 139, 141, 260, 261; familial forms of, 121; homeownership and, 58; pathological, 85; poblador, 238–39
Beltran, Mario Hugo, 169, 170, 295n13
Benavides, César Raúl, 183–84
Benjamin, Walter: states of emergency and, 161, 162
Berman, Marshall: modernity and, 46
Blomley, Nicholas, 26
boundaries, 3, 209; management of, 165; spatial, 27, 117; transgression of, 251–52
buildings, seizing, 118–19, *118*
Buín Regiment, 145–46
bureaucracy, 47, 62, 63, 82, 169, 237, 276n21; decline of, 235; financial, 171; growth of, 60; infrastructure and, 114; legitimacy in, 114; role of, 183; struggles with, 75, 76; transnational development, 4, 7–8

callampas, 58, 64, 83, 88, 89, 91, 97, 268, 282n34
Campamento Cardenal Juan Francisco Fresno, photo of, 208
Campamento Cardenal Raúl Silva Henríquez, 207, 208
Campamento Herminda de la Victoria, 77, 78, 281n19; committees from, 93; land seizures and, 79, 98, 115

335

Campamento Huamachuco, 12, 140, 158, 160, 205, 257; military coup and, 144–45
Campamento Juan Francisco Fresno, 207, 208
Campamento Las Palmeras, 122, 125, 140, 158, 195, 196, 197–98, 211; confrontation in, 199–200; military coup and, 145–47; raids on, 144
Campamento Lenin, 122, 124, 125, 140, 157, 242, 260, 261, 292nn27–28; establishment of, 201; military coup and, 145–47; Pastenes and, 146
Campamento Lo Boza, 14, 16–17, 202, 222, 224, 230, 239; housing stock of, 223; mediaguas for, 235; moving from, 237; needs of, 23; photo of, 15, 223; poverty in, 233–37; resources for, 238
Campamento Lo Velásquez, 13, 14, 197, 199, 200–201, 203, 256, 299n8; allegado in, 245–50; conditions in, 260; crime in, 252; eradication programs of, 242; La Maule and, 202; photo of, 198; protest in, 200, 242; security in, 201
Campamento Nueva La Habana, 140, 300
Campamento Nuevo Amanecer (New Dawn), 140, 300n33
Campamento Primero de Mayo, 12, 95–96, 99, 140, 143, 160, 205, 211, 257, 260, 265, 285n81, 287n23; military coup and, 137, 144–45; photo of, 94; pobladores in, 97; protest at, 213
Campamento Violeta Parra, 79, 93
campamentos, 7, 9–10, 11, 13, 17, 18, 32, 39, 64, 65, 72, 73, 83, 89, 91, 95, 98, 99, 101, 112, 115, 120, 121, 124, 125, 139, 160, 165, 170; allegados and, 189; defined, 14–15, 197, 222–25; emergency, 162, 179; eradication of, 84, 136, 152, 172, 173, 175, 177, 197, 219, 220, 221, 233, 237; establishment of, 155, 178–79, 251; female participation in, 235, 236; governing projects and, 24; home searches in, 141–47, 210; improving, 109, 149; irregular, 84, 116, 179, 186; land seizures and, 127; land status of, 156; legal status of, 93, 146, 293n56; living in, 96, 97, 174–75, 204; poblaciones and, 15, 82, 193, 195–203, 209; police and, 136; poverty and, 265; protests in, 14, 211, 214, 215; segregation and, 175; services of, 187; transformation of, 108, 136, 154, 235; villas and, 15, 82, 237–41
capital: flight, 105; flows, 204; foreign/domestic, 130; investment, 177–78, 230; capitalism, 47, 49, 82, 165; agrarian, 46; global, 10, 221, 227; injustices of, 111
Carsten, Janet: housing/kinship and, 273n7
Castro, Fidel, 125
Caupolicán, resistance by, 111
Caupolicán Theater, demonstrations/meetings at, 216
Center, 66, 209; ideological projects of, 67; popular classes and, 81–82
Center-Left Concertación, 23, 62, 217, 220, 221, 225, 227, 230, 231, 233, 241
Central Bank, 157
Centro de Desarrollo Social de América Latina (DESAL), 283n39

Chakrabarty, Dipesh, 29, 271, 295n6
charities, 14, 48, 221, 222, 236; Catholic, 57; low-income groups and, 49
Chatterjee, Partha, 268, 304n4
Chicago Boys, 151, 221, 293n43
Chile Barrio, 23, 219, 302n27
Chilean Chamber of Commerce, 223, 283n49
Chilean Chamber of Construction, 62, 63, 88, 119, 177, 231–32
Chilean Communist Party (PC), 12, 54, 60, 73, 79–80, 86, 93, 137, 160, 207, 211, 265; dictatorship and, 214; favelas and, 280n60; formation of, 65, 72; land seizures and, 80, 116, 280n61
Chilean Constitution: of 1980, 193, 227; of 1925, 5
Chilean Copper Miner's Confederation (CTC), 209
Chilean Path to Socialism, 23, 102, 103, 104, 106, 111–12, 114, 116, 125, 130, 131
Christian Democratic Party, 66, 78, 282n23
Christian Democrats, 82, 91, 113, 120, 151, 177, 193, 284n56, 285n86; Allende and, 129; homeless and, 81; housing and, 88–89; land seizures and, 118–19; low-income groups and, 85; pobladores and, 86, 96; popular classes and, 81; programs of, 87, 90, 266; reform programs of, 87; reformism of, 12; "Revolution in Liberty" and, 81
citizens, 267; low-income, 35, 277n1; mobilization of, 85; participation by, 23, 154, 227; rights of, 217–18; threats/guarantees to, 281n9
citizenship, 30–33, 34, 35, 45, 74, 100, 244, 269, 271; benefits of, 108; claims to, 28, 250; dynamics of, 8, 26; governance and, 267; home and, 25, 54; housing and, 29; ideals of, 234; liberal notion of, 6; obligations of, 124; privileges of, 58; promises of, 41, 67, 195; property and, 27; propriety and, 40, 189; rights of, 5, 29, 30, 31, 38, 58, 80, 82, 126, 267; squatters and, 25, 268; state formation and, 27, 40; state-led development and, 64; subjectivities to, 130
civic associations, 40, 50, 52, 54, 60, 67
civil code (1857), 48
civil war, 119, 142, 277n3, 291n20
Clarke, Arthur, 180, 182, 183
clothing store, opening of, 171, 172
Cold War, 23, 25, 81, 264, 274n1, 282n25; conflicts of, 33; housing and, 64–67
Comisión Nacional de Verdad y Reconciliación. *See* Rettig Commission
Comisión Nacional sobre Prisión Política y Tortura. *See* Valech Commission
Communal Command of the Homeless of Renca, 73, 76, 79, 99
Communist Youth, 71, 72, 76
communists, 66, 77, 139, 284n52; social welfare state and, 61
compadrazgo, 1, 18, 158, 245, 256, 274n18
conflicts, 66, 253; activism and, 100; contradictions and, 28; drug, 254; ideological, 26, 36,

50, 67, 81–88, 270; social, 41, 53, 129, 138; sociopolitical, 26, 33–35, 233; construction, 57, 62, 231, 279n35; consumer credit, 247–48
consumption, 11, 31, 47, 60, 122, 137, 229, 257–58; capitalist forms of, 130; kinship and, 248; production and, 102, 104, 107, 286n5; revolutionary, 107–10
conventillos, 59, 64, 124, 165, 170, 279n27; improvement of, 45; as national shame, 54; prestige in, 47
copper, 43, 61, 179, 279n45; controlling, 81; growth in, 165; nationalization of, 105, 286n2; revenues from, 59–60, 105
corruption, 35, 37, 41, 55, 58, 179, 237; petty forms of, 2; real estate, 267
Cortés, Carlos, 109, 114
counterrevolution, 33, 131
covert operations, United States, 105–7
criminality, 2, 10, 17, 143, 249–50, 252
Cuban Revolution, 24, 81

De Cristo, Hogar, 57
De la Victoria, Herminda: death of, 77, 78–79
De Soto, Hernando, 7–8, 28, 304n2
debt burdens, 180, 247–48, 249
deindustrialization, 152, 228
democracy, 6, 52, 125, 129, 171, 203, 302n29; achieving, 23; demise of, 24, 107, 129, 131; equality and, 101; transition to, 138, 194, 217–18, 220
Democratic Alliance, 215, 217
detention, 138, 141, 210, 215
development, 42, 66, 75, 136, 165, 189, 200, 221, 226; commercial, 230; economic, 152; historical, 11, 33; home, 41, 120, 122, 184, 245, 255; neighborhood, 57, 91, 154, 155, 156, 236, 242; social, 3, 32, 236; spatial, 3, 167, 204; state-led, 58–64, 67; urban, 7, 17, 52, 59, 62, 91, 109, 174, 178, 180, 189, 197, 217; vision of, 23, 91, 189
development companies, 189, 221–22
dictatorship, 24, 136, 162–63, 171, 194, 221, 225; campamentos and, 196; criticism of, 189, 206; housing subsidies and, 182; human rights abuses and, 265; legitimacy for, 175–76; neoliberal restructuring and, 151–56, 167; patriarchy and, 206, 216; PC and, 214; power of, 144, 213; reactionary ideology of, 166, 270; stigma during, 226; unemployment and, 176
dignity, 3, 16, 17, 83, 169, 236, 243–44, 261, 262; ideals of, 243, 245, 260; life of, 24, 28, 38, 39, 270, 271; question of, 37–39, 240–41; vision of, 234
DINAC. See National Directorate of Distribution and Commerce
domestic relations, 49, 61, 71, 103, 114, 122, 127, 130, 216, 236, 252, 257, 262, 267; strain on, 255–56
Donoso, Andrés, 82, 95; Operación Sitio and, 89–90; protests and, 99; survey by, 94

Dorfman, Ariel, 101
Douglas, Mary, 295n6
drug abuse, 17, 255, 256, 257–58, 261, 303n6
drug trafficking, 201, 252, 254
dueñas de casa, 130, 200, 236, 256, 258; bloated bourgeoisie and, *127*; described, 36; home development and, 122, 184; homeless committees and, 92; managing crises as, 159–60; neighborhood development and, 113; protest by, 199; rights of, 126

economic activities, 48, 49, 103, 104, 177, 266, 269
economic depression, 10, 56, 107, 161, 162, 163
economic growth, 8, 42–43, 163, 165, 167, 179, 189, 193, 204, 225, 227, 228, 229, 266; education and, 229; equity and, 229; rates of, 228
economic problems, 119, 161, 174, 188, 204, 217, 242, 302n23
education, 175, 234, 293n51; access to, 60, 240; economic growth and, 229
emergency: campamentos, 162, 179; housing, 57, 159, 168, 276n20; humanitarian/medical understanding of, 290n8; poblaciones, 152, 153, 162, 276n20. *See also* states of emergency
employment, 60, 107, 205; bureaucracy and, 60; domestic, 64; flexibility of, 228; seasonal, 176
Engels, Friedrich: on housing question, 270–71
equality, 216; democracy and, 101
eradication programs, 23, 84, 136, 152, 173–75, 177, 183–84, 189, 197, 198, 199, 201, 219–22
European Union, 171, 226, 237

family, 36, 144, 158, 281n5; allowances, 61; apolitical notion of, 184; harmony of, 169; importance of, 280n54; nuclear, 48, 96, 124, 157; proper, 254–59; relations, 3, 19, 48, 256, 257, 304n19; sanctity of, 102; strengthening, 180
feminism, 36, 216, 273n6; Left and, 124
financial issues, 1, 2, 3, 19, 166, 189, 301n15
First Congress of the Movement of Pobladores *Ukamau*, 240
Foucault, Michel, 32
Frei Montalva, Eduardo, 23, 24, 81, 82, 114, 138, 284n65, 287n13, 287n15; housing crisis and, 83, 98; land seizures and, 73, 116
Frei Ruiz-Tagle, Eduardo, 233
Fresno, Juan Francisco, 207
Friedman, Milton, 151
Fuentes, Humberto, 281n10

Garcés, Mario, 52
gender, 91–92, 140, 149, 252, 271, 286n3; claims making and, 36–37; dynamics of, 35, 274n6; ideology of, 139, 274n6; violence and, 25
Global South, 29, 33, 267, 269
governance, 5, 24, 32, 37, 120, 130, 165, 166, 177, 182, 197, 265; attitudes toward, 53; categories of, 167; citizenship and, 267; criticism of, 244;

liberal forms of, 138, 270; limits of, 103–7; norm of, 45, 267; property and, 26–30; protection of home and, 210; revolutionary, 111–16
Grandin, Greg, 33, 34, 139, 262
Green Valley, 112, 113, 116, 288n29; Women's Committee, 112, 114
gross national product (GNP), 103, 152, 165, 204
Grovogui, Siba N.: dignity and, 243–44
Guevara, Che, 123, 140, 145

Han, Clara, 4–5, 248
Harvey, David, 25, 271
health care, 23, 60, 175, 205, 236, 293n51; coverage, 249, 254, 303n5
Hiriart de Pinochet, Lucía, 180, 184; photo of, 181
history, dynamics of, 29, 171, 274n9
Holston, James, 28, 30, 33–34
home, 247; citizenship and, 25; normalization of, 147–51; political debates and, 125; private property and, 272; protection of, 210; searches, 141–47; social world and, 120
home life, 67, 71, 74, 163; creating, 102–3; expectations of, 102; improper, 131; moral, 102; proper, 126; quality of, 54; sanctity of, 29; secure, 179, 197; underside of, 186
homeless, 73, 78, 79, 80, 83, 90, 97, 99, 100, 114, 141, 221, 224, 240, 267, 268; appeal by, 75, 180; land seizures and, 91, 93, 124, 126; mobilization of, 74, 116–20; moral requirements of, 122; responding to, 81; sanctions/prosecutions for, 76; survey of, 95; as wedge issue, 82
homeless committees, 96, 115, 116, 121, 284n55, 284n62, 285nn73–74; marginality to, 100; negotiating with, 78; organization of, 92; tactics of, 80; work of, 73, 74, 76, 77, 80
homeownership, 37, 55, 57, 122, 171, 180, 185, 197, 206, 237, 243, 269; achievement of, 201, 270; attitudes toward, 53; behavior and, 58; citizenship and, 54; colonial period and, 40–41; declining property values and, 204; demands for, 221; development of, 62, 275n16; dignity and, 244; dominant notion of, 29; extension of, 63; legally recognized, 121; limits of, 6–10; pobladores and, 38, 39, 75, 179; rate of, 4; squatters and, 26; state power and, 238
housing, 3, 14, 48, 96, 115, 150, 154, 155, 158, 168, 175, 178, 180, 182, 185, 196, 217, 221, 223, 224; "acceptable," 8, 30, 31, 35, 54, 55, 87, 120, 187, 240, 269; access to, 37, 60, 120, 156, 258; assigning, 186; citizenship and, 29; Cold War and, 64–67; construction of, 61, 120, 188, 205, 226–27, 231, 232, 240, 251, 270, 301n12; credit for, 62; debates over, 271; defining, 183; demands for, 54, 59; developed, 202; emergency, 57, 159, 168, 276n20; financing for, 231; homes and, 120–25; hygienic, 279n26; illegal, 4, 49; informal, 30–33, 44, 49, 56, 250; low-income, 5, 7, 46, 61, 63, 88, 89, 92, 157, 164, 177, 225, 232, 264, 302n24; maintaining, 245, 297n45; "minimal" forms of, 57, 120, 153; photo of, 13, 14, 198; pobladores and, 27, 28, 38, 39, 59, 64, 158, 271, 289n55; providing, 100, 120, 233–34, 236; public discussion of, 38; recipients of, 177; reform, 53–58, 62; "regularizing," 187; rental, 55; seeking, 25, 170; shortage of, 32, 76–77, 88, 169, 178, 231, 263; single-family, 84, 110; social, 7, 168, 237, 295n13; standards for, 99; starting, 119, 178; state, 35, 53, 266, 296n24; subsidized, 9, 53, 72, 83, 85, 88, 90, 92, 107, 169, 182, 183, 201, 207, 225, 231, 232–33, 260, 268; surveys, 114; urban, 4, 11, 34, 41–42, 64–67, 82, 109, 187, 266, 282n38; well-constituted, 92, 114, 120, 186
housing activism, 6, 8, 10, 37, 71, 90–91, 100, 116, 185, 208, 243, 266; pobladores and, 3–4; repression of, 270
housing conditions, 97, 263; challenging, 5, 180; low-income, 274n17; minimally accepted, 80; poor, 59
housing cooperatives, 54, 56, 57, 58, 105, 156, 179, 302n23; land seizures and, 118
housing development, 4, 11, 35, 52, 57, 232; low-income, 177; middle-class, 16
housing laws, 41, 55, 56, 167
housing markets, 239; insecure/corrupt, 41; low-end, 157; mass-consumer, 122
housing policies, 53, 62, 84, 157, 232; neoliberal, 274n10; state, 4, 54
housing programs, 55, 57, 82, 91, 92, 94–95, 109, 124, 202, 204; administration of, 179–85; debates about, 4; government-sponsored, 96, 98; low-income, 3, 4; patronage and, 179–85; pobladores and, 233; progressive, 301n6; public sector, 283n49; social policy and, 239; state, 9, 56, 180, 182; stipulations of, 293n57
housing question, 65, 270–71, 273n5; state-led development and, 58–64; unresolved, 239–41
housing rights, 5, 29, 30, 32, 37–39, 57, 77, 148, 208, 218, 239, 240, 244, 264, 269, 277n1; acquisition of, 241; limits of, 6–10; movement for, 34, 39; squatters and, 75; human rights, 24, 178, 205, 207, 216, 225
human rights abuses, 31, 137, 143, 161, 189, 227; dictatorship and, 265; exposing, 226
human rights movement, 24, 161, 294n69, 300n31

Ibáñez del Campo, Carlos, 60
IDB. *See* Inter-American Development Bank
identity, 213; class-based, 11; cultural, 11; national, 50, 138, 149, 194; place-based, 11; social, 34
ideologies, 5, 26, 30, 34, 35, 36, 60, 67, 81–88; gender, 139, 274n6; reactionary, 166, 270

Independent Democratic Union (UDI), 185, 220
industrialization, 60, 66
inequality, 10, 166, 185, 221; class, 49; income, 86, 229; mass, 10, 35, 131
infrastructure, 63; bureaucracy and, 114; developing, 109, 251; services, 154, 155, 157, 177, 178, 179, 199, 224, 239
insecurity, 10, 162, 189, 244; labor, 227, 254, 255; neighborhood, 250–54
Inter-American Development Bank (IDB), 13, 63, 82, 85, 105, 176, 177, 197, 286n92
international development institutions, 166, 176, 177, 201
International Monetary Fund (IMF), 240

JAPs. *See* Supply and Price Control Committees
Jara, Victor, 78, 282n20
justice, 30, 37, 179, 186; social, 23, 66, 82, 234, 271

Kast, Miguel, 153–54, 155, 176
kinship, 1, 48, 58, 304nn18–19; consumption and, 248; fictive, 254–59, 304n17; housing and, 273n7
Klein-Saks Mission, 60

labor, 12, 41, 42, 48, 176, 179, 205, 216, 221; agricultural, 60; changes for, 229; collective, 110, 228; construction, 57; exploitation of, 65; industrial, 49; militancy, 61, 261; mobilization of, 34; undermining, 176, 189; women and, 254
labor relations, 152, 254
Lagos, Ricardo, 220, 225, 226, 227, 233, 234, 238, 301n11, 302n24; health care coverage and, 303n5; housing and, 231
land seizures, 13, 37, 57, 65, 71, 96, 110, 121, 151, 183, 188, 194, 207, 220; activism and, 73, 99; condemning, 90; goal of, 120; homeless and, 91, 126; homes and, 186; impact of, 74, 115, 116, 117, 118–19, 127, 206; justifying, 76–81; neighborhoods and, 97; pobladores and, 19, 66, 73, 77, 80, 98, 114, 124, 206, 207, 242; problem with, 111–16; squatters and, 91, 206; symbolism of, 93; urban, 74, 90, 102, 111, 117, 159, 280n4
land tenure, 5, 7, 8, 26, 35, 57, 66, 276n27; legal, 179, 274n12; politics and, 391 security of, 200–201, 237, 269; squatters and, 35, 250
landownership, 34, 47, 159; duties/responsibilities of, 31; squatters and, 117
Las Condes, 171, 172, 174, 177, 230; economic growth in, 229; land seizures in, 117; pobladores in, 175; poverty in, 173
Las Cuncunas, 121–22, 125
Lavín, Joaquín, 220
Law 7600 (1943), housing construction and, 61
Law for the Permanent Defense of Democracy, 65

Law of Affordable Housing, 55, 56, 58
Law of Worker Housing, 53
Lefebvre, Henri, 240–42
Left, 12, 66, 85, 106, 115, 129, 131, 138, 209, 215, 243; feminism and, 124; formation of, 52; ideological projects of, 67; land seizures and, 16; pobladores and, 33; popular classes and, 81–82; radical transformation and, 60–61; sponsorship of, 135
leftists, 12, 13, 34, 60, 61, 64, 66, 71, 74, 91, 116–17, 127, 131, 139, 140, 142, 143, 146; activism of, 78, 81, 111, 143, 291n21; criticism by, 128–29; histories of, 72; housing crisis and, 83; militancy of, 125; mobilization of, 101; youth culture, 289n63
legal codes, 4, 27, 156
Lewis, Oscar, 283n47
Ley de Arrendatarios, 55
Ley de Habitaciones Baratas, 55
Ley de Habitaciones Obreras, 53
liberation theology, 206
living conditions, 30, 41, 50, 60, 120, 126, 165, 186, 199, 204, 265
Locke, John, 28, 29, 275n13
Lomnitz, Larissa, 1, 273n1
low-income groups, 3, 6, 29, 107; home life for, 71; stigmatization of, 85
low-income housing, 7, 46, 61, 92, 157, 164, 177, 225, 264, 296n32; development of, 88, 89, 302n24; politics of, 5

Manuel Rodriguez Patriotic Front, 213, 214
Map of Extreme Poverty, 153, 186, 195, 222
Mapocho River, 45, 57, 129, 143, 226
Marches of the Empty Pots, 106, 125, 126, 149, 210, 211; photo of, 212
marginality, 11, 64, 85, 86, 87, 100, 170, 244
Marginality School, 85–86, 87, 283nn46–47
Marín, Gladys, 76, 77, 79, 93, 95, 116, 282n21
market practices, 167–70, 189, 271
Marxism, 135, 137, 138, 139, 142
Marxists, 81, 82, 99, 148
May Day land seizure, 12, 73–74, 79, 93–99, 141, 265, 284n61, 286n90
mediaguas, 158, 183, 223, 235, 240, 255
Milanich, Nara, 48, 304n17
military coup, 24, 116, 135, 137, 149, 281n8; conditions following, 162; popular activism and, 261
military government, 156, 162, 168; changes and, 165; crisis conditions and, 137, 152–53; resistance to, 215. *See also* dictatorship
Ministry of Housing and Urbanism (MINVU), 76, 78, 79, 82, 87, 92, 95, 108, 109, 111, 112, 113, 120, 151, 152, 157, 164, 182, 186, 195; acquisition by, 285n80; campamentos and, 97; decree law and, 298n60; demonstration at, 99; eradica-

tion and, 219; establishment of, 62; housing and, 84, 89, 90, 98, 156, 159, 169–70, 180; IDB and, 177; land seizures and, 115, 116; land tenure and, 179; organization by, 97; Popular Promotion and, 85; *sanear* and, 83; savings and loan institutions and, 88; squatters and, 116, 187–88; survey by, 94
Ministry of Public Works and Transportation, 164, 168, 226
Ministry of the Interior, 78, 152, 153, 160; housing and, 156; land tenure and, 179; riot police of, 66; squatters and, 225
MINVU. *See* Ministry of Housing and Urbanism
MIR. *See* Movement of the Revolutionary Left
Mitchell, Timothy: on de Soto, 8
mobilization, 74, 85, 93, 100, 101, 113, 140, 161, 193, 210, 213, 214, 215, 216, 217; aggressive, 130, 231, 233; citizen, 42, 240; concentration of, 211; decline in, 225; homeless, 116–20; labor, 67, 228; mass, 203–6, 264; pobladores, 37, 86, 110, 154, 194, 270; popular, 41, 50–52, 131, 225, 233, 240, 274n17; social, 102; social crisis and, 203–6; women's, 37, 206
modernity, 46, 49, 75, 271; capitalist, 165; expectations of, 304n3; myths of, 25
modernization, 61, 108, 165, 182, 264; theory, 86, 283n45
Molina, Sergio, 150–51, 154
moral economy, 51, 193, 251–52
morality, 26, 37, 58, 126, 137, 207, 250, 261–62
mortgages, 62, 63, 114, 124–25, 157
Movement for Unitary Popular Action (MAPU), 284n56
Movement of Revolutionary Pobladores (MPR), 289n48
Movement of the Revolutionary Left (MIR), 13–14, 105, 139, 145, 146, 172, 211, 214, 261, 289n46, 291n18, 300n33, 300n35; activism of, 123–24; campamentos and, 117, 122; land seizures and, 116, 117, 289n46; organization/discipline of, 117; strength for, 123–24
Muñoz, Heraldo, 226, 227
Muñoz Vargas, Patricio, 195

National Center of Information (CNI), 208, 265
National Command of the Homeless, 282n20
National Directorate of Distribution and Commerce (DINAC), 127; poster for, *128*
National Office of Emergencies, 153, 293n47
National Planning Office (ODEPLAN), 153, 195
National Women's Secretariat, 184, 292n34
nationalism, 24, 135, 184
neighborhood councils, 108, 109, 114, 188; personal conduct and, 122–23
neighborhood organizations, 54, 91–92, 105, 118, 120, 236, 237, 238, 262; power of, 298n64; problems for, 235

neighborhoods, 50, 54, 100, 115, 200; irregular, 14; land seizures and, 97; legally sanctioned, 238; outreach, 236; squatters and, 289n57; underdeveloped, 158
Neira, Luis, 77
neocolonialism, 103–4
neoliberalism, 23, 24, 34, 62, 135, 137, 138, 156, 166, 175, 204, 207, 217, 218, 220, 227, 239, 254, 266, 274n10, 276n26, 302n29; consolidation of, 167; impact of, 221, 228; limiting, 6; problems with, 232–33; transition to, 264
neoliberal model, 225–27, 227–30
neoliberal period, 234, 239, 296n23; dictatorship and, 151–56
neoliberal policy, 8, 10, 38, 164, 239, 269, 273n1
neoliberal reforms, 157, 159, 173–74, 189, 262; dictatorship and, 151–56, 167
neoliberal state, inventions/retreats of, 175–79
Neruda, Pablo, 247
NGOs. *See* nongovernmental organizations
nitrates, 43, 47
Nixon, Richard, 105
nongovernmental organizations (NGOs), 12, 160, 185, 206, 219–21, 223, 224, 239, 249, 252
normalization, 147–51, 159

ODEPLAN. *See* National Planning Office
olla común, 160, 205
Operación Limpieza, 215
Operación Sitio, 89–90, 179, 285n86, 286n92
Operation Winter, 109
order, 67; aesthetic of, 43, 47, 167, 168, 189; cracks in, 156–59; underside of, 185–89
organization, 235; advocacy, 62; citizen, 221; housing, 109; pobladore, 149, 156; political, 265; popular, 40; social, 157, 210; spatial, 97, 139

Parliamentary Republic (1891–1924), 50
Patria y Libertad, 106, 116, 126
patriarchy, 61; dictatorship and, 206, 216
patronage, 31, 182; housing programs and, 179–85
Paula (magazine), 122; pages from, *123*
PC. *See* Chilean Communist Party

peñas, 280n3
Pereira Law (1949), 62
Pérez Yoma, Francisco, 232
personhood, 5, 30, 244, 245, 269, 273n7; concept of, 259; property and, 260
phantom subdivisions, 55–56, 57
Piñera, José, 166
Pinochet, Augusto, 13, 32, 125, 171, 221, 296n29, 298n55; Alameda and, 164; arrest of, 225; bank accounts of, 179; cityscape and, 167; economic growth and, 165; governing project of, 166; housing and, 178, 204; Molina and, 151; photo of, *181*; plebiscite and, 217; regime of, 4, 23,

65, 225; on right-wing women, 148; Rodriguez and, 150; Santiago and, 226; social housing and, 7; supporters of, 200
Pisagua (concentration camp), 208
planning, 84, 100, 113, 154; UP, 106, 108, 114; urban, 52
Plaza de Armas, 46, 48
poblaciones, 11, 12–13, 16, 17, 18, 72, 73, 83, 95, 98, 124, 136, 143, 160, 178–79, 219, 222, 247, 252; campamentos and, 15, 193, 195–203, 209; confrontation by, 206; described, 13, 204; emergency, 152, 153, 162, 276n20; female participation in, 235, 236; housing in, *13*, *14*; land seizures and, 127; low-income, 172; marginal, 170; protests in, 211, 214, 215; raids of, 142, 210; segregation and, 175; stigmatization of, 16; villas and, 15
pobladores, 11, 12, 18, 25, 32, 37; challenges by, 5; condemning, 16, 17; defined, 41–42, 58, 81; difficulties for, 6, 79, 98, 162; status of, 53–58
polarization, 23, 24, 82, 107, 155, 179, 185, 194, 214
police, 27, 43, 57, 136, 216; confrontation with, 213; special operations by, 65
policía, as government paradigm, 43–45
political parties, 40, 60, 64, 67, 91, 185, 200
political relations, 16, 25, 44, 52, 131, 240
politics, 37, 62, 91, 115, 125–26, 127, 156; discussing, 184; global relevance for, 29; land tenure and, 39; mass, 50; public, 4; radical, 75; urban, 25, 207
poor, 59; housing for, 52; urban, 4, 6, 18, 41–42, 58, 85–86, 87, 266, 267
popular classes, 81–82, 109, 278n15
Popular Front, 61, 280n50, 280n53
popular power, 12, 75, 100, 101, 124
Popular Promotion, 81, 85, 90, 283n39
popular sovereignty, 33, 44, 52, 91, 268
Popular Unity (UP), 99, 131, 152, 206, 284n56, 291n18; feminist opposition to, 290n67; support for, 101; victory for, 112
Popular Unity (UP) government, 101, 119, 123, 139, 216; challenges for, 102, 104, 106, 116, 117; housing and, 158; land seizures and, 111, 117, 124; minority support for, 104–5; planning by, 106, 108, 114; programs by, 109; protests against, 148, 212; shortages and, 127; social crisis under, 137; squatters and, 187
population growth, 33–34, 59, 88
poverty, 32, 41, 86, 87, 108, 165, 206, 230; campamentos and, 265; culture of, 11, 283n47; eradicating, 7, 173, 179, 200, 220, 227, 233; extreme, 153, 154, 173, 176, 179, 189, 200, 217, 218, 220, 224, 228; levels, 254, 293n51; locating, 154, 155; organization against, 33–37; rate of, 229; reducing, 8, 10, 82–83, 177, 178, 180, 189, 201, 217, 224, 227, 228, 236, 244, 270; squatters and, 154; understandings of, 155, 221, 224; urban, 64, 85, 175

power, 27, 36, 37, 144, 213; popular, 12, 75, 100, 101, 124; purchasing, 13, 110; sociopolitical, 25; state, 42, 75, 130, 238, 264, 271; transformative, 67, 155
Primero de Mayo, 12, 13, 128, 286n92
private life, 18, 29, 135, 142
private property, 55, 206, 225; dominance of, 35; home and, 271; laws, 4, 65; rejection of, 28; significance of, 26
privatization, 27, 48, 175
production, 271; capitalist forms of, 130; consumption and, 102, 104, 107, 286n5
property, 110, 220, 262; citizenship and, 27; dynamics, 30; governance and, 26–30; individual, 260; interrelationships of, 27; Lockean/Hegelian traditions of, 28; personhood and, 260; propriety and, 25, 26–30, 40, 61, 75, 157, 177, 241, 245, 260, 266, 270; residential forms of, 269; social order and, 27; urban, 14, 40, 41, 46, 67. *See also* private property
property regimes, 29, 41, 49, 253, 268, 269, 270; constructed nature of, 27
property relations, 26, 27, 39, 245, 266; improprieties of, 28; state-sanctioned, 35
property rights, 8, 33, 65, 121, 177
property titles, 10, 35, 57, 92, 154, 176, 179, 196, 221, 222, 224, 235, 266, 268; access to, 239; granting, 188; lack of, 178; pobladores and, 38; provision of, 166, 177, 180; right to, 75
propriety, 67, 91, 95, 96, 244, 248, 256; boundaries of, 3; citizenship and, 40, 189; expectations of, 29, 250, 259; politics of, 5, 25, 34, 37, 38, 39, 40, 82, 87, 157, 163, 166, 183, 194, 222, 239, 240, 241, 243, 245, 259–63, 270; principles of, 179; property and, 25, 26–30, 40, 61, 75, 157, 177, 241, 245, 260, 266, 270; state function and, 40; stigmatization and, 16–19; vision of, 234
protests, 52, 161, 189, 193, 217, 261, 300n41; fractious unity of, 209–16; identity/camaraderie and, 213; photo of, 212; pobladores and, 203, 213–14
public, 19; private and, 29, 273n4
public health, 52, 62, 207, 277n5, 295n6
Puerto Montt, 90; massacre in, 111, 284n56

radicalism, 66, 75, 87, 104, 114, 193
rancherías, 46, 48, 55, 56
Ravinet, Jaime, 220
real estate, 62, 177, 232; growth, 59, 166, 174, 296n23; markets, 4, 41, 171, 231
Recabarren, Emilio, 72
reconstruction: apolitical, 148; national, 159, 184
Red Week, 52
reform, 33, 43, 46, 48, 53–58, 62, 67, 87; neoliberal, 151–56, 157, 159, 167, 173–74, 189, 262; state, 42, 88–91; suppositions of, 81–88; urban, 32, 62, 166

relationships, 159, 245; citizen, 24, 271; dialectical, 189; unregulated, 250
Renca, 12, 17, 55, 72, 185, 195, 196, 197, 198, 211, 222, 223, 230, 242, 248, 254; campamentos in, 145, 146, 158, 236; experiences in, 244–45; growth for, 59; homeless in, 73, 76, 77, 79, 80, 92, 95, 141; housing problem in, 94; indigence in, 229; pobladores in, 175
Renters' Law, 55
Renters' League, 54
repression, 152, 173, 214, 261; objects of, 137–47; state-sponsored, 176
residential spaces, 44, 67; social class and, 175
resources, 66, 238; distribution of, 27, 38, 235
responsibility, 157, 248, 257; citizenship, 30, 31, 243; domestic, 126; sharing, 183–84
Rettig Commission, 290n6, 290n10, 291n13, 291n17, 291n21, 292n28
revolution, 65, 67; continuity and, 99–100; legacies/contradictions in, 130–31; vision of, 107
Revolution in Liberty, 81, 90
Right, 66; Allende and, 129; ideological projects of, 67
Rightist National Party, 66, 86, 113
Rodríguez, Manuel, 93, 111

San Bernardo, 112, 255
sanear, 45, 46, 57, 65, 83, 108, 136, 166, 178
sanitary huts, 89, 283n51, 286n92
Santiago: changes for, 19, 42, 43, 46–47, 173–74, 226; economic growth in, 229, 230–31; land seizures in, 66; state relations in, 41–50; zones in, 46
savings plans, 85, 87, 93, 180, 197
Schild, Verónica, 239, 297n48
security, 143, 173, 200–201, 262, 270, 271; celebration of, 165; housing and, 276n24; physical, 170
security forces, 96, 118, 144, 171
security state, 24, 159, 264
segregation, 162, 165, 168, 240; residential, 41, 46, 126, 166, 175, 230; socioeconomic, 10
self-possession, 244, 250, 257, 259, 260, 262; earning, 275n13; notions of, 245
services, 38, 84, 55, 168, 176, 196; access to, 100, 262; gains in, 240; housing and, 87; infrastructure, 154, 157, 177, 178, 179, 199, 224, 239; lack of, 178; low-level, 64; provision of, 56, 57, 109, 144, 251; social, 207, 223; urban, 31, 89, 188, 279n31
settlements: illegal, 73, 267; informal, 92; irregular, 293n50. *See also* squatter settlements
Seven Modernizations, 189
shortages, 149, 152, 263; consumer goods, 31; housing, 32, 88, 169, 178, 231, 263; responding to, 125–30
Silva Henríquez, Raúl, 207
single motherhood, 254–59
slums, 264, 275n17, 301n1; removal of, 10, 166, 168, 174, 176, 188, 197, 201, 230
social body, cancer in, 137–41
social crisis, 137, 203–6
social democracy, 24, 39, 154
social environment, 102, 107, 179, 276n22
social fragmentation, 24, 110, 220, 242
social homogeneity, 167, 168, 174, 186
socialism: Chilean path to, 23, 102, 103, 104, 106, 111–12, 114, 116, 125, 130, 131; strands of, 50
Socialist Party, 60, 105, 193, 285n84; land seizures and, 116
socialists, 77, 101, 139, 284n52; social welfare state and, 61
social justice, 23, 66, 82, 234, 271
social landscapes, 58, 97, 155, 221, 269
social life, 103, 104, 139, 175; degradation of, 215; normalization of, 151; reshaping, 135
social movements, 5, 29, 34, 71–100, 193–241
social order, 27, 37, 136, 266
social relations, 10, 27, 29, 49, 87, 129, 131, 148, 260, 270, 271; commodification of, 47, 262; polarized, 107
social rights, 29, 154
social security, 61, 143, 175, 254
social spending, 168, 175
social status, 166, 168, 170, 199
social structures, 30, 85, 150
social workers, 11, 169, 183, 186, 297n45
sociospatial relations, 25, 37, 52, 67, 270
solidarity, 72, 98, 103, 135, 161, 206, 240, 251, 252, 256; communal, 262; memories of, 172; networks of, 76; social, 262
spaces: modernization of, 182; present/(ir)relevance of past in, 170–75; production of, 271
spatial relations, 24, 25, 26, 29, 30, 58, 221, 271
squatter settlements, 4, 57, 109, 273n3, 276n26; consolidation of, 277n35; informal, 30; legislation/law and, 32; services for, 136; swindlers/speculators and, 31
squatters, 32, 33, 34, 56, 57, 66, 89, 92, 115, 158, 200, 222, 264, 265, 269; acceptance of, 35; dignity of, 39; illegal, 121, 187–88, 298n60; ingenuity of, 304n2; interests of, 6; mobilization of, 37; negotiations with, 95; organized, 206–9; removing, 225; rights for, 35; risks by, 114; rupture caused by, 35; state assistance for, 75; status for, 64, 116; survey of, 95; urban, 31, 131, 266; work for, 207
standards of living, 50, 120; improving, 88, 103, 108
state formation, 74, 100, 111, 167, 271; capitalist, 130, 193; citizenship and, 27, 40; elements of, 28, 30; property and, 40
state relations, 41–50, 52
states of emergency, 32, 64, 136, 159, 224, 264, 265, 268; declarations of, 162; locating, 161–63; violence and, 162
states of exception, 32, 136, 137

states of siege, 135, 162, 166, 216
Stern, Steve, 138–39, 274n4, 277n36, 286n6, 292n35, 292n37, 300n41
stigmatization, 49–50, 87, 112, 116, 170, 214, 252; homelessness and, 83; pobladores and, 16, 205; propriety and, 16–19; social, 10, 49, 265
strikes, 52, 54, 106, 176
subsidies, 59, 60, 182, 231
subsidized housing, 9, 53, 83, 90, 92, 107, 182, 207, 225, 231, 232, 268; applying for, 169
Supply and Price Control Committees (JAPs), 127–28, 129
"Survey of Precarious Settlements," 222, 233

tariffs, 59, 60, 152
Teitelboim, Volodia, 116
terror, 24, 156, 294n70
Thompson, E. P.: moral economy and, 193
Toledo, Eduardo, 87–88
torture, 138, 141, 142, 148, 210, 215, 249, 265
transportation, 194; public, 149, 199, 200, 210, 301n11
Trivelli, Marcelo, 219, 220

UN HABITAT, 275n17
Un Techo para Chile, 235, 236, 237
underdevelopment, 86, 116, 152, 264
underemployment, 60, 267
unemployment, 50–51, 56, 60, 160, 225, 229, 249, 255, 267, 296n26; increase in, 152, 204, 273n2; mass, 59; rate of, 176
unions, 52, 60, 61, 101, 105, 152, 193, 206, 289n45; formation of, 278n17; land seizures and, 93; undermining, 176
United Nations, 8, 207, 301n16
UP. *See* Popular Unity
urban development, 7, 52, 62, 91, 109, 174, 178, 189, 197, 217; concrete and, 17; forms of, 59; impact of, 180
urbanism, 32, 62, 63, 82, 114, 115, 150, 163, 166, 167, 168, 177, 180, 185, 220; housing and, 11, 109, 187
urban landscape, 44, 48, 56, 58, 165, 167, 244, 245, 262, 269; coming to terms with, 10–16; fractured, 10, 11

urban poor, 4, 58, 87, 266, 267, 273n1; experience of, 18; homes for, 6, 41–42; Marginality School and, 85–86
urbanization, 30, 33–35, 39, 41–50, 112, 277n2
US Agency for International Development (USAID), 8, 63, 82, 85, 176, 296n29

Valdés, Ana, 72, 129, 140, 141, 161, 185, 280n2, 285n83, 285n86; on Frei, 98; homelessness for, 73, 76; housing and, 99; human rights abuses and, 265; land seizure and, 128; military regime and, 205–6; PC and, 71, 73; problems for, 159–60; unemployment and, 160
Valdivia Ortiz de Zárate, Verónica, 184–85
Valech Commission, 291nn15–16, 292n23
Vicuña Mackenna, Benjamin, 220, 277n5; policía and, 44–45; projects of, 42, 46–47; reforms by, 48; Santiago and, 43, 45
Villa Antumalal, 237, *238*, 239
villas, 11, 90, 219, 222, 232, 245, 252; campamentos and, 15, 82, 237–41; described, 15–16; low-income, 172; moving to, 237; poblaciones and, 15
violence, 6, 50, 137, 141, 143, 162, 163, 173, 175; domestic, 39; drug, 254; gender and, 25; reactionary, 269; state-sponsored, 160
Viveros, Minister, 156–57
Vuskovic, Pedro, 107

Wacquänt, Loïc: lateral denegration and, 252
War of the Pacific (1879–1883), 12, 42–43
War with the Peruvian-Bolivian Confederation (1836–1839), 42
welfare, 168, 175, 186; social, 10, 61, 71, 154–55, 301n13
Williams, Raymond, 271
Winn, Peter, 131, 289n45
Women's Power, 126, 148
World Bank, 8, 105, 176